PRODUCTION FOR GRAPHIC DESIGNERS

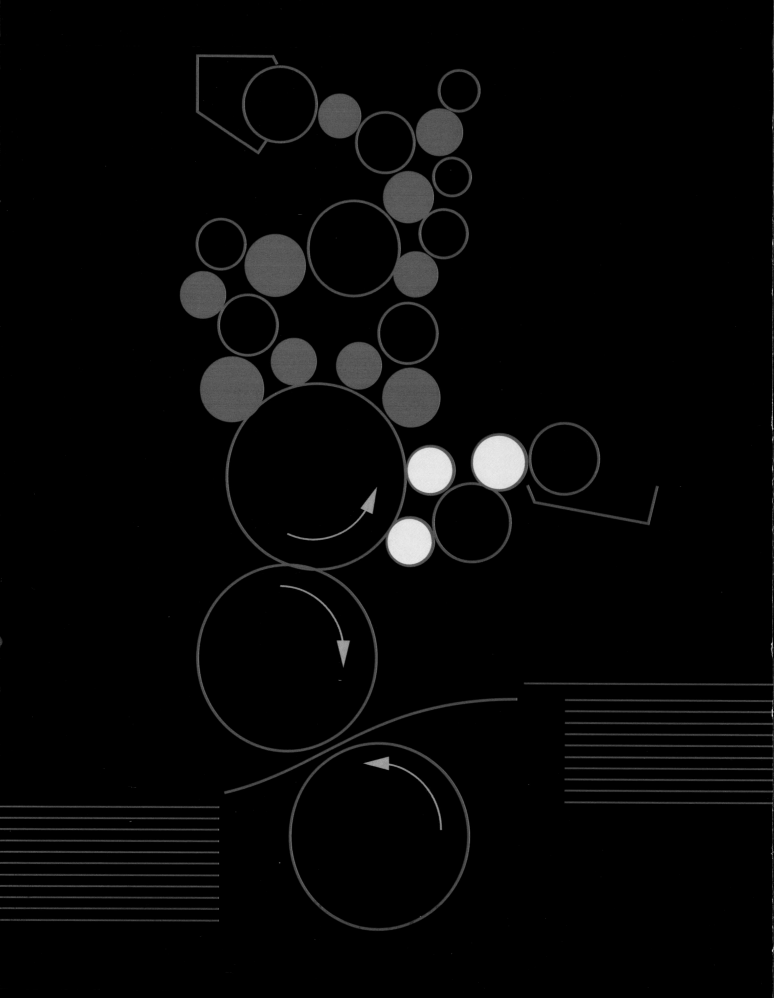

PRODUCTION FOR GRAPHIC DESIGNERS

ALAN PIPES

SECOND EDITION

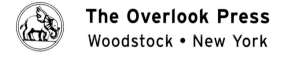

The Overlook Press
Woodstock • New York

First published in the United States in 1998 by
The Overlook Press, Peter Mayer Publishers, Inc.
Lewis Hollow Road
Woodstock, New York 12498

Library of Congress Cataloging-in-Publication Data

Pipes, Alan
Production for graphic designers/Alan Pipes. − 2nd ed.
p.   cm.
Includes bibliographical references (p.) and index.
1. Printing−Great Britain. 2. Printing−United States.
3. Graphic arts−Great Britain. 4. Graphic Arts−United
States. I. Title.
Z244.P57   1997   686.2'0941−dc21   97-19717

Printed in Hong Kong

ISBN 0-87951-815-4

9 8 7 6 5 4 3 2 1

This book was designed and produced by
Calmann & King Ltd, London

Design by Cara Gallardo, Area
Editorial work by Damian Thompson
Picture research by Mirco de Cet and Graham Moore
Typesetting by Marie Doherty
Photography on cover and chapter openers by
Toby Macfarlan Pond

About the typefaces used in this book
Main text: 9/12pt Interstate regular

Designed by Tobias Frere-Jones in 1993, Interstate is based on
the signage alphabets of the United States Federal Highway
Administration, alphabets that we read every day as we drive.
In 1994, he expanded it for the Font Bureau to full character sets
in a full range of weights, prepared for both text and display.

Caption text: 7.5/9.8pt ATRotis serif 55

Rotis Serif was designed by Otl Aicher in 1989 for Agfa
Compugraphic, part of a family comprising Sans, Semi Sans, Semi
Serif, and Serif. The styles are matched for weight and height to
give consistency when matched. Certain round characters have a
distinctive calligraphic treatment, which is apparent in all styles.

Other production notes

Screen ruling: 175 lines
Text paper: 115 gsm Korean Shin Ho
Jacket: 140 gsm glossy art and polypropylene lamination
Binding: Sewn in 16-page sections, separate ends applied, fully cased
in self-colored arlin over 3.5 mm boards, blocked on spine, rounded
and backed, head and tail bands attached and jacketed

CONTENTS

▶

2

72 DESIGN TRAILBLAZERS ◆ ERIK SPIEKERMANN

3   ILLUSTRATION 74

100 DESIGN TRAILBLAZERS ◆ LUCILLE TENAZAS

4   MECHANICAL PREPRESS 102

▶

▶

7   THE INTERNET 200

PREFACE

When the first edition of this book was published, computers were being used in graphic design – mainly for producing newspapers and magazines – but the predominant means of layout was the mechanical. Now computers are commonplace in every area of the design-to-production cycle. The drawing board has been confined to the corner, and that once so expensive PMT camera consigned to the scrapyard. Mechanicals are still being used – by small-scale or small-town printers, for example, and to update standing jobs. But as time goes by, the computer is taking over. Every month they get cheaper and more powerful, and there are no excuses left for not buying one.

In prepress, too, that once analog world of photographic emulsions and baths of chemicals has gone digital. Direct computer-to-plate, and even plateless print, are becoming more familiar. Xerography is being used to produce short-run jobs on demand. And it won't be long before all the paraphernalia of prepress, currently the province of the service bureau, can be brought in-house.

And even more startling, in the past few years a completely new medium (to designers at least) has shot to prominence – the Internet. There was no mention of the Internet in the first edition of this book. It is now deemed important enough to deserve its own chapter. Through the Internet, and that other emerging technology, the CD-rom, designers are able to break the bounds of traditional print and incorporate dynamic online resources that could only have been dreamt about when the first edition was put to bed.

This completely revised edition addresses the exciting changes that have taken place since *Production for Graphic Designers* was first published. There is now an even greater need to master the fast-moving world of computing. Pre-digital methods of production are still important to know, but have here been abbreviated and repositioned into a more appropriate historical and pedagogical context. Another new development has been to include, in-between chapters, inspirational profiles of important practicing designers along with showcases of their work. And, as a bonus, we have studded the text with "hot tips and cool tricks," expert practical solutions to help you power through some common production challenges.

I should like to thank the friends and colleagues who helped in the production of the first edition, particularly my editor Ursula Sadie at Calmann & King, picture researcher Elizabeth Loving, designer Richard Foenander, Chris Myers at Bookworm Typesetting, and Rosemary Bradley, who commissioned me to write it. Grateful thanks are also offered (almost alphabetically) to Aldus UK (now Adobe) for a copy of FreeHand (now back with Macromedia) with which to produce the line drawings; Joty Barker at Face to Face; the staff of Brighton Polytechnic (now the University of Brighton) Library at St. Peter's House; Jane Brotchie for access to her HP DeskWriter; Roger Burg of Monotype Typography; John Christopher of Strong Silent Type;

Ellie Curtis, formerly at the Royal College of Art, London, now in Cairo; Bob and Sue Harrington of RH Design; Nikki Morton and Ruth Jindal for their help in locating and retrieving books; Stan Noble of Towers Noble Design; William Owen; Kanwal Sharma of Lewis Sharma Design; Martin Shovel for the use of his StyleWriter; and Elvis the goldfish for his or her calming influence.

For the second edition I should like to thank my editor Damian Thompson at Calmann & King, whose enthusiasm for and commitment to the project contributed far more to the "look and feel" of the new edition than can be guessed from this small credit, and designer Cara Gallardo at Area for making my text and picture ideas a joy to read. Cara also art directed the cover and chapter opening spreads, and I should also like to acknowledge and thank: photographer Toby McFarlan Pond; London Graphic Centre for the use of the keyboard introducing Chapter 2; Peripheral Vision, London, for the circuit board (Chapter 5) and cable (Chapter 7); and The Pale Green Press, London, for the printing inks introducing Chapter 6; I would also like to mention Philip and Dave Clark of Brighton Print Centre for tirelessly explaining to me the finer points of practical printing. And finally, thanks go to Lesley Ripley Greenfield, editorial director at Calmann & King, for commissioning me to write this substantial update.

Alan Pipes
Spring 1997

1 INTRODUCTION

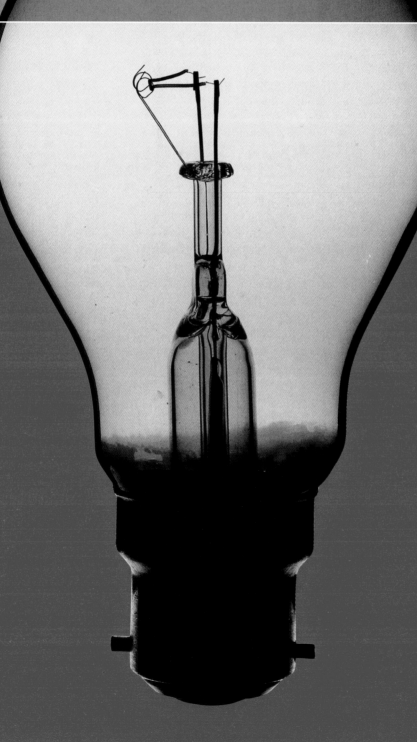

Words and pictures. Paper and ink. These are the raw materials of the graphic designer. They are about to meet, go on a journey, and undergo several transformations, before ending up in a printed and finished publication that you designed. Something that will communicate ideas and images to large numbers of people.

But how do words and pictures get on to the printed page? Printing has always been a mysterious craft. And until quite recently, graphic designers were excluded from its secrets. The purpose of this book is to demystify and help you understand some of those arcane processes.

There is a long-standing misconception that to learn the craft part of any profession can be a chore. The temptation is to jump right in there and get on with the creative stuff. Print production, in particular, with its many different stages and processes, can seem dull, the very sound of words like "mechanical" conjuring up visions of production lines of automatons cutting and pasting like galley slaves. On the other hand, there are some designers, and many typographers, who are so in love with the process that they forget the purpose of the job they are doing. What use is a beautiful piece of design or typography, without meaning or content? The graphic designer's role, first and foremost, is that of communicator. But if you can communicate cost-effectively with wit, economy and elegance, then you are a very good graphic designer indeed.

In graphic design, free expression cannot exist in isolation from the process. Walter Gropius, the modernist architect and founder of the Bauhaus — a German art school that has become the model for most of our present schools of art, communications, and design — suggested in his manifesto of 1919 that art cannot be taught, but that craft can

"A foundation in handicraft is essential for every artist," he said. "It is there that the primary source of creativity lies."

Graphic designers are both artists and craftspeople. This book does not major on how to be an artist, but it will tell you much that you need to know about the craft of printing. And when you have learnt all about print production, the creativity will be able to come shining through. A sound understanding of all stages of the print production process will at the very least prevent your designs from failing for technical reasons.

The chapters are arranged to follow the tracks of both the design process and the print process — from the choosing of type and the preparation of illustrations and photographs, through their arrangement on the mechanical or inside the electronic page make-up program, to the printing and finishing of the publication. The design process may follow a linear path, but many of the design decisions up front are affected by processes downstream. Every stage of the print production process will exert some influence on your design.

The choice of paper and print technology, for example, will affect the kind of typefaces you can use and the way in which halftones are treated. In turn, the size of print run determines the print technology. You may be asked to design a range of product labels, for example — some to be printed on paper stock using high-quality litho presses, while others will be printed directly on to plastic yogurt pots using flexography or screenprinting. You may even be expected to "repurpose" the designs for multimedia or the Internet. Your designs will have to work well across a range of substrates and media.

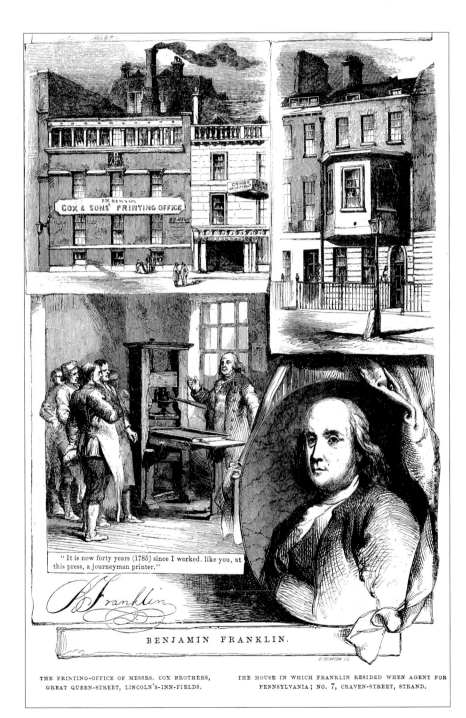

THE PRINTING-OFFICE OF MESSRS. COX BROTHERS, GREAT QUEEN-STREET, LINCOLN'S-INN-FIELDS.

THE HOUSE IN WHICH FRANKLIN RESIDED WHEN AGENT FOR PENNSYLVANIA; NO. 7, CRAVEN-STREET, STRAND.

1.1 Benjamin Franklin (1706–90) is perhaps America's most famous printer. This wood engraving shows him at the London print shop of Cox & Sons in 1785; note the wooden screw press.

When you open the parcel from the printer, and you look at the finished copy of your design, it is as well to pause and appreciate that this printed product is a tribute to every advance in printing technology since the first wooden block was inked and pressed against a sheet of paper.

The history of printing began in the East: in China, Korea, and Japan. Paper was invented in China – its invention was officially announced to the Emperor by Ts'ai Lun in AD 105 – and printing using wooden blocks had become a flourishing fine art by the tenth century. The oldest known printed book, the *Diamond Sutra*, is dated at AD 868, though books were almost certainly being printed a century before. Words and pictures were carved together on to the same wooden blocks, and a fresh set of blocks had to be cut for each new book. Printing presses with type cast from individual pieces of clay that could be used time and time again were in use in China by AD 1041, and Korean printers were casting metal type before AD 1400. But because the languages of the East use symbols for whole words – some tens of thousands of them – rather than putting together words from relatively few characters in an alphabet, the development of so-called "movable" type was not so significant there as it later was in Europe.

Textiles have been printed in Europe since at least the sixth century, and playing cards were certainly being printed, using wooden blocks similar to those of the Chinese printers, by the 14th century. But it is Johannes Gutenberg (1398-1468) who is credited with the invention of printing in the West, some time before 1440.

Gutenberg was a goldsmith by trade, living in Mainz, in what is now Germany. All the technology necessary for the invention of printing was in place at the time – it was just waiting for the right mind to put all the pieces together. He knew how to cast objects in metal, there were presses already available (for wine making), he had ink and paper. And he saw a market opportunity for mass-produced books, to stock the libraries of all the universities being founded at that time.

Before that, in the Middle Ages, all books were created by hand. Scribes and artists worked together to create one-off books, often copying from existing texts. They were beautiful objects, mostly "illuminated" with ornamental letters, paintings, decorative borders, and gold blocking. There was even a form of mass-production in operation. In scriptoria, a chief scribe would dictate aloud the text to be copied by a team of under-scribes. Nevertheless, it was a slow process, and their books could be possessed only by the very rich.

Gutenberg's invention was the process of letterpress: the concept of casting individual letters that could be assembled into words, printed, then cleaned and put away, and used over again. First he cut a

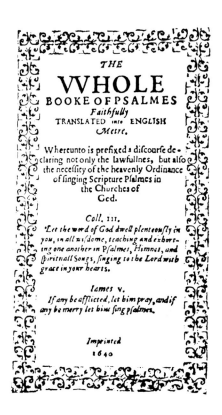

THE
WHOLE
BOOKE OF PSALMES
Faithfully
TRANSLATED into ENGLISH
Metre.

1.2 Title page from *The Whole Booke of Psalmes* (1640), the first book to be published in North America, by Stephen Daye of Cambridge, Massachusetts.

steel punch for each character and punctuation mark. This punch was then struck into a softer metal to form the matrix in which the type was cast. Finally lead, with the addition of some antimony for hardness and tin for toughness, was poured into the mold and the type cast. The most original part of Gutenberg's process was a mold of adjustable width, used to hold the different sizes of matrix. (See Chapter 2, p. 61, for a fuller description of the process of hot-metal typesetting.)

Gutenberg's original idea was to imitate in type the handwritten books of the scribes (but without the graphic embellishments). To do that he had to create a set of over 300 characters, including all the variations of letterforms and joined letters that a scribe might use. In comparison, a modern printer's alphabet might contain only 50 or so characters.

The invention of printing spread across Europe. The first book in English was printed by William Caxton, who learnt his craft in Cologne, Germany, and set up a press in London in 1476, using Flemish equipment. Printing was brought to America by Joseph Glover, who imported a press and three printers from Cambridge, England, to Cambridge, Massachusetts. Sadly, Glover died on the voyage, but the press was installed by Stephen Daye and his two sons in 1638, and operated under the auspices of Harvard College (Fig. **1.2**).

Progress in the technology of printing was slow until the Industrial Revolution. Wooden wine-type presses with huge screws (Fig. **1.1**, p. 13) were gradually replaced by iron presses operated by a simpler lever mechanism. The first was developed by Earl Stanhope in 1804, and this was followed by the more ornate Columbian and Albion presses. By 1812, there were presses in operation powered by steam, and huge rotary machines followed soon after.

Printing became a more industrialized process with the invention of automatic typesetting machines, first from Linotype in 1886, and from Monotype in 1887. Until the beginning of this century, however, it was very difficult to combine type and pictures on the same printed page.

▶ **1.3** Until the end of the 18th century, the only way to print type and illustrations combined on the same page was by using woodcuts. These have period charm but lacked the capacity for fine detail, as is obvious from this depiction of the 1456 visit of Halley's comet, from Conrad Lycosthenes' *Prodigiorum ac ostentorum chronicon*, 1557.

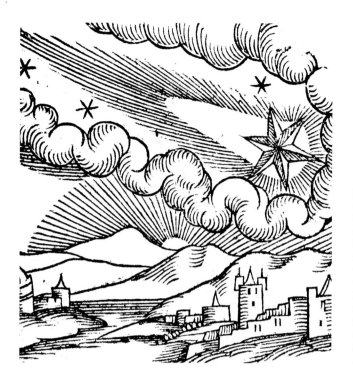

Printing pictures

Letterpress is a relief method of printing, in which a raised surface is inked and pressed against the paper. However, throughout the early history of printing almost every method of reproducing images used the **intaglio** process. The only exception was the woodcut – a relief process that predates printing – which could be used for decorative initials and simple illustrative work (Fig. **1.3**). Woodcuts are made with a knife on the long grain of the wood. The result is a rather rough image, but one that can be printed with the type.

For fine illustrative work, the only alternative was the intaglio process. Intaglio is the opposite to relief. Here it is the incised lines that print. A plate is inked, wiped almost clean, and the ink that remains in the grooves is drawn out, under pressure, to form the image on the dampened paper. Both engraving and etching are intaglio methods of printing (Fig. **1.4**).

So, before the Industrial Revolution, letterpress was used for printing text, in large print runs. Intaglio was used for refined work, where the print run was relatively small and the expense not so crucial. Artists had been making engravings on copper plates since the Renaissance. By the 18th century, the process was used commercially for printing invitation cards, banknotes, and stamps. The engravers used a sharp instrument called a burin to incise lines on to copper plates. And because any lettering had to be drawn by hand, it was often very elaborate. Hence the term "copperplate" is now used for a

▼ **1.4** Because etching is an intaglio process, illustrations had to be printed separately from the text and were "tipped in" when the book was bound. This baker's shop, 1635, comes from a series of 22 etchings on the arts and crafts by Jan Joris van der Vliet.

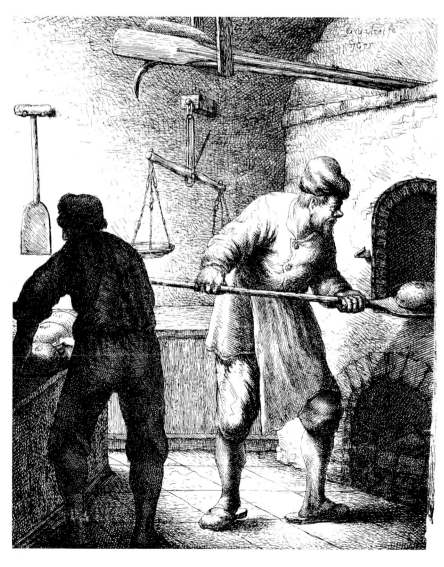

1.5 Etchings and engravings were originally made on copper plates, which quickly wear out. In the 19th century, the problem was overcome by coating them with steel. This steel engraving of emigrants to America crossing the Plains was first published in New York in 1869.

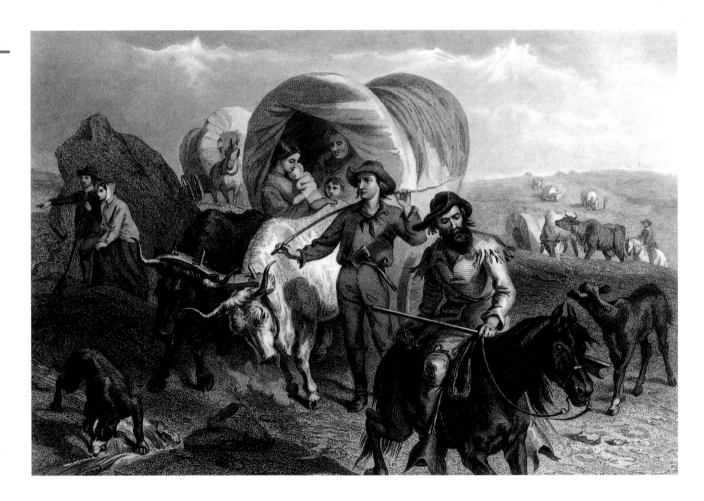

particular kind of formal handwriting. In the late 19th century, methods were developed for engraving on steel plates (Fig. **1.5**), which are more durable than copper.

A later development was etching, in which marks are made with a needle or any other sharp instrument to scratch off an acid-resistant coating on the surface of a copper plate. This is then placed into a bath of acid, and the drawing is etched chemically into the surface of the plate. The image on an etched plate was usually tidied up and detail added by hand, by engraving directly into the plate with a burin.

Another intaglio process was mezzotint, in which a burnisher is used to smooth the rough texture on the surface of the plate, created previously by the action of an abrasive "rocker" (the smooth areas would be white on the finished printed material). Aquatint is a type of etching that builds up tones using resin and stopping-out varnish. **Resist** is applied to the plate to prevent the non-printing areas from etching. Both these latter processes were used mainly to reproduce watercolor paintings. All of these

methods are still used today by artists to produce limited edition prints, but are no longer used by commercial printers.

From Gutenberg's time until the Industrial Revolution, it was common for images in books to be printed separately from the text using an intaglio process. They were tipped-in (inserted among the text pages) during the binding process.

Things improved, however, when Thomas Bewick (1753–1828) developed the art of wood engraving (Fig. **1.6**). At last publishers had at their disposal the means to print

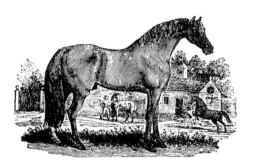

1.6 An Arabian horse from Thomas Bewick's *General History of Quadrupeds*, 1790. Bewick had the bright idea of cutting boxwood on the end grain, and thus invented wood engraving. Despite its name, this is a relief method, which is capable of a dazzling tonal range and delicacy of line.

4   HISTORY OF QUADRUPEDS.

THE ARABIAN HORSE.

THERE is fcarcely an Arabian, how poor foever in other refpects, but is poffeffed of his Horfe, which he confiders as an invaluable treafure. Having no other dwelling but a tent, the Arabian and his Horfe live upon the moft equal terms : His wife and family, his mare and her foal, generally lie indifcriminately together ; whilft the little children frequently climb without fear upon the body of the inoffenfive animal, which permits them to play with and carefs it without injury. The Arabs never beat their Horfes ; they fpeak to, and feem to hold friendly intercourfe with them ; they never whip them ; and feldom, but in cafes of neceffity, make ufe of the fpur. Their agility in leaping is wonderful ; and if the rider happen to fall, they are fo tractable as to ftand ftill in the midft of the moft rapid career.—The Arabian Horfes, in general lefs than the Race-Horfes of this country, are eafy and graceful in their motions, and rather inclined to leannefs.—It is worthy of remark, that, inftead of

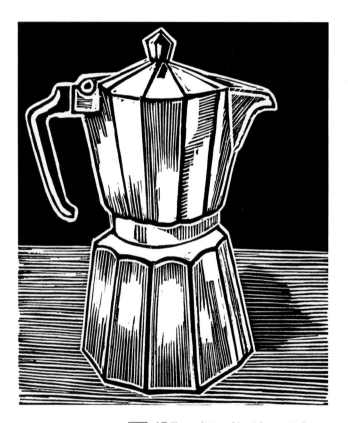

1.7 The tradition of Bewick is carried on today by contemporary wood engravers such as Nick Day, who are more likely to be seen cutting vinyl floor tiles than boxwood.

fine line work and areas of rich black, in among the text.

Wood engraving is a relief process, despite the similarity of its name to copper engraving, which is an intaglio process. Wood engravings are made with tools similar to those of the engravers, on the end grain of boxwood (Fig. **1.7**). Scratchboard, or scraperboard, is a contemporary method of illustration that simulates the appearance of a wood engraving.

By the middle of the 19th century, wood engraving had become an industry, and engravers such as Joseph Swain and the Dalziel brothers were as famous as the illustrators whose work they interpreted. Magazines such as the *Illustrated London News* used a system of separating large blocks into more manageable pieces, sending them out to a team of engravers, then reassembling them – an overseer had the job of disguising the joins. Journalistic accuracy came second to visual impact, with the same blocks used over and over, whenever there was a public hanging or a shipwreck.

1.8 The process of lithography revolutionized print production, but it was a long time coming. Early lithographic illustrations, like engravings, had to be printed separately from the text, but were used extensively for color work. This express train was first published in 1870 by Currier & Ives in New York as a color lithograph. Note that here it has to be reproduced as a halftone from a photograph of the original.

Enter lithography and photography

In fact, there was a process that could quite easily combine type and pictures on the same page, and it had been around since the end of the 18th century.

It was lithography (Fig. **1.8**), invented in Prague by Alois Senefelder around 1796–9. Neither a relief nor an intaglio process, it is better described as a planographic process. It is based on the principle that oil and water do not mix (much more in Chapter 6), and in effect everything happens on a flat surface.

Ironically, it was the versatility of the process that prevented it from being taken up more universally. Almost any greasy mark made on

the lithographic stone, or, from the end of the 19th century, on a prepared metal plate, will print. Illustrators could at last work directly and spontaneously. By the end of the 19th century, greetings cards, postcards, decorative "scraps," maps, sheet music, and posters were all being mass-produced by lithography.

Offset lithography – in which the image is transferred from the stone or plate to a rubber roller, and then to the **substrate** – entered the scene surreptitiously. The process was first used in around 1875 for printing ornamental decorations on to tinplate, for applications in packaging.

Type produced by letterpress could be transferred on to the stone using special transfer paper, but this was not a totally satisfactory pro-

cess. One more ingredient was necessary before lithography could take over from letterpress as the most versatile of all the printing processes: the invention of photography in the late 1830s.

Photography is the basis for every print production process in use today. The first application of photography to the reproduction of illustrations was quite modest, however. It was used to sensitize the surface of the boxwood used for wood engravings. These still had to be cut by hand, but the illustrator's original drawing could be preserved and, furthermore, the method could be used to reproduce photographs.

Early photographers were eager to reproduce their work in large numbers. They were an extremely

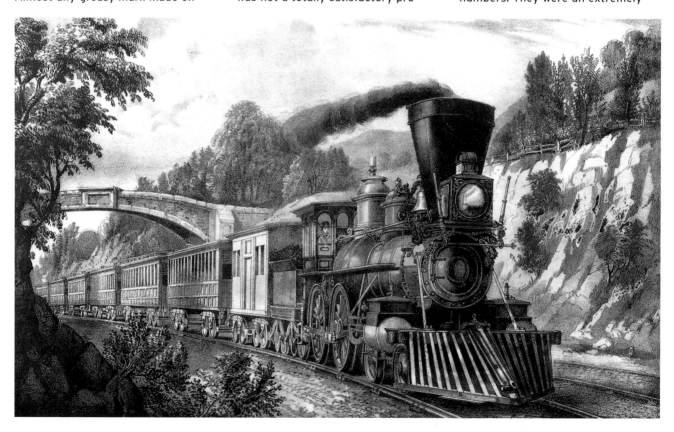

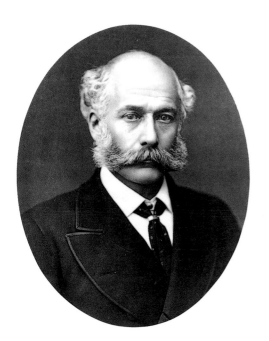

1.9 It was the experimental photographers of the late 19th century who pushed forward the technology of print production, inventing better methods of reproducing continuous-tone artwork and the technique of producing color separations. This picture of Joseph Bazalgette, the architect of London's sewerage system, was first reproduced by Woodburytype – a form of collotype patented by Walter Bentley Woodbury in 1866 – a process said to produce hard and brilliant prints.

experimental group of individuals, and much of the pioneering developments in print production were made by them. Collotype (Fig. **1.9**) was the first method used for reproducing photographs, and this slow and expensive process was soon followed by photogravure.

Collotype – the name comes from the Greek word for glue – uses a plate coated with photographically sensitive gelatin which hardens in proportion to the amount of light falling on to it. A negative is exposed in contact with the plate, which is then moistened and absorbs more water where there was less light. Impressions are taken using greasy ink, as in lithography. Collotype gives an almost facsimile reproduction of pencil, pastel, and crayon. To date it is the only commercial process that can print continuous-tone originals without having them first converted into a pattern of dots, by screening.

Photogravure, first developed in 1852, is an intaglio process characterized by rich tones and the absence of regularly patterned dots. However, the process does involve a form of screening to create the "grains" on the plate or cylinder. On etching, the grains are eaten away in proportion to the tone values on the original – the blacks become the deepest and

the whites the shallowest. On printing, the darker areas are created by a greater amount of ink being deposited on the paper, and the grains are obliterated by the spread of the ink. The process relies on quick-drying spirit-based inks, and for this reason many of the early reproductions appeared in sepia or green. Photogravure is used widely to this day, and is discussed more fully as a printing process in Chapter 6.

The breakthrough that allowed images to be printed by letterpress was the development of the process block. The line block, for black and white work, was invented in Vienna by Paul Pretsch in 1853 and used a process resembling collotype – the softer portions of sensitized gelatin on the surface of the plate swell into relief. An electrotype cast is made, and the resulting plate is mounted on to a wooden block (hence the name – the block brings it up to the height of the type). This can then be assembled with the type. By the

mid-1880s, zinc plates were being etched photographically from original artwork, and the profession of process engraving, or blockmaking, was born.

The early process blocks could handle only relatively simple areas of black and white, and the style of illustrators such as Aubrey Beardsley owes much to the constraints of the process (Fig. **1.10**). For the first time, an illustrator was free to draw at larger sizes than the work would be appearing in print.

Tints could be added by the blockmaker (see Fig. **3.2**), where indicated by the illustrator. Ben Day tints, the first commercially available tints, were introduced in 1901. These were sheets of celluloid stretched in wooden frames. Each sheet was embossed with a pattern and was transferred to the block, before etching, using a roller inked with lithographic ink. Areas not requiring a tint were first painted out with gum to repel the ink.

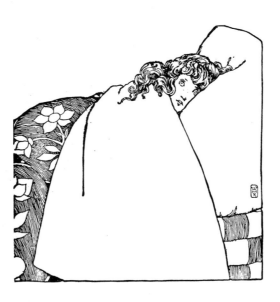

1.10 The line art of William Heath Robinson was as much influenced by the invention of the process block as by the importation of Japanese art at the end of the 19th century. At last an artist's spontaneity could be reproduced directly from artwork – as can be seen in this illustration from Hans Andersen's *Fairy Tales* (1913).

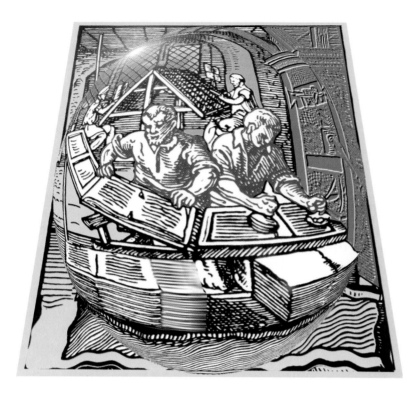

1.11 Old meets new. This 16th-century woodcut of printers at work is given a contemporary treatment courtesy of Photoshop, the image manipulation program from Adobe.

The reproduction of continuous tone by means other than collotype had to await the invention of the halftone screen. The photographer Fox Talbot first suggested in 1852 that tones could be reproduced by means of "photographic screens or veils." But it was Frederick Ives of Philadelphia who patented a method of converting a photograph into dots. This was refined in 1882 by George Meisenbach, who used a single-lined screen that was turned 90 degrees during exposure. Ives, in collaboration with Louis and Max Levy, replied in 1890 with the first cross-lined screen. Now illustrations and photographs could be freely combined with type on the same page, and printed together at the same time.

The invention of the halftone screen also paved the way for full-color printing, using three and later four "process" colors to reproduce all the colors of the rainbow (see p. 87).

The first rotary offset lithography machine for printing on paper was introduced in 1906 by Ira W. Rubel, but it was not until the 1950s that it began to take over from letterpress.

Photocomposition systems could set type, not in pieces of lead, but on rolls of photographic bromide paper or transparent film. These could be cut and pasted into designs that could then be transferred directly to a lithographic plate and printed. This technological breakthrough, and the explosion of print that followed, gave a huge boost to the young profession of graphic design. Over the years, the printing industry had become fragmented – there were separate typesetters, process engravers, and printers – and someone had to step in to plan and coordinate printing projects. That job fell to the graphic designer.

There was greater creative freedom too. No longer were graphic designers constrained to what could be done with metal type and process blocks. Type on paper could be positioned anywhere, alongside any images that could be recorded by the camera.

It was the age of camera-ready artwork – the mechanical. And the introduction of display faces in the form of dry-transfer rub-down lettering such as Letraset liberated the adventurous designer even further. What you saw on the mechanical was what you got in the printed product.

It was a natural next step to want to design on the computer screen, once WYSIWYG (what you see is what you get) displays became available in the early 1980s. Both text and graphics could be treated equally in the eyes of the computer, and could be subjected to an almost infinite variety of manipulation (Fig. **1.11**).

The introduction of PageMaker for the Apple Macintosh in 1984, along with the PostScript page-description language and the LaserWriter, were just some of the many recent milestones in the history of print production for graphic designers.

Now, as the Internet emerges from the domain of computer scientists to become a mainstream medium in its own right, so once again graphic designers are liberated, set free to expand their horizons beyond the world of printed ink on paper and into digital screen-based multimedia applications.

As with the invention of lithography, it is often difficult to foresee the effect of an isolated discovery on the overall history of printing. Lithography had to wait for the development of photography before it could become a commercial proposition. In the same way xerography, invented in 1938 by Chester Carlson, has leapt forward with laser and computer technology. Put these together and we can predict, with some confidence, that xerography will become the dominant printing technology of the early 21st century and that the Internet will become as commonplace as the telephone and television, complementing print-based media with a degree of interactivity and immediacy undreamt of by Gutenberg.

AD 105 Paper invented in China by Ts'ai Lun

868 *Diamond Sutra*, first printed book, in China

1041 First presses with clay movable type in China

1150 First paper mill opened in Europe, in Xativa, Spain

1400 Koreans printing with metal movable type

1445 Johannes Gutenberg printed first book in Europe

1446 Earliest known copper engraving: *The Scourging of Christ*, by a German artist

1477 William Caxton issued first dated printed book

1638 First American press established by Stephen Daye at Harvard College

1690 First American papermill established in Germantown, Pennsylvania, by William Rittenhouse

1790 Thomas Bewick perfected process of wood engraving

1796-9 Lithography invented by Alois Senefelder

1798 Papermaking machine invented by Nicholas-Louis Robert

1804 Iron press devised by Earl Stanhope

1810 First Fourdrinier paper-making machines in operation

1812 *The London Times* printed on steam press

1822 First photographic image made by J. N. Niepce

1829 Amos H. Hubbard's mill at Norwich, Connecticut, was first American papermill to install a Fourdrinier machine.

1837 Invention of Daguerre photographic process

1839 Negative/positive photo-graphy invented by Fox Talbot

1852 Photogravure invented by Fox Talbot

1853 Line block invented by Paul Pretsch

1860 Photographically sensitized boxwood process developed by Thomas Bolton

1860 Principle of color separation by filters demonstrated by Clerk Maxwell

1861 First color photograph by Clerk Maxwell

1872 Process line block invented by Alfred Dawson

1875 Offset litho used for printing on tin

1881 Halftone process invented by Frederick Ives

1884 Punch-cutting machine invented by Linn Boyd Benton

1886 Linotype machine invented by Ottmar Mergenthaler

1886 First Linotype installed at *New York Herald Tribune*

1887 Monotype machine invented by Tolbert Lanston

1890 Four-color separation process invented

1890 Aniline coal-tar process (later called flexography) demonstrated at Bibby, Baron & Sons in Liverpool, England, but later abandoned

1901 Ben Day mechanical tints introduced

1906 First rotary offset litho machine invented by Ira W. Rubel

1920s Aniline process developed for printing on non-absorbent stock such as cellophane

1938 Xerography invented by Chester Carlson

1948 Color scanner invented by Kodak

1952 Name flexography coined for aniline coal-tar process

1955 Linofilm photocomposing system introduced

1959 First Linofilm installation at *National Geographic*

1960 Laser invented at Hughes Laboratory

1967 Computerized Linofilm typesetter introduced

1968 Crosfield Magnascan four-color scanner introduced

1969 ARPAnet, the precursor to the Internet, established

1971 Email invented by Ray Tomlinson of BBN

1981 IBM PC announced

1982 Lisa, the precursor to the Macintosh, introduced by Apple

1984 Apple Macintosh and Linotronic 300 laser image-setter launched

1985 Adobe PostScript used to set type on LaserWriter and Linotronic imagesetter at different resolutions

1985 Aldus PageMaker launched, and term "desktop publishing" coined by Aldus founder Paul Brainerd

1987 Mac II and QuarkXPress launched

1990 Windows 3 released by Microsoft

1991 TrueType format and System 7 introduced by Apple

1992 Tim Berners-Lee of CERN develops software for the World Wide Web (WWW)

1993 NCSA releases Mosaic, the first WWW browser

1993 Intel introduces the 80 MHz Pentium chip

1993 Motorola ships the first 80 MHz Power PC 601 chip

1994 First PowerPC Macs launched

1994 Aldus and Adobe merge

1994 Netscape Navigator launched by Mosaic Communications

1995 Windows 95 released

1996 Internet Explorer released by Microsoft

GETTING STARTED: STUDIO EQUIPMENT

Some graphic designers claim to get by with just a pad of layout paper, a pencil, and a book of type specimens. The typographer Erik Spieker-mann (see p. 72) used to boast (before he bought his Apple Macintosh) that he could communicate clearly with his typesetter by means of a written set of instructions. This was a type specification that could be dictated down the telephone, if need be – with no graphic layout necessary. Well, you may argue that typographers have it a lot easier than graphic designers. They don't have to deal with pictures, or color.

So maybe in the past the more unprofessional graphic designers just sent rough layouts covered in key-lines and instructions to the printer and hoped for the best. These days, it is more likely that you will present your computer-generated design to an imagesetting bureau or repro house on a removable hard disk, or down the telephone wire via a modem. And you will already have a very good idea of how the printed result is going to look.

What do you need to get started? A sturdy tabletop or, better, a draw-ing board with an adjustable angled surface and built-in parallel motion (a straight edge that moves up and down, always perfectly horizontally) is essential. The drawing board has become synonymous with the cycli-cal nature of the design process. How many times have you heard the phrase "back to the drawing board" when pernickety clients changed

their mind about what they really wanted? Even in design studios with computers, drawing boards are still seen – they are good places at which to plan and think, to scale and crop illustrations, and are ideal for spreading around the design ele-ments during the sketch stage of design.

A surgical scalpel and a heavier-duty craft knife (such as an X-acto) are useful for cutting paper and board. Use a cutting mat with a "self-healing" surface for trimming artwork and typesetting, and clean off any stickiness regularly with lighter fuel. For sticking and mount-ing you will need rubber cement, which can be spread thinly with an applicator or spatula. Surplus gum can be removed cleanly when dry using a homemade "eraser" of dried-up gum. Some designers prefer aerosol adhesive, such as Scotch Spray Mount, for wrinkle-free mount-ing. For safety's sake, adequate ventilation is essential while using spray glue. Buy a brand that uses a CFC-free propellant, to protect the environment. Many graphic design-ers prefer hot-wax coaters, such as

Letraset's Waxcoater, for sticking paper to board; they will also keep the studio warm in the winter! Low-tack masking tape and matte frosted "magic" tape are useful for mending, and for attaching tissue or acetate overlays to delicate artwork.

Other accessories include plenty of non-reproducing light-blue pencils, including some greasy pencils (Chinagraphs) for writing on glossy surfaces, and maybe an electric pencil sharpener. A large soft brush is indispensable for removing debris from the work in progress, and a supply of talcum powder will come in handy for degreasing and "lubricating" surfaces. However, keep it away from finished work! A bulk stock of paper towels is useful to mop up spillages. It is always good policy to keep things clean and tidy.

Paint called process white is used by designers for correcting mistakes and adding highlights to drawings. It is still considered good advice to buy the finest-quality sable brushes (sizes 00, 1 and 3 would be a good selection). Look after them – they should be washed and rinsed straight

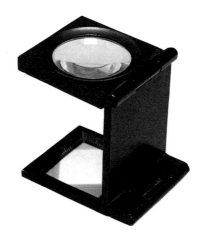

1.12 A loupe, or linen tester, is a magnify-ing glass which is useful for examining transparencies and proofs for imperfections, often in conjunction with a lightbox.

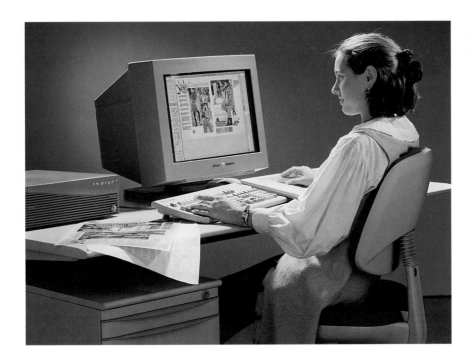

after use (they must never be left point down in a jar of water) and stored with the points upward. There are some very good synthetic substitutes available.

A loupe, linen tester, or eyeglass (Fig. **1.12**) is a mounted magnifying glass that will prove its worth over and over. It can be used to check the dots in a halftone, examine a color transparency for suitability and any defects, and to scrutinize proofs for printing problems.

A lightbox that fits on the tabletop, and comprises a translucent surface illuminated from below by fluorescent lights conforming to the **standard lighting conditions** used by printers, is invaluable for properly examining the color temperature of transparencies. It is also a great aid to experimentation. You can try out different designs on a lightbox, tracing over those parts of an original design you wish to retain. A lightbox can also be used to check the registration on color separations. Some corner of the studio, too, should be set up according to **standard viewing conditions**, with the light source surrounded by neutral gray, if you are to be checking and correcting color proofs.

A proportional scale, or just a plain old calculator, will help you work out percentage reductions and enlargements. And there are all kinds of other measurement devices. A stainless-steel pica rule will become a lifelong companion, and there are plastic rules available for measuring the depth of type in different sizes, useful for casting off (calculating the length of a text) and copy fitting (making sure your typesetting will fit the space you have left for it in the layout). A transparent grid will assist you in checking that design elements are square, and well aligned. A photocopier capable of enlarging and reducing is a very useful addition to any studio, as is a fax machine to keep in visual touch with the client and printer.

Then there's the computer (Fig. **1.13**). And here's a word of warning, right at the start of the book. A computer can be a tireless and uncomplaining assistant, but you cannot talk to it in such subjective terms as "increase the spacing here" or "less orange there" as you would with a typesetter or the scanner operator at your repro house. Compositors and scanner operators have had years of experience in

delivering results they think you want. They can almost read your mind. They have a common understanding of what is acceptable, and what is good. The computer, on the other hand, can do either nothing or anything – depending on what instructions you give!

The computer might never question your unusual requests and never charge you for changes of mind. But it will expect you to do all the thinking, and be able to tell it exactly, to the thousandth of an inch, centimeter, or percentage point, where things should be moved. Not only does that make more work for you, but you have to know in minute detail exactly what you want – and you will have to take responsibility for the outcome.

Typesetters were in fact some of the first users of computers – they could recognize a good thing when they saw it. Your computer is not going to replace the printer, and they will probably always be one step ahead of you. So think of your system as complementing their computers, acting as a front end to their systems.

Use your computer responsibly, to improve the quality of design communication between your studio – the ideas house – and the printers – the production house. Their centuries of hard-won expertise are there to be used. And they will appreciate the knowledge you have of their processes, gained from reading this book.

ZUZANA LICKO

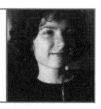

LIFE STORY Zuzana Licko was born in 1961 in Bratislava, Czechoslovakia, and emigrated to the United States at the age of seven. She graduated with a degree in graphic communications from the University of California at Berkeley in 1984.

In the same year Licko, together with her Dutch-born husband Rudy VanderLans, started *Emigre* magazine, a journal for experimental graphic design. The magazine garnered much critical acclaim when it began to incorporate Licko's digital typeface designs – Emperor, Emigre, and Oakland – that were created on the Macintosh computer. The 128k Macintosh was launched as the second edition of *Emigre* was in production. The exposure and success of these typefaces in *Emigre* magazine led Licko and VanderLans to set up Emigre Inc. to manufacture and distribute the fonts to a wider audience.

When Licko designed her first fonts for the Mac (the Emperor, Emigre, Oakland, and Universal families) in 1984, bitmap fonts were the only kinds available. Her intention was to create a series of legible fonts for the 72 dpi computer screen and dot matrix printer. After laser printers and outline fonts were introduced, she imagined that these bitmaps would be relegated to the status of novelty fonts, but with current interest in multimedia CDs and the World Wide Web, they have been re-evaluated.

As a graphic design team, Emigre has worked for clients ranging from large multinationals such as Apple Computer to independent art organizations such as San Francisco's Artspace. Their work has been published in *Blueprint*, *Baseline*, *Axis*, *ID*, *Eye*, *Communication Arts*, *Print*, and numerous design magazines and books throughout the United States, Britain, the Netherlands, Germany, and Japan. Their writing has been published in the *AIGA Journal, ID, U&lc* and *How*. Selections of their work are included in the permanent collections of the San Francisco Museum of Modern Art, the Design Museum in London, the National Design Museum in New York, the Italian traveling exhibit, "Pacific Wave," and in the Walker Art Center design retrospective, "Graphic Design in America."

Emigre was the 1994 recipient of the prestigious Chrysler Award for Innovation in Design, and in January of the same year, New York publisher Van Nostrand Reinhold published a ten-year retrospective book entitled: *Emigre: Graphic Design into the Digital Realm*, which is currently in its third printing.

As well as designing fonts such as Base-9 and Base-12 (see spread), Mrs Eaves (based on Baskerville), Matrix, Modula, and Senator – many of which are evocative of letterpress type – Licko also makes and sells stoneware pots with the same restraint and simplicity of design as her typefaces. To see the vases, check out the web page at: <http://www.emigre.com/VASES.html>.

> "Integrating design and production, the computer has reintroduced craft as the source of inspiration"

MANIFESTO Puzzles
"Ever since I was first introduced to graphic design, I heard everybody say how bad digital type looked and how it was impossible to make it look any better. This really intrigued me. Whenever anyone makes a statement like that, I have difficulty agreeing. I was reading books on the history of graphic design and in the final chapter they would always mention something about digital type and show typefaces like OCR A and B. Some of them were interesting but never really any good for setting text.

"So I saw that here was something unexplored and interesting and I wanted to try my own hand at it. But every time I asked for advice, people kept telling me it was really a lost cause, that it couldn't be done. So I thought that anything I would do would be better than what was out there.

"I enjoy things that are like puzzles; anything that is tremendously restrictive, where there are very few choices but you have to make it work. If I get too many choices, I become overwhelmed, I just don't have the time and patience to look at every possible scenario. This is the problem I have with graphic design. I never got the feeling that I found the final solution to a problem. Although I now design more traditional and less modular typefaces, I still get most of my creative energy out of solving these problems. When nobody is able to make something work, I get inspired to find out what I might do with it.

"Integrating design and production, the computer has reintroduced craft as the source of inspiration. Because the computer is an unfamiliar medium, designers must reconsider many basic rules previously taken for granted. This has brought excitement and creativity to aspects of design that have been forgotten since the days of letterpress. With computers many alternatives can be quickly and economically reviewed. Today's designers must learn to discriminate intelligently among all of the choices, a task requiring a thorough understanding of fundamentals."

WORKSTATION
• Emigre's web site is at <http://www.emigre.com>
• Rudy VanderLans and Zuzana Licko, *Emigre: Graphic Design into the Digital Realm*, Van Nostrand Reinhold, 1994.
• *Emigre* (the magazine): published quarterly by Emigre Inc., 4475 D Street, Sacramento, CA 95819, USA.

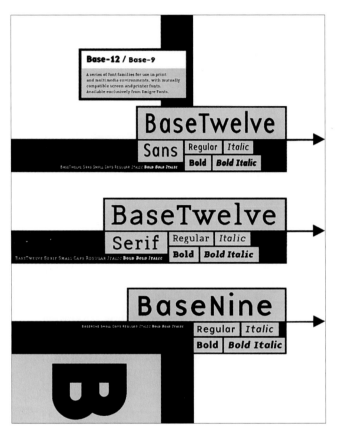

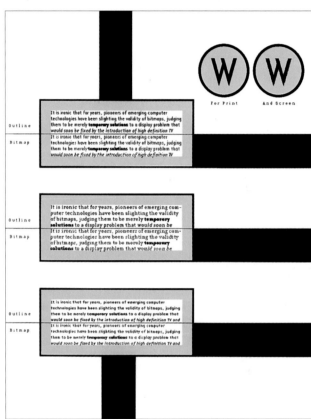

Base-9 and Base-12 These fonts were designed by Zuzano Licko in 1995. The basic concept for the Base-12 family started with the 24- and 36-point screen fonts that Licko designed for use on the Emigre web site. Licko had identified a need for a family of screen fonts with companion printer fonts. The result was one serif and one sans serif family based on 12 point screen fonts called Base-12, and one family based on 9 point screen fonts named Base-9 — a total of 24 individual faces.

PostScript fonts come in two parts (see p. 68): the screen font or bitmap and the device-independent outline font or printer font. Usually, the printer font characters dictate the look of the screen font characters, but Licko tackled the problem from the opposite direction, designing the screen fonts first to set the exact character widths within which the outline characters were adjusted to fit.

The first step, then, was to choose the most appropriate screen font size. For various reasons, 12 point proved to be the most useful. It is the default size for most applications and Web browsers, and 12 point is cleanly scaled to many of the standard sizes, namely 24 and 36.

The greatest challenge in harmonizing the legibility of screen fonts with printer fonts is that of spacing. Traditional screen fonts are adjusted to fit the shapes and widths of the printer fonts, but because of the limited number of pixels available to play with, the width of a bitmap character has to be rounded off. When lines of text are composed, many page layout programs match the line length on screen to the printed line length by adding in the cumulative effect of these left-over fractions. As a result, extra pixels of space are inserted between characters here and there, causing uneven spacing: some characters may be moved a pixel to the left or right, overriding the spacing intentions of the designer.

Emigre's collection of 152 Whirligigs contains 126 concentric illustrations, ten sets of symmetrical borders, and six connecting illustrations. These pictorial elements have been created using font technology and can be combined to create an almost limitless number of kaleidoscopic patterns of increasing complexity.

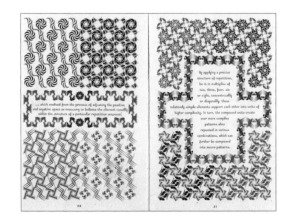

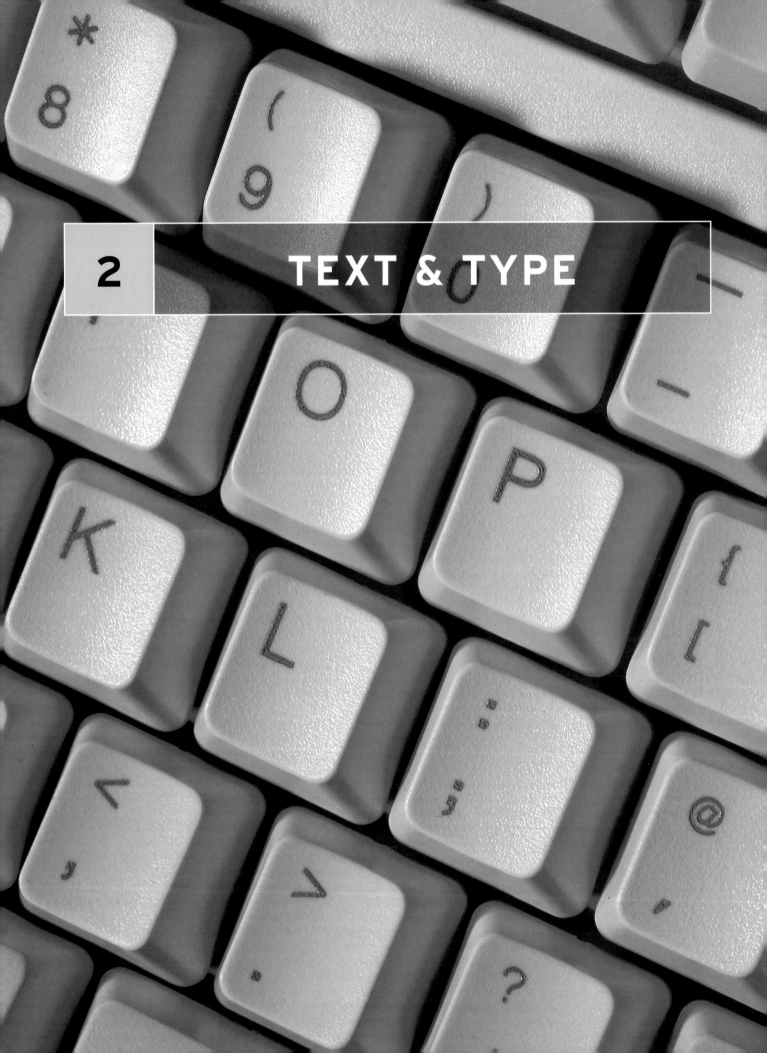

2 TEXT & TYPE

The ability to use type effectively is an essential skill for successful graphic design. Just a few basic principles open the way to an infinite variety of design possibilities for all kinds of printed products. Graphic designers must make type work hard, in harmony with other graphical elements, such as illustration, photography, and color. They are dealing with practical situations, in the real world of tight deadlines, specific briefs, and competitive pitches.

Since the introduction of digital design systems, the graphic designer has been confronted with a bewildering choice of typefaces, as well as the means to manipulate them. It has never been more important for graphic designers to become familiar with the craft and knowledge of the printers and typographers who have gone before.

People like Gutenberg designed their own type, cut the steel to make it, cast it into lead type, composed it into pages, printed their own books, and bound them. They concocted their own ink, and probably made their own paper as well.

Computers give graphic designers the opportunity to take back the responsibility for almost as much of the production process as they are willing, or capable enough, to handle. But to go forward, one must first know what is possible.

This chapter aims to give the graphic designer an insight into type and how it is used. It will explain the vocabulary of print and typography, both ancient and modern. For in print production we commonly use both terminology handed down through generations of printers and typesetters, and jargon introduced from computing and digital prepress.

The chapter is divided into three sections. In the first we talk about type itself — letters and words, the basic building blocks with which graphic designers work. We see how type originated from the

▶

handwriting of medieval scribes, detail the work of pioneering printers, and learn the all-important methods of measuring type.

Then we turn to the relationship between text and house style, investigate how different typefaces are recognized, and discover how to choose the best typeface for the job.

Finally we learn how type is created. Here we discuss the systems of typesetting — from hot metal, through photosetting, to the computer systems that make the craft of typography accessible to anyone possessing a power socket.

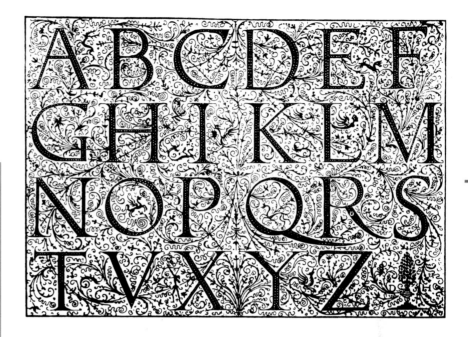

2.1 A decorative alphabet drawn as a sampler by Daniel Hopfer of Nuremburg, Germany, dated 1549. The letterforms are based on the lettering on Trajan's Column in Rome. Note the absence of J, U, and W.

What equipment do you need to get started?

- a sturdy tabletop or drawing board
- type specimens
- a pad of layout or tracing paper
- a supply of fibertip pens (ballpoints may damage artwork) and soft black pencils
- a pencil sharpener
- a non-reproducing light-blue pencil
- a stainless-steel pica rule or plastic typescale
- a set of standard proofreaders' marks
- a calculator

and optionally:

- a computer: an Apple Macintosh, an IBM PC, or PC compatible such as a Compaq
- a photocopier capable of enlarging and reducing
- a fax machine to keep in visual touch with the client and printer

TYPE

The essence of writing and lettering, according to typographer Fernand Baudin, is to make language visible and retrievable. Spoken words pass away; written words are here to stay.

Type is the basic building block of print production. The design of type is a very subtle craft, dealing with the sometimes microscopic details that distinguish one typeface from another. It is also a thankless and humbling profession. "The best typography never gets noticed," American typographer Herb Lubalin has been quoted as saying. (Typographer means here a person who designs type and designs with type. The term **compositor** is used for someone who sets type.)

Or, as another famous American typographer Beatrice Warde has pointed out, perhaps more eloquently: "Good typography is like a crystal wine glass, thin as a bubble and just as transparent, its purpose to reveal rather than hide the beautiful thing it is meant to contain. Good graphic design and typography should help people communicate with all the clarity an idea deserves."

When we are taught to write the alphabet at school, it probably never occurs to us that there are thousands of ways that 26 simple letters can be constructed. It is only through looking at printed matter in later life that we begin to realize that a letter g, for example, comes in two main varieties: g and g.

And while an alphabet with 26 letters and eight punctuation marks will be adequate for a message on a noticeboard, a set of over a hundred different characters and marks may still fall short of some tasks facing the graphic designer.

Some history

Our Western alphabet was invented by the Phoenicians around 1100 BC somewhere on the eastern shores of the Mediterranean Sea. Capital letters derive from Roman incised lettering, with its distinctive serifs (the little marks made by the chisel to neaten the ends of letters), slanted stress, and variations in stroke thickness. The chiseled capital letters carved on Trajan's Column in Rome (Figs **2.1** and **2.3**, p. 30) in around AD 114 are still regarded as the "perfect" **roman** letters. Lower-case lettering comes from a more rounded form of handwriting, known as the uncial, developed for everyday use in the fourth century.

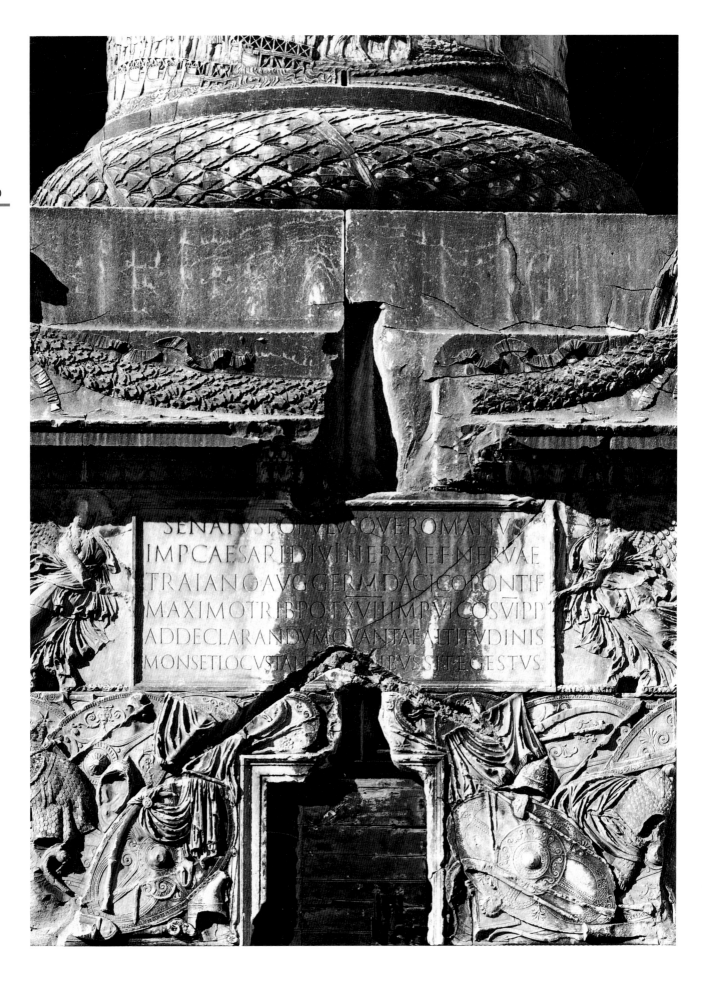

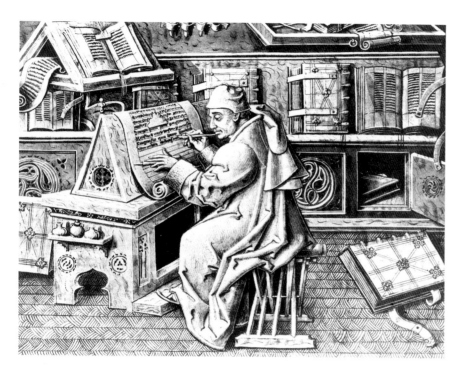

2.2 In medieval times all books were created individually, copied out slowly but lovingly by scribes. Books could only be afforded by the very rich.

In the Middle Ages, scribes created all books by hand, usually copying from existing books (Fig. **2.2**). They were beautiful objects, often "illuminated" with ornamental letters, paintings, and gold blocking (Fig. **2.4**).

The commonest form of writing in those days was called textura, or black letter, and sometimes Gothic because of its resemblance to the pointed architecture in fashion at the time.

ABCDEFGHIJ KLMNOPQR STUVWXYZ& 1234567890$

2.3 (left & opposite page) The lettering on Trajan's Column is the prototype for most present-day roman typefaces, including Adobe's display typeface (left) designed in 1989 by Carol Twombly and called, appropriately enough, Trajan. Note how our serifs derive from the chiseled finishing-off marks made by the Roman stonecutter.

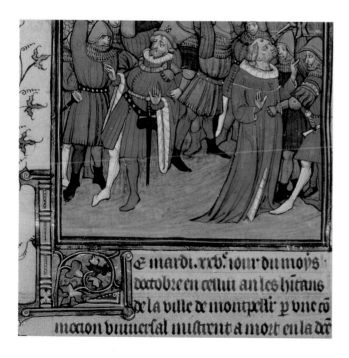

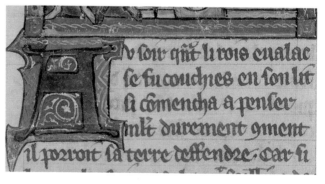

2.4 Some medieval books were illustrated or "illuminated" with watercolors and gold embellishments. The names of the artists and scribes are long forgotten, and those with recognizable styles are now known only by the names of their patrons – the Master of Mary of Burgundy, for example. To squeeze as many words as possible on to a page, most scribes used the up-and-down form of writing called textura lettering, as on this French depiction of the Montpellier riots of 1379 (left). Other manuscripts, like the 14th-century Lancelot Grail (above), used a freer, open, rounded form of script more akin to uncial, or roman lower case, writing.

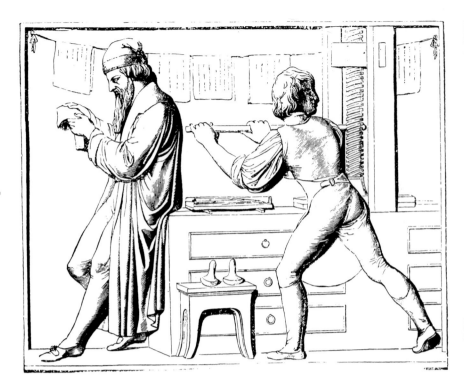

2.5 Johannes Gutenberg is credited with the invention of movable type in the western world. No portraits survive from the period; this artist's impression in woodcut, made much later from the carvings on his tomb, shows him reading proofs while his assistant works the printing press.

2.6 To imitate the lettering of the scribes, Gutenberg's font had to contain a set of over 300 characters, whereas a modern printer's alphabet might contain only 50 or so.

The first movable type in the western world, invented by Johannes Gutenberg (Fig. **2.5**), closely imitated the writing of the scribes. He created a set of over 300 characters, to accommodate all the variations of letterforms and **ligatures** (joined letters, such as fi and fl) that a scribe might need to use (Fig. **2.6**).

Gutenberg's masterpiece, known as the 42-line Bible, was an impressive achievement by any standards. Each two-volume work (48 copies survive from an estimated print run of 200) comprises 1286 pages, and was probably Gutenberg's financial undoing.

But his major legacy was the process of **hot-metal setting**. The first step is the cutting of a steel punch for every character and punctuation mark. This punch is then struck into a softer metal to form the **matrix** in which the type is cast. Finally lead, with the addition of some antimony for hardness and tin for toughness, is poured into the mold and the type cast.

Lead was used because it melts easily, flows evenly into the matrix, and expands slightly to make an exact replica of the punch. It hardens sufficiently to print repeatedly with

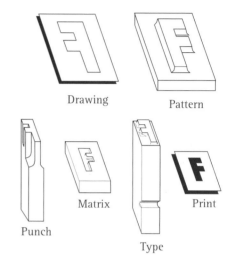

2.7 The design for a hot-metal letterform had to go through many stages on its way to the printed page, and at each successive stage the image had to be reversed (laterally inverted).

Drawing

Pattern

Punch

Matrix

Type

Print

acceptable levels of wear. Type for letterpress was always designed "the wrong way round" in mirror image, the production sequence being: drawing (wrong), pattern (right), punch (wrong), matrix (right), type (wrong), print (right) (Fig. **2.7**).

The fact that, in letterpress, characters have initially to be carved from steel has had a strong influence on type design ever since. It was only with the introduction of photo-setting, in the 1950s, that some of the constraints were lifted.

The condensed upright and angular letters of "black letter" type have almost no curves. Paper and vellum (the prepared skins of calves, sheep, or goats) were expensive then, and the scribes were encouraged to fit as many letters to a line as possible. The result is a closely packed page, with much more black than white.

In Italy, however, the humanist scholars favored the lighter roman style of lettering. As the skills of printing spread across Europe, craftsmen adapted their type to match the kind of lettering their customers preferred. William Caxton, the first printer in England, learnt his craft in Cologne, Germany, and bought Flemish equipment, so his books adopted the textura type.

Caxton's first book was printed in 1477. By 1509, English printers were already using roman type, mainly because of French influence. Shakespeare's plays were first printed in roman type (Fig. **2.8**), and "black letter" is now rarely seen – outside of German-speaking countries – except on newspaper mastheads, certificates and diplomas, on signs advertising "Ye Olde Worlde Shoppes" and for the logos of heavy rock bands.

Italics began life as separate typefaces in their own right. They were a derivation of the "chancery script" practiced by Italian legal scribes as a speedy alternative to regular writing. The first italic face was cut in Venice by Aldus Manutius in around 1500. It was not until two centuries later that it became partnered with roman, or plain text, and an essential part of the type family.

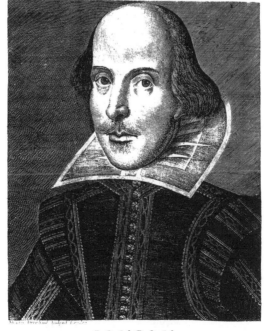

2.8 The title page of a Shakespeare edition of 1623. By the time his plays were being published, the more readable roman humanist style of type – still in common use today – had replaced the denser textura faces of the scribes.

2.9 A complete font. This font – ITC Clearface – is based on a face originally designed for American Type Founders by Morris Fuller Benton in 1907, and was redesigned in 1979 by Victor Caruso.

The language of type

A **font** is a complete set *in one size* of all the letters of the alphabet, complete with associated ligatures (joined letters), numerals, punctuation marks, and any other signs and symbols (Fig. **2.9**). The word font, or fount as it is spelt in Europe, derives from "found" as in type foundry, and reminds us of the days when molten metal type was cast in molds.

Typeface, often shortened to **face**, is the name given to the *design* of the alphabet and its associated marks and symbols. Every typeface has a name. This can be the name of its designer, for example Garamond, Bodoni, or Baskerville. It can take the name of the publication it was originally designed for, for example Times New Roman or Century. Or it may just have a fanciful name intended to convey the "feel" of the face, for example Optima, Perpetua, and Futura.

The letters of the alphabet, the numerals, and all the associated marks and symbols are collectively known as the **alphanumeric character set**. Individually, they are known as **sorts**. The expression "out of sorts," meaning unwell or depressed, comes from the typesetters finding that they have run out of a particular sort when composing a job.

The two words "font" and "typeface" are often used interchangeably. This has come about because in hot metal there will be a different font for each size of type. In photosetting, as we shall see later, it is common for one design to be enlarged or reduced to make all the sizes. This confusion is compounded in a digital page-layout system or word processor, in which a computer menu item labeled "font" will display to the user a list of available typefaces.

ABCDEFGHIJKLMNOPQRSTUVWXYZ
abcdefghijklmnopqrstuvwxyzfifl.,"-:;
()ÆæŒœ?&–$£1234567890

ABCDEFGHIJKLMNOPQRSTUVWXYZ
abcdefghijklmnopqrstuvwxyzfifl.,"-:;
()ÆæŒœ?&–$£1234567890

ABCDEFGHIJKLMNOPQRSTUVWXYZ
abcdefghijklmnopqrstuvwxyzfifl.,"-:;
()ÆæŒœ?&–$£1234567890

A complete set of sorts will also include some or all of the following:

- alternative letters, for the ends of lines, for example, and ornamented or "swash" capitals, such as

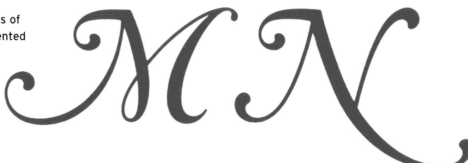

- diphthongs, such as æ and œ
- ligatures, such as fi and fl (in books of poetry, you may even see a ligature between c and t, see right)
- accented letters or "floating" accents for setting foreign languages, such as à (grave), é (acute), ô (circumflex), ü (diaresis), ç (cedilla), ñ (tilde)
- numerals or figures, which can be lining or non-lining (sometimes called "old-style" numbers). Some fonts have both (Fig. **2.10**)

1234567890

1234567890

◄ **2.10** Lining and non-lining ("old-style") numbers. The old-style ones have more charm, but lining numerals are easier to incorporate into tabular matter.

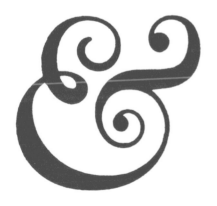

- punctuation marks, such as , (comma) and ; (semi-colon)
- reference marks, such as * (asterisk) and ¶ (paragraph)
- fractions and mathematical signs, also known as **pi characters**, such as + (plus) and = (equals)
- and other signs and **dingbats**, such as & (ampersand, see left), ☞, and © (copyright)

A font of roman type will comprise three alphabets:

- capitals, also called majuscules or upper case, so named because of the position of the letters in the compositor's typecase (abbreviated to caps or u.c.)
- small letters, also known as minuscules or lower case (abbreviated to l.c.)
- and perhaps small capitals, which are the height of a lower case letter (see left)

ABCDEFGHIJKLMNOPQRSTUVWXYZ
abcdefghijklmnopqrstuvwxyz
ABCDEFGHIJKLMNOPQRSTUVWXYZ

Helvetica Roman
Helvetica Italic
Helvetica Bold
Helvetica Bold Italic

Helvetica Heavy
Helvetica Heavy Italic
Helvetica Black
Helvetica Black Italic

◀ **2.11** A type family contains all the fonts associated with a particular design.

Italic and bold fonts contain just two alphabets: capitals and lower case.

A **family** is a set of fonts related to the basic roman typeface which may include italic and bold plus a whole spectrum of different "weights" (Fig. **2.11**). These range from ultra light to ultra bold. It will also include different widths, ranging from ultra condensed to ultra expanded.

Univers, for example, was designed by Adrian Frutiger in 1957 to have 21 fonts, in five weights and four widths (Fig. **2.12**). In the original numbering system for Univers, the tens figure indicates the weight, the units figure the width. Odd numbers are roman, even numbers italic.

A **series** is a complete range of sizes in the same typeface.

How type is measured

The way type is measured dates back to the days of hot metal. Type sizes used to have quaint names such as nonpareil, long primer, minikin, minion, and brevier. Only "pica" remains in common usage.

In 1737, the Frenchman Pierre Fournier *le jeune* invented the **point** system of measurement, by dividing the French inch into 12 "lines" which were further subdivided into six points. Some half century later, around 1785, another Parisian, François-Ambroise Didot, settled on a standard – the **didot point** – that is used in Europe to this day.

In the USA, the point was standardized by the American Type Founders' Association in 1886 to be 0·013837 inch (or 0·3515 mm). Recently, the point has been further rationalized to make it exactly $\frac{1}{72}$ inch (0·01389 in or 0·3528 mm). This may seem like splitting hairs, but it means in practice that the pica rules and typescales (Fig. **2.13**) designed for traditional typesetting will give inaccurate readings when used with digital layout.

There are 72 points to the inch. A **pica** is 12 points, and so measures $\frac{1}{6}$ inch. (The didot equivalent to the pica is the cicero.) Although with computerized systems type can be of any height, its size is still generally measured in points, abbreviated to pt.

The use of points to specify size refers back to metal letterpress type. When a font is described as 6 pt or 18 pt, what is really being measured is the height of the body of lead that the letter sits upon (Fig. **2.14**). This is the total height from the lowest extremity of a **descender** (the long vertical stroke of a p or q) to the top of the tallest **ascender** (the long vertical stroke of a k or d), with a little extra space top and bottom. Thus in Linotype Times, for example, the distance from the top of a 10 pt letter k to the

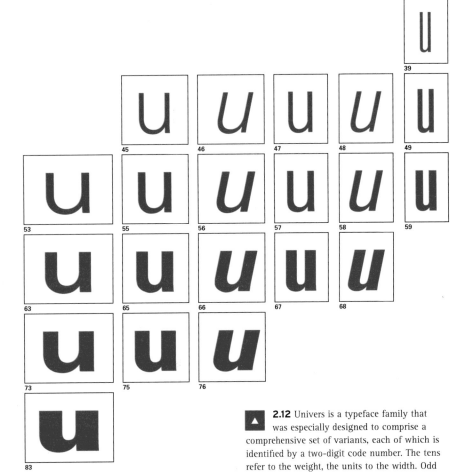

▲ **2.12** Univers is a typeface family that was especially designed to comprise a comprehensive set of variants, each of which is identified by a two-digit code number. The tens refer to the weight, the units to the width. Odd numbers are roman, even numbers italic.

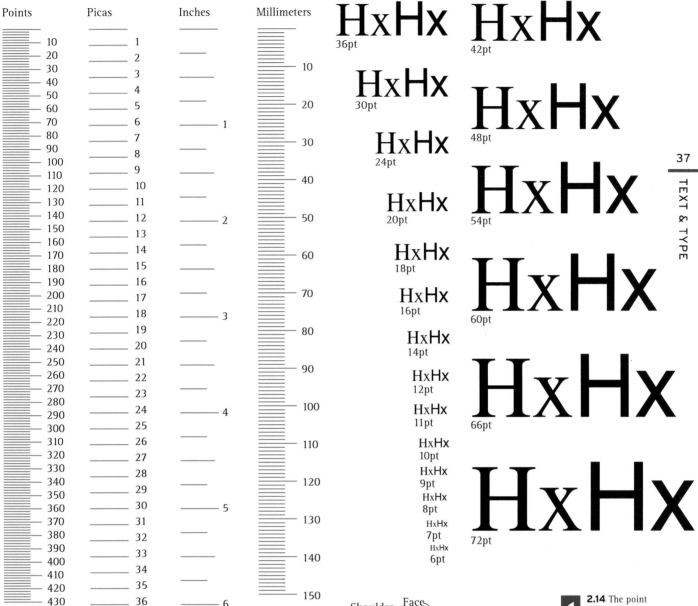

Points	Picas	Inches	Millimeters
10	1		
20	2		
30	3		10
40	4		
50	5		
60	5		20
70	6	1	
80	7		30
90	8		
100	9		
110	9		40
120	10		
130	11		
140	12	2	50
150	13		
160	14		60
170	14		
180	15		
190	16		70
200	17		
210	18	3	
220	19		80
230	19		
240	20		
250	21		90
260	22		
270	23		
280	24		100
290	24	4	
300	25		110
310	26		
320	27		
330	28		120
340	29		
350	29		
360	30	5	130
370	31		
380	32		
390	33		140
400	34		
410	34		150
420	35		
430	36	6	

HxHx 36pt
HxHx 42pt
HxHx 30pt
HxHx 48pt
HxHx 24pt
HxHx 54pt
HxHx 20pt
HxHx 18pt
HxHx 60pt
HxHx 16pt
HxHx 14pt
HxHx 12pt
HxHx 66pt
HxHx 11pt
HxHx 10pt
HxHx 9pt
HxHx 8pt
HxHx 72pt
HxHx 7pt
HxHx 6pt

▲ **2.13** (left and right) Type is still mainly measured in points and picas. There are 12 points to the pica, and 72 points to the inch. Here the two most commonplace fonts – Times New Roman and Helvetica – are shown in various point sizes.

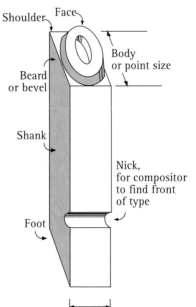

Shoulder · Face
Body or point size
Beard or bevel
Shank
Nick, for compositor to find front of type
Foot
Width, or set

◄ **2.14** The point size of a font refers back to metal type – to the top-to-bottom size of the body that the letter sits upon, not the distance from the uppermost part of a letter to the lowermost.

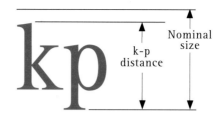

 2.15 A more logical method for measuring the size of type is to measure from the top of a letter k to the bottom of a letter p: the so-called k–p distance.

kpx | x-height

kpx | x-height

2.16 Different typefaces have different proportions of ascender/ descender in relation to the bowl, say, of a letter b. So two faces of the same point size may appear to be different sizes in print. The x-height – the height of a typical lower case letter – is a good guide to the apparent size, and thus legibility, of a particular typeface.

bottom of a letter p (the **k-p distance**, Fig. **2.15**) is not 10 pt but only 7·973 pt. The k-p distance of a named face can vary depending on its source, so the only sure way to identify type size is to compare your sample with suppliers' example settings.

A more exact way of defining point size is to say that it is the distance from **baseline** to baseline when type is set solid (without leading – see p. 40).

Some typefaces have longer ascenders and descenders than others, so it is quite possible for two typefaces to be exactly the same point size but to appear smaller or larger. A more visually accurate method for describing size is to use the **x-height** (Fig. **2.16**). The letter x is used because all its terminals touch a line of measurement.

Type below 14 pt is called **body type**, text, or book type. Type above 14 pt is called **display type**. Some display types are so decorative as to be unsuitable for text setting and are available in capitals only.

Width and spacing

The width of a letter is called the **set**. Every character sits on a body (real in hot metal, imaginary in computer systems) that is a number of "set points" wide, each set point being the same as the point which defines the height of the type. Typefaces with a narrow set, such as Bembo, will fit more words per page than wider typefaces, such as Baskerville.

On a regular typewriter, each letter, whether it is a thin i or a fat W, occupies the same width. The carriage moves forward the same distance each time a key is struck. The design of a typewriter font accommodates that shortcoming to

some extent. Look at the length of the serifs on a typewritten i, for example, or on a t (Fig. **2.17**).

Some letters are naturally wider than others, so, in typesetting, the "body" (the letter itself plus some space either side) is divided into vertical slices or **units**. In hot metal, an 18-unit system is employed. Thus the letter i occupies 5 units, whilst an M occupies the maximum of 18. Numerals are normally all 9 units wide, for ease of setting tables.

A regular typewriter uses a 1 unit, or monospaced, system. A "proportionally spaced" typewriter, such as the IBM Selectric, uses a 9-unit system. In comparison, photosetting systems use as

2.17 In a typewriter face such as Courier, all the letters are of equal width – note how the i is elongated to match the m. In more sophisticated typefaces, the width of letters varies, from the slim-line l to the more expansive w. Thus different letters are allocated different numbers of units according to their set, or width.

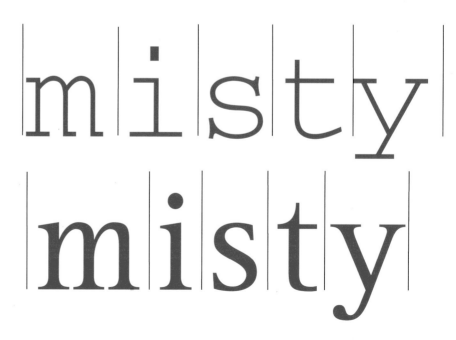

2.18 Letterpress type was kerned by cutting away parts of some metal sorts, and by placing parts of others to overhang the body of the type.

many as 96 units, the subtleties being apparent only in the very largest sizes of type.

In graphic design, the space around type is often as important as the letterform itself. When characters are allocated units, they are also given units either side to prevent consecutive sorts from touching. These are called **side bearings**, and the information about horizontal spacing built into a typeface is known as its **font metrics**.

Ems and ens

The width of a line of setting, or the column width of a publication, is called the **measure**, and is usually measured in picas. Other dimensions, particularly relating to page size and the positions of blocks of type, are generally measured in inches or millimeters.

Another convenient method of measurement is the **em**. This is the width of a capital M (or, strictly speaking, the width of a square space called an em **quad**). Half an em is an **en**, which is the width of a capital N. A complete font also provides the graphic designer with two types of dash, an en rule and an em rule – this book uses spaced em rules.

The em is not an absolute measurement like the pica. Its size will vary depending on the set of the typeface and its point size. A one em indent in 10 pt type is 10 points; a one em indent in 18 pt type is 18 points. But it is often convenient to ask the typesetter for a paragraph indent of say an em, so that it will always be in proportion with the rest of the setting. A column width should never be specified in ems,

however, for it will be different for each different font used. A 12 pt em is called a **pica em** – not to be confused with a regular pica!

Kerning and tracking

By overriding the unit allocation for pairs of certain letters, such as L and T, it is possible to bring them closer together and improve their visual appearance. This is called **kerning** (Fig. **2.19**).

In hot metal, kerning is only possible by physically cutting away, or mortising, the metal body of the type. Kerning characters are made with portions of the face overhanging the body (Fig. **2.18**). With computer systems, there are no restrictions on the extent of kerning possible. Most systems have routines already pre-programmed to adjust the spacing between kerning pairs automatically.

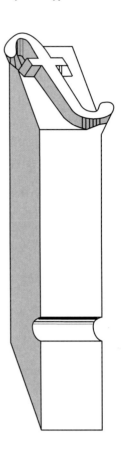

2.18 Letterpress type was kerned by cutting away parts of some metal sorts, and by placing parts of others to overhang the body of the type.

Yo! World.
Yo! World.

2.19 To improve the visual spacing between certain pairs of letters, especially those with overhanging parts, they are kerned according to rules laid down by the type designer. It is also possible to fine-tune the kerning later, by eye, depending on the context and on the size of the type.

▶ **2.20** Normal tracking leaves the spaces between letters as the type designer intended them to be. Negative tracking puts the letters closer together; positive or open tracking spaces them out.

Adjusting the spacing between *all* the letters is called **tracking** (Fig. **2.20**). Tracking should not be confused with kerning, which only takes place between pairs of letters.

Tracking was never really feasible with hot-metal setting, except in special places such as the title pages of books. On the rare occasions when it was, different materials were used to make spaces between letters: brass for 1 pt, copper for ½ pt, stainless steel for ¼ pt, and paper for the finest letterspacing of all.

In computer systems, it is common practice to use negative tracking to tighten up the spacing of text, particularly with sans-serif faces.

Jo was very busy in the garret, for the October days began to grow chilly, and the afternoons were short. For two or three hours the sun lay warmly in the high window, showing Jo seated on the old sofa, writing busily, with her papers spread out upon a trunk before her, while Scrabble, the pet rat, promenaded the beams overhead, accompanied by his oldest son, a fine young fellow, who was evidently very proud of his whiskers. Quite absorbed in her work, Jo scribbled away till the last page was filled, when she signed her name with a flourish, and threw down her pen, exclaiming:

"There, I've done my best! If this won't suit I shall have to wait till I can do better."

▲ ROTIS SERIF 55 12/13PT NORMAL TRACKING

Jo was very busy in the garret, for the October days began to grow chilly, and the afternoons were short. For two or three hours the sun lay warmly in the high window, showing Jo seated on the old sofa, writing busily, with her papers spread out upon a trunk before her, while Scrabble, the pet rat, promenaded the beams overhead, accompanied by his oldest son, a fine young fellow, who was evidently very proud of his whiskers. Quite absorbed in her work, Jo scribbled away till the last page was filled, when she signed her name with a flourish, and threw down her pen, exclaiming:

"There, I've done my best! If this won't suit I shall have to wait till I can do better."

▲ ROTIS SERIF 55 12/13PT NEGATIVE TRACKING

Jo was very busy in the garret, for the October days began to grow chilly, and the afternoons were short. For two or three hours the sun lay warmly in the high window, showing Jo seated on the old sofa, writing busily, with her papers spread out upon a trunk before her, while Scrabble, the pet rat, promenaded the beams overhead, accompanied by his oldest son, a fine young fellow, who was evidently very proud of his whiskers. Quite absorbed in her work, Jo scribbled away till the last page was filled, when she signed her name with a flourish, and threw down her pen, exclaiming:

"There, I've done my best! If this won't suit I shall have to wait till I can do better."

▲ ROTIS SERIF 55 12/13PT POSITIVE TRACKING

2.21 The space between lines of type is called leading after the strips of lead that were used in letterpress. Thus 12/12 pt is said to be set solid. The 12/13 pt has 1 pt leading. Type can also be set with negative leading, producing lines with ascenders and descenders touching.

Leading

Spacing between lines of type is called **leading**, pronounced "ledding," and named after the strips of lead that were placed between lines of type in hot-metal setting (Fig. **2.21**). **Set solid** means without leading, for example, written 10/10 pt and spoken ten on ten point. To write 10/11 pt means to ask for 10 pt type with a 1 pt space (leading) between the lines, although in hot metal it actually meant to cast 10 pt type on to an 11 pt body. To aid legibility (see p. 56) it is now common always to use 1 pt or 1¹/₂ pt leading in text setting.

With computer systems, it is now allowable to specify all measurements in either inches or millimeters, or even mixtures of the two. However, against all odds, the point and pica persist!

Jo was very busy in the garret, for the October days began to grow chilly, and the afternoons were short. For two or three hours the sun lay warmly in the high window, showing Jo seated on the old sofa, writing busily, with her papers spread out upon a trunk before her, while Scrabble, the pet rat, promenaded the beams overhead, accompanied by his oldest son, a fine young fellow, who was evidently very proud of his whiskers. Quite absorbed in her work, Jo scribbled away till the last page was filled, when she signed her name with a flourish, and threw down her pen, exclaiming:

"There, I've done my best! If this won't suit I shall have to wait till I can do better."

▲ ROTIS SERIF 55 12/11PT

Jo was very busy in the garret, for the October days began to grow chilly, and the afternoons were short. For two or three hours the sun lay warmly in the high window, showing Jo seated on the old sofa, writing busily, with her papers spread out upon a trunk before her, while Scrabble, the pet rat, promenaded the beams overhead, accompanied by his oldest son, a fine young fellow, who was evidently very proud of his whiskers. Quite absorbed in her work, Jo scribbled away till the last page was filled, when she signed her name with a flourish, and threw down her pen, exclaiming:

"There, I've done my best! If this won't suit I shall have to wait till I can do better."

▲ ROTIS SERIF 55 12/12PT

Jo was very busy in the garret, for the October days began to grow chilly, and the afternoons were short. For two or three hours the sun lay warmly in the high window, showing Jo seated on the old sofa, writing busily, with her papers spread out upon a trunk before her, while Scrabble, the pet rat, promenaded the beams overhead, accompanied by his oldest son, a fine young fellow, who was evidently very proud of his whiskers. Quite absorbed in her work, Jo scribbled away till the last page was filled, when she signed her name with a flourish, and threw down her pen, exclaiming:

"There, I've done my best! If this won't suit I shall have to wait till I can do better."

▲ ROTIS SERIF 55 12/13PT

Jo was very busy in the garret, for the October days began to grow chilly, and the afternoons were short. For two or three hours the sun lay warmly in the high window, showing Jo seated on the old sofa, writing busily, with her papers spread out upon a trunk before her, while Scrabble, the pet rat, promenaded the beams overhead, accompanied by his oldest son, a fine young fellow, who was evidently very proud of his whiskers. Quite absorbed in her work, Jo scribbled away till the last page was filled, when she signed her name with a flourish, and threw down her pen, exclaiming:

"There, I've done my best! If this won't suit I shall have to wait till I can do better."

▲ ROTIS SERIF 55 12/14PT

TABS AND PARAGRAPHS
Try to use the tabs and paragraph commands in your word processor to format text, rather than taps on the spacebar. Type will line up better and won't cause problems later if it has to be reflowed. Better still, learn how to use the style sheet commands included in most word processors – it will save you time in the long run, and ensure consistency within the document.

Most word processors and page layout programs let you specify left, right, and first-line indents for paragraphs (a paragraph to a computer is all the text until you reach a carriage return, and includes headlines). So try to kick the typist's habit of hitting the tab key when you begin a new para – give the paragraph a first-line indent.

And if you're setting text that's ranged left and want to move a sticking-out word over to the next line, use a forced break (shift-return) rather than a return or lots of spaces.

2.22 Type is commonly set ranged left (ragged right). It can instead be ranged right, centered, or asymmetrical. If type is to be set justified – neatly aligned on both left and right sides – variable spaces must be introduced between words to make each line the same length. Failing this, some words must be broken, or hyphenated.

Justification and hyphenation

A regular typewriter produces rows of type that line up on the left-hand side but give a ragged appearance on the right. In typesetting, this is called ragged right, **ranged left**, or flush left. Type can also be set ragged left, **ranged right**, centered, or asymmetrical (Fig. **2.22**).

In books and magazines, it is usual to see columns of type with neat edges on both sides. This is called **justified** setting, and it is achieved by introducing variable amounts of space between the words. More often than not, especially with the narrow columns used in newspapers and magazines, it is not possible to justify a line merely by increasing the space, and so words must be divided, or **hyphenated**.

Compositors have been taught to break words according to certain rules, as found in handbooks such as *Hart's Rules for Compositors and Readers*. A word is usually hyphenated between syllables, pairs of consonants, or pairs of vowels. The part of the word left at the end of a line should also suggest the part commencing the next line. Thus starva-tion is to be preferred to star-vation. Other rules instruct to hyphenate before -ing, except in ring, and unless preceded by d, t, or h.

Rules for hyphenation can be programmed into computer systems, along with tables of exceptions, to avoid **bad breaks**. However, it is still common to see howlers. Some careless word breaks can create unwanted meanings: the-rapist is a memorable example.

It is also generally considered good design to avoid too many consecutive hyphens. Three lines ending with

For two or three hours the sun lay warmly in the high window, showing Jo seated on the old sofa, writing busily, with her papers spread out upon a trunk before her, while Scrabble, the pet rat, promenaded the beams overhead, accompanied by his oldest son, a fine young fellow, who was evidently very proud of his whiskers.

▲ RANGED LEFT

For two or three hours the sun lay warmly in the high window, showing Jo seated on the old sofa, writing busily, with her papers spread out upon a trunk before her, while Scrabble, the pet rat, promenaded the beams overhead, accompanied by his oldest son, a fine young fellow, who was evidently very proud of his whiskers.

▲ RANGED RIGHT

For two or three hours the sun lay warmly in the high window, showing Jo seated on the old sofa, writing busily, with her papers spread out upon a trunk before her, while Scrabble, the pet rat, promenaded the beams overhead, accompanied by his oldest son, a fine young fellow, who was evidently very proud of his whiskers.

▲ CENTERED

For two or three hours the sun lay warmly in the high window, showing Jo seated on the old sofa, writing busily, with her papers spread out upon a trunk before her, while Scrabble, the pet rat, promenaded the beams overhead, accompanied by his oldest son, a fine young fellow, who was evidently very proud of his whiskers.

▲ ASYMMETRICAL

For two or three hours the sun lay warmly in the high window, showing Jo seated on the old sofa, writing busily, with her papers spread out upon a trunk before her, while Scrabble, the pet rat, promenaded the beams overhead, accompanied by his oldest son, a fine young fellow, who was evidently very proud of his whiskers.

▲ JUSTIFIED

hyphens or other punctuation marks is the maximum that can be tolerated. The designer should also be on the look-out for **rivers** of space running vertically in the middle of chunks of type. And for **widows** and **orphans** (Fig. **2.23**).

A widow is a single word on the last line of a paragraph carried over to the top of a column, and is best avoided by asking the copywriter or author to lose a word from earlier on in the paragraph. Orphans are single words, or small groups of words, left at the ends of paragraphs. There will be more discussion on the principles of layout in Chapter 4 (p. 106).

A revival from medieval manuscripts is the **drop cap** (Fig. **2.24**), mainly because it is easy to do on a computer system. A drop cap is an initial letter signaling the beginning of the text. It is usually enlarged to a size equivalent to three or more lines of type, with the type adjacent to the drop cap indented to make room. Drop caps work best when the first sentence begins with a single letter, such as A or I. Failing that, avoid short words, especially ones with only two letters. And take care with those words that form different words when the initial letter is removed, such as T-he, E-very and S-elf. Another common error is to forget to remove the first letter of the body text that follows.

¶ Type *Tymes*

An occasional Newsletter for graphic designers, printers, and typographers that is published once a millennium, if ever at all.

Alphabet soup

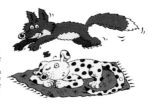

Writing text that is meant to represent body type in layouts and type specimen books is probably the most difficult task a writer can ever be asked to undertake. Ideally, the text should contain examples of all the letters and sorts – in Roman, *italic* and **bold** – and include a range of words of average length so that it looks right. Above all, it shouldn't draw attention to itself. The text is not meant to be read, merely looked at – but invariably someone somewhere will grab a magnifying glass, read it and then criticize any attempted jokes therein.

Some designers take the easy route and use real or bogus Latin text, most often a famous piece of text that begins: "Lorem ipsum dolor sit amet, consectetur adipscing elit, diam nonnumy eiusmod tempor incidunt ut labore et dolo... " These are, according to the FAQ (frequently asked questions) of the newsgroup **comp.fonts**, the slightly jumbled remnants of a passage from Cicero's *de Finibus Bonorum et Malorum*, written in 45 BC, a treatise on the theory of ethics, which begins: "Neque porro quisquam est qui dolorem ipsum quia dolor sit amet, consectetur, adipisci velit..." (There is no one who loves pain itself, who seeks after it and wants to have it, simply because it is pain.)

This text has been the industry's standard dummy text ever since some printer in the 1500s took a galley of type and scrambled it to make a type specimen book; it has survived letter-by-letter essentially unchanged except for an occasional "ing" or "y" thrown in. The nonsense Latin was as incomprehensible as Greek: so the phrase "it's all Greek to me" and the term "greeking" have common semantic roots!

But this does contain some strange, to English eyes, letter combinations. Few, if any, English words contain the sequence "eiu," for example. When short pieces of text are called for, try to make a sentence containing all the letters of the alphabet with as few duplications as possible. These are called *pangrams*.

Whatever else you do, try always to avoid widows.

The classic pangram used by typographers is: "The quick brown fox jumps over a lazy dog". Good score: all 24 letters of the alphabet in a 33-word sentence that makes sense. "Pack my box with five dozen liquor jugs" is better, with one letter less. Another common albeit longer one is: "How razorback-jumping frogs can level six piqued gymnasts!"

This one is not so good: "In the vocation of typesetting, dexterity can be gained by means of quiet, judicious and zealous work." It is more appropriate to the printing trade, but comprises 83 letters! And what about this: "Wherever civilization extends, the services of expert and judicious typographers and printers must always be quickly called upon". Is that grammatically correct? I don't think so. Or this: "The bank recognizes this claim as quite valid and just, so we expect full payment". Hmm.

Probably the shortest French pangram, at 29 letters, is: "Whisky vert: jugez cinq fox d'aplomb." Some pangrams of exactly 26 letters do exist, but rely heavily on the kind of obscure words that Scrabble players collect plus the odd Welsh and Hebrew word, such as cwm (a Welsh valley) and qoph (the nineteenth letter of the Hebrew alphabet) and, of course, proper nouns (which could in fact be made up from the left-over letters): "Vext cwm fly zing jabs Kurd qoph" is a good example. And try not to leave any orphans!

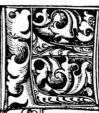**2.23** One of the general rules of good layout is to avoid creating "orphans" – one or a few words alone on a line at the end of a paragraph – or worse still, a "widow" – a single word floating at the top of a new page or column.

For two or three hours the sun lay warmly in the high window, showing Jo seated on the old sofa, writing busily, with her papers spread out upon a trunk before her, while Scrabble, the pet rat, promenaded the beams overhead, accompanied by his oldest son, a fine young fellow, who was evidently very proud of his whiskers.

For two or three hours the sun lay warmly in the high window, showing Jo seated on the old sofa, writing busily, with her papers spread out upon a trunk before her, while Scrabble, the pet rat, promenaded the beams overhead, accompanied by his oldest son, a fine young fellow, who was evidently very proud of his whiskers.

2.24 A drop cap is an embellishment found at the beginning of a chapter in a book or in the opening paragraph of a magazine article, in which the first letter is enlarged and set into the body of the text. Its historical precedent can be found in illuminated medieval manuscripts like the ornamented title page of 1496 from the Cistercian monastery at Zinna reproduced above.

44

TEXT & TYPE

TEXT

Text is the "meaning" part of type: just plain words plus the spaces between them, devoid of any information about the typefaces, sizes, measures, or weights being used. In print production, raw text is called **copy**.

One of the designer's tasks is **copy preparation**: adding the instructions that define how the text is going to look, either by keying them directly into the computer or by **marking up** the manuscript for the typesetter (Fig. **2.25**).

For type to remain consistent within a long document, or from issue to issue of a magazine, the graphic designer will write down and send to the compositor a **style sheet** or **type specification** (Fig. **2.26**). This will define the size, typeface, and measure of the body text, captions, headlines, and so on. In this book, for example, the text is set in 9/12.5 pt Interstate Regular, headings in various sizes of Interstate Bold, and chapter titles in 32 pt Interstate Bold.

The type spec may also lay down a **grid** (see pp. 106–7) which restricts type to certain areas of the page.

2.26 The style sheet for this book.

Correcting text proofs

~~Proofing and proof correction~~

Once type has been set, it must be checked to make sure that it has been keyed correctly. The old proofreaders on newspapers were adept at reading type back to front, but for mere mortals, a proof must be taken. The first proof is called the galley proof. Several pulls are made so that the various professionals involved in the production can each read the proof. The printer's reader is the first, and ~~he or the~~ marks the printer's mistakes to be corrected, usually in green ink.

[Run on] One proof is designated the **master proof**, and others *[bold]* *of the galley* go to the author or copywriter and to the copy editor, who decides which corrections should be incorporated on to the master proof. So-called **author's corrections** are *[bold]* marked in blue and have to be paid for, while any other printer's errors are marked in red. *[n.p.]* Typing errors such *[¶]* as transposed letters are called **literals**, and probably *[bold]* constitute the bulk of the corrections. Note that it is possible in hot metal and photosetting to introduce new, more serious errors into a text when attempting to correct a relatively trivial one! So that there can be no chance of misunderstanding between the copy editor and the compositor, corrections are marked neatly both in the setting and with an accompanying marginal symbol, according to an internationally agreed convention 2.28 (Fig. ~~2.5~~). *If something is wrongly corrected and needs to be reinstated, it should be marked with dotted underlining and the word stet written in the margin.*

Although there are no physical galleys in photosetting, the

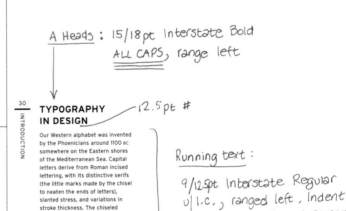

A Heads : 15/18pt Interstate Bold ALL CAPS, range left

30 INTRODUCTION

TYPOGRAPHY IN DESIGN   *12.5pt #*

Our Western alphabet was invented by the Phoenicians around 1100 BC somewhere on the Eastern shores of the Mediterranean Sea. Capital letters derive from Roman incised lettering, with its distinctive serifs (the little marks made by the chisel to neaten the ends of letters), slanted stress, and variations in stroke thickness. The chiseled capital letters carved on Trajan's Column in Rome around AD 114 are still regarded as the "perfect" Roman letters. Lower-case lettering comes from a more rounded form of handwriting, known as the uncial, developed for everyday use in the fourth century.

In the Middle Ages, scribes created all books by hand, usually copying from existing books. They were beautiful objects, often "illuminated" with ornamental letters, painting, and gold blocking.

Running text :
9/12.5pt Interstate Regular u/l.c., ranged left. Indent first line of new paragraphs by 12.5pts (hyphenate to even out spacing)

12.5pts #

Some history

Our Western alphabet was invented by the Phoenicians around 1100 BC somewhere on the Eastern shores of the Mediterranean Sea. Capital letters derive from Roman incised lettering, with its distinctive serifs (the little marks made by the chisel to neaten the ends of letters), slanted stress, and variations in stroke thickness.

B Heads: 12/15pt Interstate Bold u/l.c., range left

Ems and ens

Our Western alphabet was invented by the Phoenicians around 1100 BC somewhere on the Eastern shores of

C Heads: 9/12.5pt Interstate Bold u/l.c., range left

2.27 Once the marked-up copy returns from the typesetter in the form of galley proofs, it must be read, checked, and marked for correction using standard proof correction signs, as shown overleaf. Here we show the original marked-up copy (Fig. **2.25**), the typesetting after being marked for correction (right), and, after another journey to the typesetter's, the resulting "clean" setting (below), incorporated into the layout.

Correcting text proofs

Once type has been set, it must be checked to make sure that it has been keyed correctly. The old proof-readers on newspapers were adept at reading type back to front, but for mere mortals, a proof must be taken. The first proof is called the galley proof. Several copies are made so that the various professionals involved in the production can each read the proof. The printer's reader is the first, and marks the printer's mistakes to be corrected, usually in green ink. One of the galley proofs is designated the **master proof**, and others go to the author or copy-writer and to the copy editor, who decides which corrections should be incorporated on to the master proof (Fig. **2.27**). So-called **author's corrections** are marked in blue and have to be paid for, while any other printer's errors are marked in red.

Typing errors such as transposed letters are called **literals**, and probably constitute the bulk of the corrections. Note that it is possible in hot metal and photosetting to introduce new, more serious errors into a text when attempting to correct a relatively trivial one! So that there can be no chance of misunderstanding between the copy editor and the compositor, corrections are marked neatly both in the setting and with an accompanying marginal symbol, according to an internationally agreed convention (Fig. **2.28**, p. 46). The marginal symbol is most important because compositors run their eyes down the edges of proofs to locate corrections. If something is wrongly corrected and needs to be reinstated, it should be marked with

BOOKWORM TYPESETTING
4 Harthill Street, Manchester
T: 0161-832 3034

Calmann & King
Production for Graphic Design
24.2.97 [Own Disc & Pi]
David Newton [254G]

W9808FIG.FOL

Correcting text profs

Once typo has been set, it must be checked to make sure that it has been keyed correctly. The old proof-readers on newspapers were adept at reading type back to font, but for mere mortals, a proof mst be taken. The first proof is called the galley proof. Several pulls are made so that the various proffessionals involved in the production can each read the proof. Several pulls are taken so that the various proffessionals involved in the production can each read the proof The printers reader is the first, and marks the printer's mistakes to be corrected, usually in green ink.

One of the galley proofs is designated the **master proof**, and others go t the author or copywriter and to the copy editor, who decides which corrections should be incorporated on to the master proof. So-called **author's corrections are marked in blue and have to be paid for, while any other printer's errors are marked in red.**

Typing errors such as transposed letters are called *literals*, and probably constitute the bulk of the corrections. Note that it is possible in hot metal and photosetting to introduce new, more serious errors into a text when attempting to correct a relatively trivial one! so that there can be no chance of misunderstanding between the copyeditor and the composor, corrections are marked neatly both in the setting and with an accompanying marginal symbol, according to an internationally agreed convention (*Fig.* **2.27**). If something is wrongly corrected and needs to be reinstated, it should be marked with dotted underlining and the word stet written in the margin. Although there are no physical galleys in photosetting, the same procedure applies. The designer and/our copy editor usually will receive a set of photocopies of the bromide print, which is treated in exactly the same way as the hot metal galley proof. Once corrected, another proof may be sent, but it is more likely that the next chance to check that the corrections have been made will be on the page proof, a proof of the mechanical complete with running headlines, captions, and line illustrations in palace.

With apologies to Bookworm Typesetting, who set the galley proofs very cleanly.

dotted underlining and the word **stet** written in the margin.

Although there are no physical galleys in photosetting, the same procedure applies. The designer and/or copy editor will usually receive a set of photocopies of the bromide print, which is treated in exactly the same way as the hot metal galley proof. Once corrected, another proof may be sent, but it is more likely that the next chance to check that the corrections have been made will be on the **page proof**, a proof of the page layout complete with running headlines, captions, and illustrations in place.

With a digital design system, it is tempting to go straight to page layout once the text has been input. It is much safer to print out the text and to read it as if it were a galley proof. In this way there is **hardcopy** – a record of the corrections made. Better still, get a colleague to read the proof – mistakes are often invisible to those who make

STANDARD PROOF CORRECTION SIGNS

EXPLANATION	MARGINAL MARK	TEXT MARK
Delete letter(s) or word(s)		I've done my best
Close up; delete space		I've done my best
Delete, and close up word		I've done may best
Let it stand as it is	stet	I've done my best
Insert space	#	I've done my best
Equalize spacing	eq #	I've done my best
Insert hair space	hr #	1398–1468
Letterspace	LS	I'VE DONE MY BEST
Begin new paragraph	¶	I've done my best! If
Don't begin new paragraph; run on	no ¶	I've done my best! If this won't suit
Move type one em		I've done my best
Move type two ems		I've done my best
Move right		I've done my best
Move left		I've done my best
Center		I've done my best
Move up		I've done my best
Move down		I've done my best
Flush left; range left	fl	I've done my best
Flush right; range right	fr	I've done my best
Straighten type; align horizontally		I've done my best
Align vertically		I've done
Transpose; swap the order	tr	I've done my best
Set in *italic* type	ital	I've done my best
Set in roman type	rom	I've done my best
Set in bold type	bf	I've done my best
Set in lower case	lc	I've done MY best
Set in UPPER CASE (capitals)	cap	i've done my best
Set in SMALL CAPITALS	sc	I've done my best
Remove blemish	x	I've done my best
Make superscript figure		1024 is 210
Make subscript figure		101012
Insert comma		There I've done my best
Insert apostrophe or single quotation mark		Ive done my best
Insert period		I've done my best
Insert question mark	?	Have I done my best
Insert colon	:/	She exclaimed "I've done
Insert hyphen	/=/	Black and-white print
Insert en dash		1398 1468
Insert em dash		I've done my best
Insert parentheses	(/)	I've done my best
Insert brackets	[/]	I've done my best

2.28 To ensure that designers, proof readers, editors, and typesetters can communicate with each other effectively, an internationally agreed standard for proof correction symbols has been developed.

Casting off and copy fitting

Casting off is estimating the number of words in a manuscript. **Copy fitting** is assessing how much space text will take up in a printed document. Both are tedious and produce only approximate results, but are important in ensuring that you do not end up with pages of **overmatter**. Traditionally, one would encourage the author to type the same number of lines per page, and across a measure containing a round number of characters that is straightforward to calculate.

A regular typewriter does not have proportional spacing, so each letter takes up the same amount of space. Rule a pencil line down the right-hand edge of the typing, placed so that the visual area of the type to the right of the line equals the area of white space to the left. This establishes the average number of characters per line. A less accurate method is to count the number of characters per line for the first, say, ten lines and find the average. Then count the number of lines, marking, say, every hundredth line in pencil. It is assumed that, in English, an average word is five letters plus one space long, so the number of characters divided by six gives the number of words.

Most word processors use proportional spacing, which makes character counting more difficult. However, most now have built-in word counters. These are often approximate, depending on what the program decides constitutes a word. Different programs can give different word counts for the same piece of text.

them. And beware of computer spell checkers – they can give a false sense of security. For example, if a word is wrong but spelt "correctly," i.e. you typed "cat" but meant "cut," it won't be picked up by a spell checker. Irritatingly, spell checkers also stop at every proper noun and most numbers!

Collectively, a text document is called a **manuscript**, abbreviated to Ms. A single sheet is called a **folio**. (A folio is also the term given by publishers to the page numbers in books.) Each folio should be numbered and identified with a tag or catchline, usually the name of the author or job,

in case the Ms is dropped or blown about by a passing breeze. It is also customary for short pieces of setting to indicate on each folio whether (*more follows* or that the copy (*ends*.

Copy should always be clean and legible, typed or printed out on one side of the paper in double spacing with wide margins, leaving enough room for the copy editor's corrections. Some publishers provide authors with templates, sheets printed with faint blue guidelines, for the purpose. Any matter not to be printed, such as instructions to the typesetter, should be encircled.

2.29 Copy-fitting tables help estimate the space needed by copy in a particular typeface and point size. The above old-style table is for Century. In the two-part table below, each typeface is given a value. A number from the first table is used to read off characters per pica from the second.

Characters per line

Font size	Pica Measure												
	18	19	20	21	22	23	24	25	26	27	28	29	30
8 pt.	59	62	65	68	72	75	78	81	85	88	91	94	98
9 pt.	52	55	58	60	63	66	69	72	75	78	81	83	86
10 pt.	46	48	51	53	56	58	61	64	66	69	71	74	76
11 pt.	42	44	47	49	51	54	56	58	61	63	65	68	70
12 pt.	38	40	43	45	47	49	51	53	55	57	60	62	64

The amount of space required when the text is set into type will vary depending both on the type size and the typeface. For hot metal and photosetting, the type foundries supply copy-fitting tables (Fig. **2.29**), which will give you the information that, for example, 11 pt Bembo averages 66 characters (11 words) in a line 24 picas long. It is thus possible to find out how many pages the copy will fill once set in type.

For smaller jobs, a plastic type gauge can be used to measure the number of lines that a particular size of type will occupy. If you calculate that five lines of text will give you seven lines of type, for example, it is possible to count them off using the gauge. Many type gauges also have scales with which to count typewritten characters. On typewriters, the number of characters per inch is called the **pitch**: the normal 10 pitch is called pica (no relation to the typographic pica!), and the smaller 12 pitch is called elite. Always overestimate the number of words, to be on the safe side. It is easier to deal with white space than to find room for unexpected text.

With computer setting, there is a lot of variation in set width between the same named typeface from different suppliers. The only way to be safe is to base your calculations on a piece of sample setting from your chosen font and use *exactly* the same font for the eventual setting. This is particularly important when using a bureau which may claim to hold the same font; when the proof arrives you may find the words are not where you wanted them.

It is all too easy to make copy fit an awkward space by altering the tracking, the size of type, or the leading by just the tiniest amount, with a resulting inconsistency of "color" within the document. This is a temptation that should be resisted.

House style

There are few absolutes in life, and in some cases a usage is neither right nor wrong. But **house style** is a way of standardizing spelling and codifying the way, say, that ships' names, like the uss *Enterprise*, are always italicized. There will normally also be guidelines to avoid sexist and racist usages creeping into print.

House style will regulate how the date should be written, and will also include instructions as to whether acronyms should be given periods or not (dots per inch as d.p.i. or dpi, or even dots/in), set all caps or all lower case (both WYSIWYG and wysiwyg, for example, could be used to mean "what you see is what you get").

The keyword is consistency – within a publication, and within an organization.

Alphabet lengths for different sizes
Laufweitenkennzahl für verschiedene Schriftgrößen
Longueur d'alphabet pour différents corps

	pt	6	7	8	9	10	11	12	14	16	18	20	24	30	36	42	48
	mm	2,25	2,63	3,00	3,38	3,75	4,13	4,50	5,25	6,00	6,75	7,50	9,00	11,25	13,50	15,75	18,00
	85	51	59	68	76	85	93	102	119	136	153	170	204	255	306	357	408
	87	52	60	69	78	87	95	104	121	139	156	174	208	261	313	365	417
	88	52	61	70	79	88	96	105	123	140	158	176	211	264	316	369	422
	90	54	63	72	81	90	99	108	126	144	162	180	216	270	324	378	432
	92	55	64	73	82	92	101	110	128	147	165	184	220	276	331	386	441
	93	55	65	74	83	93	102	111	130	148	167	186	223	279	334	390	446
	95	57	66	76	85	95	104	114	133	152	171	190	228	285	342	399	456
	97	58	67	77	87	97	106	116	135	155	174	194	232	291	349	407	465
	98	58	68	78	88	98	107	117	137	156	176	196	235	294	352	411	470
	100	60	70	80	90	100	110	120	140	160	180	200	240	300	360	420	480
	102	61	71	81	91	102	112	122	142	163	183	204	244	306	367	428	489
	103	61	72	82	92	103	113	123	144	164	185	206	247	309	370	432	494
	105	63	73	84	94	105	115	126	147	168	189	210	252	315	378	441	504
																449	513
																453	518
																462	528
																470	537
																474	542
																483	552
																491	561
																495	566
																504	576
																512	585
																516	590
																525	600
																533	609
																537	614
																546	624
																554	633
																558	638
																567	648
																575	657
																579	662
																588	672
																596	681

(left margin label: alphabet length ref. no. at 10 pt / Laufweitenkennzahl in 10 pt / Référence de longueur d'alphabet en 10 pt)

Characters per line (Pica)
Zeichen pro Zeile (Pica)
Caractères par ligne (Pica)

Pica	1.00	10	12	14	16	18	20	22	24	26	28	30	32	36	40	45
50	6.74	67	81	94	108	121	135	148	162	175	189	202	216	243	270	303
52	6.48	65	78	91	104	117	130	143	156	168	181	194	207	233	259	292
54	6.24	62	75	87	100	112	125	137	150	162	175	187	200	225	250	281
56	6.02	60	72	84	96	108	120	132	144	156	168	181	193	217	241	271
58	5.81	58	70	81	93	105	116	128	139	151	163	174	186	209	232	261
60	5.62	56	67	79	90	101	112	124	135	146	157	168	180	202	225	253
62	5.43	54	65	76	87	98	109	120	130	141	152	163	174	196	217	245
64	5.27	53	63	74	84	95	105	116	126	137	147	158	168	190	211	237
66	5.11	51	61	71	82	92	102	112	123	133	143	153	163	184	204	230
68	4.96	50	59	69	79	89	99	109	119	129	139	149	159	178	198	223
70	4.81	48	58	67	77	87	96	106	116	125	135	144	154	173	193	217
72	4.68	47	56	66	75	84	94	103	112	122	131	140	150	168	187	211
74	4.55	46	55	64	73	82	91	100	109	118	127	137	146	164	182	205
76	4.43	44	53	62	71	80	89	98	106	115	124	133	142	160	177	200
78	4.32	43	52	60	69	78	86	95	104	112	121	130	138	156	173	194

(left margin label: determined alphabet length ref. no. / ermittelte Laufweitenkennzahl / Référence de longueur d'alphabet déterminés)

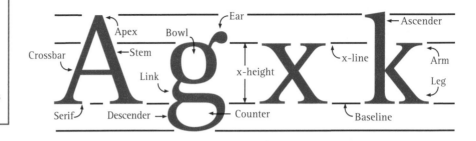

RECOGNIZING TYPEFACES
To recognize a typeface you're not familiar with, look at the capital Q, the lower-case g and the ampersand (&) first for the earmarks (distinguishing features) of the face. Collect as many type sample books as you can – catalogs are often given away by type foundries – and, if you have time, try asking your supplier: some type vendors offer a type-recognition service.

Choosing and recognizing typefaces

To be able to choose the right type-face for the job, one must first know something about how typefaces are constructed and classified (Fig. **2.30**).

Each face has its own personality (Fig. **2.31**), and typefaces are des-cribed by typographers in the same hallowed tones used by connoisseurs to talk about wine. Garamond is said to be "quiet"; Bodoni "sparkles."

Each has its place in the graphic designer's toolkit: for a bank's annual report, for example, you may wish to use a well-established "classic" face like Garamond to convey tradition and solidity; a music magazine aimed at young people will look better with a fashionable type like Meta. Some typefaces are chosen for practical reasons. Newspapers tend to use faces with large x-heights and open counters, because the ink spread on low-grade paper would fill in less robust faces.

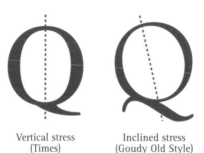

Vertical stress
(Times)

Inclined stress
(Goudy Old Style)

2.30 Each letter has its own anatomical details, and knowing the names for the component parts of a letterform is a great aid to identifying and specifying a particular typeface.

Establishment
Times New Roman

Professional
Rotis serif 55 ·

Fun and Friendly
Dolores Bold

Bland but safe
Helvetica

Traditional
Baskerville

Powerful
Franklin Gothic Heavy

Fashionable
Meta

Elegant
Garamond Italic

2.31 Some typefaces are so familiar as to be virtually invisible – Times and Helvetica are the main culprits – while others, such as Futura and Gill, come regularly in and out of fashion every few years.

 **2.32** All typefaces can be classified according to whether they do or do not have serifs. Some serifs have brackets – smooth "fillets" between the horizontal and upright – and some do not. The size of the serif can range from slab to hairline.

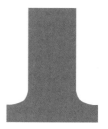

Sans serif (without serifs)   Square or slab serifs   Bracketed serifs

Thin or hairline serifs   Round serifs

Serif or sans serif?

The most obvious distinguishing feature of a typeface is whether it has a serif or not (Fig. **2.32**). **Serifs** are marks or flourishes around the extremities of letters, on the baseline and at the top, usually at right angles to the direction of the stroke. They help to make type more readable (see p. 56), and take several different forms: bracketed, with a smooth curved "fillet" between the serif and stem; slab, with sharper corners and almost the same thickness as the stem; hairline; or wedge.

A typeface without serifs is called **sans serif**, or just sans. The old name was grot, from grotesque, and in America they are also known as Gothic faces. The first sans typeface for text was cast in 1835 and called Seven Lines Grotesque, though sans faces have long been used for display setting and for signwriting. It did not become popular until the beginning of this century, first with Edward Johnston's 1916 typeface – still in use – for London Transport. Later came Univers, and Max Miedinger's Helvetica, perhaps one of the most popular typefaces currently in use.

Earmarks

Each typeface has its own distinctive characteristics, called **earmarks** (Fig. **2.33**), named after the distinctive "ear" on the lower case g. These enable us to identify one design from another. To distinguish Helvetica from Univers, for example, look for the vertical downstroke in the capital G, the curly tail of the lower case y, and the angled tail through the bowl of the Q.

Soon you will be spotting the more subtle differences. For other

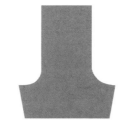

Novelty serifs

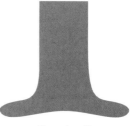

Cupped serifs

GgyQa&3
Helvetica

GgyQa&3
Univers

GgyQa&3
Futura

GgyQa&3
Gill

GgyQa&4
Clearface

GgyQa&4
Times

GgyQap&3
Baskerville

GgyQap&3
Garamond

typefaces, a good strategy is to start with the Q (a letter so infrequently used that typographers often have fun with it, making it their trademark), then the ampersand, then the J, G, and W. Try the lower case g, then a, j, and y. For numbers, look first at 3, then 7, 5, and 2. Real italics, not the sloped oblique versions of roman type found in computer systems, are usually distinctive and easy to identify.

2.33 Earmarks are the distinguishing features of a typeface design. Easily identifiable letters include the capital Q and the lower case g, and don't forget the ampersand.

Group 1: Humanist

These faces are characterized by an inclined bar on the lower case e, which points to their calligraphic origins. They are light in weight, with bracketed serifs, and an oblique stress. Also known as Venetian. An example is Centaur.

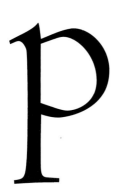

2.34a Humanist: Centaur.
Mind your Ps & Qs
ABCDEFGHIJKLMNOPQRSTUVWXYZ
abcdefghijklmnopqrstuvwxyz
1234567890
(.,:;*?$["&"]'%'!)

It was after sun-up now, but we went right on and didn't tie up. The king and the duke turned out by and by looking pretty rusty; but after they'd jumped overboard and took a swim it chippered them up a good deal. After breakfast the king he took a seat on the corner of the raft, and pulled off his boots and rolled up his britches, and let his legs dangle in the water, so as to be comfortable, and lit his pipe, and went to getting his "Romeo and Juliet" by heart.

Group 2: Garalde

The faces in this group still have an oblique stress, but are less script-like, with a horizontal bar on the e. The name Garalde is a contraction of *Gara*mond and *Ald*us, though where the e comes from is a mystery. Other examples include Bembo, Plantin, and Caslon (Fig. **2.35**).

Collectively, Humanist and Garalde are called "old face" or "old style." Old style, however, does not mean old-fashioned: Galliard is a face designed with the aid of a computer by Matthew Carter in 1978-81.

2.34b Garalde: Caslon.
Mind your Ps & Qs
ABCDEFGHIJKLMNOPQRSTUVWXYZ
abcdefghijklmnopqrstuvwxyz
1234567890
(.,:;*?$["&"]'%'!)

It was after sun-up now, but we went right on and didn't tie up. The king and the duke turned out by and by looking pretty rusty; but after they'd jumped overboard and took a swim it chippered them up a good deal. After breakfast the king he took a seat on the corner of the raft, and pulled off his boots and rolled up his britches, and let his legs dangle in the water, so as to be comfortable, and lit his pipe, and went to getting his "Romeo and Juliet" by heart.

Other features that help distinguish different typefaces are the overall proportions (the relation of x-height to ascenders and descenders, for example), the stress (is it oblique or vertical?), the contrast between thick and thin strokes, the formation of the serifs. Are the characters wide and loose fitting, or compact and tight? Some are easy: script and "black letter" faces, for example, stand out from all the others. To the untrained eye, others look virtually indistinguishable.

Type has long been classified into groups, such as "old face," "transitional," and "modern." These sometimes vague classifications have been codified, first by French typographer Maximilien Vox, and later by national and international standards, into nine groups (Fig. **2.34**). The categories may not seem at first sight to be of great use to the graphic designer when choosing type, but they are a considerable aid to communicating with the typesetter and printer.

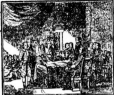

2.35 The US Declaration of Independence, 1776, set in Caslon.

Group 3: Transitional

Here the axis of the curves has become vertical, with bracketed oblique serifs. The construction of each letter is based on a mathematical formula, and the major example is Baskerville, which is wide for its x-height.

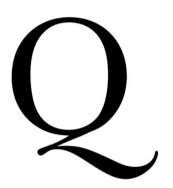

2.34c Transitional: Baskerville.
Mind your Ps & Qs
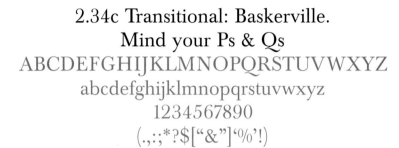
ABCDEFGHIJKLMNOPQRSTUVWXYZ
abcdefghijklmnopqrstuvwxyz
1234567890
(.,:;*?$["&"]'%'!)

It was after sun-up now, but we went right on and didn't tie up. The king and the duke turned out by and by looking pretty rusty; but after they'd jumped overboard and took a swim it chippered them up a good deal. After breakfast the king he took a seat on the corner of the raft, and pulled off his boots and rolled up his britches, and let his legs dangle in the water, so as to be comfortable, and lit his pipe, and went to getting his "Romeo and Juliet" by heart.

Group 4: Didone

There is an abrupt contrast between the thick and the thin strokes; the axis of the curves is completely vertical; and serifs are horizontal, unbracketed, and hairline. This grouping is also called "modern." The name is a contraction of *Dido*t and Bo*doni*, and other examples include Caledonia.

P

2.34d Didone: Bodoni.
Mind your Ps & Qs
ABCDEFGHIJKLMNOPQRSTUVWXYZ
abcdefghijklmnopqrstuvwxyz
1234567890
(.,:;*?$["&"]'%'!)

It was after sun-up now, but we went right on and didn't tie up. The king and the duke turned out by and by looking pretty rusty; but after they'd jumped overboard and took a swim it chippered them up a good deal. After breakfast the king he took a seat on the corner of the raft, and pulled off his boots and rolled up his britches, and let his legs dangle in the water, so as to be comfortable, and lit his pipe, and went to getting his "Romeo and Juliet" by heart.

2.34e Mechanistic: Rockwell.
Mind your Ps & Qs
ABCDEFGHIJKLMNOPQRSTUVWXYZ
abcdefghijklmnopqrstuvwxyz
1234567890
(.,:;*?$["&"]'%'!)

It was after sun-up now, but we went right on and didn't tie up. The king and the duke turned out by and by looking pretty rusty; but after they'd jumped overboard and took a swim it chippered them up a good deal. After breakfast the king he took a seat on the corner of the raft, and pulled off his boots and rolled up his britches, and let his legs dangle in the water, so as to be comfortable, and lit his pipe, and went to getting his "Romeo and Juliet" by heart.

Also known as slab-serif or Egyptian, these faces have heavy square-ended serifs, with or without brackets. Examples include Clarendon, Melior, and Rockwell.

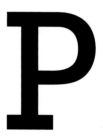

2.34f Neo-grot sans serif: Helvetica.
Mind your Ps & Qs
ABCDEFGHIJKLMNOPQRSTUVWXYZ
abcdefghijklmnopqrstuvwxyz
1234567890
(.,:;*?$["&"]'%'!)

It was after sun-up now, but we went right on and didn't tie up. The king and the duke turned out by and by looking pretty rusty; but after they'd jumped overboard and took a swim it chippered them up a good deal. After breakfast the king he took a seat on the corner of the raft, and pulled off his boots and rolled up his britches, and let his legs dangle in the water, so as to be comfortable, and lit his pipe, and went to getting his "Romeo and Juliet" by heart.

Group 6: Lineal
Better known as sans serif, these faces are further subdivided into:
- Grotesque, the original 19th-century faces with a "closed" appearance, e.g. Grot and Headline;
- Neo-grot, which are rounded and open with a monoline weight, e.g. Helvetica and Univers;

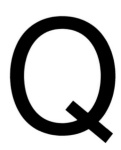

Group 6: Lineal continued
- Geometric, based on the geometric shapes promoted by the Bauhaus, such as circles and straight lines, e.g. Futura;
- Humanist sans serif, based on more classical proportions, e.g. Gill Sans and Optima.

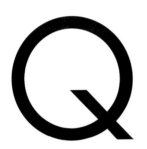

2.34g Geometric sans serif: Futura.

Mind your Ps & Qs
ABCDEFGHIJKLMNOPQRSTUVWXYZ
abcdefghijklmnopqrstuvwxyz
1234567890
(.,:;*?$["&"]'%'!)

It was after sun-up now, but we went right on and didn't tie up. The king and the duke turned out by and by looking pretty rusty; but after they'd jumped overboard and took a swim it chippered them up a good deal. After breakfast the king he took a seat on the corner of the raft, and pulled off his boots and rolled up his britches, and let his legs dangle in the water, so as to be comfortable, and lit his pipe, and went to getting his "Romeo and Juliet" by heart.

Group 7: Glyphic
These faces look chiseled rather than written, with blunt elephant's foot serifs. The example shown here is Albertus.

ABCDEFGHIJKLMNOPQ
RSTUVWXYZ
abcdefghijklmnopqrstuvwxyz
1234567890

Group 8: Script
Script faces imitate cursive or "copperplate" writing. They can be formal, e.g. the Berthold Script shown here, or informal, e.g. Flash. They are not normally used as text faces, but are reserved for jobs such as wedding invitations or menus.

ABCDEFGHIJKLMNO
PQRSTUVWXYZ
abcdefghijklmnopqrstuvwxyz
1234567890

Group 9: Graphic
This group includes faces that look as if they have been drawn, rather than written. Examples are Dom Casual (shown here) and Klang.

ABCDEFGHIJKLMNO
PQRSTUVWXYZ
1234567890

ABCDEFGHIJKLMNOPQRSTUVWXYZ
abcdefghijklmnopqrstuvwxyz

ABCDEFGHIJKLMNOPQRSTU
VWXYZ
abcdefghijklmnopqrstuvwxyz

ABCDEFGHIJKLMNOPQRSTUVWXYZ
abcdefghijklmnopqrstuvwxyz

ABCDEFGHIJKLMNOPQRSTUVWXYZ
abcdefghijklmnopqrstuvwxyz

ABCDEFGHIJKLMNOPQRSTUVWXYZ
abcdefghijklmnopqrstuvwxyz

ABCDEFGHIJKLMNOPQRSTUVWXYZ
abcdefghijklmnopqrstuvwxyz

◀ **2.36** Many classic letterpress typefaces have been redesigned over the years, first for phototypesetting and lately for digital systems. Note how recent versions often have greater x-heights, thicker serifs, and a more condensed appearance. This is to accommodate changing needs in both technology and fashion. Shown contrasted here are Monotype's Century Old Style and ITC's Century Book, and both Monotype and ITC versions of Garamond and Garamond Italic. (ITC faces are printed in red.)

To this classification scheme ought to be added a group to include the digital faces created recently on computer systems (see pp. 63-7) mainly for the style magazines of the 1980s, e.g. Modula and Emigré, and the so-called "intelligent" faces such as Beowulf.

Despite the best efforts of the classifiers, there still remain some typefaces that defy categorization, and which can only be described as being "hybrids." These include the best known typeface of all – Times New Roman – which has to be described as a Garalde/Didone hybrid. There are two other points to make about typefaces: first, not all versions of a named typeface are the same (Fig. **2.36**). There are many versions and interpretations of Univers and Times for example, and if you are not precise in specifying a particular vendor's Univers, you may be in for a surprise, especially when an accurate cast-off has been attempted.

Second, for copyright reasons, the same design of typeface may have a different name (often thinly disguised to give a clue to its origin) when obtained from a source other than its originator. For example, Bitstream's version of Plantin is called Aldine 721, Linotype's Futura Book is called Spartan Book and Compugraphic's Helvetica is renamed Helios.

TEXT & TYPE

2.37 Maximum legibility is always required for warning signs. This poster, dated 1851, was printed by letterpress — the word "CAUTION" using wooden type, the rest in metal.

Legibility and readability

One of the most important concerns of the graphic designer is to ensure that any type used is legible and readable. The intention, after all, is to communicate the author's or copywriter's ideas to the reader as efficiently as possible. If the type makes an aesthetically pleasing "picture" on the page as well, then that's a bonus.

For legibility, context is everything (Fig. **2.37**). Novels, cookery books, and telephone directories are all read in different ways. The designer has to know the conditions in which the type will be read, who will be reading it, and why.

Faces with quirky letters, like the Q in Bodoni and the *g* in Galliard Italic, can begin to annoy when set in continuous text. And a display face for advertising or a logo has a completely different purpose to that of a face for a children's book. A logo, for example, may initially be harder to read, but in the long term is more memorable and recognizable. The instant legibility of type on freeway signs is a matter of life and death.

Legibility, however, is a cultural matter. Unless they are German-speaking, many people find "black face" lettering difficult to under-stand. Graffiti on subway trains are unreadable by most people over 15. Designers such as David Carson (see p. 118) are often attacked by purist typographers for alleged illegibility, but in cases like *Ray Gun*, where the style is often more important than the content, a more adventurous approach to type is often expected.

There has been much research on the legibility of sans versus seriffed faces. The outcome seems to be that, with some exceptions, faces with serifs are easier to read continuously over long periods than those without. Serifs serve several purposes. They help letters to keep their distance. They link letters to make words, for we read by recognizing the shapes of words. They also help to differentiate letterforms, particularly the top halves, which are apparently more critical for rapid recognition. Faces with a large x-height, favored by newspapers, do not guarantee legibility, for the relatively short ascenders and descenders may have a negative effect on the overall shape of a word.

Sans serif faces, especially geometric ones like Futura, have a (purposely) high degree of similarity between sorts. Try to distinguish for example 1, l, and I out of context! For some faces there are versions specially designed for continuous setting. Futura Book, for example, is just such a version of Futura. But the matter is highly subjective. Some assert that sans serif faces set in blocks of text look monotonous and hence intrinsically less attractive.

Italic is said to be less legible than roman, so much so that the typographer Sir Francis Meynell recommended that poetry be set in italic because it ought to be read slowly!

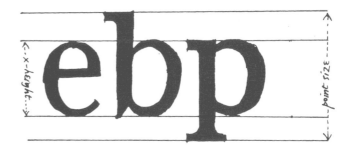

Above: Letters with a small x-height. On the facing page letters with a large x-height. The size is identical in both cases. The difference is in the contrast between the normal letters and the ascenders & descenders. All ascenders line at the top. All descenders line at the bottom. But the normal letters are much deeper on the facing page. And the descenders & ascenders are shorter accordingly. Traditionally the smaller x-height is for book-typography. The Italian Renaissance marked a return to the Carolingian alphabet & the progressive elimination of Gothic letter-

forms. The black-letter, however, was never totally eliminated. In Germany, in Switzerland it is ever-present. Nor is it absent in Britain & the U.S. It would be a real loss for typography & calligraphy if it were to disappear altogether. A larger x-height has been popularised by newspapers. The poor quality of newsprint & the speed of the printing process combine to fill in the bowls of a b d e g o p q. Technology may change. Not so the letterforms, the text columns. For more than a century the newspaper has met the expectations of millions. It is therefore easier to carry on than to try to change their visual habits.

For print to be legible, words should be set close to each other, and certainly closer than the space between lines of type. If the gap between words is too great, the eye will skip to the next line rather than the next word. So all continuous text matter is made easier to read by increasing the leading. Of course, there are some exceptions to this rule — for television graphics and on traffic signs, for example.

Legibility also has a part to play in deciding the width of columns. If the line is longer than about 12 words (or seven words in newspaper setting), the eye will have difficulty in returning to find the next line.

Black on white setting, too, is considered to be more readable than **reversed out** white on black (abbreviated WOB), where hairline serifs, for example, can be lost and horizontal spacing can look too cramped. Text all set in capitals, as in telexes, can be very tiring on the eye. On the Internet, text that is set all in capitals means you're shouting!

Legibility can be achieved by observing common-sense rules like these. Readability is something else.

It entices readers to continue reading what you have designed, and that takes care, skill, and talent!

TYPESETTING SYSTEMS

There are many ways of producing type. Most graphic designers will eventually be using offset lithography for print, and this process demands input in the form of film — a photographic image of the page to be printed. This may be made from a mechanical (see Chapter 4) or come direct from a computer system. The typesetting used as raw material in compiling the mechanical may in turn come from metal type, in the form of a reproduction proof, or it may be a bromide print from a phototypesetting machine, a laser print, or a piece of hand lettering.

Other print technologies, such as flexography and silkscreen, rely on similar processes — some newspapers even print on letterpress machines from phototypeset mechanicals. Each method of typesetting has its role and its place,

2.38 Text does not necessarily have to be typeset. Typographers like Fernand Baudin are very fond of their own handwriting, as demonstrated in these pages from his manual *How Typography Works (and Why it is Important)*.

though some methods (e.g. so-called "strike-on" from the IBM Selectric typewriter) have become obsolete, and are discussed here only for the sake of completeness.

Hand lettering and calligraphy

It is an amusing exercise to try to work out the very least expensive way to produce a book, magazine, or any other publication. If you have all the time in the world, the cheapest production method of all must be to handwrite every single copy. Fernand Baudin's book *How Typography Works (and Why it is Important)* has been produced almost entirely by reproducing the author's best handwriting (Fig. **2.38**). Since the development of photolithography and, more recently, the introduction of

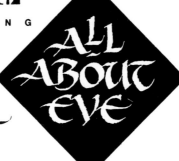

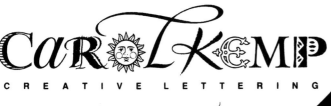

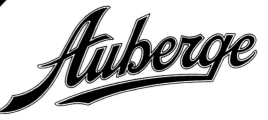

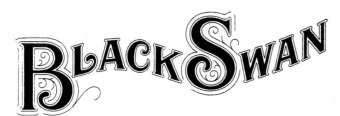

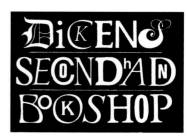

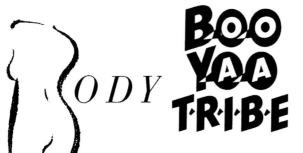

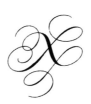

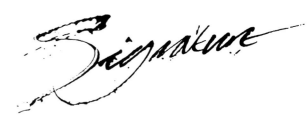

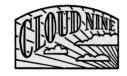

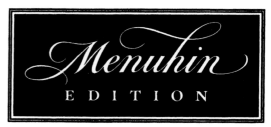

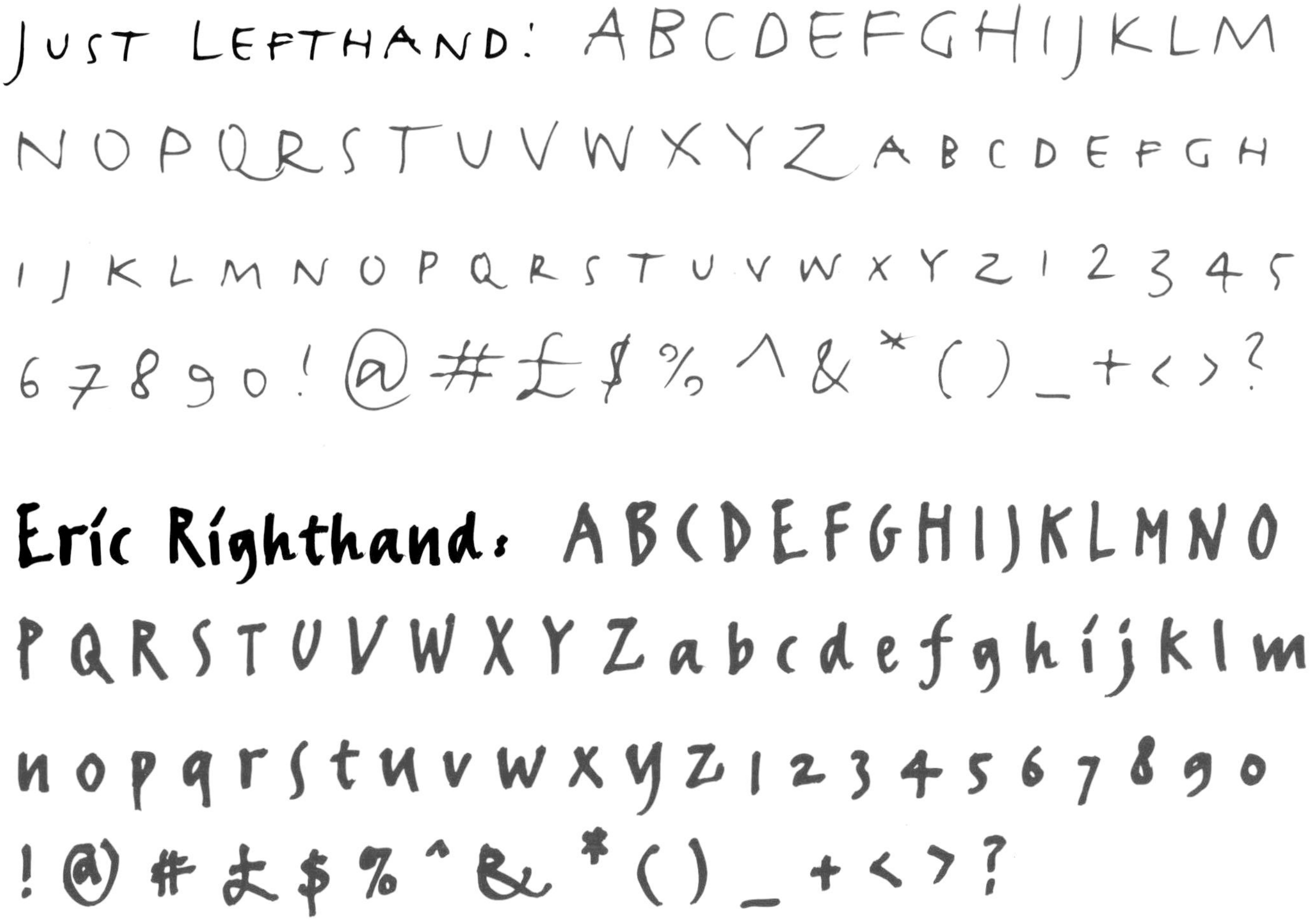

JUST LEFTHAND: ABCDEFGHIJKLM
NOPQRSTUVWXYZ ABCDEFGH
IJKLMNOPQRSTUVWXYZI2345
67890!@#£$%^&*()_+<>?

Eric Righthand: ABCDEFGHIJKLMNO
PQRSTUVWXYZabcdefghijklm
nopqrstuvwxyz1234567890
!@#£$%^&*()_+<>?

fast high-quality photocopying machines, the idea of handwriting a whole book is not as crazy as it may first appear. Many books have been produced this way, and curiously it is often typographers who tend to favor this quirky approach.

Calligraphy is handwriting's beautiful cousin (Fig. **2.39**), and is often used on the title pages of books. A grounding in calligraphy is essential for a proper understanding of good typography and graphic design, and its practice is to be encouraged.

The famous German designer Jan Tschichold wrote in 1949, "All my knowledge of letter spacing, word spacing, and leading is due to my calligraphy, and it is for this reason that I regret very much that calligraphy is so little studied in our time."

Handwriting and calligraphy have long been copied in type. Script and brush faces are "cleaned-up" versions of hand lettering. And with computers it is possible to invent your personal font based on your own hand (Fig. **2.40**).

2.40 Software can turn your handwriting into a usable font, as demonstrated by these commercially available typefaces from two Dutch designers: Eric van Blokland's Eric Righthand and Just van Rossum's Just Lefthand.

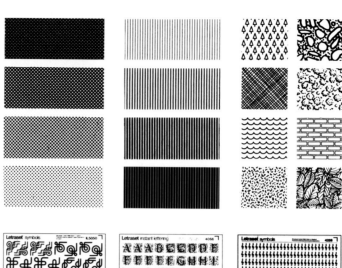

2.41 Rub-down lettering, from suppliers such as Letraset, revolutionized graphic design in the 1970s. It had to be applied carefully to prevent break-up.

"Strike-on" or "cold-metal" setting

Cutting and pasting of existing type, as in the punk blackmail-style designs of album covers by Jamie Reed in the late 1970s, is a form of **cold-metal setting**. Another form is the rub-down dry-transfer lettering used for display type from vendors such as Letraset. The vinyl letters are transferred one by one on to paper or board, and then pressure is applied through the backing sheet to "fix" the lettering in place. This is called **burnishing** (Fig. 2.41).

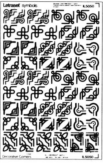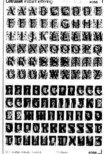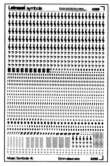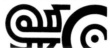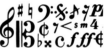

With **strike-on setting**, the marks made at the time of setting are those that will go under the camera for printing by the offset litho process. There is no intermediate processing required.

Type *can* be set using a regular typewriter (for menus, for example). Typeset-quality typewriters designed for the purpose were introduced during the 1960s. The IBM Selectric had fonts of 88 characters arranged around a "golfball" print head. It used a 9-unit system of proportional spacing, and had "real" fonts such as Univers and Times. For justified setting, each line had to be typed twice, as the first attempt was used to calculate the amount of space needed between words.

The VariTyper had an open carriage, to tackle greater widths of setting than the IBM, and could handle two fonts at a time, each of 99 characters. These machines represented a breakthrough at the time, and replaced hot metal for many low cost jobs, but by today's standards the setting looks crude and poorly spaced.

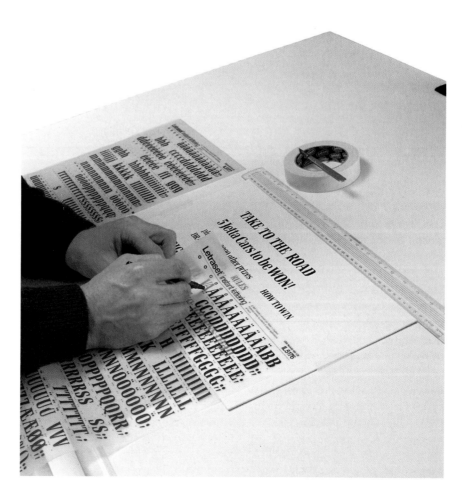

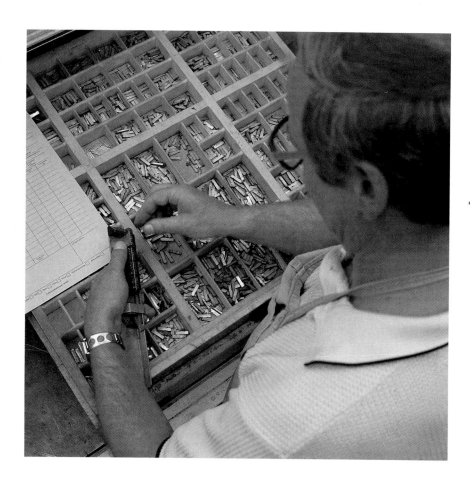

2.42 Inserting sorts from the lower typecase into the composing stick, where type is set, line by line, before being transferred to the chase.

Hot metal: hand and machine setting

The method of setting type from hot lead remained virtually unchanged from the time of Gutenberg until the invention of the punch-cutting machine by the American Linn Boyd Benton in 1884. This paved the way for the Linotype machine in 1886 and the Monotype machine a year later.

But whereas machine setting has been superseded by phototype-setting, handsetting is still used whenever beautiful typography is demanded for high-quality publications and limited-edition poetry books.

For handsetting, the compositor takes individual metal sorts and spaces from a typecase and places them one by one into a **composing stick** (Fig. **2.42**) that has been adjusted to the correct measure. Capital letters are taken from the upper case, and small letters from the lower case. The sizes of the compartments in the typecase reflect the popularity of certain sorts. You will need more "e"s for example than "z"s in an average job. Less frequently used fonts are kept in drawers under the typecase.

When the composing stick is full, the setting is transferred to a **galley** on the **imposing table**, and the compositor returns to the typecase to set the next couple of lines. When the galley is full, a **proof** is taken on a hand-operated **proofing press**, and any mistakes are picked up and corrected by the proofreader, the designer, or copy editor.

A galley proof is a long thin strip of paper, and gives the designer an

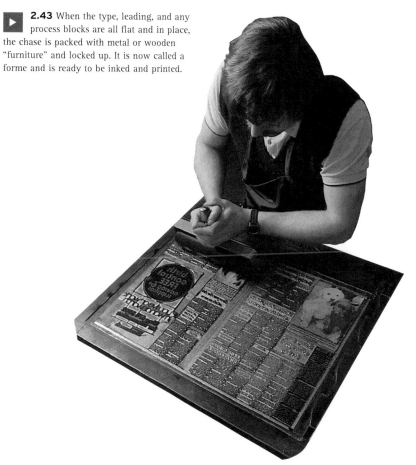

2.43 When the type, leading, and any process blocks are all flat and in place, the chase is packed with metal or wooden "furniture" and locked up. It is now called a forme and is ready to be inked and printed.

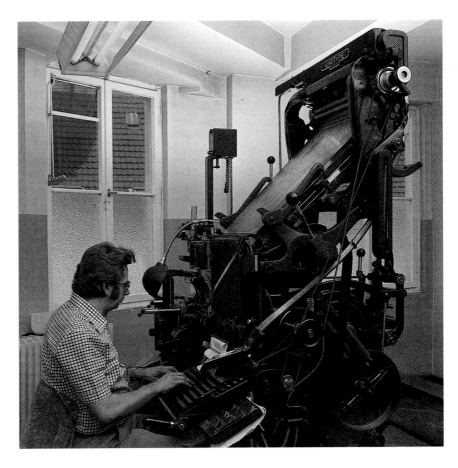

2.44 The Linotype machine automated hot-metal setting. As the compositor keyed in the text, matrixes would fall into place and the type was set line by line from molten lead.

opportunity to see the setting before it is divided up into pages. This proof, when corrected, may be good enough to be used as a **reproduction proof**, or **repro**, if the setting is going to be cut up using a scalpel and incorporated into a mechanical.

If the setting is going to be printed – and hot-metal setting is the only kind of setting discussed here that *can* be printed directly – then the type is taken from the galley and placed into a page-sized contraption called a **chase**, and "locked up" (Fig. **2.43**, p. 61). The spaces and leading used to fill up the rest of the chase, often of wood, are collectively known as furniture. The locked-up chase is called a **forme.**

For small runs, the printing is made direct from the type in the chase. But for large jobs, and for newspapers and magazines, for example, where the type must be wrapped around a cylinder, a one-piece duplicate of the type, called a **stereotype** or **stereo** (Fig. **2.45**), has

to be made from a *papier-mâché* mold called a **mat** or **flong**.

Once the stereo has been made, or the pages printed, the type is then cleaned and returned (the word used in the trade is "distributed") to the typecases. Extra care has to be taken to get this right, compositors being told "to mind their 'p's and 'q's."

The **Linotype** machine (Fig. **2.44**) was invented by Ottmar Mergenthaler of Baltimore in 1886 to automate the casting of type. Whole lines of type (hence the name from line o' type) called **slugs** are set in one operation. A compositor keys in the text, and as it is typed, molds of the letters to be cast fall into place. Wedge-shaped spacers are inserted between words, and when a line is complete, the compositor pulls a lever and these push the words apart to fill out the justified measure. Lead pours into the assembly, and out comes a slug of type. After the setting has been used, the slugs are melted down for re-use.

The **Monotype** machine, developed by Tolbert Lanston of Washington DC in 1887, sets type in individual sorts and, unlike the

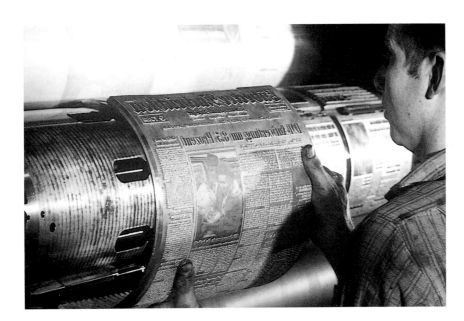

2.45 Metal type cannot be used directly on a rotary letterpress machine. It must first be made into a curved plate known as a stereotype, which is then wrapped around the press cylinder ready for printing.

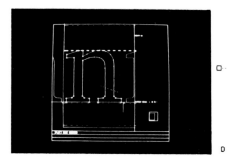

2.46 A screen shot of a letter outline being designed for phototypesetting. Note that the space between the letter n and the next letter is an integral part of the design of the "font metrics."

2.47 A bitmap of a Baskerville Bold capital B, showing how individual pixels are edited for optimum appearance at the laser printer resolution of 300 dpi.

Linotype, uses a two-stage process. The compositor sits at the keyboard and inputs the text, which is coded on to a perforated roll of paper. When the end of a line approaches, a bell rings and it is left to the compositor's skill to calculate the spaces needed between words to justify the line. This information is keyed in at the end of each line. When the job is complete, the roll of paper is inserted into a typecasting machine *back to front*, so that the spacing information precedes the text it adjusts, and the type is cast individually.

The advantage of the Monotype machine over the Linotype one is that corrections can be made using precast sorts. This is especially useful for book production. With the Linotype method, the whole line has to be reset and replaced. As a consequence, Linotype machines were mostly used for newspaper and magazine work where speed is of the essence, and where the effect of spilling the type, a catastrophe known as "printer's pie," is minimized.

Phototypesetting

The popularity of offset litho as a printing process led to the development of new ways of setting type. With letterpress it is not easy to mix text with illustrations and photo-graphs, and the opportunities for creative design are limited.

Phototypesetting, or **photo-setting**, was first demonstrated to the American Newspaper Publishers' Association in 1949 by Rene Higgo-net and Louis Marius Moyroud, but did not become popular until the 1960s. Like a Monotype system, it comprises two separate parts. The compositor sits at a keyboard and generates paper or magnetic tape. This is then transferred to the **imagesetter**, where the bromide or film is exposed. In the earliest systems, light was projected through a matrix of tiny photographic nega-tive images of the font's sorts on to photosensitive bromide paper or film. Later, the fonts were stored digitally, and reconstructed using CRTs (cathode ray tubes); now lasers are used (Figs **2.46** and **2.47**).

Photosetting provides the designer with many advantages over hot metal. Letters can be set closer together. They can be set touching, or even overlapping.

It is also possible, by means of mirrors and prisms, to distort type. Oblique (slanted) letters can be created from roman type, and head-lines can be condensed or expanded to fit a given width.

Type produced by photosetting is sharper than the equivalent hot-metal setting. Hot metal is always proofed to paper, and no matter how carefully the ink is applied, it will be squeezed between the face of the type and the paper and there will be some spread. A typeface such as Bodoni, with its extremely fine serifs, was designed to be pressed into paper – photoset versions of Bodoni had to be redesigned with thicker serifs.

With photosetting, type can be set ahead of a type specification – the text is keyed in and the size, face, and measure are added later. The same text can be used over and over, in different forms. Any metal type to be reused had to be stored as "standing matter." This was costly and took up lots of space. With photosetting, type for dictionaries and telephone directories, for exam-ple, could be stored on tape, and updated later.

Computer systems

A photosetting machine may look like a regular computer, but setting is all it can do. A computer system, on the other hand, makes use of a standard off-the-shelf PC or Mac to produce a hard disk full of infor-mation that is then input to the imagesetter that generates the bromide paper or film. It does much more besides.

More choice of typefaces
Perhaps the most apparent effect of computers on graphic designers is that they have a much greater range of typefaces to choose from. With early photosetting, and even more so with strike-on technology, the user was offered any typeface ... so long as it was Times, Univers, or Helvetica.

THE COMPUTER IS NOT
A TYPEWRITER
Beware of typists' bad habits, like placing two spaces after a full stop and
inserting a carriage return at the end of
each line. You can remove these using
the "search and replace" command in
your word processor. On the Internet,
however, particularly in email and newsgroups, you'll have to remember to put
those carriage returns back in!

▶ **2.48** Photosetting and digital software can concoct a kind of italic by slanting the roman font. This is better termed an oblique variant, as a true italic has different designs from the roman for most letters, with more cursive serifs.

Roman & afg
Oblique & afg
Italic & afg

64

TEXT & TYPE

There are currently many thousands of different typefaces available that can be used with computer systems. So-called "expert sets" add ligatures, small caps, swash caps, non-aligning numerals, fractions, and superior/ inferior figures to the basic fonts.

To produce a typeface in hot metal was an enormous and costly undertaking, requiring a huge invest- ment in both time and money. Most of the great typographers of the past are known for just one or maybe two typefaces. The same is true for photosetting. Particular typefaces were tied to particular machines. Thus if you had a Linotype machine, you could use only faces from the Linotype library. Similarly, if you had a Berthold machine, you could use only type from Berthold.

If a typographer went to Berthold with a new idea for a typeface, its production would be extremely expensive and its distribution limited to the number of Berthold machines in operation worldwide.

But with a computer system it is possible to design a brand new face, copy it on to a CD-rom or upload it to the Internet and distribute it for use by thousands of other designers within days.

Quality and flexibility of digital type

The pace of progress in computing means that the few advantages of other technologies are fast disap- pearing. Computers are being adopted by both the printing and the design industries. Yet hot metal has always held one advantage over photosetting, that of visual quality.

In hot metal, each size of a type- face has been designed individually. Thus, for the sake of legibility, the small sizes have a relatively larger x-height and a wider set width. Bigger sizes have daintier serifs and more subtle distinctions between the parts of the letterform, created by enlarging or reducing one of these **font masters**.

In computer systems, all sizes are created by **scaling** (enlarging or reducing) one font master, usually 12 pt, designed as the best compro- mise. There have been some conces- sions to creating different designs for different sizes. Times Ten Roman, for example, is a version of Times New Roman that works better at small sizes. But the problem of legi- bility at smaller sizes has usually been solved by tracking.

Photosetting machines can be used to expand and condense type, but this always distorts the overall proportions of the letterform. A Futura E, for example, when condensed, will have a vertical stroke thinner than the horizontals.

By sloping roman letterforms, a photosetting system can create an oblique – but not an italic – version of the typeface. A true italic font has entirely different designs for many of its letters. Look at the a, f, and g of an italic face (Fig. **2.48**).

Any computer system can perform these kinds of distortions. They can embolden letters too, and produce combinations of italic, bold, outline, and shadow (Fig. **2.49**). But the results bear little aesthetic rela- tionship to the original "plain" letter- forms. The design intention of the typographer will have been lost.

Multiple Masters from Adobe is a technology that incorporates non- linear scaling into typefaces. It uses

SET ALONG A PATH
OUTLINE
OR AROUND A CIRCLE
BUMP
BLUR
ROUGHEN
STROKE & FILL
ZOOM
REVERSE
SOFT SHADOW

◀ **2.49** Computer software can also take a roman font and "style" it in various ways. Most programs can create bold, outline, shad- owed, and reversed-out variants. More special- ized software, such as FreeHand, can be used, for example, to set type along a curve, and to apply "fill and stroke" to a letterform.

2.50 New custom fonts can be designed letter by letter using programs such as Fontographer. These programs can also import existing typefaces, which can then be adapted to your own taste.

2.51 Software such as Macromedia's FreeHand can be used to distort letters and words mathematically. Previously, the lettering would have to have been drawn laboriously by hand or distorted photographically.

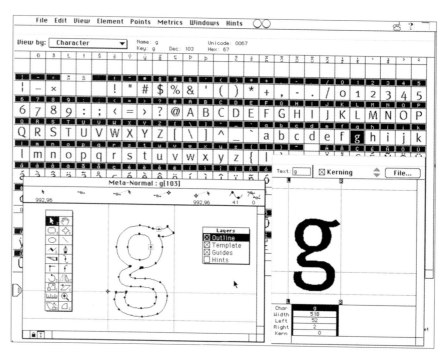

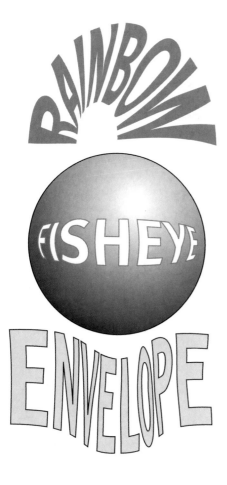

mathematical formulas to retain relationships between the stroke weights of individual letterforms, and inter-character spacing is adjusted appropriately. It is possible to encode a font master with information that describes the shapes of small, medium, and large versions of the typeface, and the computer will interpolate all the gradations in between.

With computer setting, the graphic designer has never been restricted to the small and standard list of point sizes available from the hot-metal type foundries. In page-layout systems such as Adobe PageMaker and QuarkXPress, for example, type can be set at any size in any increment, leading can be defined in increments or percentages, and letters can be kerned interactively. Multiple Master fonts – Adobe Sans MM and Adobe Serif MM – are mainly used in Adobe's Acrobat PDF (Portable Document Format) to simulate the appearance of a designed document. They will automatically generate an accurate weight/width shape variation for any specified size.

Apple's QuickDraw GX promises the possibility of 65,000 different "glyphs" (PostScript and TrueType can only handle 256) plus the intelligence to auto-substitute ligatures, swashes, and diphthongs without causing problems for spell checkers. This is especially good news for designers working in languages other than English, making available all kinds of accents and characters, and for those designing with non-Roman scripts like Arabic and Hindi.

Type manipulation and custom font design

Page-layout systems, such as Adobe PageMaker and QuarkXPress, are able to adjust the size of type to fit a certain space, condensing or expanding it to the limits of legibility.

Drawing programs (more of which in Chapter 3, p. 95), such as Macromedia's FreeHand and Adobe Illustrator, allow text, for example, to be set around an ellipse or along a freeform curve. Plug-ins and "xtras," such as MetaTools' Vector Effects, permit more extreme distortions (Fig. **2.51**). The designer is able to create graphical "envelopes" into which the text is squeezed and contorted to fit.

With programs such as Fontographer (Fig. **2.50**), you can tweak existing faces to your own preferences or create entirely new faces from scratch. It is this power that horrifies traditional typographers. Here, a knowledge of typography, however rudimentary, is essential to prevent the novice from falling into the pitfalls learnt the hard way throughout the history of type.

Most digital fonts are revivals of traditional fonts, adapted to the limitations of the technology. There are

Column 1

McVAY S.T,
  18 Swan Copse,Mansfield Rd 25..708 0761
  T, 9 Hollington Cres 33 ....784 7037
McVEAGH J.G.R, 211 Castle La,Solihull..743 3266
  W, 69 Damson La,Solihull 705 7866
McVEICH S, 171 Jayshaw Av 43 ....357 5933
McVEIGH A, 63 New Coventry Rd 26 ..742 8955
  D.F, 5 Bernard Pl,Brookfield Rd 18 ..554 2068
  G, Warwick Rd,Solihull 705 6922
  J, 16 Harvington Rd,Oldbury 422 4789
  J.D, 17 Winton Gro,Sutton Coldfield ..351 4406
  J.M, 99 Miranda Clo 45 ....453 9681
  J.P, 49 Round Moor Wlk 35 ....747 8542
  M.F.P, 27 Prospect La,Solihull 744 5227
  R.M, 8 Chiseldon Croft 14 ....474 5165
McVEIGHTY D, 82 Audley Rd 33 ....786 2946
  D, 39 Este Rd 26 ....783 0454
  D, 67 Hilleys Croft 37 ....770 1737
  R, 62 Clarence Rd 13 ....444 4088
McVEITH T, 37 Frankley La 31 ....478 0534
MACVENAN M, 15 Overbrunton Clo 31 ....477 2547
McVERRY B.P, 4 Chalybeate Clo 45 ...453 8277
  D, 24 Goodrest Croft 14 ....430 4084
  D.J, 17 Duncalfe Dv,Sutton Coldfield ..308 5672
McVEY C.F, 19 Brownley Rd,Shirley ..745 1015
  J, 31 Beeches Wy 31 ....477 8434
  J, 158 Jayshaw Av 43 ....357 4988
McVICAR A.J, 158 Swan Gdns 23 .....373 0289
  E.W, 38 Moorfield Dv,Sutton Coldfield ..373 8366
McVICKER N.M, 78 Northdown Rd,Solihull ..705 8822
  R.P, 43 Heybarnes Rd 10 ....773 7558
MACVIE F.E,
  Fiddlers Gn,Blackford Hl....Henley-in-A 2819
  Mrs M.H, 72 Marsh Hl 23 ....373 2702
McVITTY P.J, 312 Sarehole Rd 28 ...777 5575
McWALTER I.M,
  30 Upper St. Mary's Rd,Smethwick 429 1297
  J.W, 66 Hawkstone Rd 29 ....475 6246
  S.G, 207 Court Oak Rd 17 ....427 9694
McWALTERS S.B,
  11 Chadwick Rd,Sutton Coldfield..378 3693
McWATTS A.C,
  6 Bannersgate Rd,Sutton Coldfield..355 1647
McWEE R.M, 29 Stanmore Gro,Halesowen..422 7767
McWEENEY L, 114 Junction Rd 21 ...523 3828
McWHINNEY S.J, 6 Longmore Rd,Streetly..353 7526
McWHINNIE J.R.K,
  282 Eachelhurst Rd,Sutton Coldfoield..351 2022
J.R.K,
  282 Eachelhurst Rd,Sutton Coldfield..351 3382
  W.R, 22 Widney Manor Rd,Solihull..705 8842
McWHIRTER D,
  9 Spring Ho,Cooks Ct,Chester Rd 36..770 0970
  D.C, 30 Greenfield Rd 17 ....427 9679
  D.L, 24 Fugelmere Clo 17 ....429 4883
  J, 28 St. Michaels Rd,Sutton Coldfield..354 6521
  John D, 23 Maxholm Rd,Streetly ...353 2850
  P.J.K, 92 Devon Rd,Smethwick 429 1213
  R, 17 Aldbourne Wy 38 ....459 4503
  R.M, 127 Manor La,Halesowen 550 1718
  W.H.P, 188 Northfield Rd 17 ....427 1736
McWILLIAM A.R, 30 Waldrons Moor 14 ..444 2414
  I, 38 Corbridge Rd,Sutton Coldfield ..354 2558
  I.R, 50 Meriden Rd ....Hampton-in-A 2015
  J.W, 55 Colesbourne Rd,Solihull ...742 3228
  R, 108 West Av 20 ....554 4261
  R.C, 20 Galton Tower,Civic Clo 1 ...236 4901
McWILLIAMS A.G,
  32 Sandhills Cres,Solihull..704 9547
  B, 126 Kingswood Rd 31 ....477 6225
  B.V, 4 Dornton Rd 30 ....444 3788
  C, 203 Albert Rd 6 ....328 4676
  C.P, 20 Hatherton Gro 29 ....427 6854
  E, 20 Somerset Rd 23 ....384 4951
  G, 306 Prince of Wales La 14 ....430 3917
  J.B, 18 Milner Rd 29 ....472 7085
  J.D, 3 Newells Rd 26 ....742 1801
  K, 103 Ashbrook Rd 30 ....472 5807
  N, 98 Manor Ho La 26 ....743 2498
  P.W, 56 Hodge Hill Rd 34 ....783 7477
  R, 28
  R, 5
  R, 13
  S, 48
  W.K,
MACWI
MACZK
MADAH
  J.S, 1
  T, 84
MADAN
  V.P,
MADDA
MADDA
  A.D,
  B.M,
  D.G,
  G.W,
  H, 41
  J, 21
  J.L, 2
  M, 1 Chantry Dv,Halesowen 422 4339
  R.G, 714 Hagley Rd Wst,Oldbury ...422 7826
  Sidney C, 4 Griffins Brook Clo 30 ..459 3814
  T.A, 212 Highters Hth La 14 ....430 2472
MADDEN A, 54 Strathdene Rd 29 .....472 1469
  A, 2 Wilford Gro,Sutton Coldfield ..351 3998
  A, 256 Witton Ldg Rd 23 ....350 6119
  A.C, 41 Galton Tower,Civic Clo 1 ...233 2935
  B, 113 Heather Rd 10 ....771 2140
  C, 4 Sycamore Terr,Vicarage Rd 14 ..444 0919
  C, 257 West Boulevard 32 ....427 6313
  C.A, 548 Bromford La 8 ....786 2021
  C.W, 6 St Johns Rd,Oldbury 544 7941
  D, 23 Court Oak Gro 17 ....427 9851
  D, 12 Elmwood Rd,Sutton Coldfield ..353 3807
  D, 40 Middle Dv 45 ....445 2002
  D, 73 St. Agathas Rd 8 ....327 2379
  D, 4 Sunnydale Wlk,W Bromwich ...525 1518
  D.M.J, 40 Sheldonfields Rd 26 .....743 4350
  D.S, 134 Kingsdown Av 42 ....357 6662
  E, 23 Eileen Rd 11 ....449 0807
  E, 105 Manor Ho La 26 ....742 6515
  E, 1/4 Ward End Pk Rd 8 ....327 6308
  F, 34 Cecil Rd 24 ....373 4542

Column 2

MADDEN H.A, 85 Naseby Rd 8 ....327 5567
  I, 11 Boldmere Clo,Sutton Coldfield ..350 6027
  I.M, 74 Worlds End Rd 20 ....554 7649
  J, 44 Amberley Gro 6 ....356 8558
  J, 266 Galton Rd,Smethwick 429 6179
  J, 140 Knowle Rd 11 ....777 8672
  J, 37 Roughley Dv,Four Oaks 308 4882
  James, 347 St. Benedicts Rd 10 ....772 0748
  J, 68 Tomey Rd 11 ....772 0813
  J, 137 Wellsgreen Rd,Solihull 743 2015
  J, 5 Welwyndale Rd,Sutton Coldfield ..373 6653
  J, 61 Windmill La,Smethwick 565 3634
  J, 21 Windsor St Nth 7 ....359 0115
  J.A, 91 Pinewood Dv 32 ....422 0066
  J.E, 64 Pitts Fm Rd 24 ....350 5780
  J.T, 100 Alston Rd,Solihull 704 1390
  K.W, 37 Varlins Wy 38 ....458 6997
  L, 26 Chartley Rd 24 ....328 3751
  L, 7 Clodeshall Rd 8 ....328 3186
  L, 51 Ercall Clo 23 ....356 0845
  L, 331 Yardley Wood Rd 13 ....449 8241
  M, 12 Cecil Rd 23 ....373 8447
  M, 323 Guardian Ct,
    Francey Beeches Rd 31..477 5078
  Michael, 101 Livingstone Rd 20 ....356 0701
  M, 55 Norfolk Rd 23 ....373 0753
  Michael, 232 Somerville Rd 10 .....773 9922
  M, 7 Yew Tree La 26 ....706 6797
  Michael A, 51 Courtenay Rd 44 ....360 4605
  M.A, 75 Harrow Rd 7 ....472 1056
  M.J, 48 Brookvale Rd,Solihull 706 3076
  M.J, 29 Link Rd 16 ....454 7864
  M.J, 50 Moorend La 24 ....384 4518
  N, 88 Pritchett Tower,Arthur St 10 ..773 8947
  P, 21 Ebley Rd 20 ....523 9924
  P, 7 Rawlins Croft 35 ....749 3961
  P.B, 101 Clodeshall Rd 8 ....328 7530
  P.J, 48 Broadway Ave,Halesowen ..550 7879
  P.J, 135 Oxhill Rd 21 ....523 9704
  R.F, 55 Hill La,Sutton Coldfield 308 4990
  R.J, 3 Whitwell Clo,Solihull 744 7724
  R.N, 303 Dovedale Rd 23 ....382 7236
  S, 27 Gladstone Rd 26 ....706 5469
  S.D, 14 St. Michaels Rd,Sutton Coldfield..355 5701
  S.J, 376 Queslett Rd 43 ....360 1421
  T, 228 Millhouse Rd 25 ....784 0182
  T, 30 Station Rd 21 ....554 2344
  Timothy, 16 Westbury Rd,Wednesbury..526 3558
  T.A, 22 Avenue Rd 14 ....444 1597
  T.H, 53 Allcroft Rd 11 ....778 1379
  T.J, 68 Hazelbeach Rd 8 ....326 0974
  T.S, 8 Daniels Rd 9 ....773 1741
  W, 7 Hilldrop Gro 17 ....426 3667
  W.A.L, 340 Hagley Rd Wst,Oldbury..422 8554
MADDERS G.R, 37 Quarry La,Halesowen..550 5409
  G.T, 23 Rowton Dv,Streetly 353 6668
  J.L, 9 Stourton Clo,Sutton Clodfield..329 3193
  Max A, 6 Selly Clo 29 ....472 1670

  41 Mounbsley Ho,Baverstock Rd 14..474 3139
MADDIX C, 8/8 Broadmeadow Clo 30 ..459 4724
  D, 33 Calder Tower,Birchfield Rd 20 ..356 5853
  Martin, 15 Heanor Croft 6 ....328 3670

  E.L, 16 Harbury Rd 12 ....440 2185
  F.M, 512 Kingsbury Rd 24 ....350 2007
  G, 31 Daimler Clo 36 ....747 0199
  I.F, 824 Pershore Rd 29 ....472 2636
  J, 1 Denise Dv 17 ....427 2395
  J, 28 Tinmeadow Cres 45 ....453 5355
  J.C, 1 Overbury Clo,Halesowen 550 4642
  M, 8 Raven Hays Rd 31 ....477 2201
  N, 29 Marsham Rd 14 ....430 5180
  P, 38 Daisy Fm Rd 14 ....474 5939
  P, 18 Middle Pk Rd 29 ....476 9146
  P, 1 Pagnell Gro 13 ....443 3851
  R.A, 178 Franklin Rd 30 ....458 7198
  R.C, 119 Bell Holloway 31 ....477 3973
  R.S, 178 Gregory Av 29 ....477 3312
  S, 34 Hodgetts Clo,Smethwick 429 2362
  S, 25 Pettit Clo 14 ....430 5011
  S.C, 48 Rowheath Rd 30 ....459 0944
  V, 8 Cherry Tree Ct,Woodfall Av 30 ..451 3284
  W, 73 Longford Rd 44 ....354 5745
  W.L, 129 Kineton Gn Rd,Solihull ...708 2684
MADDON J, 229 Manningford Rd 14 ..430 6295
MADDOX A, 192 Farnborough Rd 35 ..747 8584
  A, 12 The Hurstway 23 ....382 5280

Column 3

MADDOX B.T, 235 Hay Green La 30 ..475 6050
  C.D, 347 The Ridgeway 23 ....331 4687
  C.R, 37 Coniston Av,Solihull 743 6397
  C.R, 26 Libbard Ho,Stonebow Ave,Solihull..705 8876
  D, 1 Alcombe Gro 33 ....784 9496
  D, 20 Ashton Rd 25 ....784 5873
  D, 73 Newlands Rd 30 ....451 2736
  D.C, 38 Duncumb Rd,Sutton Coldfield..378 3508
  D.M, 71 Babbington Rd 21 ....523 0145
  E, 139 Garretts Green La 26 ....742 5777
  E, 149 Nuthurst Rd 31 ....476 6364
  E, 2 Arbor Ct,Penns La,Sutton Coldfield..351 5636
  E.S, 89 Monmouth Rd 32 ....475 1892
  F.C, 49 Milstead Rd 26 ....784 6434
  G, 54 Harleston Rd 44 ....360 2212
  G, 57 Surrey Cres,W Bromwich 502 1184
  G, 26 Elm Croft,Windmill La,Smethwick..565 1169
  H, 15 Bucknall Cres 32 ....550 5836
  H, 5 Middleton Rd,Shirley 744 4732
  I, 41 Ansell Rd 24 ....373 1003
  J, 8 May La 47 ....Wythall 824209
  J.R, 142 Birdbrook Rd 44 ....360 1132
  John W, 18 Elmfield Rd 36 ....747 5667
  K, 2 Ingram Gro 27 ....778 2433
  K.A, 28 Britwell Rd,Sutton Coldfield..355 3522
  K.J, 2 Linford Gro 25 ....783 5073
  L, 801c Warwick Rd 11 ....706 1305
  L.L, 9 Ferndale Rd,Streetly 353 7885
  M.E, 83 Stanton Rd 43 ....358 7530
  M.I, 510 Chester Rd 36 ....770 5083
  M.K, 42 Teesdale Ave 34 ....730 2350
  M.P, 48 Amberley Gro 6 ....356 7517
  N, 3 Western Rd,Sutton Coldfield ..354 9278
  P.W, 31 Marlborough Rd 36 ....554 0517
  R, 78 Grestone Av 20 ....554 0267
  R, 197 Newton Rd 43 ....357 1863
  Roy A, 182 Northfield Rd 17 ....427 3322
  R.L, 33 Wharf Rd 30 ....459 2660
  S, 2 Greenway Clo 43 ....360 5791
  S, 50 Vimy Rd 13 ....444 1945
  S.L, 12 Boldmere Clo,Sutton Coldfield..373 3765
  W, 3 Westholme Croft 30 ....472 8782
MADDRELL Simon, 48 Ellesmere Rd 8..326 8979
MADDY K.P, 3 Merehill Av,Solihull ..745 5813
MADELEY A, 128 Dudley Rd Est,Oldbury..552 4887
  A, 7 Walton Ct,High Farm Rd,Halesowen..503 0184
  A.C, 98 Triumph Wlk 36 ....749 2685
  A.E, 56 Farnhurst Rd 36 ....328 3619
  B, 7 Dauntsey Covert 14 ....458 6910
  B.W, 27 Leaford Rd 33 ....784 0412
  C.E, 17 Marldon Rd 14 ....444 7677
  D, 89 Braemar Rd,Solihull 706 0366
  D, 30 Macmillan Rd,Rowley Regis ..559 2793
  D.H, 252 Coleshill Rd 36 ....747 4575
  E, 5 Pryor Rd,Oldbury 544 4518
  E.A, 17 Mynors Cres 47 ....Wythall 826651
  E.G, 27 Queens Ct,Alderham Clo,Solihull..705 6750
  E.S, 117 The Ridgeway 23 ....356 7835

  J, 2/24 Taylor Rd 13 ....444 0057
  J.M, 1 Chartwell Ct,Beardmore Rd,
    Sutton Coldfield..373 1815
  J. M, 40 Dower Rd,Sutton Coldfield..308 1476

  I, 449 Lugtrout La,Solihull 704 9849
  Theo M, 38 Redthorn Gro 33 ......783 7684
  W.E, 126 Spouthouse La 43 ....357 6503
MADELIN A.E,
  305 Beaconview Rd,W Bromwich..588 2099
  D, 152 Powis Av,Tipton 557 7026
  H, 55 Glebefields Rd,Tipton 557 9450
  K, 415 Sycamore Rd,Tipton 520 4748
  M, 20 Kipling Clo,Tipton 557 5572
MADEN M.A, 44 Steel Rd 31 ....476 6493
MADER R, 107 Birmingham Rd 48 ...445 2366
MADEW E.A, 39 Witton Ldg Rd 23 ...350 0522
  J.T, 226 Rectory Rd,Sutton Coldfield..378 3905
MADGE A,
  60 Bampfylde Pl,Thornbridge Av 42..358 2139
  C, 19 Andrew Rd,W Bromwich 588 6693
  C.J, 5 Rectory Pk Av,Sutton Coldfield..378 0353
  G, 1 Ravenhill Clo 34 ....748 7534
  G.H, 78 Hathersage Rd 42 ....360 2845
  H, 118 Finchley Av 34 ....355 4840
  H.E, 36 Homecroft Rd 25 ....783 4867
  H.S, 11 Parkhall Croft 34 ....748 5736
  J, 27 Walsham Croft 34 ....745 5737
  J.E, 86 Preston Rd 26 ....708 0883

Column 4

MADGE M.J, 1 Station Approach,Vesey Ldge,
    Sutton Coldfield..353 6347
  W.H, 68 Drayton Rd 14 ....443 2047
MADGWICK D.J,
  239 Ulverley Green Rd,Solihull..706 1349
  G, 3 Beresford Cres,W Bromwich ...553 3637
  H.A, 78 Coopers La,Smethwick 558 8623
MADHAL C.S, 11 Raglan Rd,Smethwick..565 1487
MADHAS N, 34 Chantry Rd 21 ....554 7075
MADHOO G, 10 High Trees 20 ....523 8532
MADIGAN A, 693 Hagley Rd Wst 32 ..421 3971
  E.G, 183 Bucklands End La 34 .....747 8988
  E.J, 206 Gravelly La 23 ....350 7814
  J.J, 48 Cranmore Rd,Shirley 745 4407
  J.J, 48 Shakespeare Rd,Shirley 745 1712
  M, 711 Kingstanding Rd 44 ....355 5221
  M.J, 4 R.A.F Houses,Chester Rd 35 ..748 6327
  S, 175 Balden Rd 32 ....429 3689
  W, 18 Blakeland Rd 44 ....356 9967
MADILL W, 64 College Rd,Sutton Coldfield..354 8566
MADIN J, 34d Wentworthrd 17 ....427 7430
  M.L.K, 182 Lightwoods Hl,Smethwick..429 2530
  W.H, 131 Park Hl Rd 17 ....427 1634
MADISON J.O, 132 Raglan Rd,Smethwick..558 4789
  N.A, 34 Teesdale Av 34 ....748 1201
MADKINS A.H,
  76 Somerville Rd,Sutton Coldfield..355 3613
  A.J, 39 South Gro 23 ....350 8551
  P.E, 20 Hinton Av 48 ....445 2966
  T.W, 433 Birmingham Rd,Walsall ..358 1512
  W.E, 110 Meadthorpe Rd 44 ....360 3535
MADLAM K, 73 Caldwell Gro,Solihull..711 1215
MADLEY Gwyn, 48 Neville Rd,Shirley..744 4881
MADOURIE C, 31 Glendower Rd 42 ...356 1081
MADRELL K.W, 95 Silhill Hall Rd,Solihull..705 2477
MAECHER Pictureproducts
    Ltd...Snodland 243450
MAEER C.W, 5 Lingard Ho,Fox Hollies Rd,
    Sutton Coldfield..351 7629
  F.W.C, 70 Clay Pit La,W Bromwich ..553 2571
  G, 3 Park La 21 ....525 3628
  J.E, 12 New St,W Bromwich 556 0285
  K.M.F, 81 Riland Rd,Sutton Coldfield..378 5549
  M.A, 42 New St,W Bromwich 502 1718
MAEERS G.A, 119 Kingsbury Rd 24 ..373 3909
MAER G.J, 14 Spiral Ct,Monkskirby Rd,
    Sutton Coldfield..378 1979
MAESE R, 34 Southcote Gro 38 ......459 8562
MAETINEAU B.E,
  Good Rest Camp Site,Good Rest La 38..459 1481
MAFFIN R.W, 64 Woodgate Gdns 32 ..422 1769
MAFLAHI M, 11 Birkdale Gro 29 .....471 4011
  M.S, 22 Aubrey Rd 10 ....773 8415
MAGAHRAN E, 46 Doveridge Rd 28...744 5756
MAGAR K.S, 2 Greenside Rd 24 ......373 3709
MAGDZIARZ A, 14 Hamstead Rd 19 ..554 1014
MAGEE A, 20 Holte Rd 6 ....327 0796
  ...7957
  ...9226
  ...8046
  ...2119
  ...0339
  ...8640
  ...1630
  ...1666
  ...5134
  ...0260
  ...1923
  ...5979
  ...9070
  ...7482
  ...8897
  ...6654

  R, 20 The Scotchings 36 ....747 9215
  R.H, 153 Castle La,Solihull 743 9893
  T, 11 Pavilion Av,Smethwick 429 5635
GEEAN J.J, 9 Leatherhead Clo 6 .....359 8471
GEED R, 27 Whetstone Clo 15 ....454 3927
GEN J.W, 80 Coronation Rd 43 ......358 6283
GENIS I, 52 Oxford St 30 ....459 8501
GGS B.E, 389 Warwick Rd,Solihull ..704 3235
  .D, 20 Greenwood Clo 19 ....443 4936
  .I, 10 Harleston Rd 44 ....350 5654
  , 32 Pitleason Clo 30 ....451 2997
  .O, 3 Garnett Av 43 ....360 3103
  .D, 7 Meerhill Av,Shirley 745 9427
  .R, 21 Whitley Ct Rd 32 ....422 0127
  V.J.T, 17 Nevison Gn 43 ....325 0098
  V.S, 24 Cherrywood Ct,Solihull 743 5528
GILL B, 11 Inkberrow Rd,Halesowen ..550 4366
  .R, 24 Morven Rd,Sutton Coldfield ..354 2746
  red, 172 West Hth Rd 31 ....475 4518
  , 201 Wyndhurst Rd 33 ....783 2748
  , 114 Clent View Rd 32 ....422 1576
  .G, 2 Bishbury Clo 15 ....455 0101
GINLEY T.H, 57 St. Peters Rd 20 ....523 3415
GINNIS A.F, 10 Chapel St,Halesowen..501 3269
  A.R, 22 Cross St,Halesowen 550 4024
  J.E, 14 Grosvenor Rd,Solihull 704 2707
  L.A, 43 Barcheston Rd ....Knowle 6840
  T.W, 676 Chester Rd 36 ....770 7022
MAGNAY Dr A.R, 18 Crosbie Rd 17 ..427 3433
MAGNER P.F, 74 Fredas Gro 17 .....427 9846
  R.D, 10 Lottie Rd 29 ....472 7916
MAGNESS C.R,
    50 Slater Rd,Bentley Hth...Knowle 3189
MAGONS F, 61 Burney La 8 ....783 6389
MAGOR D.C,
    6 Linden Ct,Hampton La,Solihull..704 9722
  M, 7 The Avenue,Rowley Regis 559 1674
MAGOWAN S.C, 21 Tansy Badgers Bank Rd,
    Sutton Coldfield..308 3265
MAGRATH G.F, 90 Wentworth Rd 17 ..426 2485
MAGRAW W.L,
  42a Maney Hl Rd,Sutton Coldfield..354 5063
MAGRIS S, 69 Tedstone Rd 32 ....427 5127
MAGRIS G.L,
  5 Far Highfield,Sutton Coldfield..378 2470
MAGSON A.G, 109 Stoney La 25 .....783 0170
  A.M, 243 The Avenue 27 ....707 3712

also several fonts designed specifically for the process, and for the changing needs of the graphic designer. Erik Spiekermann's Meta (Fig. **2.53**) is described as an ecological face, designed to look attractive even in small sizes on problematic papers such as coarse, thin, and recycled stocks. Designers Banks and Miles developed an economical typeface for British Telecom's telephone directories and managed to achieve savings in paper of over 10 percent (Fig. **2.52**).

Some typographers are using the power of the computer to incorporate "intelligence" (or rather, chaos) into their typefaces. Beowulf from Dutch designers Erik van Blokland and Just van Rossum, for example, is a "random" font in which the letterforms mutate subtly each time a character is produced (Fig. **2.54**). Three versions of Beowulf have differing levels of randomness built in, and they imitate the effects of wear and tear on metal and wooden type.

In a way, faces like Beowulf are a modern counterpart to Gutenberg's efforts to emulate the scribes' humanized typography. A similar point could be made about computer simulations of hand lettering in comics.

2.52 The condensed typeface designed by Colin Banks of London-based designers Banks and Miles also addresses green issues. It allows four columns per page of the telephone directory and this, along with the decision not to repeat surnames, has resulted in huge savings in both paper and ink. As only one size (5·75 pt) was required, Banks was able to design the bitmaps pixel by pixel. Note the **traps** in some letters to prevent ink spread from filling in the junctions.

Meta Normal:
ABCDEFGHIJKLMNOPQRSTUVWXYZ
abcdefghijklmnopqrstuvwxyz
1234567890!@#£$%^&*()_+<>?

META CAPS:
ABCDEFGHIJKLMNOPQRSTUVWXYZ
ABCDEFGHIJKLMNOPQRSTUVWXYZ
1234567890!@#£$%^&*()_+Ø≠?

Meta Bold:
ABCDEFGHIJKLMNOPQRSTUVWXYZ
abcdefghijklmnopqrstuvwxyz
1234567890!@#£$%^&*()_+¨Æ?

R21: ABCDEFGHIJKLMNOP
QRSTUVWXYZabcdefghijk
lmnopqrstuvwxyz1234567
890!@#£$%^&*()_+<>?

R22: ABCDEFGHIJKLMNOP
QRSTUVWXYZabcdefghijk
lmnopqrstuvwxyz1234567
890!@#£$%^&*()_+<>?

R23: ABCDEFGHIJKLMNOP
QRSTUVWXYZabcdefghijk
lmnopqrstuvwxyz1234567
890!@#£$%^&*()_+<>?

ABC ABC ABC

2.53 Erik Spiekermann's ecological face Meta was designed as a reaction to the overuse of Helvetica, which he describes as "the Federal font" because of its widespread use by German business and government.

2.54 Building randomness into a font's characteristics creates subtly mutating type. Beowulf from Dutch designers Erik van Blokland and Just van Rossum was the first "anarchistic" font.

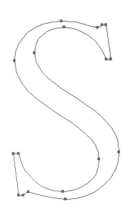

PostScript and TrueType

Almost every machine or device in print production encountered today – from computer screens and scanners to high-resolution imagesetters – works on the **raster** principle. A raster (from the Latin for "rake") is the line that makes up the picture on a television screen. On digital devices like a computer screen, each line is divided into a series of dots called **pixels**, and the **resolution** of the screen is described in terms of the number of pixels horizontally by the number of lines vertically. Thus the screen of a 14-inch Apple Macintosh monitor has a resolution of 640 x 480.

Another way of measuring resolution is by the number of dots per inch, or **dpi.** Thus, measured in this way, the Mac's screen has a resolution of 72 dpi.

The higher the resolution, the better the quality. A laser printer typically has a resolution of 600 dpi. A production-quality imagesetter, such as the Scitex Dolev 800, has a resolution of 2550 dpi.

The same type has to look good (or at least be recognizable) on all kinds of different devices with all kinds of resolutions. A designer may work initially on the computer screen, proof the results on a laser printer, and then send off a disk containing all the type information to a bureau for high-quality bromide prints or film.

Type descriptions have to be stored in a device-independent format, and converted to a form readable by the particular device as and when necessary. **PostScript**, developed by Adobe, is such a format (Fig. **2.55**).

PostScript describes the outline of the letterform in terms of vectors (lines and curves) rather than dots, and this outline is converted by software into a pattern of dots specific to each output device. PostScript is, strictly speaking, a page-description language (more in Chapter 5; see p. 135) that describes not only letterforms, but also drawings created on the computer, and the layouts of type and drawings on pages.

As PostScript is a proprietary piece of software, anyone wanting to make PostScript-compatible typefaces or printing devices has to pay Adobe a license fee. To try to break Adobe's monopoly, Microsoft, the developers of Windows for the PC (personal computer), and Apple developed a rival format called **TrueType** (Fig. **2.56**).

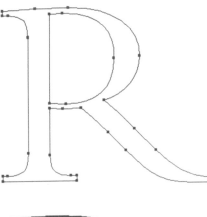

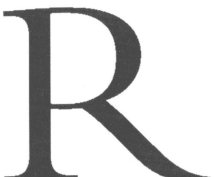

2.55 PostScript is an outline description format, developed by Adobe and adopted worldwide as a de facto standard. Letterforms are described in terms of outlines using the math of Bézier cubic spline curves. These outlines are then converted to bitmaps appropriate to the resolution of the output device.

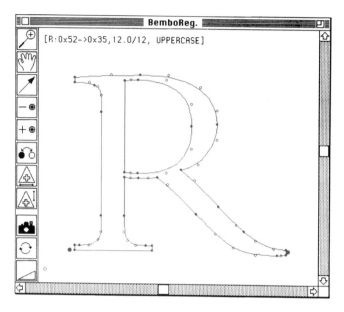

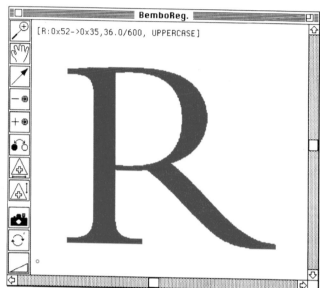

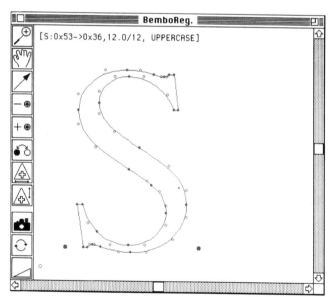

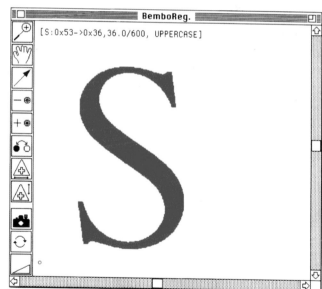

▲ **2.56** TrueType is a rival format to PostScript, developed jointly by Apple and Microsoft. It is similar in principle to PostScript, but its mathematical basis is different – it uses quadratic curves. It is linked to Apple's System 7 operating system, but also runs under Windows on an IBM PC. These samples were produced using TypeMan from Type Solutions, Inc.

The two systems will work together in the same document, but PostScript fonts will not print on the cheaper TrueType printers.

Before PostScript and TrueType, fonts were stored as arrays of dots called **bitmaps** (Fig. **2.57**). These can, when printed, be every bit as good as the equivalent PostScript version, but you will need a separate bitmap for every font and every resolution of target device. With PostScript you need just two: a screen font to give an idea of the look of the typeface on the relatively low resolution of the computer screen; and a printer font, to cover all the different kinds of output device. TrueType uses the printer font to generate the screen font.

ATM (Adobe Type Manager) is a package that improves the appearance of scaled-up fonts on the computer screen and on low-resolution printers. It has been developed purely for use with Adobe's own fonts or those from Adobe licensed suppliers such as Linotype, Monotype, Agfa, and AM Varityper.

Adobe's licensed fonts are called Type 1 PostScript fonts. Other PostScript fonts are called Type 3. There is no Type 2! Type 1 fonts have **hinting** (Fig. **2.58**), which subtly changes the shape of a character so that it better fills the pixel grid of the target device. It is not the same as non-linear scaling. Apple's QuickDraw GX adds yet another font format to PostScript and TrueType – non-GX applications will be able to use GX fonts, but without access to that font's extended character set.

2.57 A bitmap is a pattern of dots that approximates the outlines of a letterform. On a low-resolution device, such as a computer screen or dot-matrix printer, a bitmap looks crude and jagged. But on a high-resolution device, such as an imagesetter, the dots would be too small to see.

72 dpi   144 dpi   300 dpi

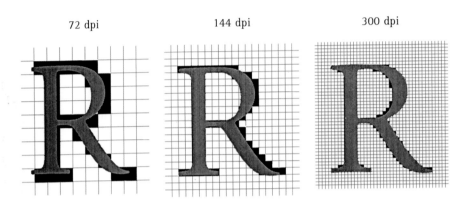

2.58 Hinting is the name given to the process of slightly adjusting the pixels in a scaled bitmap to give a consistent weight and to make the letterform more legible at smaller sizes.

Inconsistent weights   Consistent weights

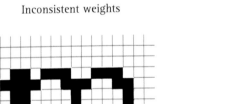

144 dpi
12 point
bitmap
scaled

2   1   1   2   2   2

Without hints   With hints

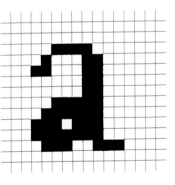   144 dpi
12 point
bitmap
scaled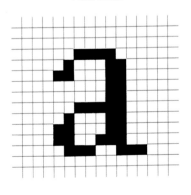

SUMMARY

What, then, are the pros and cons of the various typesetting technologies?

Hot metal or letterpress

■ **Advantages** Quality: each font designed specifically for its particular size; printed result gives an impressed look and feel which conveys care and expense. Uses original type designs. Can be quick to set up for small jobs such as business cards. Nowadays reserved mainly for short-run prestigious invitations, overprinting diplomas, and for private press editions of poetry books.

■ **Disadvantages** Handsetting is labor-intensive, and thus costly. Must hold a large inventory of metal type, which takes up space. Can run out of sorts in the middle of a job. Machine setting is noisy and highly skilled. Metal type is inflexible, does not enlarge well, and cannot be set close. Limited availability.

Cold metal or strike-on

■ **Advantages** Quick and direct setting by relatively unskilled operators. Inexpensive.

■ **Disadvantages** Poor selection of typefaces, crude intercharacter spacing. Justified setting difficult. Low quality.

Photosetting

■ **Advantages** Fast and relatively inexpensive. Wide range of typefaces. Letters can be set closer than in hot metal. Set by skilled compositors, ensuring a good-quality result.

■ **Disadvantages** All sizes produced by one font master. More "sterile" look than hot metal. Mechanicals usually needed to produce pages.

Computer setting

■ **Advantages** Wide range of typefaces available. Type can be adjusted and manipulated in different ways. Type can be imported directly to page make-up systems, so no intermediate mechanical stage required. Possibility of "do it yourself" setting, so no typesetting costs.

■ **Disadvantages** Designs of traditional typefaces vary between suppliers. Unless set by skilled compositor, possibility of errors going unchecked. Choice of sizes, leading, tracking can result in unimaginative use of defaults. New skills to be learnt.

ERIK SPIEKERMANN

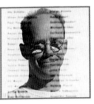

LIFE STORY Erik Spiekermann was born in 1947, in Stadthagen, Germany. He funded his own studies, in art history at the Free University in Berlin, by setting metal type and operating a printing press from the basement of his home.

Spending seven years working freelance in London in the 1970s, principally for Wolff Olins and Pentagram, he also lectured at the London College of Printing, consolidating his involvement with all aspects of typography, including type design. Spiekermann calls himself a typographic designer. "A typographic designer starts from the word up; a graphic designer starts from the picture down." His trademark signature is a "tectonic" narrow rectangle or bar bleeding off the confines of the page, usually in just one of two colors: black or red, with type dropped out in white.

Never long away from Berlin, Spiekermann also developed a successful relationship with Berthold AG, which led in the late 1970s to commissions to redraw and digitize some of their classic typefaces. He returned to work in Berlin, founding MetaDesign with Uli Mayer and Hannes Krüger in 1979. The first Mac computer arrived in 1985. MetaDesign now employs 120 designers working in the Kreuzberg district of Berlin. It is the largest design studio in Germany with major design contracts for BVG, Berliner Verkehrsbetriebe, the Berlin public transport system (see spread), Apple, Adobe, Hewlett-Packard, IBM, Texas Instruments, VW, Audi, the city of Berlin itself, and the German Green Party.

In 1992 Spiekermann co-founded MetaDesign West in San Francisco, with Terry Irwin and Bill Hill, ostensibly because he needed "a work excuse to spend more time in California." In 1995, to close his typographic circle

> "When the design of information is left to chance, the result is information anxiety"

Spiekermann formed a partnership with Tim Fendley and Robin Richmond in London, completing what has become an international network. Two of these three offices sit within strong-framed 19th-century industrial buildings: old homes to printing presses.

As a type designer, Spiekermann is best known, so far, for ITC Officina and FF Meta (see p. 67), which he once described as the "Helvetica for the 90s" and which is now approaching a Helvetica-like ubiquity. Meta began life as a corporate typeface for the German post office to try and end the "chaos" created through the use of dozens of versions of Helvetica in the organization, but ended with the client's decision to stick with Helvetica because to change would "cause unrest."

No conference about type and typography is complete without an appearance by Erik Spiekermann. If not in person then on tape or by satellite link, the typographer immediately strikes the newcomer in the audience with his articulate English and then by his humor, at once acerbic and self-deprecating. His ability to communicate ("not called speaker-man for nothing") has speeded his international recognition.

MANIFESTO You Cannot *Not* Communicate
"Each single solution has to function in every small detail," says Spiekermann, "while at the same time being seen as part of a larger total. Nothing is irrelevant: a picture chosen arbitrarily, sloppy printing, inappropriate choice of paper or messy typography can destroy even the most profound design concept."

Spiekermann's specialty is creating order from chaos: information design. His work testifies to the fact that clear signage can be informative and pleasant to look at. MetaDesign's timetables, maps, and signs for the BVG provide clear evidence of his approach. This is achieved through care in type selection, sometimes type creation, and especially through typographic clarity. He espouses, and adheres to, the use of asymmetric layouts, carefully spaced text, both in terms of character fit and linespacing, and unjustified setting (with very specific attention to word breaks and line shapes), taking as much care with the spaces as with the type.

"We're constantly bombarded by messages," says Spiekermann, "all trying to make us look, to make us listen, to make us react. Some of these messages, however, are more important than others. Often the information we need isn't provided in a way we can readily understand: think of all the instruction booklets, road maps, highway signs, electricity bills, and tax forms you've tried to read that never seem to have the answer to your questions. These familiar forms of communication all contain information which may not necessarily excite or even interest you, but not understanding it could be expensive. How you interpret some information could even be a matter of life or death. The difference between being a survivor and a casualty may be as simple as finding the "Way Out" sign.

"When the design of information is left to chance, the result is information anxiety. And when things become too complex, when an environment defies common sense, when technical requirements are allowed to prevail over human considerations, then someone has to intervene."

WORKSTATION
- *Emigre* 11, 1989, Ambition/Fear issue.
- Erik Spiekermann, *Rhyme and Reason: A Typographic Novel*, H. Berthold AG, Berlin 1987
- Erik Spiekermann and E.M. Ginger, *Stop Stealing Sheep and Find out How Type Works*, Adobe Press, Mountain View, California, 1993
- Mike Daines, "Erik Spiekermann: Serious but Not Solemn," *Baseline*, 19, 1995, pp. 22-27
- William Owen "Meta's tectonic man," *Eye*, 18, 1995, pp. 34-45 *ID* magazine, Jan/Feb 1996, p. 78
- Web site: <http://www.metadesign.com/>

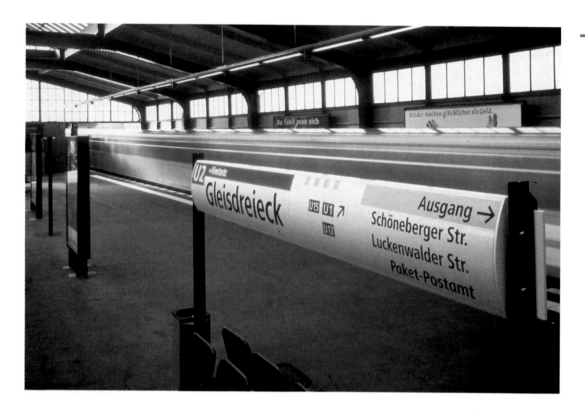

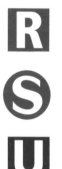

After the fall of the Berlin Wall, public transport in the unified city needed new passenger information. Signs, schedules, maps, bus stops, stations, and printed matter had to be redesigned for people in the East and West; after thirty years apart they had nothing much in common any more. By late 1990, MetaDesign had developed an information system that worked well enough for other transport corporations in the Berlin region to adopt it for their own systems. The design work was awarded the German Design Prize in 1991, which encouraged the team to continue towards a complete corporate design program — from letterheads to new tramcars and even complete subway stations. Spiekermann's familiar bleeding rectangle was forbidden by the client.

Today the Berlin Transport system sports friendly colors, with clear up-to-date messages showing a new attitude and regard for the customers. The strategy has also led to changes within the company: for example, by standardizing seat covers and other fittings across a wide range of vehicles and developing a modular signage system it has been shown that good design can also save money.

In March 1994, *Fortune* magazine recognized the BVG corporate design program with the prestigious Beacon award.

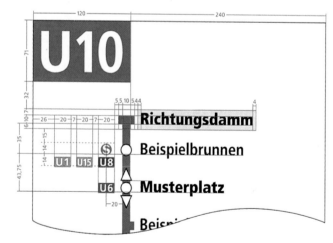

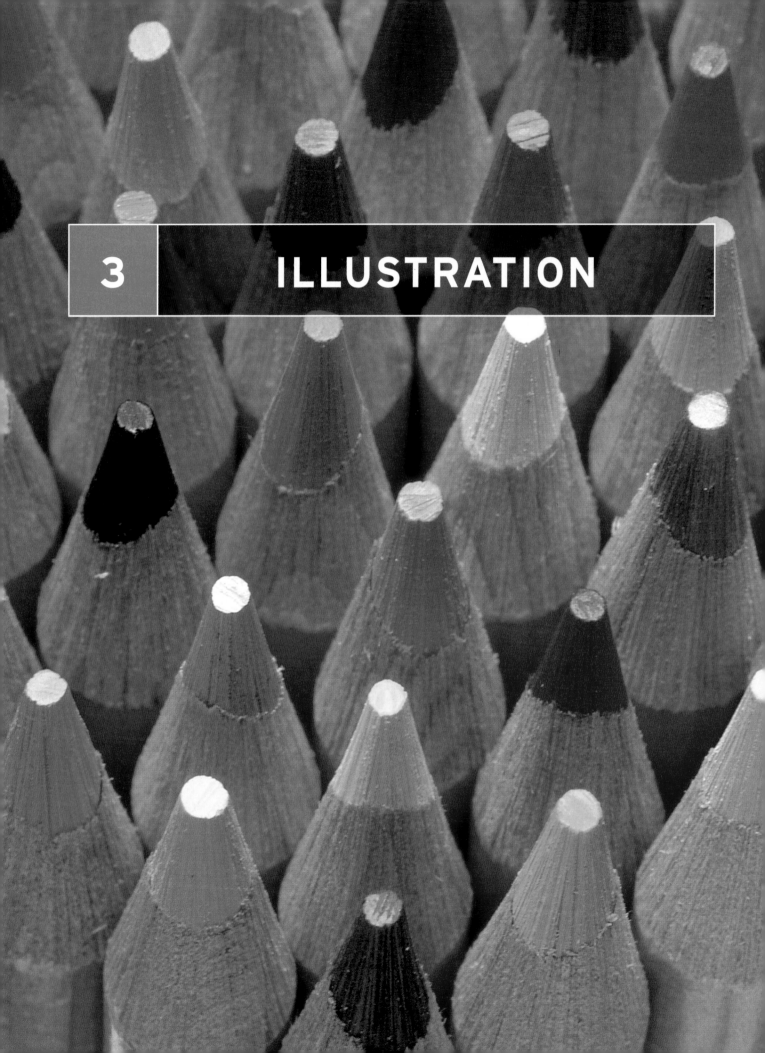

3 | ILLUSTRATION

A picture is worth more than a thousand words," says the ancient Chinese proverb. Well, that may be a gross undervaluation in our image-rich and visually literate society. And while beautifully set typography can have "shape," "form," and "color," there is nothing to compare with the real thing.

Words and pictures are the raw material of the graphic designer. We have looked at the print production of words, and now it is the turn of images in all their diversity.

Until the middle of the nineteenth century, there were very few ways that images could be combined with type. Today, any image is immediately accessible to the resourceful graphic designer. How individual designers choose to communicate the message of their particular publication is no longer limited by printing technology. But an understanding of the process is essential if designers are to realize their dreams.

We explore the differences between line and tone, find out the finer points of flat color and the four- and six-color processes, learn the secrets of successful screening, and discover how the digital scanner "sees" the copy we put before it. We look at practical methods of sizing and cropping images, and investigate the best ways of preparing artwork and photographs for the service bureau, repro house, or printer. We also develop some winning ways to get the best from our professional colleagues, the illustrators and photographers.

LINE AND TONE

Line, to the printer, is any copy that will print in a single color requiring no other intermediate treatment. When the printer mixes ink, the machinery is not capable of diluting it to produce grays, or tints of a color. Black cannot become gray; dark green cannot become pale green. The ink is either there on the paper or it's not. Line means solid areas, dots, or lines of a single color, with no gradation of tone.

There are ways of fooling the eye into perceiving tints and tones. Illustrators use techniques such as stippling or cross-hatching to simulate tones. Victorian engravings can look almost photographic, but look closely and you will see only lines and dots of one color (Fig. **3.1**).

The line process is both the cheapest and the most satisfactory for printing on inferior papers. As mentioned in Chapter 1, the line

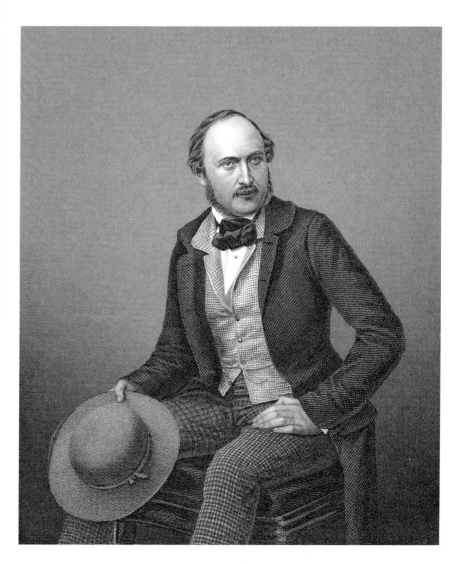

▶ **3.1** Line art includes much more than just black lines on paper, as can be seen in this Victorian engraving of Prince Albert by D. J. Pound, from an original photograph by Mayall. Look closely at the full picture and at the detail opposite and you will not be able to see anything that cannot be reproduced directly.

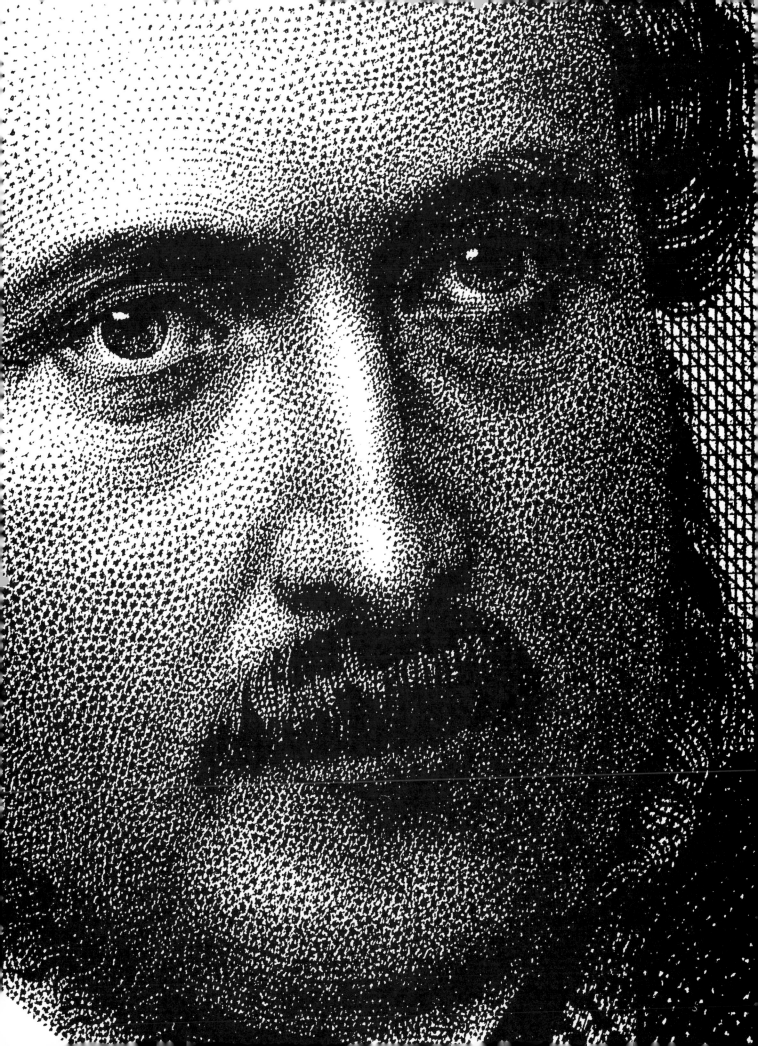

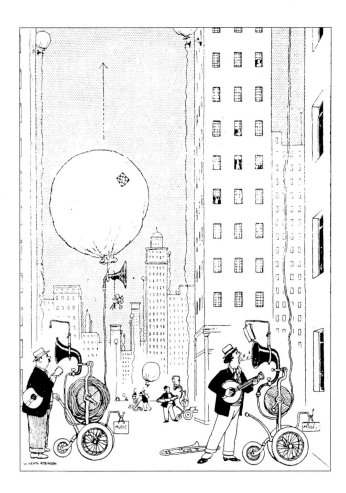

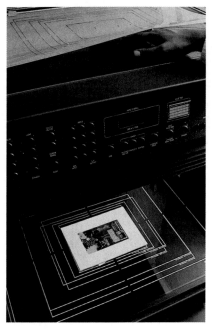

3.2 "Overcoming the difficulties of serenading in New York City," a cartoon with a mechanical tint, from William Heath Robinson's 1934 collection *Absurdities*.

3.3 Before computers, graphic design studios used a combination of process camera, like this WLTC 184, and PMT machine to produce enlarged or reduced copies of line art good enough to use on the mechanical.

block for letterpress was invented by Paul Pretsch in 1853, and, by the mid 1880s, zinc plates mounted on wooden blocks were being used to reproduce black-and-white illustrations in newspapers and books.

For the first time, an illustrator was able to work at larger sizes than the image would appear in print; any imperfections of the line would thus be proportionally reduced. It became common, therefore, to work "half-up" – at 45 x 30 to become 30 x 20 – or "twice-up" – at 60 x 40 to become 30 x 20. Too great a reduction, however, can lose much of the original quality and spontaneity of the work, and over-reduced lines may break up or disappear under the pressure of printing.

From 1901 onward, the block-maker could add Ben Day **mechanical tints** to a line drawing as indicated (usually with a blue wash on the original) by the illustrator (Fig. **3.2**). Later, self-adhesive film

such as Letratone, printed with various tints and patterns, could be added to line work to achieve the same effect.

For offset litho, line illustrations were reproduced photographically on high-contrast **bromide** paper, usually reduced down in size from the original. This print was then pasted on to a board along with the typesetting. Bromide prints can also be produced as **PMTs** (photomechanical transfers), or **diffusion transfers**, by a proprietary method developed by Kodak (Fig. **3.3**). It is a much drier process than the original method, in which the bromide paper was processed in trays of photographic chemicals in a darkroom.

To produce a PMT, original artwork was exposed on special negative paper through a process camera. This negative was then fed into a processor which activated the inbuilt developer and then laminated it to a receiving sheet of paper or

film. After a short delay, the two sheets were peeled apart and the line image was revealed. It was also possible to obtain reversed-out (white on black) images using appropriate paper.

If more than one copy was required, or there was a need for the image to be retouched, a negative film was first made from the original. (It is easier, for example, to clean marks on the white areas of an image by opaquing out the black areas on a negative.) This was then used to produce contact prints on bromide paper, by means of the conventional and messy method of processing.

For low-cost work, it is also possible (and much cheaper) to reduce artwork on a laser photocopier using smooth good-quality paper.

Screens and halftones

A **halftone** is any photograph or piece of artwork that contains tonal values other than just plain black and white (Fig. **3.4**). Before an original containing continuous or intermediate tones can be printed, it must first be converted to "line" – into a form in which there can be either ink on the paper or not. The most common method is to use a halftone **screen**, which converts the continuous tone original into a pattern of single-colored dots (Fig. **3.5**).

This is done digitally these days, but used to be achieved by placing a screen between the lens of the process camera and the bromide paper or film being exposed. As mentioned in Chapter 1, the method devised by George Meisenbach in 1882 used a single-lined screen that was turned 90 degrees during exposure. The first cross-lined screen was introduced in 1890 by Frederick Ives, in collaboration with Louis and Max Levy.

Halftone screens came in two varieties: glass screens and the cheaper plastic contact screens. Glass screens had a finely ruled grid pattern and were situated between the lens and the film. Contact screens contained a pattern of vignetted holes and were placed in direct proximity with the film. The term halftone is perhaps a misnomer: they are thus named because half of the tone is eliminated during the process. Half the image maybe – but *all* of the tone.

The optics of how this happens is not really important to know. Suffice to say that different tones are converted into dots varying in size, shape, and number, which when viewed from a distance seem to melt back into continuous tone.

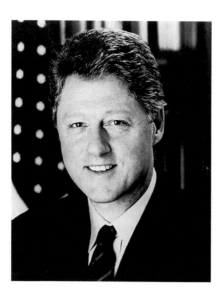

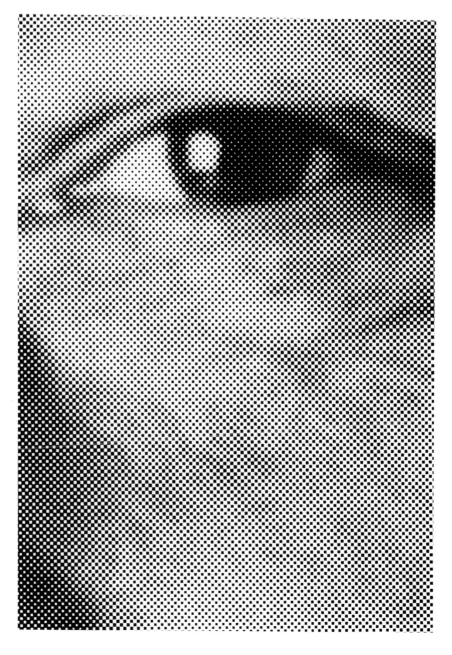

◄ **3.4** Tone art, such as this print of President Clinton, has to be converted into a pattern of dots before it can be printed, by a process called screening.

▼ **3.5** A conventional halftone contains dots of different sizes, but in a regular array conforming to the screen being used. Light areas are represented by small black dots. At 50 percent, you will see a checkerboard of black-and-white squares, while the darker tones appear as white dots on black. It is rare to find either pure white (no dots at all) or pure black (a solid area of black) on a halftone.

3.6 Imagesetters can make various shapes of dot electronically. Elliptical dots score over conventional ones, as they are less prone to dot gain – the abrupt darkening of areas where the dots are beginning to join up.

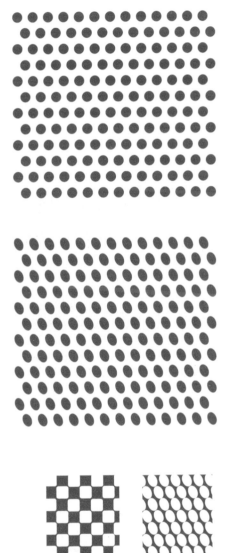

3.8 Detail of Rajarani Temple at Bhuvanesvar, India, at screen rulings of 65 (coarse), 120 (general purpose), and 175 (the ruling used throughout this book).

3.7 When two screens are super-imposed and are not quite in alignment, there is a good chance that moiré patterns will result. This happens most commonly when a previously screened halftone, cut from a magazine, for example, is put through another screening process.

that produce kite-shaped dots that join first in one direction, then the other, giving a much smoother gradation in the middle tones.

On modern electronic imageset-ters, the dots are "written" on to the bromide paper or film directly by a laser beam – no screen is involved. These machines are capable of producing any shape of dot you like: square, round, or elliptical (Fig. **3.6**). The operator at the repro house will choose the best type of dot for the printing process and paper stock being used, and the tonal quality of the original.

Halftone screens are measured in lines per inch (lines per cm in conti-nental Europe), usually abbreviated to **lines** or lpi (Fig. **3.8**). The higher the number of lines, the finer the dot pattern, and the better the quality of the reproduction. But there is a trade-off. Newspapers, for example, use cheap rough paper and thin ink that is prone to spread. Too fine a screen, and the dots in the darker areas of the image will merge and **fill in**. Thus, for newsprint, a coarse dot pattern of 55 or 65 lines for letter-press and 100 or 120 lines for offset is standard. Magazines are printed on smoother papers, and so a finer screen of, say, 150 lines can be used. The very finest screens are reserved for glossy art papers (see Chapter 6, pp. 159–69, for an in-depth discus-sion about paper).

The lines of the screen are usually aligned at 45 degrees to the horizon-tal, as this seems to produce the pattern that is easiest on the eye. There are dangers, however, when screening photographs containing regular patterns, on a person's cloth-ing, for example. The screen dots and the pattern in the picture can inter-fere with each other to produce **moiré** (wavy or basket-weave) patterns (Fig. **3.7**). This can be avoided or lessened by adjusting the angle of the screen. The moiré effect is put to good use in devices that can tell you what screen is being used in a printed publication.

There are also special-effect screens available that convert

The traditional crossed-line screen of 1890 gives a round dot, which becomes a square in the midtones – a checkerboard pattern at 50 percent density. More recently, vari-ous shapes of dot have been tried. An improvement on the conventional screen is one with elliptical holes

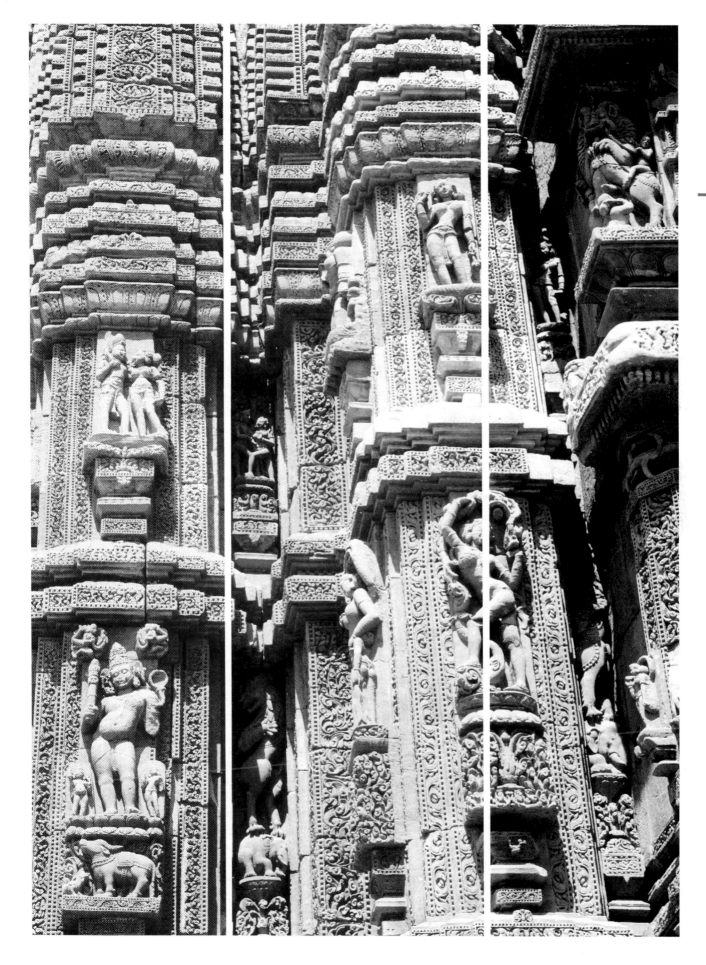

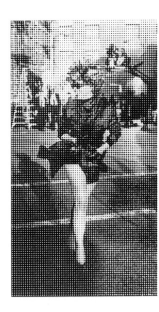 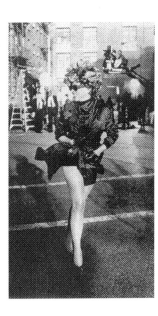 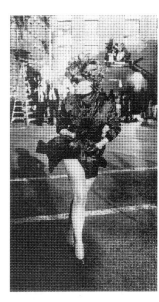 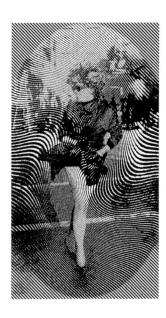

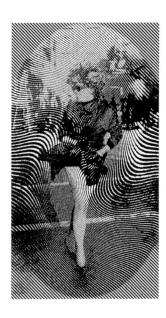
3.9 Publicity shot of Tina Turner. It does not have to be dots! But use special effect screens with discretion!

continuous tone into straight lines of varying weight, wavy lines, concentric circles, and textures that simulate canvas, linen, and random grain (Fig. **3.9**).

Conventional screening is now referred to as **AM** (amplitude-modulated) screening: the dots are arranged in regular columns and rows, but vary in size. In **FM** (frequency-modulated) screening, all the dots are same size, but they are randomly scattered (Fig. **3.10**). This eliminates the possibility of moiré patterns, and produces much smoother vignettes. And because the final image is built from single pixels, rather than composite halftone dots, the imagesetter can be run at lower resolutions. However, subsequent platemaking is so sensitive it must be carried out in almost "clean-room" conditions. Note the absence of the familiar rosettes you see when you magnify areas of constant color in four-color work. FM screening is also sometimes called **stochastic** screening, from the Greek for "random." Linotype-Hell's Diamond Screening and Agfa's Cristalraster are examples of FM screening.

Halftones are generally squared up, i.e. rectangular in shape. Sometimes you might want to specify a thin black line around them to define the edge. There are other effects

that can be used by the discerning graphic designer (Fig. **3.11**). These include **cut-outs**, in which extraneous matter is opaqued out (by hand, or using an image-manipulation program such as Photoshop); **drop-outs**, in which the dots in the very whitest areas are eliminated to accentuate the highlights; and **vignettes**, usually oval, in which the image fades gradually to nothing at the edges.

In work destined for offset lithography, halftones are usually made into negative film and are "stripped-in" later, occupying the clear holes on the negative page left by black squares placed on the artwork. For some jobs, however, it is cheaper and more convenient to be able to put correctly sized halftones into place along with the type and line, and shoot the whole page in one operation.

A **velox** is the halftone equivalent of a PMT – a halftone on bromide paper. Do not be alarmed if a velox appears slightly lacking in contrast, because each time an image is copied, it gains contrast. It will look fine when printed. The screen for veloxes should be as coarse as can be accepted, and should never exceed 120 lines.

Sometimes it may be necessary to produce a halftone from copy that

has already been screened. It may not be possible to locate the original of an old illustration from a book, for example. To put a screened picture directly under the camera will more often than not result in unwanted moiré patterns, but there are way of avoiding this.

Use your **loupe** (eyeglass) to see if the dots on the original are sharp and black. If the screen does not exceed 120 lines, it can be shot as line copy. This is called **dot-for-dot** reproduction, and will often result in an increase of contrast. Where this method is not possible, try rotating the screen angle 30 degrees from the original and shooting slightly out of focus.

Where lines and tones appear on the same piece of artwork, for example in a pencil drawing or an ink and wash illustration, a compromise has to be made. Either the whole illustration is treated as tone, in which case the white of the paper will appear light gray and the black lines will lose their crispness. Or the artwork is shot twice, as line and as tone, and combined at the film or platemaking stage as a **line and tone combination**.

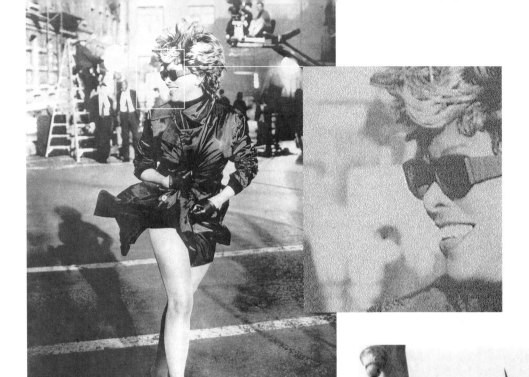

3.10 Publicity shot of Tina Turner. FM or stochastic screening uses a random scattering of spots to reproduce tone, rather than the regular pattern of dots used in AM screening.

83

ILLUSTRATION

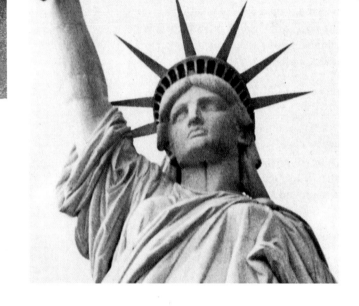

3.11 A halftone is not always "squared-up." It can also be cut-out around a profile, have the highlights dropped-out, or it can be made into a vignette with the usually elliptical edges fading away to white. (Bartholdi's Statue of Liberty at the entrance to New York harbor.)

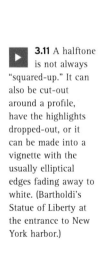

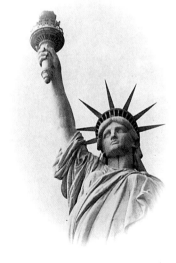

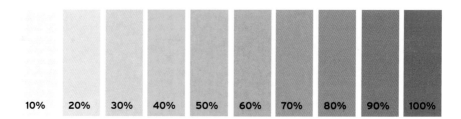

3.12 Color tints are effective when used under typesetting to draw attention to a particular passage, quotation, or checklist.

| 10% | 20% | 30% | 40% | 50% | 60% | 70% | 80% | 90% | 100% |

84

ILLUSTRATION

COLOR

The use of color in printing is almost as old as printing itself, but the process has always been labor-intensive and has required painstaking amounts of skill. The chromolithographs of the mid-19th century sometimes used as many as 12 separate hand-drawn plates. This created correspondingly enormous problems of positioning the successive printings into correct alignment, one on top of the other – what printers call **registration**.

Flat color

Printers can mix up any color of ink you like – you will just be charged for the cost of special ink and for cleaning up the machine afterward.

An additional color used as a design element in a layout is called **flat color**, or sometimes **match** or **spot color**. In theory, you could use any number of different colors in a design. In practice, most printing presses are designed to handle two, four, or even six colors in one printing, and the more printings you ask for, the higher the cost of the job.

Printers can match almost any color – from a color chart, a piece of printed work, or even the color of

your eyes. But if it is consistency you're after, between jobs and other related printed items, you're going to have to be a little more scientific.

The **Pantone Matching System** (PMS) is an industry-standard collection of over 1000 colors that printers recognize and are comfortable using. (PMS 485 – red – is the flat color used throughout this book.) It is worth purchasing a color guide, in the form of a fan chart or **swatch book**. It will show you all the shades,

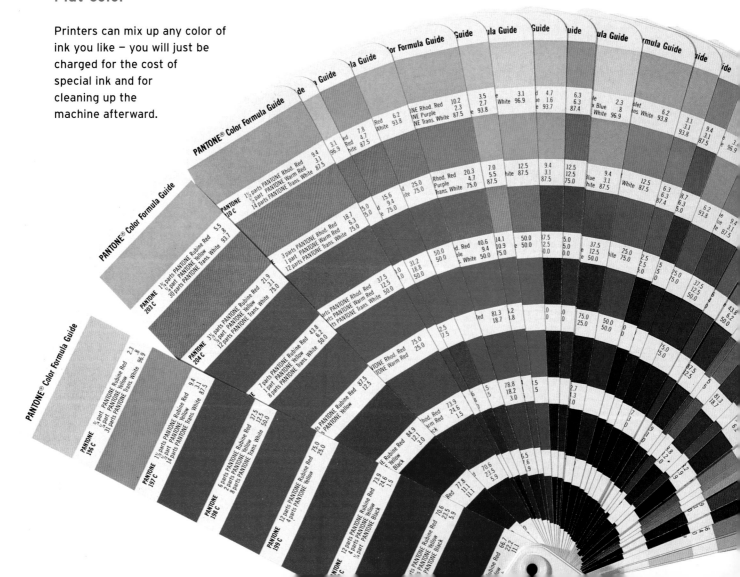

SURPRINT

REVERSE OUT

OVERPRINT

along with the formulas for mixing the ink, and the effect of colors printed on both coated and uncoated paper (Fig. **3.13**). The easiest way of specifying flat color is to give the printer the Pantone number and perhaps one of the tear-off samples that come with the swatch book.

Any color chosen from the Pantone range is made from a mixture of two or more from a set of nine basic colors: yellow, warm red, rubine red, rhodamine red, purple, violet, reflex blue, process blue, and green, supplemented by transparent white and black. There are also complementary sets of colors incorporating metallic inks, and specialist selections, such as pastel colors for packaging designers.

Flat color can be printed solid or as a percentage **tint** (Fig. **3.12**). Books are also available that show Pantone colors in a range of percentage tints. Type can be combined with a tint of flat color in three ways: **surprinted**, with the tint and in the same color; **reversed out** of a tint block; or **overprinted** in another color (Fig. **3.14**). Legibility is an issue, so check with printed samples to see what will work with different percentages of tint.

Printers do not like to have flat colors overlapping, because it slows down the rate of drying of the inks and introduces the possibility of smudging. A color will change shade, too, when printed over another one. But adjacent areas of flat color will need to overlap to a small extent to allow for misregistration (misalignment of successive printings). This allowance is called **trapping** (Fig.

3.14 Text surprinted, dropped out of a tint of the same color, and overprinted in a different color.

3.15) and is particularly important where, say, lettering is reversed out of a block of one color and printed in another. Without trapping, the slightest amount the printing slips **out of register** will cause a thin white line to appear around part of the boundary, resulting in an unwanted bas-relief effect. Generally, it is the lighter color that is extended into the area of the darker color.

3.15 If a graphic or type in one flat color has to fit with a background of another color, there is always the possibility that misregistration might cause a sliver of white where they should abut — this is called bad trapping. The prevention and cure is to add a "stroke" width all round the lighter component, which will be hidden when the darker ink is overprinted.

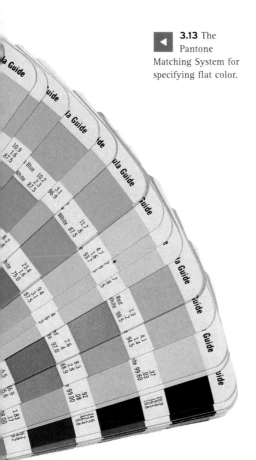

3.13 The Pantone Matching System for specifying flat color.

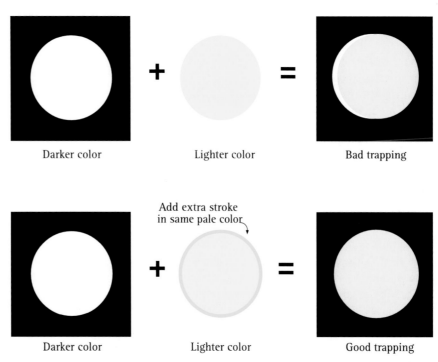

Darker color + Lighter color = Bad trapping

Add extra stroke in same pale color

Darker color + Lighter color = Good trapping

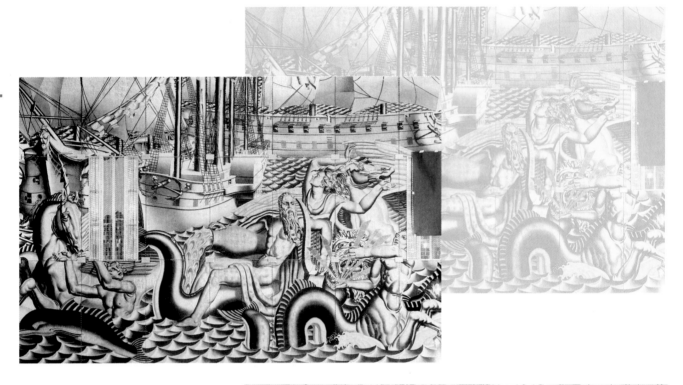

Duotones

A halftone cannot always reproduce the full tonal range of a photograph. A **duotone** is a superimposition of a contrasty black halftone over a one-color halftone, which is shot for highlights and middle tones (Fig. **3.16**), using the same image. The most commonly used color are yellows, browns, and reds. The intention is to create a rich range of tones, and at the same time add a colored tint to the result. For high-quality work, where cost is not a constraint, a duotone may even comprise two printings in black, or in black with a shade of gray. A basic shot with the screen at 45 degrees is used for the black plate, and a second shot at 15 degrees is used for the second color.

For very high-quality publications, three passes of black or gray ink may be used to reproduce the full tonal range of a halftone. A less

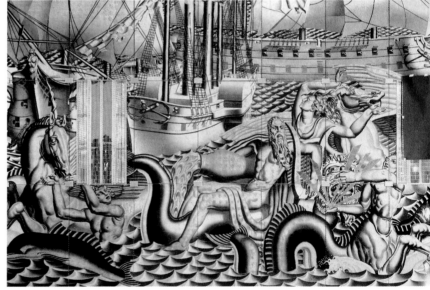

impressive duotone effect can be achieved by printing a black halftone over a color tint of the same size. This is called a **flat-tint halftone**. The tint must be kept quite light, as the highlights in the halftone can only ever be as light as the underlying tint.

▲ **3.16** A duotone is a halftone reproduction comprising two (or sometimes more) printings — one for contrast and the other for the highlights and middle tones. More often than not, the underprinting is in a color other than black. The use of cyan here enhances the sparkle in these Art Deco glass panels, now housed in the Metropolitan Museum of Art, New York, from the ocean liner *Normandie*.

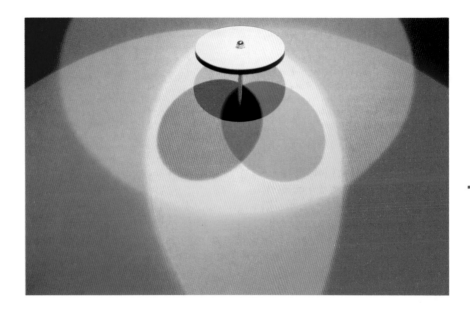

3.17 Pure white light contains all the colors of the rainbow. Add together the three primaries — red, green, and blue-violet — and you get white. Where the primaries overlap, the secondaries appear: yellow, magenta, and cyan.

Full-color reproduction

It is neither economic nor practical to mix up ink and print every individual color to be found in a piece of artwork or color photograph, so another method has to be used. It should be possible to create any color from a mixture of the three primary pigments: red, yellow, and blue. Mix any two primary colors and you have the secondaries. Thus blue and yellow produce green, red and yellow produce orange, and blue and red produce purple. Theoretically, if you mix all three, you get black. Experience tells us, however, that what we really end up with is an unpleasant muddy brown. These combinations apply to **reflected light**.

With **transmitted light** (Fig. **3.17**), things are a little better. Here, the three primaries are red, green, and blue-violet; the secondaries are yellow, **magenta** (reddish purple), and **cyan** (turquoise). Mix three such primary beams of light, and the result is pure white. Grass is green because it absorbs the red and blue-violet components of white light and retransmits the green.

The secondary colors of transmitted light — yellow, magenta (process red), and cyan (process blue) — are the ones used by printers to reproduce full-color work. In 1860, Clerk Maxwell demonstrated how colored filters could be used to record the blue-violet, green, and red constituents of any full-color subject. Filters of red, green, and blue-violet — the primaries of transmitted light, also known as **additive colors** — are used to produce **separation** negatives (Fig. **3.18**). The red filter allows only the blue and green components

through, creating cyan. The green filter allows through only red and blue, creating magenta, and the blue filter lets through only the red and green, creating the yellow. The negatives taken through these filters, known as **color separations**, are screened and the positives are then used to make plates to be printed in sequence and in register (correct alignment) in the **process colors** of yellow, magenta, and cyan.

In theory, all the colors added together should produce black, but in practice printing ink, like school paint, never does produce a pure enough black. So a fourth color — black — is added to deepen the dark areas and increase contrast. This makes the scheme a **four-color process**. In print jargon, black is referred to as **key**, so the system is known as **CMYK**. Other systems of defining color include **RGB** (red, green, blue) used for computer displays, and the more theoretical **HLS (hue, luminance, saturation)**. Hue is the part of the rainbow the color occupies — whether it is red or blue. Luminance, or **value**, is the amount of black or white that has been added, to make yellow into brown, or red into pink. Saturation, or intensity, is a measure of the color's position in the range from neutral gray to fully saturated, or bright, color.

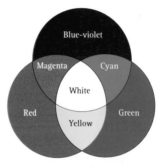

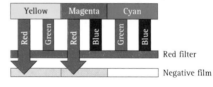

Red filter

Negative film

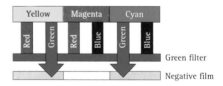

Green filter

Negative film

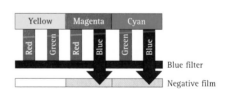

Blue filter

Negative film

3.18 All the colors in full-color copy can be reproduced from a mixture of the secondaries — yellow, magenta, and cyan — and these components of any color can be extracted using filters of the primaries red, green, and blue-violet.

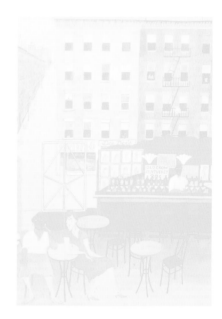

▶ **3.20** In theory, any color can be reproduced from a combination of yellow, cyan, and magenta. In practice, though, black is added for extra punch. Gray component replacement trades off some of the neutral gray created by combinations of the process colors for tints of black — it saves ink and quickens drying (see bottom row). Detail of Scene in Harlem (Simply Heavenly) by Edward Burra (1905–76).

Pantone's **Hexachrome** system uses six colors: brighter (fluorescent) versions of CYMK plus vivid orange and green. This expands the color **gamut** (the limited spectrum of colors that a particular device can reproduce) and is also referred to as HiFi color. When the image is separated, green and magenta are prevented from appearing in the same area, as are orange and cyan, so can share the same screen angles (see Fig. **3.19**) and avoid any moiré patterns. When printing, black goes down first, followed by green, cyan, magenta, yellow, and finally orange.

Color separations

A color tone original can be separated either in the **process camera** or, most commonly these days, by an electronic **scanner**. Separations by camera are made on to continuous tone film using the three color filters, and these are then converted into halftones by exposure through screens. The screens are laid out at different angles, so that the dots are kept separate − the "mixing" of the colors is done by the eye − and in a pattern designed to eliminate moiré effects (Fig. **3.19**). The screens of the main colors are orientated at 30 degrees to each other, with the stronger colors at 45, 75, and 105 degrees, and the less intrusive yellow at the "difficult" angle of 90 degrees.

Scanners work by reading the artwork as a series of horizontal lines, or rasters. The **transparency** or artwork is wrapped around the scanner's transparent drum, which revolves at around 90 miles per hour (150 km/h). A beam of light is used to pick up the three color components. These split beams are digitized, and

pass into a computer where color correction and some manipulation of the image can take place. Finally, a laser is employed to "write" the dots of the screened separations directly on to film.

Some combinations of the three process colors cancel each other out to produce neutral grays, and since black is being used anyway, this can be seen as overkill. **Gray component replacement** (Fig. **3.20**), also known as **achromatic stabilization**, is a technique used at the scanning stage for cleaning up the color and reducing the amount of ink that gets to the paper. Not all the "chromatic" gray is removed and replaced by a tint of black, however. **Undercolor addition (UCA)** is a method of returning some of the process color, usually cyan, beneath the black to add depth and density to areas of deep shadow. **Undercolor removal (UCR)** reduces the amount of color in areas of shadows, to save ink and prevent problems that may occur if a new layer of ink is printed on to ink that is not quite dry.

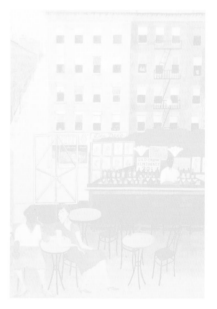

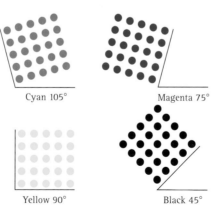

Cyan 105°   Magenta 75°

Yellow 90°   Black 45°

▲ **3.19** To prevent moiré patterns, the screens for the different color printings are set at specific angles: 45 degrees is easiest on the eye, so that is reserved for black; 90 degrees is the least satisfactory angle, so it is used for the relatively pale yellow.

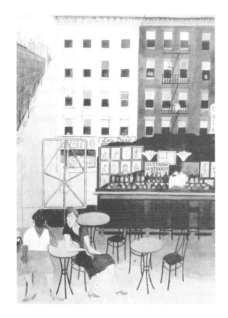
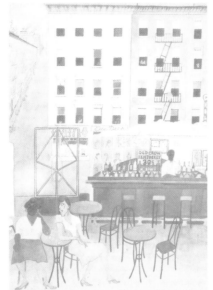
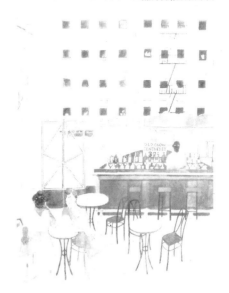

89

ILLUSTRATION

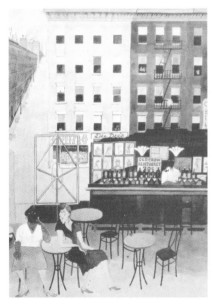
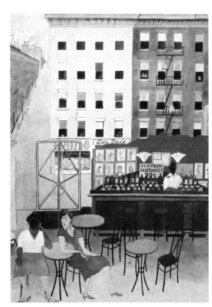
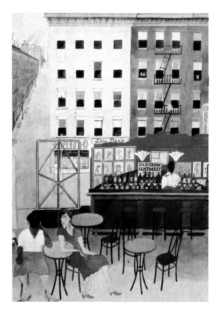

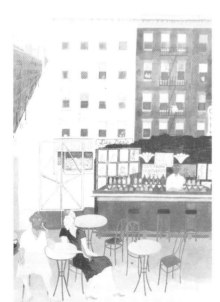

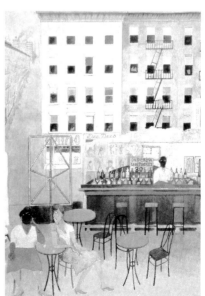

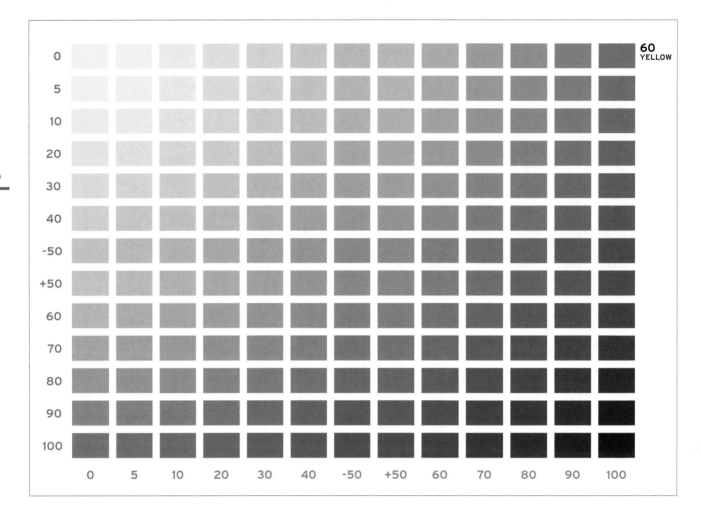

													60 YELLOW
0													
5													
10													
20													
30													
40													
-50													
+50													
60													
70													
80													
90													
100													
	0	5	10	20	30	40	-50	+50	60	70	80	90	100

If a solid area is to be printed in a Pantone shade along with four-color illustrations, it will be cheaper to match the color by using a combination of tints in two or more of the process colors. Pantone publishes charts illustrating various combinations of process tints printed one over the other (Fig. **3.21**). But if you plan to substitute in this way, check first with your clients. They may have strict rules about the use of color for corporate-identity work – the color of a company logo, for example – and may be willing to stand the cost of an extra printing in a specially mixed Pantone shade.

To prevent potential muddiness when too many colors are mixed together, a rule of thumb has evolved that the sum of percentage components of the process colors should never exceed 240. A color comprising 30% yellow, 10% cyan,

and 60% magenta (= 100%) is fine, but one containing 70% yellow, 100% cyan, and 80% magenta (= 250%) would not be allowed on the press. The color bar on a color proof has checks for this (see p. 117).

CHOOSING AND PREPARING ILLUSTRATIONS

Briefing an illustrator or photographer

Graphic designers and illustrators have much in common. The most famous illustrator turned graphic designer, Milton Glaser, has always encouraged illustrators to do as he has done. Not only will you earn more money as a graphic designer, but you can then commission yourself to do

3.21 Charts showing combinations of various percentage tints help you make the most effective use of process color in layouts. This chart shows the effect of changing the percentages of magenta and cyan while keeping yellow constant at 60 percent. Along the axes, -50 refers to dots that are not touching and +50 refers to ones that are.

the illustrations! Be that as it may, not every graphic designer can draw as well as he, nor is every illustrator as passionately interested in type.

A graphic designer may commission artwork and photography, or may be presented with a package of words and pictures to put together according to a design brief. If the graphic designer is involved at an early stage with the commissioning of illustration and photography, a careful eye can be kept on the quality and content of the finished job.

Perhaps the two most important pieces of information an illustrator

needs to know are the deadline date, and the size of the artwork required. The content and style will be different for each job, and the choice of a particular illustrator or photographer will be made on their ability to deliver what you want, on time, and to a professional standard. There are, however, some further general principles that can be outlined.

There are two kinds of original copy. Flat artwork from the hand of the illustrator, photographic prints, and PMTs are termed **reflection copy**; they are viewed by reflected light. Color transparencies and film positives are known as **transmission copy**.

Almost all copy is scanned in and separated on a drum scanner nowadays, so try to encourage illustrators to produce their artwork on flexible media that will wrap around the drum. Check with the repro house the maximum size of artwork that the scanner can take. Black-and-white line artwork is often scanned as grayscale, so if you want black line, make a point of telling the repro house that black line is what you want! An illustrator may use different densities of black ink for the outline and solid color. Under the process camera, all would come out as solid black; scanned as grayscale, you might end up with an illustration in two distinct shades of gray.

Many illustrators like to work on rigid board. There is a kind of board available with a surface that can be peeled off from a rigid base and then wrapped around the drum of a scanner. Originals sometimes get damaged and some kinds of paint crack, so it is wise to have a transparency made first, and for this to be

used in the scanning process. Bear in mind, however, that there will be a loss of quality whenever an original is copied.

Where you do have commissioning power, and when selecting images that already exist – from picture libraries, for example – insist on the following:
• Line reflection copy, such as cartoons, should be in black Indian ink on good quality artboard, with any corrections made in process white paint. The original should be drawn no larger than twice-up, unless the lines are simple and thick enough to withstand reduction below 50 percent. Scratchboard illustrations, with their sharp lines, generally reduce well. If a line-and-tone effect is required, for example in comic book illustration, the line work and lettering should be drawn on an acetate overlay, in register, over the tonal element.
• Halftone reflection copy, such as photographic prints or airbrush drawings, should have a wide tonal range with not too much contrast. Check for the correct exposure, the graininess, and whether the part of the image you require is correctly in focus. The original should ideally be same size and, at any rate, not more than half-up. Photographs should be printed on glossy paper.

If you have access to a slide scanner, or attachment to a flatbed scanner, it is possible to scan a negative directly into the computer, where it can then be turned positive using a program such as Photoshop.

Never risk scratch marks by attaching anything to a photograph with a paperclip or staple. If color copy is to be reproduced in black

and white, be prepared for a loss in clarity and contrast, and be aware that certain colors are "seen" by the process camera differently from the way the human eye perceives them. Red, for example, will print black, but light blue may not print at all. Flesh tones, particularly, will have to be compensated for. If in doubt, you can have a black-and-white internegative and print made.

Artwork intended for flat color should be supplied in black on a baseboard, with each color drawn, in register, on a separate overlay. Artwork in which the separate flat colors do not touch or overlap can be drawn on the same board, provided that the portions to be printed in different colors are clearly indicated on an overlay.

Artwork in full color should not contain any fluorescent paints or inks as they do not reproduce well when separated into process colors. Nor do very pure secondary colors, such as purples and lime greens.
• Halftone transmission copy, such as photographic transparencies, should be chosen on a lightbox equipped with standard lighting conditions. Transparencies come in various formats: 35 mm, 5 in x 4 in, and 10 in x 8 in, for example. Because they will undergo considerable enlargement when reproduced, choose as large a format as you can afford. Check for graininess – it will increase as the transparency is enlarged. And because a transparency's tonal range will be compressed by the printing process, look for detail in both shadow areas and highlights. Check for correct exposure (ask the photographer to "bracket" the exposures, by shooting

▶ **3.22** A reproduction calculator – a device for working out the size an illustration will appear on the page once it has been reduced or enlarged.

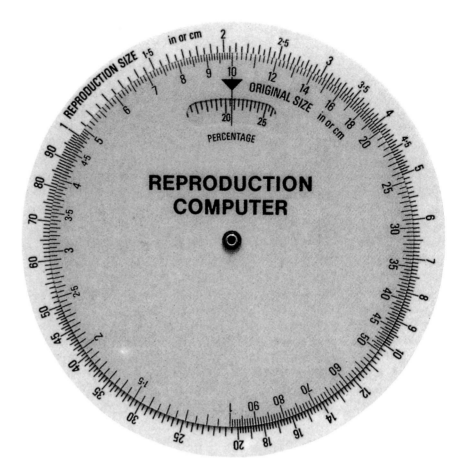

at apertures above and below the optimum f-stop, and choose the best result). Look, too, for the **color cast** found on a subject photographed against a strongly colored background. Also, scrutinize the transparencies for fingerprints, scratches, and other blemishes. Colors can be corrected to some degree at the repro house, and some retouching can be done using Photoshop, but beware – you will be charged for the service.

Ensure that each transparency is right reading – the repro house will assume that the image is correct when the transparency is viewed with the **emulsion side** facing away from you. This is not always the case, especially if the "original" is a duplicate. Double check by supplying them with a sketch of the subject on a traced overlay.

Scaling and cropping

Copy to be reproduced at exactly the same size as the original is called same size and marked S/S. More often than not, artwork will have to be reduced in size to fit your layout, and transparencies enlarged. This is called scaling, or reproportioning.

The simplest and clearest way to indicate the required size of artwork or photographs is to mark the limits of the image with a double-headed arrow and write "Reduce to 4 inches" or whatever you want the width (or height) to be. To avoid damaging the artwork, this is best done on an **overlay**, or flap, of layout paper or tissue. If you are using only a portion of the photograph or artwork, the area you need can also be

outlined on the overlay. This is called **cropping**, or recomposing.

It must be said, however, that few photographers and probably no illustrators like to have their work cropped by a graphic designer. Some sensitivity and diplomacy is required if it just has to be done. It is much better to have the size and shape of the illustration or photograph worked out in advance so that the illustrator or photographer can be briefed thoroughly. Obviously, photographs come in standard formats, and some cropping is inevitable. But give the photographers a chance to crop their images and you will be rewarded with better results.

If you are ever tempted, for the sake of a composition, to invert a photograph laterally, i.e. turn it into a mirror image of itself (and it can be done quite simply at the stripping-in stage), get out your loupe and watch out for the giveaways. These include

obvious ones such as lettering and signs, but also more subtle telltales such as clocks and maps in the background, or the position of a man's suit breast pocket, or specialized equipment with controls and buttons that the reader will recognize as inverted. Some of these can be retouched, but it is often better to prevent potential embarrassment by leaving well alone, or paying out to have the photograph reshot.

It is difficult to draw **crop marks** accurately on such a small area as a portion of a 35 mm transparency, and it is better to make an enlarged photocopy, and to mark that with your instructions. These copies can be placed in position and at the correct size on the artwork (more on this in Chapter 4, p. 111).

It is often useful to know the size an image will appear once it has been reduced or enlarged, so that you can plan your layout with confidence that the scanned image or dropped-in

▶ **3.23** Diagonal scaling is a quick and easy way of estimating the space an enlarged or reduced illustration will occupy.

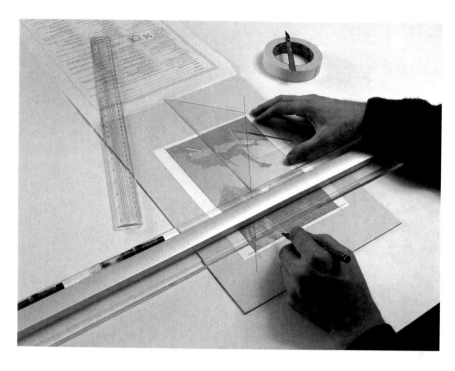

color separations will fit. There are two methods for making this calculation. The first is to use a **reproduction calculator** or **proportional scale** (Fig. **3.22**). This is a kind of circular slide rule, comprising two disks that rotate relative to each other. Find the width of the original on the inner wheel, line up the width of the space into which is has to fit on the outer wheel, and you will be able to read off the corresponding reduction or enlargement in height. It will also give you another useful figure – the percentage reduction or enlargement.

An ordinary pocket calculator can also be used to determine the size of an illustration after reduction or enlargement – just substitute your figures into the following formula:

$$\frac{\text{height after reduction (or enlargement)}}{\text{height of original}} = \frac{\text{width after reduction}}{\text{width of original}}$$

Suppose you have a photograph 10 inches high by 8 inches wide that you have to reduce so that it will fit a column 3 inches wide. What will be the resulting height after reduction? How much room should you allocate in the layout?

Using the above formula:

$$\frac{x}{10} = \frac{3}{8}$$

Now, cross-multiply and divide to find *x*, thus:

$8x = 30$
$x = 30 \div 8 = 3{\cdot}75$ in

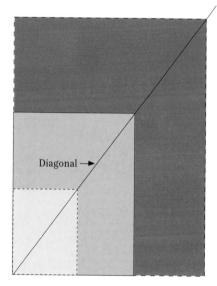

Diagonal →

The main thing to remember when using a regular pocket calculator is to ensure that your units of measurement are consistent. *All* units must be in either inches, millimeters, or picas – but never a mixture!

To calculate the percentage reduction or enlargement, divide the intended width (or height) by the width (or height) of the original and multiply the result by 100. In this example:

$$\text{percentage reduction} = \frac{3}{8} \times 100$$

$$= 37{\cdot}5\%$$

A process camera can handle images within a range of 16 percent reduction and 600 percent enlargement.

Percentages can seem confusing at first: 100 percent, for example, is same size; 50 percent is half the width or height, but a quarter the area; 200 percent is twice the width or height, but four times the area. If you increase or reduce the width, do not forget that the height will also be increased or reduced, in direct proportion. When in doubt, always mark the copy with the width (or height) at which you want the image to appear. Writing exact measurements on the copy will also make it easier to check that the correct reduction or enlargement has been made when you receive your picture proofs.

The diagonal method (Fig. **3.23**) uses geometry to help you to work out the final size of your scaled artwork. Draw a rectangle around the cropped area on the overlay, using a setsquare (triangle) or transparent grid to make sure that the corners are square. Protect the original, and draw a diagonal from the bottom left corner to the top right. If the artwork is to be reduced, measure the width you want it to appear along the bottom edge of

3.24 Digital cameras, such as this Kodak DC20, do not use film – they capture photographic images digitally. The digital information can then be input to a computer system directly, and no digitizing, scanning, or other processing is necessary.

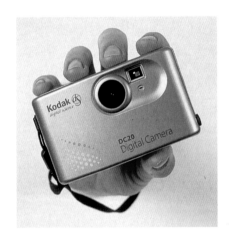

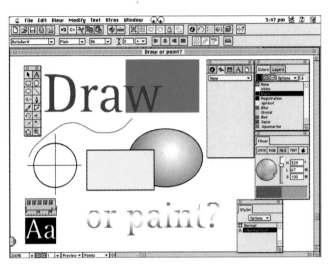

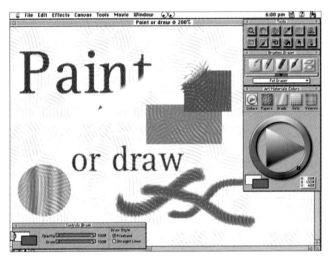

3.25 The main difference between "paint" and "draw" software lies in how the image seen on the screen is stored in the memory. A paint document is a bitmap – just a representation of the screen – whereas a draw document is stored in terms of the points, lines, and formulas used to create it. Thus a draw document is not restricted to the resolution of the screen, and the image can be "deconstructed" for editing and amendment.

the rectangle using the bottom left corner as your starting point, and draw a vertical from the other end, up to meet the diagonal. Where these two lines intersect, draw a horizontal line to meet the left vertical edge of your original box. This is the height that your scaled artwork will appear when reproduced.

If the artwork or transparency is to be enlarged, trace the crop outline to the bottom left corner of a piece of paper, draw the diagonal as before, but extending it beyond the crop rectangle. Also extend the bottom edge of the box and the left vertical. Now measure off the intended width of the enlargement, draw a line vertically to meet the extended diagonal, and read off the enlarged height.

Most pictures have to fit a specified width – a column width, for example. This method can, however, be used to calculate the width of an image that has to fit a specific height.

A Grant enlarger, or opaque projector, is a great help in scaling artwork. A lightbox, too, will make the process a lot easier.

Always label illustrations, and do so in soft pencil, preferably a non-reproducing light-blue one, or in felt-tip pen (checking first that it will not bleed through the overlay). Do not stack photographs while the marks on the back are still wet without first protecting the front, and never write on the back of a photograph with a ballpoint pen. A greasy pencil, such as a Chinagraph, is best for writing on glossy surfaces. If you will be handling a lot of transparencies, invest in some lint-free cotton gloves to avoid introducing fingerprints on to the images. And always remove transparencies from glass mounts before sending them to the printers – they will break, damaging the transparency, and showering the recipient with thin shards of glass.

Desktop scanning

Users of computer systems can bypass the PMT stage by directly scanning black-and-white artwork, using a desktop or hand-held scanner. The quality of the scanned images produced by these devices is much lower than that of illustrations originated on the drum scanners found in repro houses, but they are improving, and coming down in price all the time.

Desktop color scanners and special slide scanners are not yet considered to be up to repro quality, but they do have a place in giving the graphic designer an idea of how the layout is going to work. And they are being used as a creative tool by a new breed of computer graphics illustrators. With digital cameras

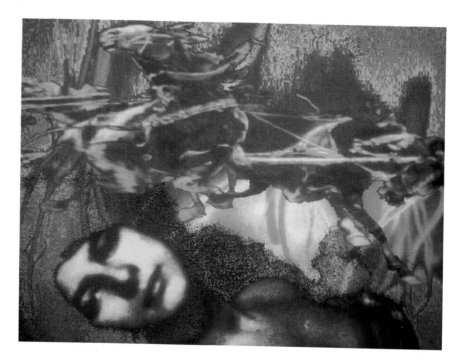

▶ **3.26** This "paint" illustration by David Wood, for an EMI Classics recording of Wagner's Die Walküre, was created on PC-based equipment at London's Central St Martin's College of Art and Design.

(Fig. **3.24**), it is possible to bypass even the scanning process, and input digitized images direct to the computer (see p. 131). With Kodak's PhotoCD, you can take a film from a conventional 35mm camera to your local film-processing lab and have the images put on to a CD-rom. These images can then be viewed and further manipulated on your computer system. It is possible to put several films on to one CD-rom over the course of several sessions.

Drawing and painting by computer

On a computer such as the Macintosh, there are two different ways of producing illustrations, referred to as "draw" and "paint" (Fig. **3.25**). A "paint" document is stored in the computer's memory as a bitmap, a one-to-one array corresponding to the pixels (dots) appearing on the screen – although the image can be much larger than the size of the screen. In a **paint program**, a circle intersected by a line, say, is just a pattern of dots and can only be moved en bloc. It is not possible to edit "globally" – modify every circle in a picture, for example – using just one command.

A "draw" document has more in-built "intelligence." It is stored in the computer's memory as a display list of the points and lines that make up the illustration, plus the formulas for any circles, ellipses, and curves. This is also known as object-oriented graphics, because every object – a circle, line, or curve – can be accounted for separately. In draw programs, it is possible to move the line without affecting the circle. And

because they are not stored in terms of bitmaps, the output resolution to, say, a PostScript plotter is independent of the image's resolution.

MacPaint was the first program for the Macintosh to use bitmapped graphics, and was good for producing freehand irregularly shaped objects and airbrush effects. MacDraw was the original object-oriented draw program.

Paint systems, such as the Quantel Paintbox (Fig. **3.27**), are best known for their use in graphic design and for producing special effects for broadcast television. There are paint systems around that

do their best to emulate real paint. Fractal Design's Painter, for example, can simulate the wet appearance of oilpaint and produce convincing chalk and pastel effects through the use of a pressure-sensitive stylus.

It is as a medium of photomontage, however, that paint systems such as Adobe's Photoshop are being put to work in most design studios (Fig. **3.26**). Originally developed for **retouching** photographic images, Photoshop is now the *de facto* image-manipulation program. It does produce very large files, however, which can bring your computer to its knees quite easily.

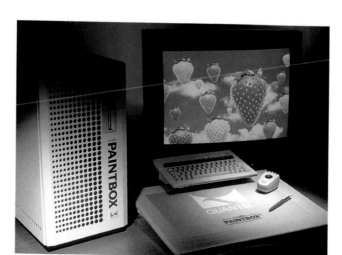

◀ **3.27** The Quantel Paintbox was originally designed for television graphics. The Graphic Paintbox has a much higher resolution, more suitable for print applications.

FREEHAND COLOR TRICKS
To change a solid fill to a gradient,
press the control key as you drag and
drop a second color on to the object;
change a gradient to a solid by pressing
shift as you drag a swatch of new color
on to the object. Placing a swatch of
new color bottom center produces a
vertical fill; central left or right
produces a horizontal fill.

96

ILLUSTRATION

3.28 Paint systems are not only used to make "paintings" from scratch; they are more usually put to work retouching or montaging photographs, as in this still from a commercial for cough drops.

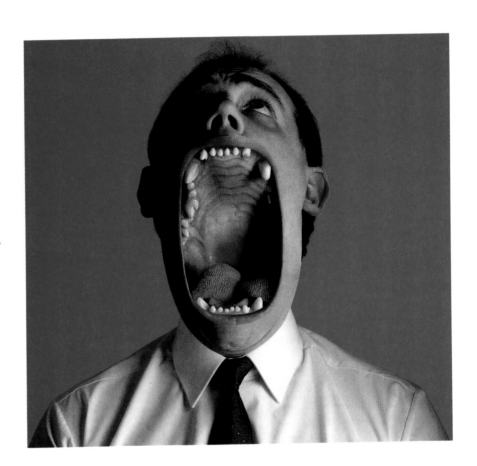

A new breed of image-manipulation programs, such as Live Picture and Macromedia's xRes, work in a different way. Instead of having the whole file in memory all the time – the way Photoshop does – Live Picture and xRes let you work on a screen-resolution version of the image while logging away the manipulations you make. When you have finished the job, the image is rendered into the format you require. Here so-called source or "reference material" (beware of copyright infringement!) can be scanned into the system, or "framegrabbed" by a video camera, to be combined, manipulated, and recolored. This is analogous to sampling and remixing musical quotations to produce today's electronic dance music.

Some graphic designers also use paint systems as a concept design tool. If you are designing packaging for a new range of TV dinners, for example, a convincing illustration can be montaged from illustrations "grabbed" from cookery books or other sources. When the concept has been approved for go-ahead by the client, these roughs can be used as a brief for the commissioning of original illustration or photography.

The power of the computer as a conceptual tool is grossly underestimated. Some designers use it for nothing else, preferring to produce finished artwork traditionally, by

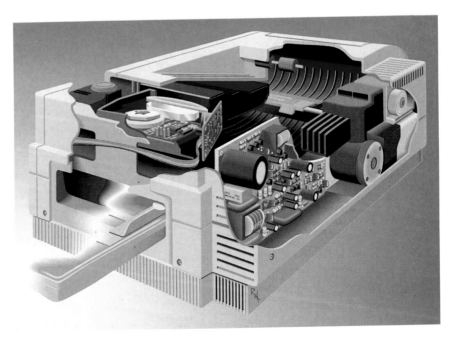

SIMPLIFY YOUR ILLUSTRATIONS

A lean and efficient illustration from FreeHand or Illustrator will output faster at the repro service bureau and save you time and money (they'll put complex jobs to the back of the line so it doesn't hold up other jobs). Use straight lines in preference to curves whenever you can. Or use paths with as few points as possible. The number of segments the output device uses to simulate curves depends on the "flatness" value. The flatness is a number between 0 and 100 and is the difference between the polygon the output device draws and the mathematical curve. The higher the number, the rougher the curve but the faster it will print. A value of 3 should be your default, but you can probably get away with a much bigger number before detecting a loss of quality. And delete any object you can't see in preview mode – it might be hidden behind another object, but it will still have to be processed!

hand. The computer allows you to play around with ideas – trying out different type, alternative positioning of elements, another color, and so on – for as long as your schedule will allow. As West Coast designer April Greiman says: "The paint never dries." And so long as you have the different versions, there is no chance of ever spoiling the original.

Retouching covers a multitude of sins: it can be as innocent as adding a few crocuses to a countryside scene, or it can be used to subvert reality completely, placing well-known characters in compromising positions, for example. Thankfully, it is mainly used to clean up images or as a purely creative medium – in fact, just as graphic designers use any other form of illustration (Fig. **3.28**). What is certain, however, is that as desktop scanners become more affordable and programs such as Photoshop are ever improved, photographs will be retouched routinely because it will be so easy to do so. And the adage that "the photograph never lies" will have even less credibility than it has now.

Draw programs such as Adobe Illustrator and Macromedia's FreeHand are now closely linked to page layout packages. They can be used not only for black-and-white or color illustration, but to manipulate type too (Fig. **3.29**).

Both use controllable freeform curves (called Bézier curves) which can be manipulated to produce complex drawings. Scanned images or bitmapped drawings from a paint program can be "imported" and traced over. However, better results can be obtained by using a specialized tracing program, such as Adobe Streamline.

Other tools are used to create boxes, lines, ellipses, and corners at any angle. Layers (overlays) are available, so that the drawing can be split up into separate elements which can be displayed and edited individually. Line attributes, pattern fills, and colors can be saved on a computer style sheet and applied to other elements later to maintain a consistency throughout a series of illustrations. There are commands for rotating, scaling, mirroring, skewing, and stretching elements. Text can be wrapped around a line or shape. Drawings thus created can be exported directly, as **EPS** (Encapsulated PostScript) files to page layout packages such as QuarkXPress or Adobe PageMaker. There they can be combined with text originated on a word processing system.

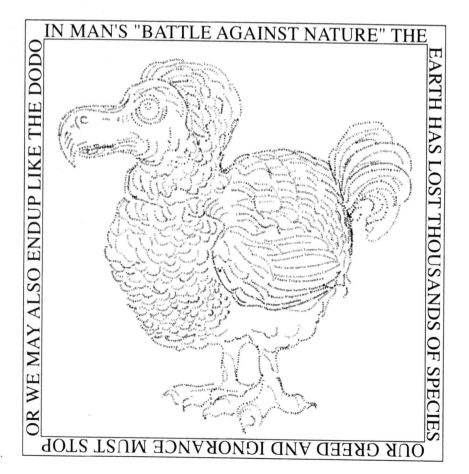

◄ ► **3.29** Illustrator Bob Harrington used Adobe Illustrator to produce this technical drawing of the Apple LaserWriter laser printer (left). Output is direct to film separations. A completely different use of a "draw" program is shown in this image by Henry Lyndsey — a dodo containing the names of 2000 endangered animals (right). It is a virtuoso demonstration of FreeHand's ability to set text along freeform lines.

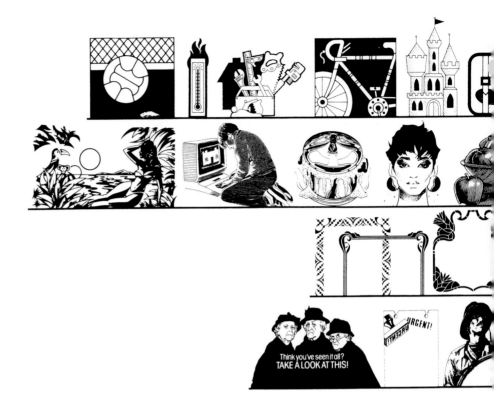

ILLUSTRATION

Clip art (Fig. **3.30**) is copyright-free artwork that can be bought ready-made and en masse on a floppy disk or CD-rom and incorporated into your layouts. It has always been around in book form, to be copied at will, but lately has proliferated. Some is good, most is awful, and none of it is either original or unique. It should be used with discretion, and never in work where clients are under the impression that they are paying for original artwork. Maps can be copied with confidence, especially when they are to be customized in a program such as FreeHand or Illustrator.

Three-dimensional design programs, such as Macromedia's Extreme 3D and Ray Dream Studio, are also increasingly being used by illustrators, especially in comic books, where cartoon characters are viewed from different angles and against different backgrounds (Fig. **3.31**). Programs such as MetaTools Bryce can be used to create fantastic fractal landscapes for use as backgrounds.

More and more, illustrators will be creating work on computer – images that can be shipped directly to page make-up programs with no intermediate artwork needed. There will always be a place, however, for original illustration and photography produced using traditional materials, and today's graphic designer will need to know how to make the best use of both, for a long time to come.

3.31 Pepe Moreno used three-dimensional graphics combined with paint software to produce the artwork for the DC Comics graphic novel Batman: Digital Justice.

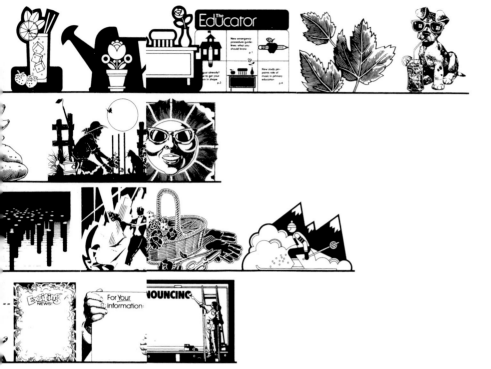

SUMMARY

Illustrations can be line or tone. If tone, they must be screened to convert the image into a pattern of dots for reproduction. Artwork can be drawn or painted conventionally, or created on a computer. Photographs can come in one of two forms: as reflection copy prints, or as transmission copy transparencies. Before origination, they will need to be scaled, and maybe cropped, so as to fit the size and shape of their position on the page layout. And they can be manipulated by computer, either on the level of merely correcting or changing colors, or in terms of undergoing more drastic treatment, using the image as a basis for a photomontage.

Whether you choose the mechanical or the digital method for the production of your illustrations will depend quite a lot on the processes being employed, and on the type of project. Conventionally drawn line work, such as cartoon illustrations, will have a sparkle and a fluidity that a computer program is unable to replicate. On the other hand, the consistent line weights and perfect geometry of a computer "draw"

program are ideal for technical diagrams. But as desktop scanners come down in price, a hybrid approach may rule: scanning-in line art drawn conventionally, to be manipulated further on the computer and output as a file ready to be placed in a page-layout program.

The constraints on black-and-white and color illustrations are different. Conventional black-and-white line drawings can be pasted directly on to mechanicals (see Chapter 4), ready for the next stage of production. If you are using a computer, it is easy enough to scan in black-and-white artwork and place it straight on to your page layout. Where photographs are concerned, the desired quality will be the decisive factor as you choose between scanning-in a coarsely screened picture or leaving its origination to the repro house. With a computer-generated or -stored illustration, there is the distinct advantage that the all-important artwork cannot get lost or damaged in the mail. It can even be sent to its destination down the telephone lines. And once the image is inside the system, it can be used over and over in different shapes and forms.

For color work, illustrations usually arrive in the form of transparencies, though original artwork can produce much better results. Whichever form they take, they must be flexible enough to be wrapped around the drum of the scanner at the repro house or printer. Desktop scanners can be used to input images intended for photomontage and other forms of creative retouching. Alternately, the scanner can produce low-resolution scans to indicate positions and crops for illustrations that will later be processed at the repro house, on better-quality equipment, as we shall discover in the next chapter.

LUCILLE TENAZAS

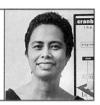

LIFE STORY Born in 1953 and raised in the Philippines, Lucille Tenazas learned at an early age to accommodate both Eastern and Western ways of looking at the world: the strong US military presence familiarized her with Western culture and she learned English alongside her native Tagalog. It is this interest in language that gives her work its distinction.

Tenazas's studies in the Philippines focused on fine and liberal arts, which broadened her understanding of the contexts in which culture and design are produced. This, coupled with design work experience at the pharmaceutical companies Bristol-Myers and Smith Kline Corporation, led her to postgraduate study in design in the United States.

Tenazas applied to Cranbrook Academy of Art in 1979, but after an initial rejection, went to California, where she studied for two semesters at the California College of Arts and Crafts (CCAC). After replenishing her portfolio and developing her skills in drawing and painting, she entered Cranbrook at the second attempt. Her work was different from that of the other students. She had brought with her the visual language of California's New Wave – bright colors, geometric shapes, and a rich textural surface.

> "The secret is to answer the client's needs as well as satisfy my desire to further my own creative exploration"

Cranbrook gave Tenazas a way of thinking about design rather than an established visual style. She moved away from her colleagues' "type 'n' stripe aesthetic" to one that displayed an elegance and formal resolution. During the mid-1980s, Tenazas continued her visual explorations at the New York corporate communication consultancy Harmon Kemp.

Now Tenazas runs her own design firm in San Francisco. Tenazas Design was responsible for the identity of the Center for the Arts at Yerba Buena Gardens, San Francisco. Her firm was also involved in the typographic design of the New England Holocaust Memorial in Boston. The studio's projects are mostly for cultural organizations: the San Francisco Museum of Modern Art, California College of Arts and Crafts, but also Chronicle Books, Esprit, and the Pacific Film Archive, architectural organization 2AES and IDEO Product development.

A recipient of many design awards, her work has been published both nationally and internationally and has been exhibited at the Pompidou Center in Paris and the Fortuny Museum in Venice. She is also an adjunct professor of design at the California College of Arts and Crafts and has been a visiting critic at Yale University and California Institute of the Arts. In 1955, she was honored as one of the "ID Forty," in *ID* magazine's third annual selection of leading design innovators.

MANIFESTO A Language of Clarity
"My early work did not investigate language as a vehicle to explore another dimension," says Tenazas. "I started to see words as objects with a physicality that can be held and touched and I seek to empower their meaning. My expression lies in the meaning, form, and content of the language. I'm interested in addressing the client's needs, but in ways that provoke the viewer to complete an unfinished idea that has been presented to them. This is one reason why my work has many layers.

"When I first came to the USA, my interest in English was as a form of verbal communication. My interest in the layers of language has evolved over the past six years. Since I came to this understanding later in my career, it has affected my way of teaching. The whole idea of authorship is important. I try to instill in my students that you have to make your voice heard. I feel that if you are aware of who you are, then you can ultimately take on the identities and problems a client may pose yet not lose your own voice."

By suggesting that art and design are compatible, Tenazas takes a controversial stance. Some designers fear that any subjectivity detracts from the effective communication of the client's message. But a designer's subjective voice gives the work distinction, and design that suppresses that voice becomes a dry exercise in problem-solving. Tenazas acknowledges the conflict: "Whether working for myself or for others, I've always seen opportunities to do something new. The secret is to answer the client's needs as well as satisfy my desire to further my own creative exploration." She is aware of the difficulty for the reader of "sifting through a lot of elements on the page" and tries "to discipline myself to use just one element." But she asks: "How does this element become interesting if it is not manipulated?"

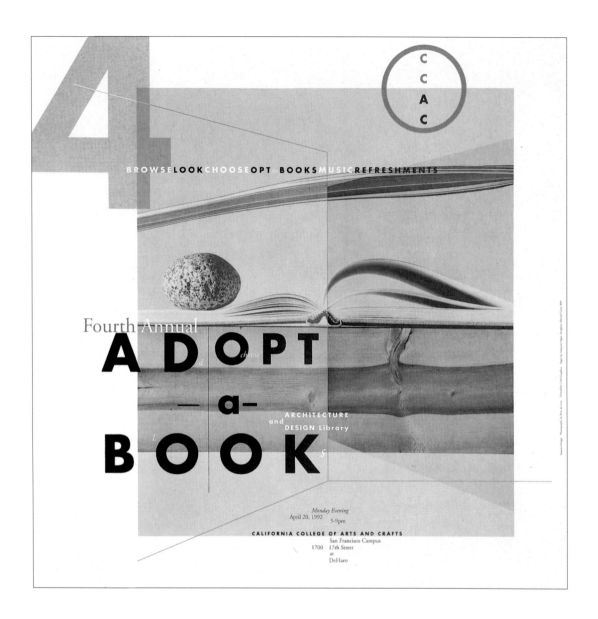

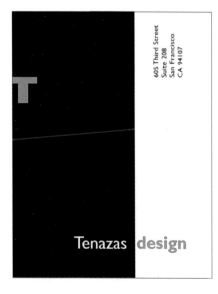

▲ **Adopt a Book**, poster for California College of Arts and Crafts, 1992. The printing is offset lithography and the paper is Simpson Evergreen Almond Cover 80#. As in her other posters, Tenazas uses a minimum of compositional elements to convey meanings and associations. She plays word games, by means of both typography and the selection of evocative words, coaxing the reader through subtle layers of interpretation. The typefaces used in the poster are Futura and Adobe Garamond, with PageMaker used for layout. The photograph was not commissioned for this project, but was appropriated from a previous project: a paper promotion brochure.

◄ Detail from Tenazas Design's address label.

WORKSTATION
• Teal Triggs, "Layers of Language," in *Eye*, **17**/95 pp. 62-71.
• Noreen Rei Fukumori, *Communication Arts*, March/April 1996 pp. 80-89.

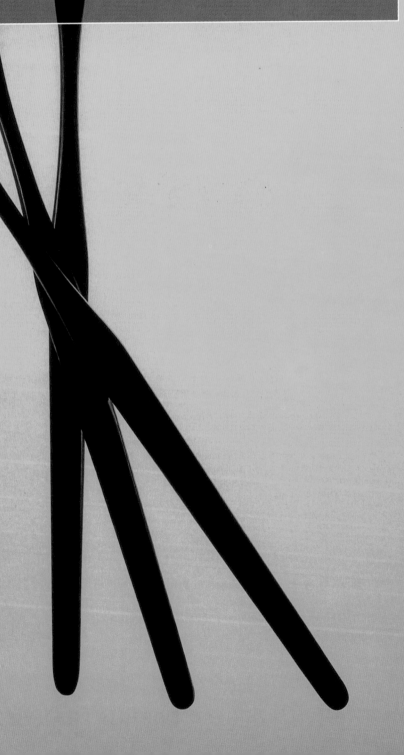

4 | MECHANICAL PREPRESS

Prepress is the part of the print process in which all the design elements – the words and the pictures – are assembled into a unified whole. It is the stage in print production that ends with the making of lithographic plates, silkscreens, or gravure cylinders. This marks the point of no return, after which the presses begin to roll.

But in recent years that decisive moment has shifted. The involvement of the graphic designer has been extended, and is now much more closely tied to the outcome. A publication used to be "put to bed" with the dispatch of the mechanicals to the printer or repro house. Now, as all the data that makes up a page is digitized and stored electronically, it is feasible (though not always desirable) to make essential changes much later in the process – right up until the exposure of the final film, in some cases.

This chapter begins by covering the principles and terminology of layout, with tips for avoiding common design pitfalls. We take a look at grids and their usefulness in providing structure to a page. They save time too. Then imposition schemes are explained – a good grounding in how and where pages are arranged on printing plates or cylinders is important for effective prepress planning. Next, a practical task: preparing the mechanical, or the camera-ready artwork. This may not be what a lot of graphic designers actually do – many leave the neat work to the typesetter. But a good knowledge of producing precise mechanicals will stand you in good stead for working on the more flexible electronic equivalent: the digital page-layout package.

Finally, we move on to repro, and look at film montage. We discuss the various methods of checking picture proofs, and outline what you can discover from a detailed examination of a proof's color bar.

¶ Type *Tymes*

An occasional Newsletter for graphic designers, printers and typographers that is published once a millennium, if ever at all.

Alphabet soup
by IMA WORDSMITH

Writing text that is meant to represent body type in layouts and type specimen books is probably the most difficult task a writer can ever be asked to undertake. Ideally, the text should contain examples of all the letters and sorts: in Roman, *italic* and **bold** so that it looks right. Above all, it shouldn't draw attention to itself. The text is not meant to be read, merely looked at – but invariably someone somewhere will grab a magnifying glass, read it and then criticize any attempted jokes therein.

Some designers take the easy route and use real or bogus Latin text, most often a famous piece of text that begins: Lorem ipsum dolor sit amet, consectetur adipiscing elit, diam nonnumy eiusmod tempor incidunt ut labore et dolo... These are, according to the FAQ (frequently asked questions) of the newsgroup comp.fonts, the slightly jumbled remnants of a passage from Cicero's *de Finibus Bonorum et Malorum*, written in 45BC, a treatise on the theory of ethics, which begins: 'Neque porro quisquam est qui dolorem ipsum quia dolor sit amet, consectetur, adipisci velit...' (There is no one who loves pain itself, who seeks after it and wants to have it, simply because it is pain.)

This text has been the industry's standard dummy text ever since some printer in the 1500s took a galley of type and scrambled it to make a type specimen book; it has survived letter-by-letter essentially unchanged except for an occasional 'ing' or 'y' thrown in. The nonsense Latin was as incomprehensible as Greek; so the phrase 'it's all Greek to me' and the term 'greeking' have common roots!

But this does contain some strange, to English eyes, letter combinations. Few, if any English words contain the sequence 'etiu', for example. When short pieces of text are called for, try to make a sentence containing all the letters of the alphabet with as few duplications as possible. These are called *pangrams*.

The classic pangram used by typographers is: 'The quick brown fox jumps over a lazy dog'. Good score: all 24 letters of the alphabet in a 33-word sentence that makes sense. 'Pack my box with five dozen liquor jugs' is better, with one letter less. Another common albeit longer one is: 'How razorback-jumping frogs can level six piqued gymnasts!'

This one is not so good: 'In the vocation of typesetting, dexterity can be gained by means of quiet, judicious and zealous work'. It is more appropriate to the printing trade, but comprises 83 letters! And what about this: 'Wherever civilization extends, the services of expert and judicious typographers and printers must always be quickly called upon'. Is that grammatically correct? I don't think so. Or this: 'The bank recognizes this claim as quite valid and just, so we expect full payment'. Hmm.

Probably the shortest French pangram, at 29 letters, is 'Whisky vent: jugez cinq fox d'aplomb'. Some pangrams of exactly 26 letters do exist, but rely heavily on odd Welsh and Hebrew words, such as cwm (a Welsh valley) and qoph (the nineteenth letter of the Hebrew alphabet) and, of course, proper nouns (which could in fact be made up from the left-over letters): 'Vext cwm fly zing jabs Kurd qoph' is a good

Page 1

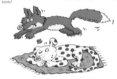

¶ Type *Tymes*

An occasional Newsletter for graphic designers, printers and typographers that is published once a millennium, if ever at all.

Alphabet soup

The classic pangram used by typographers is: 'The quick brown fox jumps over a lazy dog'. Good score: all 24 letters of the alphabet in a 33-word sentence that makes sense.

by IMA WORDSMITH

Writing text that is meant to represent body type in layouts and type specimen books is probably the most difficult task a writer can ever be asked to undertake. Ideally, the text should contain examples of all the letters and sorts: in Roman, *italic* and **bold** and include a range of words of average length so that it looks right. Above all, it shouldn't draw attention to itself. The text is not meant to be read, merely looked at – but invariably someone somewhere will grab a magnifying glass, read it and then criticize any attempted jokes therein.

Some designers take the easy route and use real or bogus Latin text, most often a famous piece of text that begins: Lorem ipsum dolor sit amet, consectetur adipiscing elit, diam nonnumy eiusmod tempor incidunt ut labore et dolo... These are, according to the FAQ (frequently asked questions) of the newsgroup comp.fonts, the slightly jumbled remnants of a passage from Cicero's *de Finibus Bonorum et Malorum*, written in 45BC, a treatise on the theory of ethics, which begins: 'Neque porro quisquam est qui dolorem ipsum quia dolor sit amet, consectetur, adipisci velit...' (There is no one who loves pain itself, who seeks after it and wants to have it, simply because it is pain.)

This text has been the industry's standard dummy text ever since some printer in the 1500s took a galley of type and scrambled it to make a type specimen book; it has survived letter-by-letter essentially unchanged except for an occasional 'ing' or 'y' thrown in. The nonsense Latin was as incomprehensible as Greek; so the phrase 'it's all Greek to me' and the term 'greeking' have common roots!

Page 1

What equipment do you need to get started?

- ✓ a sturdy tabletop or drawing board
- ✓ a supply of smooth white mounting board
- ✓ a pad of layout paper
- ✓ a supply of fibertip pens and soft black pencils
- ✓ a clean plastic eraser
- ✓ a pad of tissue or acetate for overlays
- ✓ a non-reproducing light-blue pencil
- ✓ a blue greasy pencil (Chinagraph) for writing on glossy surfaces
- ✓ a surgical scalpel or craft knife (such as an X-acto)
- ✓ a "self-healing" cutting mat
- ✓ a straight metal edge
- ✓ rubber cement and spatula, spray mount aerosol adhesive, or a hot-wax coater
- ✓ low-tack masking tape or matte frosted "magic" tape
- ✓ a large soft brush
- ✓ talcum powder for de-greasing and "lubricating" surfaces
- ✓ paper towels to mop up spillages
- ✓ process white for correcting mistakes
- ✓ sable or synthetic sable brushes, sizes 00, 1, and 3

- ✓ a loupe
- ✓ a lightbox conforming to standard lighting conditions
- ✓ a proportional scale, or calculator
- ✓ a stainless-steel pica rule or plastic typescale
- ✓ a geometry set with compasses, setsquare (triangle), and protractor for measuring angles
- ✓ circle and ellipse templates
- ✓ a transparent grid to check alignment
- ✓ a selection of type specimens
- ✓ a selection of paper samples
- ✓ a Pantone color fan and swatches

and optionally:

- ✓ a computer: an Apple Macintosh, an IBM PC, or PC compatible such as a Compaq
- ✓ page layout software, such as QuarkXPress or Adobe PageMaker
- ✓ a photocopier capable of enlarging and reducing
- ✓ a fax machine to keep in visual touch with the client and printer

---

4.1 Layouts can be symmetrical – with almost everything centered – or asymmetrical or can combine elements of both approaches. The look you decide upon is very much dependent on the sort of job in hand, the message you wish to get across, and the fashion at the time.

LAYOUT

In design, all rules are there to be broken. But first you have to know what they are. Most graphic designers are, so to speak, in the fashion business, and if asymmetrical or off-center designs are in vogue this year, then maybe a symmetrical or centered design will get noticed (Fig. **4.1**) Whenever someone writes down the rules, you can bet that someone else will come along before the ink is dry to rewrite them.

Having said that, however, there are some rules that endure and, for the majority of jobs, the desire will not be to shock, but to communicate ideas clearly, in a visual language accessible and understandable to all.

Very few designers are given a completely free hand – an open brief – to design what they will. There are always constraints, and therein lies the challenge: how to be different and eye-catching, while getting the message across, to time and to a budget. The client will expect the design to relate to the job it has to do – an annual report for a prestigious company will look very different, for example, from a newspaper advertisement for a cut-price corner store.

Designers must develop skills in communicating their concepts to the client clearly and unambiguously, through presentations, which may include rough sketches and more polished visualizations. Designers are also sometimes asked to help "sell" an idea to a client's clients by producing highly finished mock-ups or dummies that will convey a flavor of how the printed product will look.

There are technical constraints in planning your layout. Paper comes

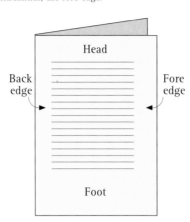

4.2 The page has a vocabulary of its own to describe the various parts of its anatomy. The blank spaces – the margins – are as important as the image and type areas: at the top is the head; at the bottom, the foot; nearest the inside, the back edge; and nearest the extremities, the fore edge.

Head

Back edge

Fore edge

Foot

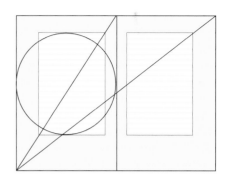

4.3 The standard proportions of medieval book pages, as discovered by the German designer Jan Tschichold. The text area and page size are in the ratio 2 : 3, the depth of text is equal to the width of the page, and the margins are in the proportions 2 (head): 3 (back): 4 (fore edge): 6 (foot).

in stock sizes, and so do printing plates. Insisting on so-called **bastard sizes** and non-standard shapes is wasteful of resources. Folding machines have their limitations too. Packaging designers, in particular, may be restricted by the print technology – for example, only two non-overlapping colors may be allowable when printing a plastic container by flexography (see p. 184).

Thankfully, the offset litho process has given designers almost complete freedom over where the design elements – the type, line illustrations, and photographs – can be positioned on the page. And computer layout systems offer the chance to try out many more potential design solutions. So where do we start?

For magazine and book work, there are certain conventions to be observed. Here we are dealing with pages. Most pages are the shape of an upright rectangle, and this orientation is sometimes called **portrait**. A page with a width greater than its height is denoted **landscape**.

Page sizes are written thus: US Letter is 8½ inches wide and 11 inches tall, and is written 8½ x 11 in. The European equivalent is called A4 (see below), and its dimensions are

written 210 x 297 mm. In inches, that is 8¼ x 11¾ in. In the USA and most of Europe, it is usual to write the width before the height; in the UK and the Far East the opposite is the case – the height precedes the width.

The white areas that frame the printed portion of the page are called the **margins** (Fig. **4.2**). The one at the top is the **head**; the one at the bottom is the **foot**. On the outer edge of the page is the **fore edge**; and the space between the printed material and the spine or fold is the **back edge**. The combined back edges of a double-page spread is called the **gutter**. It is also a term used for any vertical space – between two columns, for example. Traditionally, the foot is greater in depth than the head, and the fore edge approximately twice the width of the back edge. This means

that two facing pages will be united visually as a spread.

Much has been written about what constitutes "good" and "elegant" design. Our response to a layout is embedded in our cultural background. The German designer Jan Tschichold discovered that the margins of medieval manuscripts followed certain rules of proportion, which are still thought pleasing (Fig. **4.3**). The ratio of text area to page size was 2 : 3; the depth of the printed area was the same as the width of the page; and the head : back : fore edge : foot margins were of the ratio 2 : 3 : 4 : 6.

The famous **golden section** format of the Renaissance has proportions of 34 : 21 or 8·1 : 5. Superimposed on to a sheet of US Letter stock, the golden section is just over 1¾ inches narrower (Fig. **4.4**).

4.4 The golden section is a proportion (34 : 21) that people through the ages and in different cultures have found pleasing. It has many parallels in nature – the way a snail's shell grows, for instance. Here a sheet of paper to golden section proportions is compared with US Letter and A4 sizes.

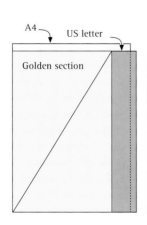

A4

US letter

Golden section

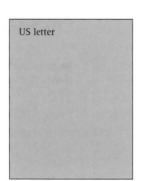

Golden section

US letter

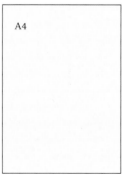

A4

MECHANICAL PREPRESS

Grids

The layout of columns, margins, and area for text and images is usually marked out as a grid (Fig. **4.5**). It also shows the positions of any repeating headlines, or **running heads**, plus the page numbers, or folios. For a one-off publication, the grid will be drawn out on to a board or sheet of heavy paper in non-reproducing blue pencil. If you often have to draw grids, it will be worth purchasing a device called a cadograph, which helps draw even grids. On regular publications or books, the grid will be preprinted on layout sheets.

4.5 The grid used for this book has been underprinted on this spread. A grid is the backbone of a good layout, and a great aid to consistency. It should not be a straitjacket, however. Too detailed and a tight grid will result in a cold and static design.

Type is set in columns. As discussed on p. 57, too wide a measure (column width) affects the readability of text. Try not to specify more than 12 words per line for books, or seven words for newspapers and magazines. Novels and most small-format books are set in one column (Fig. **4.6**). If the single column goes right across the page, you are severely restricted as to where you can place any illustrations. Two or three columns give more flexibility to illustrated books. But there again, an art book may have just one relatively wide column, situated asymmetrically, with lots of white space around it.

In newspapers and most popular magazines, white space means

4.6 While magazines and newspapers are meant to be browsed, books are generally intended for reading calmly and sequentially, hence the simple and comforting one-column format found in most fiction.

4.7 This spread from *Spy* magazine uses a versatile five-column grid, with text at either one- or two-column measure. In the glossy magazines the principles of visual variety and stylishness are often hard to reconcile with the limited space available.

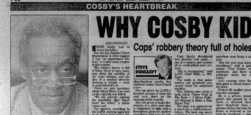

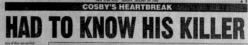

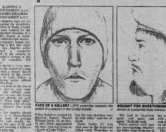

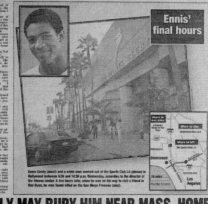

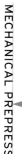

4.8 Like magazines, newspapers have relatively complex grids so as to look busy and up-to-the-minute. They tend to avoid white space altogether and use even more columns in order to cram as much text on to the page as possible. The six-column grid of this newspaper allows for flexible sizing of pictures.

wasted space, and space is at a premium. So there will typically be many narrow columns to the page, with the possibility of photographs straddling two, three, or more of them (Fig. **4.7** and **4.8**).

Horizontal lines built into the grid can be used to impose further discipline on the layout, allowing you to align the edges of photographs, say, with blocks of text. Six to eight horizontal divisions should be sufficient. Too many, and the layout will seem fussy, with no apparent thought-out design. Too few will not allow enough variety in the layout – it will appear static if the illustrations always fall in the same positions. Some grids may show a numbered horizontal line marked out for each line of type.

A grid can seem confusing at first sight, but not all the lines and divisions have to be used on every page.

Seen as an underlying structure, however, the grid can become an indispensable time-saving aid to producing clear and consistent layout, quickly and painlessly.

Design elements such as **cross-headings** (subheadings within a block of text), boxed copy, captions, rules, borders, and tint blocks are all devices for adding "color" to an otherwise "gray" layout. They will assist the readers' eyes, helping them follow the flow of the text, especially if it has been split to accommodate the placement of illustrations. And, if the copy does not fit exactly, they are useful and unobtrusive space fillers.

Lastly, a word of caution. When pasting down type, try to keep a tidy desk. There is nothing worse than having completed a tight and attractive layout, only to find an odd para-

graph that has been carelessly left out of the grand design. Keep a complete copy of the galley proofs (see p. 45) for reference, to check that paragraphs have not been pasted down out of sequence, and make any adjustments to the layout to avoid widows and orphans (see p. 42). The rest – is up to you!

If you are designing a greetings card, your first thought might
be to put the front side of it two-up on a plate; the reverse
two-up on a second plate. You can, however, print both sides
of the card using just one plate! How's it done? Using work
and turn. Say you need 1000 cards: you print 500, wait until
they're dry, flip the cards over and print the other side,
making sure that the half of the plate with the verso is back of
the half of the card's recto. Guillotine the result, and you have
two stacks of cards, both printed both sides.

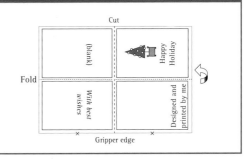

108

MECHANICAL PREPRESS

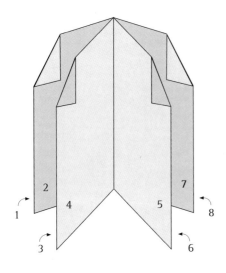

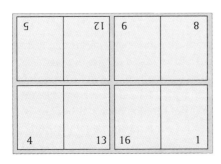

4.9 Imposition schemes can look complicated in diagram form, but all should become clear if you make a folded dummy in miniature – for your own benefit and to show the printer.

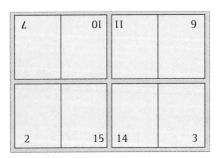

4.10 Sheetwork – the simplest form of imposition. Several pages are printed on one side of a sheet of paper, which is then turned over and printed again on the other side.

Imposition

Unless you are designing a solitary jar label, or a single-sided folder, it will help the printer considerably if you know about imposition. **Imposition** is the term used for the planning of **pagination** in folders, magazines, or books in a pattern such that when the printed sheet of paper is folded and trimmed, the resulting pages **back up** correctly and run consecutively.

A sheet of paper has two sides: front and back (Fig. **4.9**). Fold it once and – to the printer, at least – it becomes a four-page folder. Fold it again, and once one of the short sides has been cut, it becomes an eight-page folder, comprising two folded sheets, one nesting inside another. Fold a third time, and the result after trimming is a 16-page folder. It is a curious fact of the printing world that it is impossible to fold paper more than seven times, regardless of the size of the original sheet, or the thickness of the paper stock.

Most printers work in 16-page sections, with plates that print eight pages on each side. If your 16-page folder is numbered consecutively, with the first right-hand page as page 1, the first left as page 2, the numbers will fall as follows:

front: 1 4,5 8,9 12,13 16
back: 2,3 6,7 10,11 14,15

It is important to know which page numbers are on which side of the sheet, because you may wish to introduce flat color, or full color, into the publication. It will save you money if you can restrict it to one side of the sheet (Fig. **4.10**).

The odd numbers are always, by convention, on the right-hand side; the even numbers on the left. In bookwork, right or front is called **recto**; left or back is called **verso**. A 16-page section of a book is called a **signature**, and each signature will usually be marked with a **backstep mark** – a letter, number, or black strip to help the binder **collate**, or assemble, the signatures in the correct order.

If the cover of a 16-page folder is to be printed in the same stock as the rest of the publication, as a **self cover**, the first page will be the outside front cover (or OFC), page 2 will be the inside front cover (or IFC), page 15 will be the inside back cover (or IBC), and page 16 will be the outside back cover (or OBC). If, however, the cover is to be printed in heavier stock, or if it alone is to be printed in color, then it will be treated as a four-page section, printed separately. This leaves you with 16 pages for the inside, making a 20-page publication.

Generally speaking, printers like to handle only 4-, 8-, or 16-page sections (though novels are often printed in 32s and 64s). A 64-page magazine with a separate 4-page cover comprises four 16-page sections, which is convenient and economical. If you increase the pagination to 68, a 4-page section would have to be added somewhere. It is possible to add a two-page section, but not recommended. If the publication is to be saddle-stitched, this would leave an unsightly strip of paper at the other side of the wire staples. It would probably be just as economic to create another two pages.

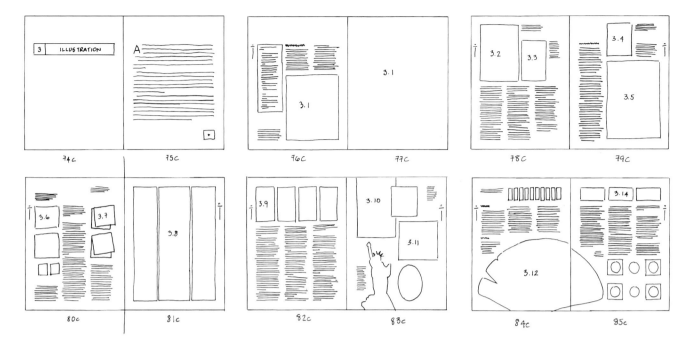

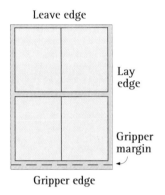

Leave edge

Lay edge

Gripper margin

Gripper edge

▲ **4.12** The way a sheet of paper goes into the printing press has a bearing on the layout. The gripper edge, for example, must contain an area free of all text or graphic material.

To help you find your way around an imposition scheme, it is common to draw out a **flatplan** (Fig. **4.11**). This shows diagrammatically what goes where in a publication. It also makes clear which sections or signatures can accommodate flat or full color to best effect. It is a good medium of communication on a magazine, for example, between the editorial, advertising, and design staff.

There are many ways of drawing up a flatplan, and it is best to consult your printers first, so as to take into account the way they are used to working, and any peculiarities of their folding machines. If in any doubt about imposition, do not be afraid of making up a folded **dummy** out of scrap paper. This would be a miniature version of your publication marked with page numbers and the position of any color.

There are two distinct ways of feeding paper through printing presses. It can be done either with pre-cut single sheets (**sheetwise**) or with a roll of paper (for **web** printing). The sheetwise method uses one plate to print the front of a sheet, and another for the back. Both sides share a common **gripper edge** (Fig. **4.12**). The gripper edge is the leading end of the sheet, and is held in place on the press by finger-like grippers. An allowance of $\frac{1}{2}$ inch (15 mm) must be made on this edge when estimating the printed area of a sheet. Opposite the gripper edge is the **leave edge**, and the left side of the sheet as it passes through the press is called the **lay edge**.

An alternative, and a method used when printing booklets or sections of publications with fewer than 16 pages, is to put both sides of the sheet on the same plate. This

▲ **4.11** Part of the flatplan for this book. It shows at a glance not only picture sizes and text position, but gives an overview of where black-and-white and color sections fall.

may sound crazy, but when it is cut and folded correctly you end up with twice as many half-size sheets.

Work-and-turn (Fig. **4.13**) is a technique in which the sheet goes through the machine first one way, then the paper is turned over sideways and printed once more, such

Cut

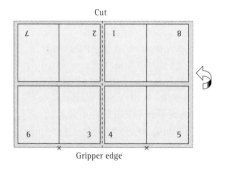

Gripper edge

▲ **4.13** Work-and-turn is an ingenious imposition scheme that gives twice as many products as you would expect using just one plate. It is often more economical to use large plates, so one side of the sheet is put on one half of the plate, the other side on the other half. The sheet is printed, and the pile is turned over and printed again on the other side. Later the pile of sheets is cut down the middle to give you two identical half-size piles of printed sheets. Both sides share the same gripper edge.

CROSSOVERS
A crossover is an image, text, or tint that extends from one page to a facing page. Unless you are designing a center spread or the center pages of a signature, the two halves of a crossover will be printed on separate sheets of paper. After trimming and binding, your crossover may well misalign – so avoid thin rules, small text sizes, and objects that are not placed horizontally. And consult your printer about imposing the two sides of a crossover, so that ink and color coverage are consistent.

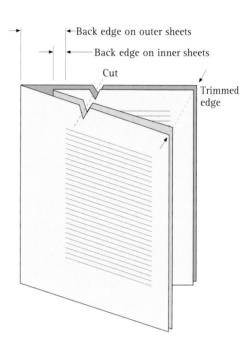

4.15 Paper creep allowance – made to counter the effect caused by the thickness of the paper in the fold of saddle-stitched publications with lots of pages. Otherwise, after the pages have been trimmed the text area will creep nearer the fore edge as the center of the publication is approached.

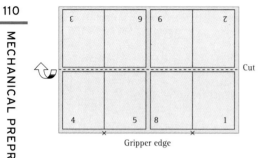

Gripper edge

4.14 Work-and-tumble is similar to work-and-turn, except the pile is flipped head over heels and the gripper edge changes ends.

that page 2 prints on the back of page 1. The gripper edge remains the same. The sheet is cut in two, and the result is two piles of paper printed on both sides that can be folded and trimmed as in sheetwise imposition. **Work-and-tumble** (Fig. **4.14**) is similarly ingenious, but the paper is flipped head over heels, and the gripper edge changes ends.

Using work-and-turn or work-and-tumble is economical. This is not only because just one plate is made and there is less **spoilage**, but also because for smaller jobs the printer can **step-and-repeat** (duplicate), a set of pages and print **two-up** – twice as many again in one printing.

With a knowledge of imposition, it is possible to arrange two or more pages of a publication on the same mechanical, saving the printer time and effort. If you are designing a whole range of stationery, to be printed in the same colors and on the same paper stock, you can make similar savings by **ganging up** the individual items on to one plate and printing **one-up**.

Web printing is usually reserved for large print runs. The possible imposition schemes are quite different from those for sheetwork. If you

are going to use this method, it is best to consult the printers at the outset.

There are other design considerations relating to the imposition scheme. A double-page spread (DPS) will be a problem if text or an image runs across two facing pages. They will only align correctly on a center spread, and even here you must take care to keep anything important – the eyes in a portrait, for example – well away from the position of a magazine's wire staples. For consistency of print density, it is best to have DPSs printed on the same side of the same section, if at all possible. **Starvation ghosting** is an unwelcome effect that results in uneven printing and is due, to some extent, to the placement of dense black elements in certain positions on the plate. If you think you may have problems, check with the printer about an alternative imposition.

There are all kinds of other imposition schemes that relate to non-standard folders and booklets – those with fan or **accordion folds**, for example, and those having unusual shapes and sizes. Computerized imposition systems arrange page files on to large sheets of film inside an imagesetter, which are then used to produce plate-ready flats.

Factors that influence the choice of a particular imposition scheme include: the total number of pages, the print run, the untrimmed page size, and the type of folding and binding. Discuss all these with the printer before you start on the mechanicals, and together you will be able to plan for the most economical sheet size, and the most cost-effective press, the lowest spoilage, the highest quality, and the fastest turnaround.

Back edge on outer sheets

Back edge on inner sheets

Cut

Trimmed edge

Paper creep allowance
A book will be bound stitched or glued in 16-page sections. A saddle-stitched publication, however, may have quite a number of sections nested one within the other. When these sections are collated, the thickness of the paper at the fold will add up to make pages toward the center stick out more than those near the covers. More paper will be trimmed from the fore edges of these pages, making them significantly narrower than those near the covers. To allow for this paper creep, you will need to vary the position of the margins, especially those at the outer edges.

A simple method of **paper creep allowance**, or shingling, is as follows (Fig. **4.15**). Make a folded dummy, using the same paper stock as the proposed publication. Looking down at the top edge of the dummy, measure off the inner margin of the

4.16 Paste-up is the act of cutting graphic elements to size with a scalpel, and pasting them down on to the mechanical using rubber solution, hot wax, or aerosol adhesive.

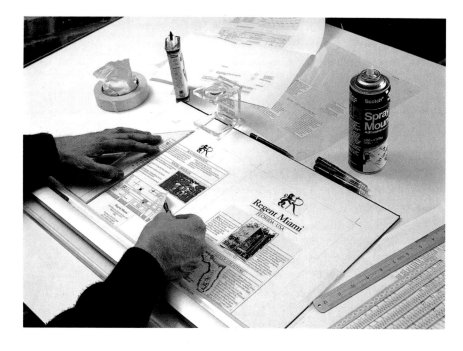

center pages and make a scalpel cut through the rest at the same point. Disassemble the dummy and use the position of the scalpel cuts as an inner margin reference on the mechanicals. It will appear to move toward the fold as you approach the center pages. It is not necessary to make an allowance on every page – a cumulative allowance can be made every few pages. Trim and center marks must remain to the same measure on all the boards, and remember to mark each mechanical "paper creep allowance made" in case a "helpful" printer decides to straighten up your seemingly wandering margins.

Page layout

The layout of the page is the graphic designer's very own domain. It is what the canvas is to the fine artist. It is the key stage in which all the copy – both text and line illustration – comes together as a unified whole ready to go to film or plate.

Some designers may produce their own finished artwork. Others may merely provide a rough cut and paste of photocopies to indicate their ideas to another professional, known as a **finished artist**, who does the neat job of preparing the layout for the later stages of prepress. For the purpose of simplicity, we assume here that you, the graphic designer, are preparing the finished artwork yourself. The procedures are exactly the same.

Before computers, designers had to prepare a **mechanical** (Fig. **4.17**), also known as **camera-ready copy** (CRC) or just plain artwork (A/W).

This skill is still relevant, though increasingly obsolete, and is something you should be familiar with before you are allowed near a computer for the first time. A mechanical is also useful for quick small jobs, old jobs that need simple updating or when you're in a hurry and the computer is down! The difference is that the mechanical is now more likely to go on to the glass of a scanner than under the lights of a process camera.

Preparing a mechanical is a manual operation using text on bromides plus PMTs or photocopies of line art and perhaps veloxes of halftones (see p. 82). These are cut to shape using a scalpel, preferably on a "self-healing" cutting mat, and pasted on to a baseboard marked with a grid (Fig. **4.16**).

The high-contrast film used in platemaking is **orthochromatic**, i.e. sensitive only to the blue end of the spectrum. The process camera "sees" red as black, and blue as white. As discussed in the previous chapter (see p. 91), the printer may have trouble with a color photograph that is to be reproduced in black and white. **Panchromatic** film, i.e. film sensitive to all colors, will have to be used if skin tones, for example, are to record correctly.

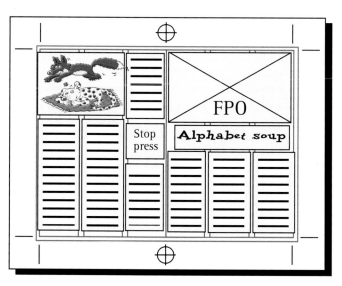

4.17 A mechanical layout can contain all kinds of design elements: text on bromide paper, PMTs or photocopies of line art, rules and boxes, and maybe even headlines created using rub-down lettering.

4.18 A keyline shows the printer where halftones, bleeds, and areas of flat color or tints are to be positioned. If they are not to print, they should appear on an overlay marked "keyline – do not print."

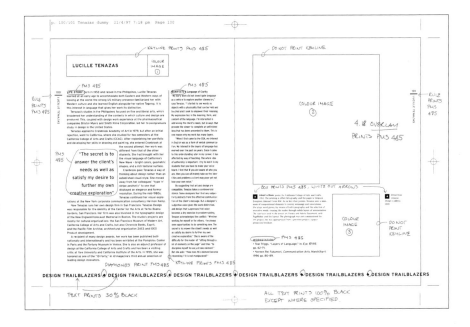

A mechanical will consist of many different kinds of paper, and the paste will have to contend with them all. Photosetting paper comes in two varieties: resin-coated (RC) bromide paper, and the cheaper stabilization paper that discolors with time (it should be avoided if the mechanical is to be used again). Typesetting from typewriters, laser printers, and photocopiers comes on plain paper, and repro proofs from letterpress setting usually come on heavy smooth art paper called **baryta**.

One commonly used type of paste is rubber cement, spread thinly with an applicator or spatula. Surplus gum can be removed cleanly when dry using a homemade "eraser" of dried-up gum. But if any remains on the mechanical, it can pick up dust and grit. It is an even worse catastrophe if gum gets on to the process camera's copyboard glass. The result is that the next few halftones processed contain annoying blemishes.

Many graphic designers use an aerosol adhesive, such as Scotch Spray Mount, which may be convenient but, unless you use a spray booth with an extractor fan, can mess up your working environment. An alternative is wax, applied to the paper from a hot-wax coating machine, such as Letraset's Wax-

coater. Wax gives a firm and even bond with no spread, and paper elements can be peeled off relatively easily to be placed elsewhere on the mechanical. Wax does not have as strong a bond as gum or spray mount, and there is a danger of small pieces falling off the mechanical.

You will need to put **trim and center marks** (Fig. 4.19) on the mechanical to indicate to the printer where the sheet is to be trimmed by the guillotine and folded. For hot metal printing, these marks always had to be kept well away from the "visible" area of the page, so that they would disappear after trimming. For offset litho, the printer uses the marks to help join several pages together, and thus a visible cross-hair mark is preferred. These will be removed before printing.

Indicate any tints on an **acetate** overlay, using a **keyline** (Fig. 4.18), accompanied by the written message, "Keyline – do not print." A keyline marks out any area to be printed in a flat color or a tint for which you are not providing separate artwork. It can also show the position of a halftone, to be stripped-in later, or can indicate a bleed.

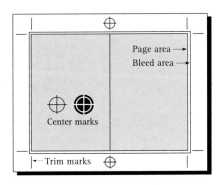

4.19 Trim and center marks are an aid to alignment of graphic elements and show the printer the extent of the printed page – everything the wrong side of the trim marks will be guillotined off and discarded.

Tints can be cut from self-adhesive sheets, from vendors such as Letraset, but once in place over text are difficult to remove if you decide that the type has been rendered illegible. This operation is best left to the printer.

For most black-and-white work, with perhaps a single underprinting in flat color (see p. 84), the mechanical will go straight under the camera. If your halftones have a screen below 100 lines (see p. 80), veloxes will suffice. Above 100 lines, it is common for the designer to draw a black square or place a piece of red film called **Rubylith** in the position the halftone will occupy, to make a **mask**. When the negative film is made, these appear as **windows**, into which the negative halftones can be placed. But to avoid any ambiguity, it is best to stick down photocopies of the halftones, marked "for position only" – they will have to be cut out anyway, as we shall see below.

Rules (lines) and boxes can be drawn directly on to the board using a technical pen filled with Indian ink (but never on to a substrate that might stretch or distort). Or printed rules can be pasted in place – they usually look neater on the final product. Do not cut them too thinly, or they will be prone to distortion. This is also true for rules that come in dispenser rolls on transparent carrier tapes. A great deal of practice and skill is needed to lay these

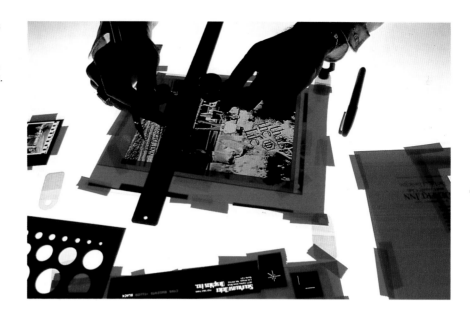

4.20 At the printer's, halftones and tints are "stripped in" to the spaces left in the text films. Opaque material such as Rubylith is used to blank out black or solid flat color areas on positive film or white areas on negative film.

down well. To create boxes, overlap the rules at the corners and cut miters through both rules, then trim away the excess.

Rule width is generally measured in points. A **hairline rule** is one narrower than half a point.

When the boards are complete, use a transparent grid lined up against the trim and center marks to check the alignment of all the pasted-down design elements. Label the boards with the name of the job and any page number. Then send them to the printer, with all the photographs and any artwork requiring special treatment, color swatches for any flat color, a folding dummy and/or flatplan to tell the printer exactly how individual pages are to be arranged, and any spare bromides or repro proofs of the typesetting for emergency repairs.

If any small-scale corrections have been made to the boards — individual letters cut and transposed, a comma added, and so on — it is prudent to circle them on the overlay. That way, the printer won't brush them on to the floor by mistake, and you will know which areas of the page proof to pay particular attention to. It is better, in any case, to replace the entire paragraph, if you have the time. There is the risk of any scalpel cuts showing up as visible shadows under the camera. They appear as white lines on the negative film, and can easily be opaqued-out using a substance called ox-blood, just so long as they are kept well away from any typematter.

If the black-and-white mechanical has been prepared at the typesetters from your rough layouts, it is most likely to be proofed on a photocopy

machine. The photocopier will be sensitive to the blue lines of the grid and will show scalpel marks too. The printer is well aware of all this, and the marks should be ignored. They won't be there when the mechanical is printed.

At the printer's, a negative film is made from the mechanical. After retouching work to opaque-out scalpel marks and any other imperfections, it is contact printed direct to a negative-working plate. Alternatively, it may first be contact printed to film to produce a positive, which is then used to produce a positive-working plate (see Chapter 6 for a fuller explanation of platemaking).

REPRO

Film make-up

For most high-quality work, and all multicolor printing, the **make-up** of the full mechanical will be bypassed, and the design elements will be assembled together on **film** (Fig. **4.20**). Paper-based mechanicals are good enough for black-and-white work, but are not considered **dimensionally stable** enough for close register work. (They will stretch and distort on their travels from the studio to the printers, as they are subjected to different environmental

conditions. The amounts are tiny, but sufficient to cause the different printings to be out of register.) It is unlikely that the average graphic designer will ever be asked to do film make-up — the **assembly** will be done by a professional called a "stripper." But graphic designers effectively have to brief the strippers with their roughs, and check the results, so it is important to know what is going on.

Film used by printers has a high-speed high-contrast emulsion on a polyester base. The emulsion side of the film is slightly duller than the other side, and it may be possible to see the image on the film if it is held up to the light and viewed at a shallow angle. If in doubt, scratch the film — well away from the image area, naturally — to discover which side the emulsion is on.

Film can be right reading, or wrong (reverse) reading. As you can view film from either side, it is important to specify "emulsion up" or "emulsion down" as well.

When the printing plates are made, the film is always put in contact with the plate for maximum sharpness. The emulsion touches the plate, i.e. the film is emulsion side down.

The type of film most commonly used is **right-reading emulsion down (RRED)**, also known as **wrong-reading emulsion up (WREU)**. The image

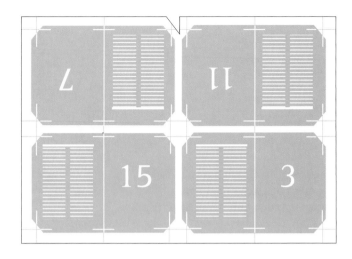

4.21 The strip-per assembles all the pages for one printing into a flat ready for platemaking, opaquing out any blemishes or marks not to be printed.

appears the correct way round (is right-reading) when the film is viewed from the shiny side, and wrong-reading from the dull emulsion side. RRED film is used for litho printing – and for all offset processes. When the film is contacted with the plate, the image is transferred so that it is right-reading. During printing, the ink on the plate transfers as wrong-reading to the rubber blanket, and then as right-reading to the paper (Fig. **4.22**; there is more about the offset litho process on p. 175).

Wrong-reading emulsion down (WRED) film, also known as **right-reading emulsion up (RREU)**, has a wrong-reading image when viewed from the shiny side and is right-reading when viewed from the dull emulsion side. WRED film is used for

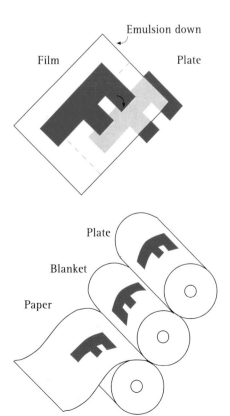

direct printing processes, such as gravure. When the cylinder is made, the image is wrong-reading. It transfers ink to the paper directly, and right-reading (see p. 182 for further information on gravure).

Pages can be assembled using positive or negative film. Negative film, with all the white space turned to black, is often too dense to use accurately. So most color **stripping-in** is done using positive film. The stripper uses a white board, on to which the grid (or layout) plus all the trim and center marks have been drawn or preprinted. A clear carrier sheet of polyester or acetate is laid on to this guide, and for each page the design elements (type, line illustrations, and halftones) on film are assembled into place with the emulsion side uppermost. The film elements are cut to size with a scalpel and attached to the base sheet with pressure-sensitive tape, in order to leave a uniformly flat surface, with none of the elements overlapping.

If the layout is quite complex, with lots of design elements stuck down with tape, a copy is made on to positive-working daylight film. This is called the **final**. Every time a duplicate is made, however, there is a

4.22 For offset litho work, strippers most often use positive right-reading emulsion down film. Thus the emulsion comes into contact with the surface of the plate; the blanket is wrong-reading; and the final printed image is right-reading.

slight degradation in quality. The best results are obtained when film is copied emulsion to emulsion. Using normal negative-working film, the image would be reversed and another copy would have to be made to right it. Special **auto-reversing film** is used instead to keep the number of steps to a minimum.

For multicolor work, a separate clear carrier sheet is used for each of the process colors. The registration (alignment) between the separate finals has to be observed meticulously, using a **pin-register** system to line up the trim marks and multicolor elements (see below). Color tints are laid down according to the formulas given in the Pantone charts.

As discussed earlier, it is generally most economical to print several pages together, in one pass of the printing press. Putting together the **flat** (Fig. **4.21**), or forme, to make a 16- or 32-page plate is the stripper's job, and here's how it is done.

A single-color flat with no registration problems to worry about is usually made up from film negatives, assembled together on an opaque orange-colored paper called **Goldenrod**. Goldenrod contains a dye that prevents ultraviolet (UV) light from passing through it, and acts as a mask to protect the non-printing areas of the flat. The negative film is placed in position emulsion side up, and the whole assembly is turned over. Windows are then cut into the Goldenrod to allow UV light to

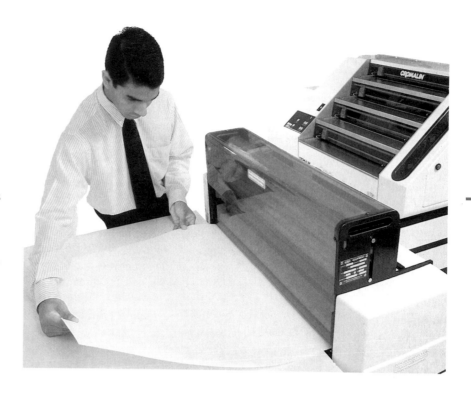

4.23 A Cromalin color proof is a "dry" proprietary system from Du Pont which gives a good idea of how a set of color film separations are going to work together on the press.

pass through the image areas. The assembled flat is placed on the press plate and exposed in a **printing-down frame**.

Goldenrod can stretch, so, for work requiring close registration, the negatives are assembled first on to clear acetate or polyester sheets, emulsion side up. The assembly is turned over and non-printing areas are masked using either Goldenrod or a red/ amber masking film.

For multicolor printing, a positive flat is made for each of the process colors. To ensure close registration, these are pin-registered (Fig. **4.24**) with pins and a special punch used to make holes in the flats. They can be correctly located with pins on the press plate, and again the plates can be located on the press cylinder with further pins and clamps.

An alternate method is called **blue and red keys**. The first flat is assembled using either the cyan or the magenta elements. This is exposed in contact with a sheet of blue or red **dyeline** film, which produces a key image of the original image in blue or red. With blue keys,

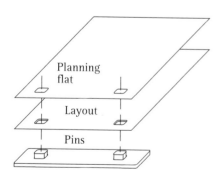

Planning flat

Layout

Pins

4.24 For color work, each printing must be in close register. Pin registration is a system of precisely placed holes and corresponding pins which ensure that all the films, flats, and plates are correctly aligned.

each color flat is registered in position using the blue to give accurate sightings. When complete, the flat is used for platemaking in the normal way, as the blue does not record on the plate. Red does record, however, so when red keys are used, the flat is assembled on to a clear acetate sheet with the red keys underneath, acting as a guide.

Picture proofing

Film for a single color is commonly proofed as a positive dyeline or **diazo** print (contact ammonia print), called an **ozalid, brownline, blueprint**, or **blue**. Blues (which may also be gray, brown, or other colors) often give the only opportunity to check the **alignment** of halftones and other elements. This is absolutely the last chance to make any changes before the job is "put to bed."

It may be necessary to see the printed quality of halftones, either all together in random order, as **scatter proofs**, or – probably more expensively – in their correct position on the page, as page proofs.

Color separations of illustrations and photographs can be proofed

photographically or digitally, as **inkjet, dye-sublimation**, or **thermal-transfer prints**, or on plastic laminate systems. These are called **prepress proofs**, or **dry proofs**, and are all approximations to the finished printed result, but will give you an idea of what to expect.

Photographic systems work by exposing each process color separation in turn on to a three-layer photographic paper, using filters. The material is then processed to produce the color proof.

One-off transfer or integral proofs, such as Du Pont's **Cromalin**, 3M's **Matchprint**, and Agfa's **Agfaproof**, take colored powders or precoated sheets representing the process colors. They are laminated in register on to white paper (Fig. **4.23**). With some systems it is possible to use the same stock as you will be using for the final printing, which is useful for checking color and inking accurately.

Plastic laminate proofs, such as 3M's **Color-Key** and Du Pont's **Cromacheck**, build up an image layer by layer on to a plastic substrate using mylar or acetate overlay film, one for each process color.

CHECKING PROOFS

Remember that contract color proofs will not reproduce exactly the way that ink will appear on your chosen paper stock: this is especially true for any varnishes, spot colors, and metallic inks. Check that colors are even and consistent and check tints to make sure they are not mottled. Use printed swatches to check spot colors. Examine the color bar for lost detail. Make sure bleeds and crossovers extend beyond the trim marks. Check for weak or breaking-up type. Use a loupe to look closely at highlights and shadows. Pay attention to flesh tones and hair. Bright reflected light in the eyes should have no dot, only paper white. On fluffy clouds, magenta and yellow dots should be as small as possible, with cyan dots only slightly larger.

MECHANICAL PREPRESS

Digital proofing systems are proliferating, and are discussed further in Chapter 5, p. 135. These produce proofs direct from the computer's memory, using inkjet, thermal-transfer, dye-sublimation, or electrostatic technologies. The Scitex Iris Realist proofers (Fig. **4.25**) use inkjet technology to produce color proofs up to 34 in x 46·8 in (863 mm x 1188 mm) in size.

A form of proofing that can be more expensive requires four plates to be made from the separations and printed on a flatbed proofing press. This should produce the most realistic representation of the finished job, and allows several sets of proofs to be made. Ensure that a complete set of color bars (see Fig. **4.26**) are run with the proof – these can later be compared with the values being recorded on the press. And ask for standard inks to be used.

A full set of **progressives** (see Fig. **3.20**) can be obtained in this way. Progressives are color proofs printed in the same order in which the process colors will be applied at press time. Each color printing is shown separately and also surprinted with the other colors. A typical set comprises the individual process colors of yellow, magenta, cyan, and black, accompanied by the cumulative combinations: magenta on yellow; cyan on yellow and magenta; and finally black on yellow, magenta, and cyan. Some printers vary the sequence by running the cyan printing before the magenta. Make sure to ask for progressives in the **laydown sequence** – the order in which the finished job will be printed.

For flat color, the printer may offer a **drawdown** – a smear of ink from a smooth blade on a particular paper stock. This should not be relied upon, however, to give an accurate impression of how a particular color will print on the press.

As mentioned above, it is important, when viewing color samples, to ask for the same paper stock as will be used for the final printing. Always make allowance for the fact that **press proofs** pulled from a proofing press will be sharper and show less dot gain (see p. 191) than a high-speed production press.

Check the proofs to see that the images are the right way round – it's amazing how often they are upside-down or reversed (**flopped**) left-to-right, or both – and at the correct resolution. Low-res images sometimes slip through! Check also for the correct crop, size, position, sharpness, and mark any obvious imperfections such as spots and scratches. Black-and-white proofs need to be checked for contrast – they should have the full tonal range from shadow to highlights.

When it comes to marking proofs for color correction, tell the printer as plainly as possible what you think is wrong. Color judgment is subjective, and there may be many routes to a better end result. Just because something has a blue cast, it does not necessarily mean that there is too much cyan – the cyan may be all right but the other colors may need taking up. It is better to say "too blue" than to instruct the printer with technical certainty to "take down the cyan."

Color bars

Color bars (Fig. **4.26**) yield vital information about the performance of both the press and the inks being used. To be able to interpret them arms you with the knowledge to improve the quality of the job without being "blinded by science" at the printer's. They contain a whole range of tests: some are visual checks; others require special instruments such as a **densitometer**. And they are totally independent of the job, thus

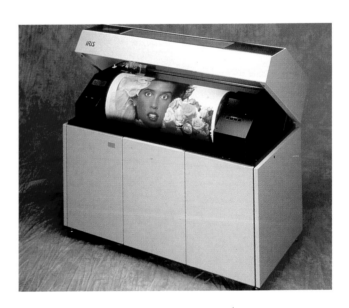

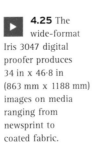

4.25 The wide-format Iris 3047 digital proofer produces 34 in x 46·8 in (863 mm x 1188 mm) images on media ranging from newsprint to coated fabric.

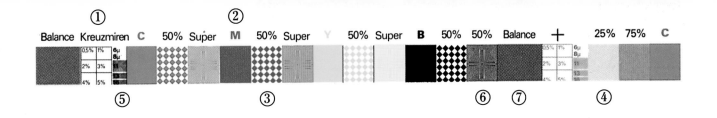

representing a consistent guide
to the standard of printing you
can expect.

Color bars comprise most or all of
the following components:
1. Printing-down controls. There will
be a series of microlines and highlight dots to assess how accurately
the job has been printed down from
film to plate.
2. Solid density patches for each
color. These monitor ink film thickness, and should be read using a
densitometer.
3. Trapping patches. These show
solid process colors printed on top of
others in different combinations, and
they test how ink is being accepted
in **wet-on-wet** printing. There will
also be a dense black made up from
100% black, 55% cyan, 42·5%
yellow, and 42·5% magenta
(= 240%, the maximum recommended percentage of tints; see
also p. 90).
4. Screen patches. Patches for each
process color at different screens
are used to monitor **dot gain.** Dot
gain happens as the ink spreads
around just joined-up dots in the
middle tones, tending to make these
areas look darker than they should
be. At one tone lighter, where the
dots are not yet touching, density
does not gain to the same extent.
This effect can cause a visible jump
in an otherwise smooth gradation of
tone. Elliptical dots can help alleviate
the problem.
5. Coarse and fine halftone scale.
This quick visual check comprises

ten steps in the form of the numerals 0 to 9 set using a screen of 200
lines, which are dropped out of a
background tint screened at 65 lines.
Dot gain shows as the numbers fill in
and become visible – the theory is
that fine tints are more sensitive to
dot gain than coarser ones.
6. Slur gauge. These patches reveal
any directional dot gain caused by
slurring or **doubling**, and take the
form of star targets and/or oblongs
containing both horizontal and
vertical lines.
7. Gray balance. If all is well, a 50%
cyan, 40% magenta, and 40%
yellow, printed on top of each other,
should produce a neutral gray.

SUMMARY

Prepress is where the text set in
type, the illustrations and photographs, and any other graphic
elements, such as rules, boxes, and
areas of flat color, all come together
in a form that can be printed. The
prepress process starts with the
page layout on to which graphic
elements – typesetting, line art and
photographs – are assembled. For
simple black-and-white work, the job
is completed.

For close-registration color work,
however, halftones must be processed on to film, and stripped in at
the printers on to flats. Paper and
board can stretch and distort; film is
more dimensionally stable.

For medium- and large-scale jobs,
it is important to give some thought

4.26 A color bar is used by printers to
assess the performance of their presses –
giving information, for example, about dot gain
and slurring. It appears away from the image
area and is trimmed off the sheets later.

to imposition schemes. Early planning in this area can have a substantial effect on the cost-effectiveness
and smooth running of a project.

The preparation of type and
graphic elements at the prepress
stage can also be carried out on a
computer. Simple black-and-white
work, and some flat color jobs, can
be done using the electronic cut-
and-paste of desktop programs such
as QuarkXPress and Adobe Page-
Maker. It can then be output by laser
printers on to plain paper, or by
higher-resolution imagesetters as
bromide prints or film.

More sophisticated systems from
Scitex, Du Pont, and Dainippon,
located at the printer's or repro
house, are used for more complex
four-color projects. But there are so-
called front-end systems available
– such as Scitex's Brisque – that
can be used by prepress operators
to communicate the designer's
layouts directly to the computers
at the printer's.

Whichever method or system is
used, it is essential to see and to be
able to understand the prepress
process of proofs and color bars, so
that you can be sure of quality … and
know that your design is the one
that is going to be printed as you
envisioned it!

DAVID CARSON

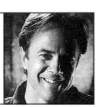

LIFE STORY David Carson was born in Corpus Christi, Texas. In the late 1970s he was a professional surfer, ranking eighth in the world. In 1977, he graduated from San Diego State University "with honors and distinction" in sociology and taught grades seven to twelve at Real Life Private School, Grants Pass, Oregon. In 1980 he took a two-week workshop in graphic design and re-enrolled at San Diego State University to study graphic design, transferring after just one month to Oregon College of Commercial Art. That same year he quit to take up an internship at Surfer Publications in Dana Point, California.

That job folded, and from 1982 until 1987 he was a sociology teacher at Torrey Pines High School in Del Mar, California – but after school, evenings, and weekends he was working on the fanzine *Transworld Skateboarding*. This was followed by a spell on *Musician*, then to the innovative but in the end financially ruinous *Beach Culture* during 1989 to 1991, to *Surfer* 1991 to 1992, and finally international success with the music and fashion magazine *Ray Gun* from 1992 until 1995. In 1993, he was honored as one of the "ID Forty," in *ID* magazine's first annual selection of leading design innovators.

> ## "Don't mistake legibility for communication"

Since 1993, he has worked as design consultant to clients such as Levi, Nike, and Pepsi and directed commercials and titling for American Express, Coca-Cola, and Sega. In 1995 he was chosen as the International Center of Photography's Designer of the Year and won best book design of the year for *Cyclops* by Vogue photographer Albert Watson, a book making full use of FM screening for the photographs, but with a typographical cover. He has since collaborated with Watson on advertising projects, including a Superbowl spot for Budweiser. Also in 1995 he set up David Carson Design in New York, with Mike Jurkovac, and Cyclops Productions with Jurkovac and Watson.

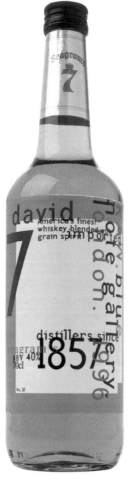

▶ **Seagrams 7**
limited edition label for sponsorship of a David Carson event in London 1996.

MANIFESTO Why Change? Why Not?
"Don't mistake legibility for communication," asserts David Carson. "David's work communicates," says former Talking Head David Byrne, "but on a level beyond words – a level that bypasses the logical rational centers of the brain and goes straight to the part that understands without thinking."

The initial reaction to Carson's magazine layouts is one of surprise, perhaps shock, and almost definitely curiosity. His work moved quickly from the subculture to become the dominant style of the 1990s. Carson has persistently pushed at the conventions of the medium, most controversially in his typography. This has raised cries that the work is illegible, despite the fact that for its target readers, the magazine communicates – otherwise they would not buy it.

Like Erik Spiekermann (see p. 72), Carson believes you cannot *not* communicate, as he seeks to explore the full range of expression possible within the page. The work integrates text, images, and the medium, forging a new way of reading across sequential pages. From the early *Transworld Skateboarding* spreads to *Ray Gun*, he has moved from one-off visual and verbal playfulness to, at times, pure graphic abstraction. Marks and color exist not as elements that build or frame pictures and sentences, but make emotional contact directly, as marks and color.

In these magazines Carson held the position of both art director and designer, being responsible not only for laying out pages, but also commissioning artwork and establishing the design rules for the publication. But it is the absence of rules that distinguish Carson's spreads. Instead of a grid, pages are freeform, each one a fresh canvas on to which type and images are applied. Instead of a limited and consistent palette of typefaces, new faces were introduced with every new issue of *Ray Gun*, not for the sake of novelty, but as a means of finding new expression for new content.

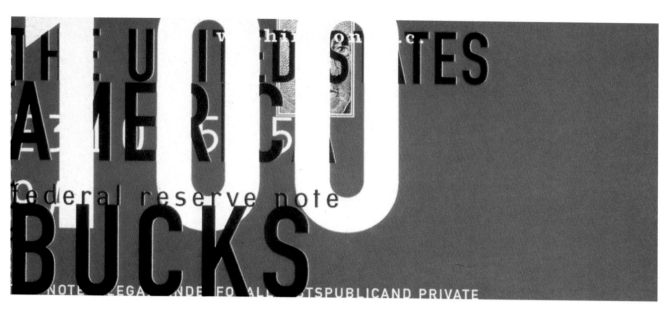

THE UNITED STATES AMERICO 100 federal reserve note BUCKS

this note is legal tender for all debts public and private

The *LA Times* asked Carson to redesign the $100 bill, one of a half-dozen artists invited as part of an article. "American money is perhaps the most boring money in the world, whereas there is some amazing money design round the world. So I got rid of existing elements, gave it an interesting color ... made sure it is what it is, 100 bucks."

Poster for a talk in San Francisco, February 1996, on the End of Print. Carson was, in part, promoting his book of the same name (see Workstation below).

The End of Print
CARSON
DAVID
A PRESENTATION BY
SAN FRANCISCO
CALIFORNIA
Thursday, FEBRUARY 15, 1996
7:00 pm
sponsored by Gannett Outdoor + chronicle books
THE AMERICAN INSTITUTE OF GRAPHIC ART + THE SAN FRANCISCO AD CLUB PRESENT
CENTER FOR THE ARTS THEATER
700 howard street at third
Info: 415 978.278 7

WORKSTATION
• *Emigre 27*, 1993, special issue on Carson.
• David Carson and Lewis Blackwell, *The End of Print: The Graphic Design of David Carson* Laurence King, London, 1995.
• David Carson and Lewis Blackwell, *David Carson: 2ndsight – Grafik Design after the End of Print* Laurence King, London, 1997.
• Rick Poynor, "David Carson revealed," *ID*, November 1995, pp. 48–53, 92, 93
• Web site: <http://www.wysiwyg.de/carson_e.html>

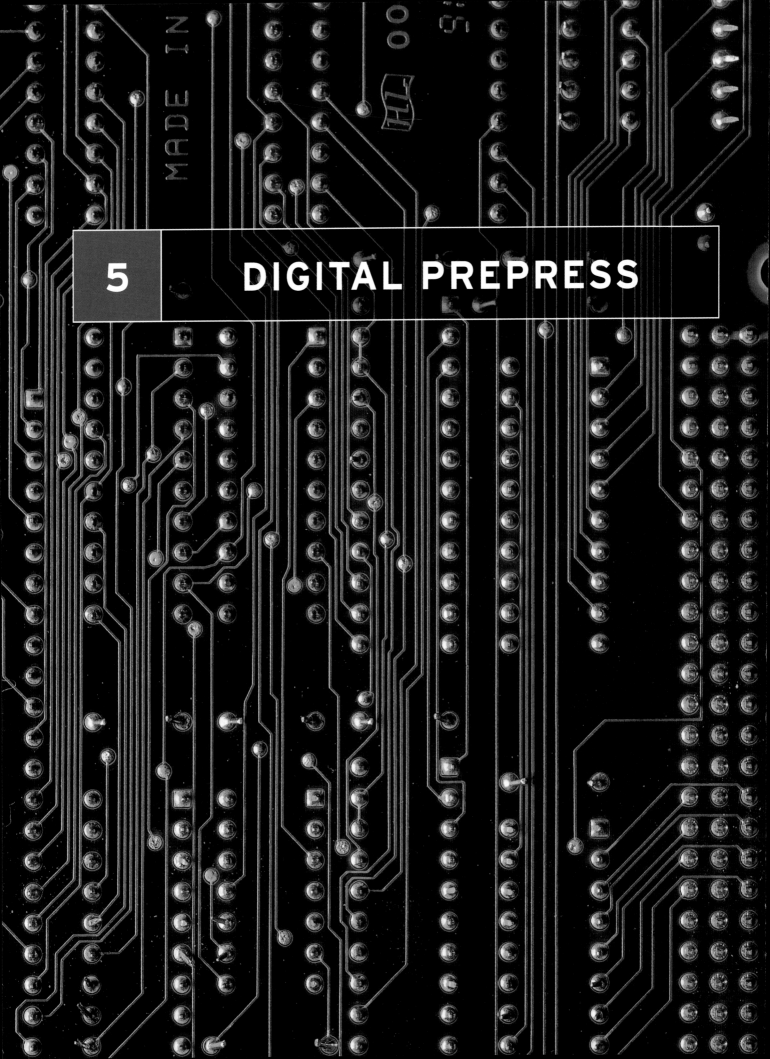

5 DIGITAL PREPRESS

ith only a few years ago, graphic designers could send corrected galleys, a rough layout, and marked-up illustrations along to the typesetter o repro shop and expect the rest of the job to be completed by others. As hey waited for ozalid and color proofs, many were blissfully unaware of the evolution taking place in print production. And the printers and compositors ʋere happy to keep things that way.

But slowly at first, and quickening all the time, that revolution has begun to nvade the designer's studio. Of course, the advances can be ignored, but it will e the designers who embrace the opportunity with enthusiasm who will ucceed in tomorrow's competitive markets.

Digital prepress can roughly be divided into what you the designer can do in ʲour studio with a computer, desktop scanner, and color printer, and what still has ːo be done at the repro service bureau or printers with their high-end drum scan ers, RIPs, imagesetters, and digital proofers. But this divide is blurring all the ime, and many large design practices are effectively bringing repro in-house.

The computer brings control and flexibility to the designer's desktop. I: ʋon't do the designing for you, of course. A computer is merely a tool, to be pu ːo work as and when necessary, alongside the pencil and layout pad. It is a: ːxtremely powerful tool, nevertheless, and it is waiting to be used.

In the past few years much of the equipment described in this chapter ha: ʲecome commonplace in designers' studios. However, it is important to knov ow it works, what it is currently capable of, what its limitations are, and wha ːrade-offs you will be expected to make. Thus forearmed, you will be able to take ɔn the suppliers' salespeople, and make sound buying decisions that will ensurɛ ː successful implementation.

Finally, the health and safety aspects of a computer installation ɑre discussed, so as to safeguard the well-being of the most valu-
ɑble component of the production system – the graphic designer

▶

Simply having a computer does not make you into a better designer. If you need any evidence, take a look at the advertisements in any computer magazine, especially for dealers and bureaux. Those people have offices bristling with computers, use all the software daily, and possess just about every font you could imagine. And still their ads look terrible.

They have fallen for the vendors' sales pitch: that with a computer, some digital prepress software, and a selection of fonts, you don't need a designer – anyone can be a designer. It's not true.

But a good designer, armed with a computer, can do wondrous things. The main advantage is almost *total control* of your design, from initial concept to finished product. There is a down side to this, though. If it is control you want, you'll have to take responsibility for all your design decisions – you won't be able to blame the typesetter, for instance, if you don't get the setting you thought you specified. And you'll have to learn something about computers.

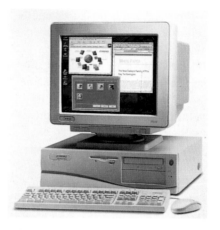

5.1 This Compaq DeskPro 4000 is an IBM PC-compatible desktop computer. It has an Intel Pentium processor with a clock speed of 120–166 MHz.

What equipment do you need to get started?

- a computer: an Apple Macintosh, IBM PC, or PC compatible such as a Compaq
- a keyboard
- a high-definition monitor, preferably of large format (17in/432 mm or more)
- a mouse (and mouse pad) or other pointing device, such as a rolling ball or digitizer
- a bubblejet black-and-white printer
- applications software, such as QuarkXPress or Adobe PageMaker

and optionally:

- a PostScript-compatible laser printer
- an inkjet, thermal transfer, or dye sublimation color printer
- a desktop scanner
- a modem
- more applications software, such as FreeHand, Illustrator and Photoshop

HARDWARE AND SOFTWARE

First, some basic definitions. The stuff you can see and touch – the computer and all the ancillary equipment, the peripherals – is the **hardware**. **Software** is the unseen factor of a system which supplements the brainpower and experience of the designer and makes the hardware come alive. It arrives on **floppy disks**, or a **CD-rom**, and is copied on to the computer's own **hard disk**. (The originals are kept in a safe place, in case anything should go wrong with the hard disk.)

The word **system** is used a lot in computer parlance. It is a catch-all term, and usually means "everything" – the hardware and software together, as in a digital prepress system. The software that looks after the internal workings of the computer is called the operating system. And an item of software can be referred to as a program, a package, or, again, a system.

Most people recognize a computer from the name it has on the front: it may be an IBM PC, a Compaq (Fig. **5.1**), or an Apple Macintosh (Fig. **5.2**). These are all **personal computers**. A personal computer is a self-contained system that sits on the desktop, that you do not have to share, and that is powerful enough to do the job you have in mind.

5.2 An Apple Power Macintosh 9500/200 uses a RISC-based 604e chip to achieve clock speeds of 200 MHz.

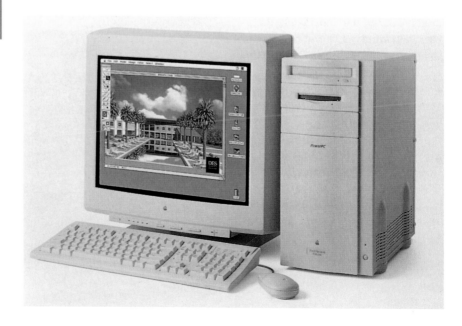

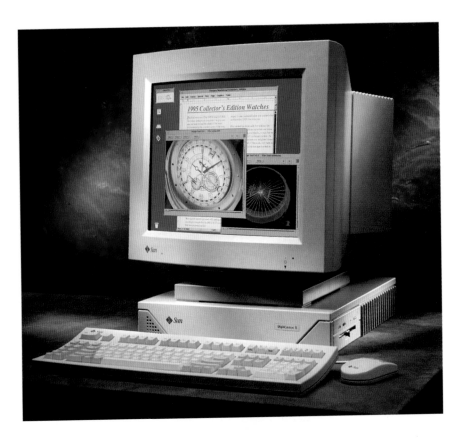

5.3 A Sun SparcStation is categorized as a workstation, and the processor box usually sits under the desk. It is based around a RISC (reduced instruction set computer) chipset.

124

DIGITAL PREPRESS

The next grade up is a computer called a **workstation**, from a supplier such as Sun or Silicon Graphics (Figs **5.3** and **5.4**). These, too, are self-contained systems, but can be linked together into networks (see p. 150). They are much more powerful than personal computers, but they take up more space and are more expensive.

The old-fashioned kind of computer that has several "dumb" terminals sharing a set of large metal boxes located in an air-conditioned room is called a **minicomputer**. The largest computers of all are called **mainframes**, and handle the payrolls for multinational companies. The average graphic designer will probably never see a minicomputer or a mainframe.

Although the abbreviation PC stands for personal computer it refers to a specific class of personal computer, namely the IBM PC and compatible computers from suppliers such as Compaq. Because IBM-compatible PCs always contain an Intel processor and mostly use the Microsoft Windows operating system, they are also sometimes referred to as "Wintel" computers.

The Apple Macintosh is a personal computer, but not a PC. It operates in a fundamentally different way to the IBM PC and compatibles. Programs designed for the PC will not work on a Macintosh, and vice versa, although *versions* of a program such as PageMaker are available for both kinds of computer and will operate in similar ways.

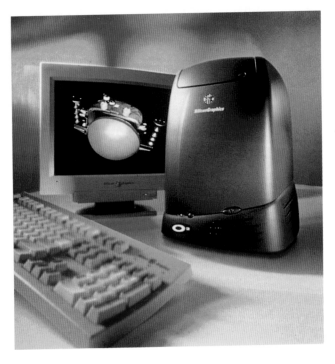

5.4 A Silicon Graphics O^2 system is a high-end workstation designed specifically for graphics applications. It is based on a 64-bit RISC chipset and runs a Unix-based operating system.

Software

There are many levels of software inside the computer which are mainly invisible to the user. At the lowest level, you need a program built into the machine that loads (or boots, as in "pull yourself up by the bootstraps") all the other programs.

At the next level is the **operating system**. This looks after the computer's internal workings, particularly the operation of the hard disk memory. It is often specific to the make of computer: PCs use MS-DOS and Microsoft Windows. The Macintosh's operating system is just a number, such as System 7.5.3. Workstations mostly use a version of AT&T's Unix, such as A/UX (the names of the variants usually have an x in them somewhere). The operating system comes with the computer when you buy it, and upgrades can be bought on CD-roms and installed on the hard disk. You usually see evidence of the operating system at work only when you switch the computer on. It checks that everything is in working order, then awaits your instructions. If anything is wrong, it will put an error message on the screen and you will have to refer to the manual and take remedial action.

The most visible level of software is the **application**, which you buy on floppy disks or CD-rom, along with an operating manual. Applications software converts the general-purpose computer, that cannot do anything, into the kind of system the user wants. It can be one of a number of things: a spreadsheet, a page layout package, paint software, or a computer game. Software suppliers each have their own methods of numbering versions. It is important to know which version you have, to ensure compatibility, for example, between your program and the one at the **service bureau**. Some of the more expensive applications come with a device called a dongle that has to be connected between, say, the keyboard and the computer. This prevents you from copying the software to a friend. New versions of software packages are being released all the time – some are really significant improvements on the previous release, some are merely "fixes" that correct bugs.

A **bug** is an error in the program, hidden away in the depths of the computer code – a mistake made by the programmer. The term was coined in the late 1950s by computer pioneer Grace Hopper, who found a real insect interfering with the working of her computer.

All programs have bugs, just as all computers do inexplicable things now and then. Thus there is all the more reason to save your current job to the hard disk as frequently as possible, rather than leave it in the short-term memory. A few but by no means all programs do this automatically. It is a good idea also to back up (copy) anything important on to an external hard disk or a removable hard disk like a Syquest at the end of every session. Then put them in a safe place.

A **virus** is worse than a bug – it is a self-replicating piece of mischief, introduced surreptitiously into your computer by malicious computer addicts called "hackers."

Software is written in a programming language. The computer's own language is called **machine code**, which is expressed in hexadecimal numbers (numbers in base 16). It is gibberish to all but the most hardened hacker. Computers "think" in binary code (using the numbers in base 2: 0 or 1, on or off), but this is too cumbersome for humans to get to grips with. Binary, however, is conveniently convertible to hexadecimal. One step up from machine code is **assembler**, which substitutes short mnemonics such as MPY for multiply, one-for-one, for the hexadecimal numbers. Easiest to use are the so-called high-level languages such as **Basic** (beginners all-purpose symbolic instruction code) and **C**. These use English words, arranged using simple grammar, which is later "compiled" or "interpreted" into machine code. Even higher-level languages are sometimes available so that users can customize (adapt) the applications software to their own preferred ways of working.

But today it is completely unnecessary to learn a programming language. The operating system of the Macintosh, for example, contains an "intuitive" **GUI** (graphical user interface; Fig. **5.5**, p. 126) that simplifies communication between the human and the computer. Commands are chosen from lists called **menus**, and most things can be done by **tools**. A pen tool, for example, allows you to draw lines on the screen. The user selects them by pointing at small pictures called **icons**, using a device such as a "mouse" (more of which on p. 131).

5.5 This screen shot from the author's Mac shows its WIMP (windows, icons, mouse, and pull-down menus) GUI (graphical user interface). Documents – drawings or text – are represented in the window by icons and are selected by pointing and clicking the mouse-controlled cursor. Software commands are chosen from pull-down menus, which can also be selected by moving the mouse pointing device.

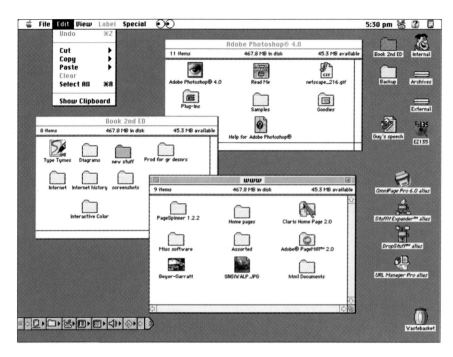

The processor

The "brain" of a computer is usually housed in a featureless box, perhaps with a floppy disk slot in the front, and with the odd light flashing to show that the hard disk is working. The display screen rests on the box. The processor may also come in a "tower" that stands on the floor or on the desk, next to the display.

At the heart of the computer is the **CPU (central processing unit)**, comprising a microprocessor silicon chip or set of chips (chipset). The main manufacturers are Intel (identified by the numbers 80286, 80386, 80486 … Pentium), who supply the chips for the PC and compatibles, and Motorola (identified by the numbers 68000, 68020, 68030, 68040), who supply the chips for the Apple Macintosh. Apple Power-Macs use PowerPC RISC (reduced instruction set computer) chips, which are the result of a joint venture between IBM, Apple, and Motorola, and are numbered 601, 603, 604, and so on. Most workstation vendors have opted for the simpler RISC architecture for their chips. Sun's version is called SPARC (scalable processor architecture).

Raw speed in computer terms is measured by the internal **clock speed**. Clock speed is measured in MHz (megahertz, or millions of cycles per second). For example, a Macintosh Classic built around a 68000 cpu chip ran at 8 MHz; a PowerMac 9500/200 has a 604e chip running at 200 MHz.

At every tick of the clock, the cpu processes an instruction, or part of one. These are not the instructions you key into the computer, though.

The computer breaks down your complicated instructions into millions of simple ones, which it calculates very quickly.

Computers for graphics applications have special requirements. Pictures take up enormous amounts of memory, compared with text, and to move them around, the cpus on these systems require some help. They are therefore augmented with various speed-increasing subsystems – such as maths coprocessors or floating-point units (FPUs). Power PCs have an FPU built-in to handle the repetitive mathematics involved in manipulating images. They also need printed circuit-boards (pcbs), or cards, to control the color graphics on the screen. On some systems, these functions are built in.

All this, however, is pure speed and, like the top figure on an automobile's speedometer, is an abstract quantity. Some computers may be able to redraw the screen after a tricky manipulation more quickly than others. But how quickly a designer actually completes a given job ultimately depends both on the efficacy of the software and on the proficiency of the operator.

Memory: ROM and RAM

Computers have two sorts of chip-based memory. **ROM (read-only memory)** chips have instructions manufactured into them, and they cannot be altered. These instructions remain on the chip even when the computer is switched off. ROM chips contain some of the computer's operating system, and give a computer its "personality."

Local memory, containing the immediate job in hand, is in the form of **RAM (random access memory)** chips which are wiped clean each time the computer is switched off (Fig. **5.6**). This, of course, includes any form of power failure, however fleeting. The amount of RAM a computer has available is measured in **bytes**, each equal to 8 **bits** (bit is short for binary digit). A kbyte, k, or kilobyte is not a thousand bytes as you may have expected, but 1024 bytes, which is equal to 2^{10} (2 to the power of 10, or 2 x 2 x 2 x 2 x 2 x 2 x 2 x 2 x 2 x 2). A megabyte, written 1 Mbyte, is more than a million bytes. A gigabyte, or Gbyte, is more than 1000 Mbytes.

The reason for the strange number 1024 is as follows. Computers

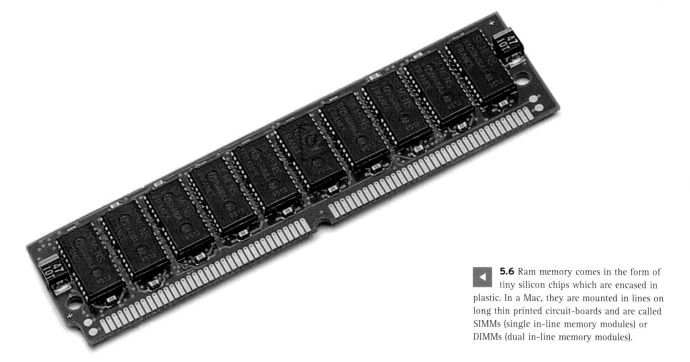

5.6 Ram memory comes in the form of tiny silicon chips which are encased in plastic. In a Mac, they are mounted in lines on long thin printed circuit-boards and are called SIMMs (single in-line memory modules) or DIMMs (dual in-line memory modules).

count in binary numbers, 0s and 1s. (Hexadecimal, referred to earlier, is easily converted to binary and is more convenient for computer scientists to deal with.) Thus, to a computer, "round numbers" are always powers of 2 (such as 4, 8, 16, 32, 64, 128, 256, 512, and 1024), and that is why you will often see these numbers associated with computers.

ASCII (American Standard Code for Information Interchange), the worldwide format for encoding alphanumeric text, allocates a single byte per character. This chapter contains over 64·5 kbytes of information. The hard disk on my computer is capable of containing 500 Mbytes, and that is quite modest by graphic design standards.

Saved data is stored in a hard (Winchester) disk drive. It is advisable to back-up important data to floppy disks, which can hold around 1.4 Mbyte chunks of information, or on to DAT (digital audio tape) drives, which use cartridges that are similar to audio cassettes.

Removable hard disks, such as a Syquest, can be added to your system. They are useful for overflow, archiving, and for transporting large files to an imagesetting bureau. For memory-intensive operations, you can buy optical drives that store many Gbytes of data. A device containing several optical disk drives is called a jukebox. CD-rom drives are compact disc players for computers which hold large amounts of bought-in data, such as fonts and clip art. CD-rom drives are now commonly built in to Macs and PCs.

Data travels round the computer on "buses," which are like clumps of wires. There are two main buses: the memory bus and the data bus. A 32-bit computer has a data bus 32 bits wide, i.e. 32 bits of data can travel around the computer and be processed at the same time. The "width" of the bus determines how much data can be processed at each tick of the clock, and how much RAM memory can be managed.

A typical home micro from the early 1980s had an 8-bit processor and a 16-bit memory bus. It could thus address only 2^{16} permutations of 0s and 1s, which equals 64 k possible memory locations in RAM. A 32-bit processor can handle several Mbytes. Some computers also have "cache memory." This is a portion of RAM that holds the most recently used data from the hard disk ready for further action, thus increasing the apparent speed of access to the user.

Frame buffers

A **frame buffer** is a short-term memory store between the processor and the screen.

The frame buffer or VRAM (video random-access memory) contains the current image in the form of a bitmap of pixels (picture elements; see p. 128). It comprises several layers or planes, with one bit (a 1 or a 0) stored for each pixel on each plane. The number of planes, and hence the number of bits allocated to each pixel, determines how many colors or "grayscale" shades the displayed pixel can be.

A mono screen, without grayscales, has 1 bit per pixel. An 8-plane system can handle 2^8 (256) different colors or grayscales. A 24-plane system can display 16·8 million, a number considered sufficient to produce realistic-looking images. A 32-bit system has 24-bits allocated to color, the rest for other things — in the Macintosh's 32-bit QuickDraw, for example, the extra 8 bits are called the "alpha channel" and are available for animation effects.

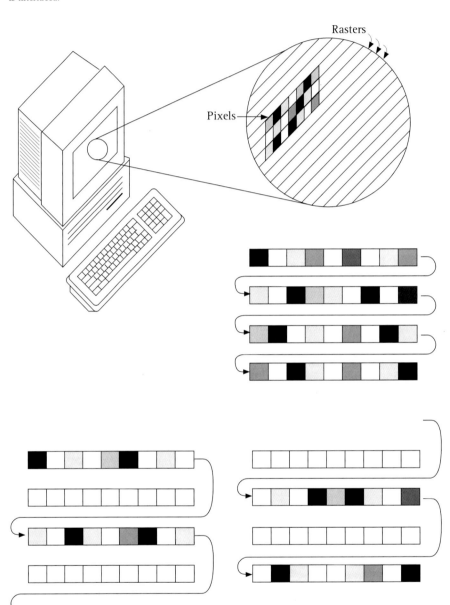

5.7 Pixels are tiny identifiable areas of the computer's display, and there is a one-to-one relationship between a pixel and a portion of computer memory. The display's electron gun scans the screen in lines called rasters. If it scans every single line in one pass, the display is non-interlaced. If it scans only every other line each pass, then the screen is interlaced.

Displays

The computer's display is the window through which we view whatever is being designed, and through which we interact with the software. It is important to remember, however, that the image on the screen is more often than not a crude representation of the page that exists inside the computer's memory. Printed output will always be crisper, in the correct typeface, and with the letter-spacing you have specified in the software. The output quality is dependent on the output device – whether it be a low-resolution laser printer or a high-resolution image-setter – not on the quality of the screen.

The majority of computer displays are based on the cathode ray tube (CRT), the tube that takes up most of the space in a television set. What make the CRT work are substances called phosphors: electrically active materials that luminesce when bombarded by electrons.

Computer and television screens are called raster displays, from the Latin *rastrum*, or rake (Fig. **5.7**). The electron gun at the back of the CRT scans the whole screen in horizontal lines, top to bottom, usually 60 times a second (60 Hz). On a non-interlaced display, every line is scanned each cycle. In a television set, alternate lines are scanned each cycle, resulting in two "fields" per cycle. This is known as an interlaced display. Most computer companies make screens that are non-interlaced, because they flicker less than interlaced screens.

Each scan line is chopped into chunks called pixels (picture elements). Pixels are the screen equivalent of dots (see p. 79), and as we have discussed earlier, each pixel on the screen is described by one or more bits in the frame buffer. The resolution (fineness) of a raster display is measured by the number of pixels horizontally by the number of scan lines vertically. The resolution of a 14-inch display is 640 x 480. For higher resolutions – 1280 x 1024, for example – you may need a plug-in graphics card (printed circuit-board) and a special **high-resolution** screen (see below). A multiscan screen can display different resolutions: from 640 x 480 to 1024 x 768, for example. To display at

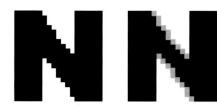

5.8 Anti-aliasing is a way of fooling the eye into thinking your screen has a higher resolution than it actually has. Low-res screens produce jagged edges, especially on diagonals. Shading the pixels near the edges with a mixture of the foreground and background colors results in a fuzziness that looks smooth at a distance.

higher resolutions, you may need to upgrade your VRAM or add a graphics card.

Other technologies, such as the liquid crystal displays found in portable computers, are smaller, slower, and of lower quality than CRTs.

Meanwhile, software optical illusions such as **anti-aliasing** (Fig. **5.8**) are used to improve the perceived resolution of their screens. Anti-aliasing smooths out the staircase effect seen on diagonal lines near the horizontal. It does so by coloring the pixels around the diagonals that actually define the line or edge in subtle shades of the current foreground and background colors.

Both the Mac and PC come with their own regular 14-inch screen as standard. If you are doing lots of design work you will need a larger-format display: either 17 inch (432 mm), or 21 inch (533 mm). Prepress operators and designers doing lots of color work will need the highest-possible quality of screen to make sure the transmitted RGB color of the screen faithfully predicts the CMYK color of the scan and finished printed page. The Radius PressView (Fig. **5.9**) is a professional prepress screen with an integral hood to prevent reflections and glare, a built-in display calibrator (note the sensor attached to the front of the screen) and color matching software – it even comes with a special cloak for you to wear to minimize ambient light reflection from your clothing!

Color display systems come in two parts: the color screen itself, and the graphics card that drives it. The monitor's tube comes from one of two major manufacturers: Hitachi and Sony. The traditional tubes,

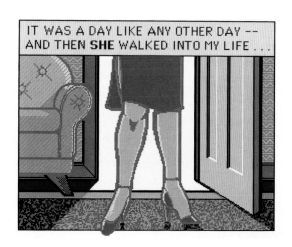

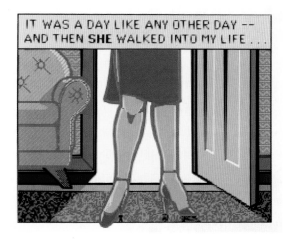

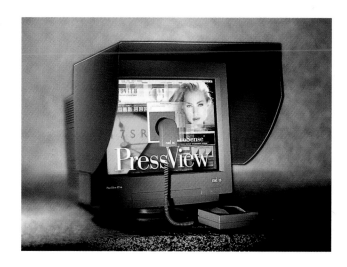

5.9 The Radius PressView is a professional prepress screen with a built-in display calibrator (note the sensor affixed to the screen) and software for matching colors.

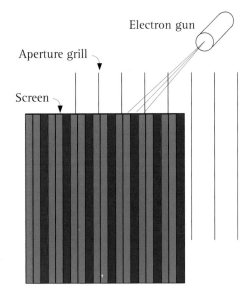

Electron gun

Aperture grill

Screen

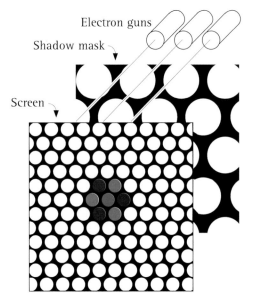

Electron guns

Shadow mask

Screen

5.10 Displays are built around two distinct technologies: those based on Sony's Trinitron with their vertical lines, and the more conventional shadowmask screens mainly manufactured by Hitachi.

which are mainly manufactured by Hitachi, have three electron guns, one each for the red, green, and blue dots on the screen (Fig. **5.10**). On their way to the screen, the beams are synchronized by a shadowmask – a metal mask with precisely placed holes through which the beams pass. A Sony Trinitron tube uses a single gun, and the shadowmask is a grid of fine vertical slots. A Trinitron tube is flatter and has a sharper, brighter picture, but it is heavier than regular screens and gives noticeable vertical lines of color. You may also be able to see two very thin dark horizontal lines: one about a quarter from the top; the other a quarter from the bottom.

The graphics card contains the frame buffer, and is either 8-bit, for 256 displayable colors, or 24-bit, for 16·7 million colors. An 8-bit card stores information about which colors are being used (the current palette) in a color look-up table. This is like an array of pigeon holes. Each contains the "address" of four numbers: an index number, plus values

for the red, green, and blue output levels that add together to display your chosen color. With 24-bit color, you have direct access to all 16·7 million colors, not just a selection of 256, and there is no need for the intermediate indexing. Each color – red, green, blue – is allocated an 8-bit value, to drive the red, green, and blue electron guns in the tube.

The color coming from a color monitor, being transmitted light, will never be the same as the color reflected from a printed page (see p. 87), and the color output will change as the phosphors age. To make the colors on the screen as faithful as possible, you must **color calibrate** your screen regularly. The Radius ProSense uses an optical sensor to take readings directly from colors on the screen (Fig. **5.11**). Software then compares them with Pantone colors and recalibrates for color "temperature" appropriate to the application and local lighting conditions. The software then makes adjustments to the color look-up

5.11 Displays must be calibrated regularly if their color reproduction is to remain faithful. A Radius ProSense color calibrator makes sure that colors on the screen bear a good resemblance to printed colors.

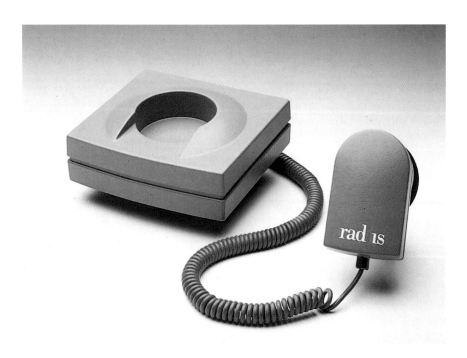

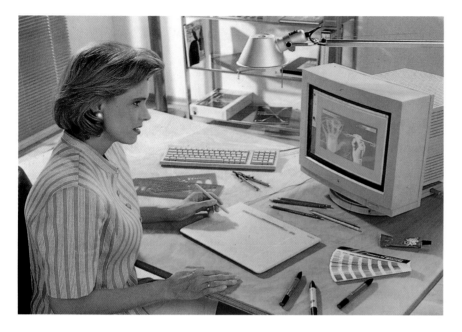

5.12 Digitizers are essential for precision drawing and tracing. Wacom's digitizing tablets are cordless, and are available with either a puck or a pressure-sensitive stylus.

The **digitizing tablet** (Fig. **5.12**) performs a dual role: it can be used to point and pick software commands from a menu, or to make pictures. Most, like the Wacom ArtPad and UltraPad, are electro-magnetic devices containing a grid of fine wires embedded into the work surface. Others make use of sonic techniques to detect the position of the stylus or puck.

A digitizer with a cordless pressure-sensitive stylus, from a supplier such as Wacom, can be used with some draw and paint programs to create images more intuitively than with a mouse and keyboard.

The mechanical **mouse** (Fig. **5.13**) suffers from friction or the lack of it (use a special mouse pad rather than the slippery surface of the desk). And, as it works in relative coordinates rather than absolute ones,

tables. Color management systems such as Apple's ColorSync and Kodak's CMS, in conjunction with application software, use device profiles supplied by the manufacturers of displays and scanners to ensure consistency between scans, what you see on the screen, and the printed product.

Input devices

The input device is the means by which the designer tells the machine and the software what to do. The particular method used for human/computer interaction is called the computer's graphical user interface (GUI). Originally, you would have had to type commands using the computer's keyboard. Apple Macintosh then introduced the "point and click" approach, and all the Mac's applications now make use of a mouse pointing device to "pull down" menus (lists of options), select icons (pic-

tures that represent tools and documents), and open and close windows (active areas of the screen). This form of GUI is gradually migrating to other systems. Microsoft's Windows for PCs and X-Windows for workstations are other examples.

Computer graphics users have long abandoned exclusive use of the keyboard that always comes with the computer, in favor of other methods for manipulating on-screen cursors and entering shape descriptions. However, keyboard-entered shortcut commands remain popular with experienced so-called "power" users, who find mouse operations slow compared with typing "command-P" to print, for example.

There are many alternatives to the mouse, however. There are rolling balls, joysticks, thumbwheels, and digitizing tablets – which come with a pen-like stylus or a mouse-like puck with buttons depending on the user's preference.

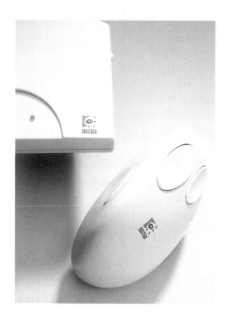

5.13 Most computers come with a standard mouse pointing device, but you don't have to stick with it.

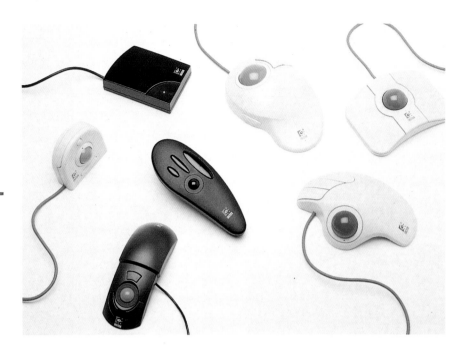

5.14 Rolling balls are more touch sensitive than mouses, have a smaller "footprint," and are more robust.

it gets lost in space. It is fine for menu picking, but little use for drawing. Turn the mouse upside down, however, and you have the **rolling ball** (Fig. **5.14**) – a device that has been used in air-traffic control for decades. These are much more sensitive to touch than joysticks. Furthermore, they are less prone to breakage, don't trap dirt, and have a small "footprint."

Digital cameras

A **digital camera** looks and feels just like a conventional analog camera, but with one big difference. Instead of capturing an image on light-sensitive film that has to be sent away to be developed and printed, or put on to a PhotoCD, a digital camera uses an array of CCD (charge-coupled device) sensors in order to convert the image into a form that can be stored in the camera's RAM and then downloaded into your computer.

The advantages are that you don't need to buy film, you don't have to wait for the film to be developed or PhotoCD made, and there is no need to scan the photograph or transparency into your computer. The disadvantages (at the time of

writing) are that digital cameras are expensive, the images are at a lower resolution that the silver crystals of photographic film, they can only store a limited number of images, and for hard copy you would have to output to a dye-sublimation printer.

The Kodak DC-50, for example (Fig. **5.15**), has a resolution of 756 x 504 pixels at three quality levels: its internal 1 Mbyte of memory can store 24 images at the lowest (com-

pressed) setting; seven at the highest quality. An optional 4 Mbyte card can increase this capacity up to 35 high-resolution pictures. For magazine print quality output, an enlargement would be limited to around 86 mm x 65 mm. If you are working away from the studio, and need to take more pictures, you will need a portable computer to use as a mass storage device. Like a conventional compact camera, it has an automatic flash, a motorized zoom lens with auto-focus, a shutter that fires at speeds of $\frac{1}{16}$ of a second to $\frac{1}{500}$ of a second and an aperture control that ranges from f2·6 to f16.

5.15 Digital cameras, like this Kodak DC-50, are already being used by realtors, photographers doing production-line pack-shot and catalog work, and by designers with not too high resolution expectations.

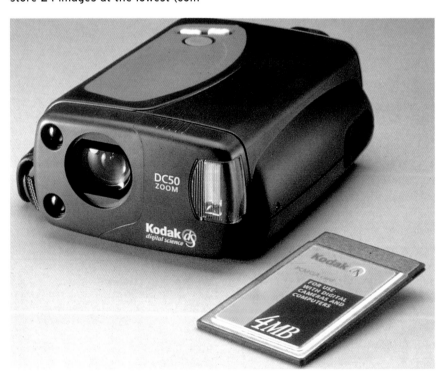

It is also possible to buy digital backs to attach to conventional 5 in x 4 in cameras. These use a single row of CCDs, and work like a scanner. These cameras have much higher resolutions than the compact versions (up to 6000 x 7520), but must be wired directly to a computer and, as they require long exposure times, must be used with a tripod and high-intensity lights. As RAM comes down in price, however, and the technology of the digital camera matures, there will undoubtedly come a time when a digital camera becomes an essential part of the designer's toolkit.

Scanners

A scanner converts flat artwork, photographs or transparencies into a form that can be "seen" by your computer software. You may have a desktop scanner in your studio and you will almost certainly have to make use of the drum scanner at your repro service bureau – very few color separations are made by process camera these days.

Desktop scanners (Fig. **5.16**) allow the designer to input already existing images into the system – commissioned photographs, drawings or images plagiarized from magazines. A **frame grabber** is another input device – a small television camera mounted above a well-lit baseboard – which can be used not only to input pictures, but also for silhouettes of small three-dimensional objects.

Scanned data, whether it comes from a television camera, a video stills camera, or a laser scanner, is in its raw form a bitmapped image (see p. 70). A bitmap is good enough for a

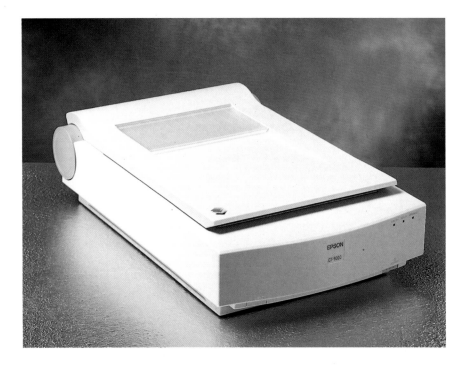

paint system to get to grips with. However, a drawing package will need some conversion, and the scanned image is best used as a background layer, to be traced over. Halftones can be input directly, in a format called **TIFF** (tagged image file format).

The most popular scanners for the studio are the single-pass flat-bed desktops, which look similar to photocopiers. The early models worked like photocopiers, with a moving scan head containing a fluorescent tube slowly moving from end to end of the original, recording a 300 dpi (dots per inch) bitmap 1 bit deep (i.e. only black or white). More recent models use CCDs (charge-coupled devices) to recognize and store images 30 bits deep at up to 600 dpi. Scanned images can be retouched using a package such as Photoshop. Import them to a page

5.16 Desktop scanners like this Epson GT9000 are useful in the design studio for inputting black-and-white line art, and for making low-resolution scans of color images which will later be replaced by scans made at the repro house.

layout package such as QuarkXPress or Adobe PageMaker, and convert them to screened halftones later in the process.

A rule of thumb says you should scan at a resolution that is twice the screen you plan to use for printing, if the image is to be reproduced at same size. So a scanner with a resolution of 300 dpi will just about be able to produce a halftone at same size with a screen of 150 lines. Although this will be good enough for newspaper or newsletter reproduction, for other jobs a scanned image should be used for position only and replaced with a

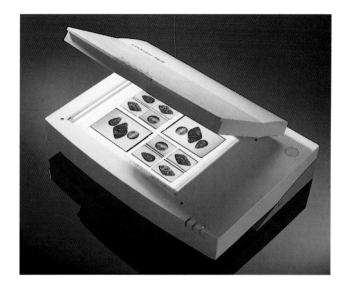

5.17 A top-end flatbed scanner, such as this Linotype-Hell Opal, can scan originals up to 38 in (150 mm) wide at 800 x 1600 dpi with a magnification of up to 600 percent.

professionally screened image at the film stage.

Desktop color scanners produce a quality far below that of the drum scanners found at repro shops (Fig. **5.17**). They work like mono scanners by scanning the image three times, using red, green, and blue lamps. At best, a desktop scanner can capture 30 bits per pixel, compared with the 48 bits a drum scanner can "see." In practice, the scanner can usually resolve no more than 6-bits per color. There are other issues to consider, as well. A 24-bit image takes up a great deal of memory: anything between 4 and 8 Mbytes when it is first scanned. Subsequent processing increases the size of the file. QuarkXPress, for example, will convert the TIFF file into five EPS (Encapsulated PostScript) files: a master preview plus data for each of the cyan, magenta, yellow, and key (black) separations. Thus a 7 Mbyte TIFF file can grow to occupy over 20 Mbytes. Multiply that by the number of color pictures in your publication, and you can begin to understand the magnitude of the problem.

5.18 This A3 size (18·5 in x 12·5 in) ICG 350i Sentinel, unlike many other drum scanners, stands vertically, thus saving space. It has a resolution of 4000 dpi and rotates at 1500 rpm. Artwork can be mounted round an external drum or transparencies can be mounted inside a smaller (18 in x 5·8 in) internal drum.

High-end scanners − the kind found at your repro service bureau − come in two distinct types: flatbed (like studio desktop scanners) that can achieve resolutions of 5000 dpi (Fig. **5.17**) and the more traditional drum scanners that can more than double that figure (Fig. **5.18**). It is important to mount the artwork very precisely. With a flatbed scanner, you just lay the artwork on the glass plate or place transparencies into a carrier with pre-cut frames and you're ready to scan. Mounting film or flexible artwork on a drum scanner is more complicated; the drum spins very quickly, so you must

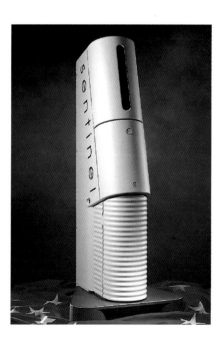

secure the film well. Oil mounting (which reduces problems created by dust and scratches on the film) can be used on drum scanners: bending the film around the drum creates tension that holds it evenly against the glass. Oil mounting on flatbed scanners isn't practical, because a flat piece of film lacks the tension it needs to maintain an even layer of oil, and air bubbles will form.

Flatbed scanners use a line of CCDs (charge-coupled devices), just like studio desktop scanners. Drum scanners use photo-multiplier tubes. Separations are made by a beam splitter, which divides the light transmitted through the transparency or off the artwork into its three color components. Each beam goes through a filter corresponding to one of the additive primaries (see p. 87) and is detected by a photocell. These signals are converted into CMYK by color correction software.

When changing levels of magnification, both types of scanner maintain a

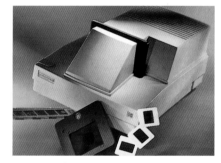

5.19 Slide scanners, such as this Kodak RFS 3570, are dedicated to scanning 35 mm and 70 mm transparencies at up to 2000 dpi. They are also useful for scanning in color negatives from regular print film.

ROTATE IMAGES BEFORE YOU IMPORT THEM
You can save time by cropping and rotating images in Photo-shop before importing them to a page-layout program such as PageMaker or QuarkXPress; it will also save time at the image-setting stage. To straighten a crooked scan in Photoshop, select the crop tool and draw a box around the image to be straight-ened, leaving plenty of room between the image and the edge of the scan. Now rotate the crop box. Once the edge of the box is parallel with the image, press Return for Photoshop to straighten and crop the image at the same time.

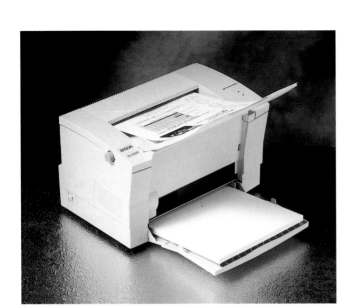

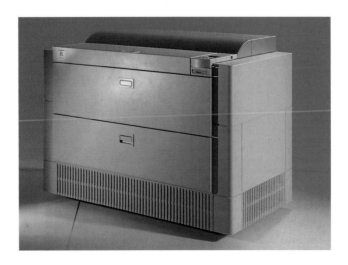

5.20 Laser printers like this Epson EPL-5500W give 600 dpi black-and-white output on plain paper, which can be good enough quality to use as camera copy for jobs such as newsletters and pricelists.

1:1 aspect ratio. To do this, drum scanners change the rate at which the optics scan across the drum. At the same time, they change the frequency with which the photo-multiplier samples the image. Scan-ning at a lower rate captures finer lines horizontally; higher-frequency sampling keeps the vertical density the same. Flatbed scanners use lenses to map a smaller or larger area of the film on to the CCDs: when a smaller area is captured, a shorter movement by the stepper motor keeps the density of pixels the same vertically and horizontally.

The time it takes to convert a PostScript file to a raster file to drive the imagesetter in the RIP (see p. 137) can work out to be extremely expensive for color, negating any advantages you may have gained by bringing color scanning in-house.

Until all photographers are equip-ped with digital cameras, there will still be a need to scan in slides or negatives. High-end flatbed and drum scanners are happiest with large-format transparencies: 35 mm slides are small and often come in mounts that lift the emulsion away from the glass and the optimum focusing distance. Dedicated slide scanners are optimized for this kind of work and can deliver high-quality 36-bit scans quickly: Kodak's RFS

3570 (Fig. **5.19**) can produce an 18 Mbyte scan in less than a minute. Maximum resolution is 2000 dpi or 2048 x 3072 pixels.

Output devices: laser printers and imagesetters

A graphic designer will be most likely to output to a nearby laser or inkjet printer for proofing, and send a Post-Script file to a repro service bureau for imagesetting on bromide paper or film. In addition, many of the out-put devices on the following pages can also be used for undemanding short printing runs.

Laser printers work on a similar principle to laser photocopiers (Fig. **5.20**). In a photocopier, the light

reflected from the white areas of an image causes a rotating drum charged with static electricity to lose its charge, so the toner doesn't stick. In a laser printer, however, there is no "original," so a laser draws a negative image on to the drum, removing charge from the white areas.

Laser printers, such as Apple's LaserWriter family and Hewlett-Packard's LaserJets, are small-format and most print in black and white only. The resolution is rarely greater than 600 dpi, which is adequate for proof-ing, producing artwork for low-grade publications such as newsletters and printing short runs of simple docu-ments. Color laser copiers are falling in price and are increasingly being used for proofing.

The original phototypesetters could only set type. With the intro-duction of PostScript, came the imagesetter, which could output graphics and pictures as well as type (Fig. **5.21**). The ability to output all page elements in position streamlined the traditional camera and stripping operations, paving the way to totally digital prepress.

5.21 High-end color image-setters such as this Scitex Dolev 800V are used to produce high-quality film separations.

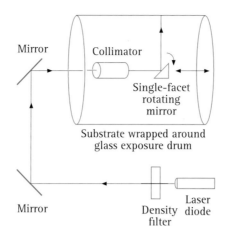

5.22 Drum imagesetter (above) and capstan (below) configurations. Each has its particular pros and cons, but the drum-based ones seem to offer the better and more consistent quality of output.

Mirror

Collimator

Single-facet rotating mirror

Substrate wrapped around glass exposure drum

Mirror

Density filter

Laser diode

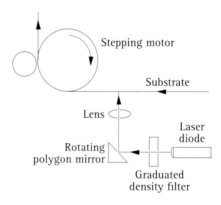

Stepping motor

Substrate

Lens

Rotating polygon mirror

Laser diode

Graduated density filter

The resolution of an imagesetter is measured in dpi (dots per inch) and these should not be confused with halftone dots, which are measured in lpi (lines per inch). A halftone dot is a cluster of many imagesetter dots (which, to avoid confusion, we'll call spots). An imagesetter might deliver a resolution of up to 4876 dpi – in other words, 847 distinct spots can be laid along a line one inch long with their edges just touching. Most, however, will output at 1200 (actually 1219) or 2400 (actually 2438) dpi.

The size of a laser's spot cannot easily be altered, and so halftone dots are built up by overlapping the spots (Fig. **5.23**). The **addressability** of an imagesetter is the accuracy with which the centers of the spots can be placed in proximity with each other. Thus an addressability of 2540 dpi means that the centers of two spots can be positioned $1/2540$th of an inch apart. So, when we talk about resolution, we are more correctly talking about addressability. Other important parameters are the dot (spot) size, measured in **mils** (thousandths of an inch) or micrometers (aka µm or microns – millionths of a meter) and the repeatability, also measured in

mils or microns, which is a measure of how well separations will register together.

We are told that the higher the resolution (but read: addressability), the better the print quality. But this is not always the case: there comes a point where there is so much overlapping of spots that any difference in quality is marginal. Similar results could probably be obtained using a lower setting.

There are two main types of imagesetter: capstan and drum (Fig. **5.22**). In an internal drum image-

setter, film enters and exits through a gap at the base of a large stationary drum. Tension rollers on either side of the gap hold the film flush against the inside of the drum. In a capstan or roll-fed imagesetter, film enters and exits the imagesetter between tension rollers, which hold the film taut and flat. Photo material – film or bromide paper – is stored in a light-tight cassette or box and then pulled across the imaging area into a receiving cassette or direct to an inline chemical processor.

Drum-based imagesetters are either internal-drum, where the film is positioned inside the drum and the imaging system moves, or external-drum systems, where the film is positioned on the outside of the drum and the drum rotates while the imaging system remains stationary. Internal drum imagesetters have an imaging laser attached to a screw that runs down the middle of the drum. As the laser spins, it slowly moves across the drum, writing the image, line by line. The film is always at the same distance from the laser. Capstan imagesetters have a stationary laser: a spinning mirror located directly above the film reflects the beam from side to side across the film.

A drum imagesetter's imaging area is limited in both width and length by the diameter and length of the drum. These imagesetters typically accept wider film sizes than do

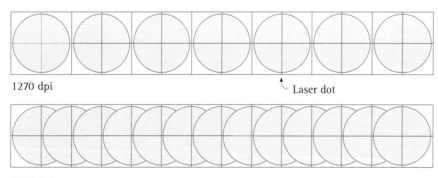

1270 dpi

Laser dot

2540 dpi

5.23 Resolution and addressability are two different, but related, parameters of an imagesetter. Resolution is the number of dots edge to edge in a line measuring an inch; addressability is a measure of how close, center to center, those dots can be placed next to one another.

capstan devices, which are limited by the tolerance to distortion at the edges of the imaging area where the laser beam is being reflected at a steeper angle. Capstan imagesetters have to use complex optical systems to ensure that the beam reaching the film or paper is uniform in strength. Imperfections in all the extra optics can lead to slurring, and loss of brightness and contrast. This results in weaker (less sharp) dots. Typically these devices use narrower film than drum imagesetters do, but can run longer lengths of film.

Drum-based imagesetters produce more accuracy and repeatability of images for each of the four films. They use sheets of film capable of four-up standard pages. Each of the four color separations can be output on one sheet of film, or four sheets can be output on four-up pages, one for each CMYK color.

Imagesetters which, along with imposition software, produce film negatives with pages in position ready for platemaking are sometimes called **imposetters**.

There must also be some means of processing the film or bromide paper, and imagesetters will have either an inline film processor attached, or cassettes of exposed film will have to be taken to a separate unit. Dry imagesetters output film without the need for wet chemicals and all the problems of recycling and disposal. Linotype-Hell and Polaroid have collaborated on the Drysetter (Fig. **5.24**). The film consists of a carrier layer and a top foil. Between these, under a laser-sensitive layer, is a layer of microscopic carbon particles. The laser combines the carbon with the laser-sensitive

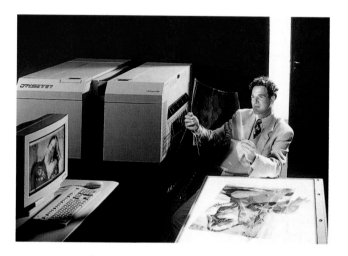

5.24 The Drysetter from Linotype-Hell and Polaroid outputs film without the need for wet chemical processing.

layer and then the foil with the surplus carbon is peeled away. Finally, a laminator seals the image to the carrier film. It has two resolutions: 2540 dpi and 3387 dpi with a dot size of 7·5 μm.

In a **platesetter**, the film is replaced by plate material. Although some imagesetters have always been able to output polyester plates for black-and-white work, these days color computer-to-plate technology is a reality (see p. 178 in Chapter 6), although it is not always possible to see a dot-for-dot proof before going to press.

To print documents containing PostScript files (see p. 68) – such as type, a page layout from Quark-XPress or PageMaker, or an image from a program such as FreeHand or Illustrator – an imagesetter has to operate with a device called a **RIP (raster image processor** – see also p. 148). These are sometimes built into the imagesetter, but are usually housed in a separate box. An RIP is a computer in its own right, and often is just that – a standard Mac or PC with lots of RAM – and all it ever

does is convert PostScript into the raster bitmap an imagesetter can read and output. The RIP also takes care of the screening of halftones. A 3600 dpi imagesetter with a spot size of 7·5 μm will have a maximum screen of 500 lpi.

To do all the "ripping" on the designer's computer would be very time-consuming. A way to get round this is to send only the text, rules, and non-scanned graphics to the RIP, along with instructions describing the size, cropping, and position on the page of the scanned pictures (the high-resolution files). This is a process known as **automatic picture replacement** (APR).

The picture commands, tagged on to the PostScript file, are part of a standard known as the **open prepress interface** (OPI), originally proposed by Aldus. A page description can thus be transferred from a Mac or PC to a faster, more powerful workstation at the repro service bureau and then to the RIP. A designer's computer is thus liberated to do what it does best – page design and layout.

5.25 Dot-matrix printers make use of straightforward mechanical technology — metal pins banging through an inked ribbon. They are cheap and reliable, but the quality of output is poor.

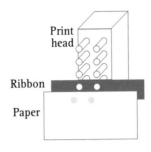

Print head

Ribbon

Paper

Hardcopy: other technologies

There are many other forms of output, especially for color, and one or more of the machines described here will be found in the designer's studio before long. If the quality of output is not important or if a quick-look plot is needed, a **dot-matrix printer** (Fig. **5.25**) like Apple's ImageWriter LQ may be good enough. They are cheap and can double-up with your word processor. The resolution is coarse, equivalent to around 72 dpi, and color fill can be messy (Fig. **5.26**).

Inkjet plotters (Fig. **5.27**) spray jets of microscopic electrically charged droplets of ink on to a moving roll of paper. These jets of ink are deflected by electromagnets – just like the electron beam in a television tube – to build up the

5.26 Here we compare the output quality of a 300 dpi Hewlett-Packard DeskWriter bubblejet printer in "best" mode (top), a 300 dpi Apple LaserWriter laser printer (middle), and a 600 dpi laser (bottom).

a new thing —
a new thing —
a new thing —

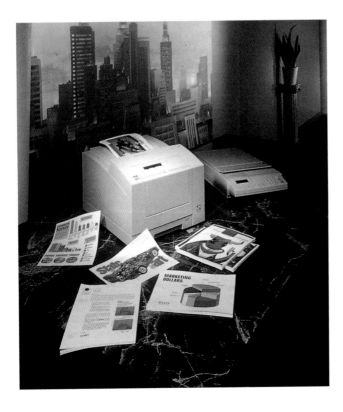

5.27 Inkjet plotters, like this Tektronix Phaser 350, work by shooting minute drops of ink at the paper. The Phaser is described as a phase-change inkjet: solid sticks of ink are melted in the printhead, squirted at the paper, then cold fused.

5.28 Inkjet and bubblejet printers produce bright, saturated colors, yet though they are often rated above laser printers in terms of resolution, the dots are bigger and more prone to smudging.

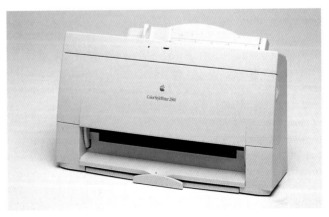

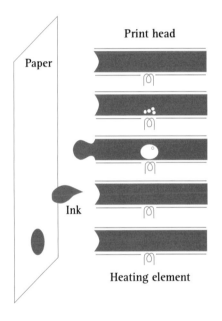

5.29 In bubblejet plotters, such as Apple's Color StyleWriter 2500, a heating element causes bubbles to form in the print head, thus forcing drops of ink to fly on to the paper.

Paper

Print head

Ink

Heating element

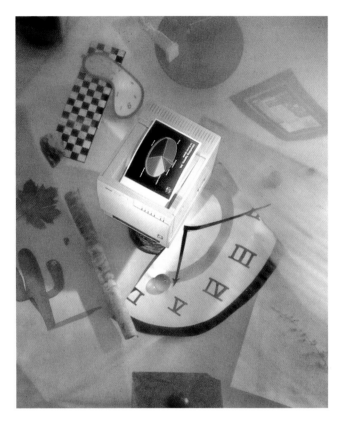

5.30 Tektronix Phaser 240 thermal-transfer plotter.

139

DIGITAL PREPRESS

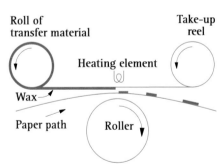

Roll of transfer material

Take-up reel

Heating element

Wax

Paper path

Roller

5.31 In the thermal-transfer process, rolls of transfer paper containing colored wax are "ironed" on to smooth paper by hundreds of individually controlled heating elements.

image. **Bubblejet plotters** (Fig. **5.28**) have an array of thin nozzles in the print head, each of which is full of ink, held there by surface tension. A small heating element causes a bubble to form which forces the ink out of the nozzle and on to the page (Fig. **5.29**). Another variation is the **thermojet plotter**, which sprays melted plastic on to the paper.

Top-end inkjet printers such as the Scitex Iris are used for color proofing and artists' prints. Large-scale inkjets can be used to print posters up to A0 in size and some can print the huge banners that hang outside buildings.

Thermal-transfer plotters (Fig. **5.30**) use an inked-roll cartridge sandwiched between the mechanism and the drawing. It acts like carbon paper, "ironing" the image on to clay-coated paper. The three process colors (and sometimes black) are applied, one at a time, by melting dots of wax on to the paper or acetate at a resolution of 300 dpi (Fig. **5.31**). Printers such as the Tektronix Phaser 240 are also used for color proofing. The machines are cleaner and dryer than inkjets, but consumables are more expensive. **Thermal-transfer machines** produce solid, bright colors, but tend to print blues and greens darker than inkjets. **Direct thermal printers** "burn" a monochrome image into specially coated paper using thermal heads.

5.32 Most output technologies can produce only one size of dot in just one intensity. This is fine for line work and flat color, but for smooth blends between colors, they have to resort to a trick called dithering, which introduces deliberate randomness into a dot pattern.

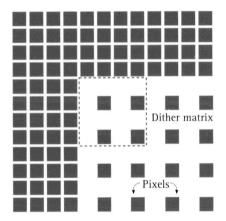

Dither matrix

Pixels

Thermal-transfer and inkjet print-ers produce all their colors by a pro-cess called **dithering** (Figs **5.32** and **5.33**), which is analogous to halftone screening. Pixels of cyan, magenta, and yellow (and sometimes black) are interspersed in regular patterns. Some printers use a fixed pattern of dithering, which results in a distinct step between colors. Others can make use of different patterns, leading to smoother gradations.

Laser, thermal-transfer, and inkjet printers are available with or without a PostScript driver, the PostScript versions being more expensive. It is possible to produce acceptable results without PostScript by using Adobe Type Manager or TrueType fonts. For most graphic designers committed to PostScript, and who need fast and consistent output, a PostScript-compatible printer will be essential.

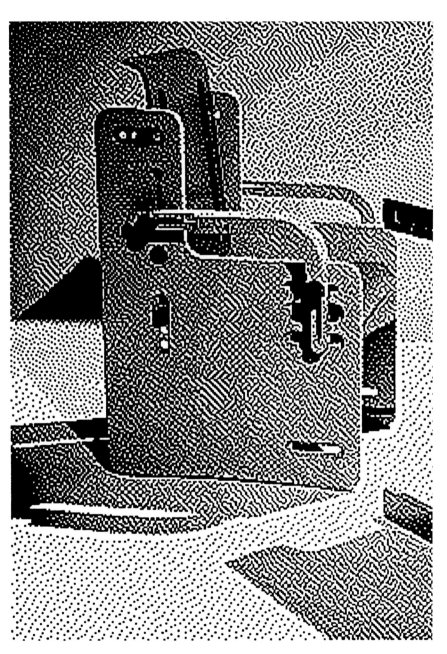

5.33 Simple 1-bit dithering can be seen in this close-up – a laser plot of a chair produced by Kanwal Sharma of Lewis Sharma Design, a studio in Bristol, England, specializing in design for disabled people.

▶ **5.34** Dye-sublimation printers can produce an almost photographic quality of output, without dots or dithering, by melting and merging the inks right on the surface of the paper.

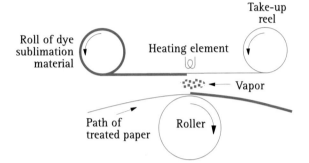

Roll of dye sublimation material

Take-up reel

Heating element

Vapor

Path of treated paper

Roller

▼ **5.35** Low-cost dye sublimation printers, such as the Fargo FotoFun, produce postcard-size images of photographic quality.

Perhaps the best contender yet for color hardcopy is dye sublimation (Fig. **5.34**). Machines from Mitsubishi and Hitachi mix the ink on the treated paper, without dots or dithering. So 16·7 million possible colors and 256 grayscales are smoothly blended together into a photo-graphic-quality image almost good enough to go as artwork straight to the printer's.

Sublimation is the phenomenon whereby certain substances go dir-ectly from a solid to a gaseous form, without the usual intermediate liquid stage. The thermal head on a dye-sublimation printer varies the tem-perature so that the amount of dye emitted is continuously controlled.

At present, both the machines and the media for dye sublimation are very expensive. With the creation of a market for digital cameras, dye sublimation will become much less expensive. Already, cheaper dye-sublimation printers such as the Fargo FotoFun (Fig. **5.35**) can pro-duce postcard-size prints of near-photographic quality.

Designers will sometimes want to take a 35 mm or larger-format transparency off the system. A **film recorder** (Fig. **5.36**), from companies such as Agfa and Lasergraphics,

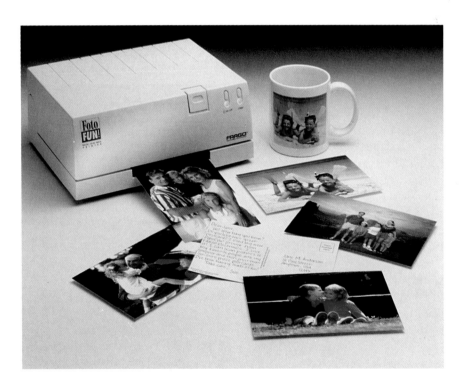

captures the image on a small flat CRT tube built into the device, making three consecutive exposures through red, green, and blue filters. The LFR Mark III from Lasergraphics, for example, has 35 mm, 120/220 and 5 in x 4 in camera backs and can process a 104 Mbyte file from a Mac or PC to produce an 8000-line (8192 x 5462) slide in 4 minutes 50 seconds.

▼ **5.36** Film recorders are used to produce photographic transparencies direct from computer disk. They work by exposing the film three times — once for each of the primary colors — using small flat cathode-ray tubes.

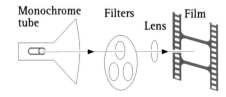

Monochrome tube

Filters

Lens

Film

A **pen plotter** will have limited use in most graphic design studios. An exception is where the graphic designer does a lot of packaging design work. The pen plotter will be used to draw out fold and cut lines for the flat-pattern development of the carton or box being designed.

A pen plotter, with a cutting knife replacing the pen or pencil, can also be used to prepare flat-color masks for silkscreen printing (see p. 185), and for cutting out vinyl letters for large-scale displays and signs (Fig. **5.37**).

There are two main types of pen plotter. Desktop plotters have the pen moving in all directions on a stationary piece of paper, held in place horizontally by a suction pump. Larger drum plotters have the pen moving in one direction and the paper in the other. These use abrasive pinch rollers to grip the edges of the paper, eliminating the necessity for sprocketed paper or film.

Roland's CAMM-1 is a desktop plotter modified for cutting vinyl and Rubylith film (see p. 112). Large format flatbed and drum production plotters/cutters are made by Zund, Wild, Aristo, and Kongsberg. Laser cutters are used for acrylics.

Plotters and cutters are vector devices, moving from point to point as on a graph, and the code that drives them conforms to a standard called HP-GL (Hewlett-Packard graphics language). PostScript is a vector format too, even though most computer devices encountered by the graphic designer work on the raster principle. PostScript to HP-GL conversion is necessary to drive a plotter directly from a PostScript package.

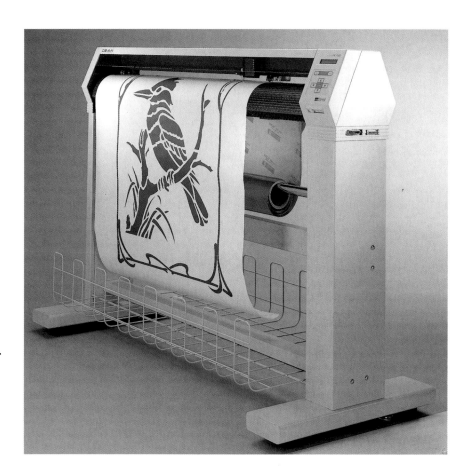

DIGITAL MAKE-UP

If you follow the conventional prepress procedure, you will have to prepare text for the typesetter, deciding on the typeface, size, and measure in advance. You will receive back a photocopied galley to use for layout. Alternately, the galley will be on bromide paper, and you will use this to paste up the finished artwork. If you change your mind, or find that the copy does not fit your meticulously planned layout, then you will have to start over, and ask for the text to be reset, or at least rerun. This can all be very time-consuming and costly.

5.37 Pen plotters are rarely used by graphic designers. An exception is when they are equipped with a cutting knife in place of the pen, like this Roland CAMM-1, and are used to produce masks for screenprinting or to cut vinyl letters for large signs.

With a computer system, it is possible to design "on the fly," though this methodology is not always recommended! What is certain though, is that you will be able to try out lots of "what-if?" layouts, and always end up with clean, seamless artwork, with no changes in density where paragraphs have been corrected, no scalpel cuts to be retouched, and no chance of

last-minute corrections dropping off the mechanical and vanishing on the printer's floor. That's the theory, of course!

In practice, however, there will be some compromise. Unless the entire process – from idea to press plate – is digital, you will probably have to use a service bureau to produce the bromides of the pages on a high-quality imagesetter. And once the bromide is back in your studio, last-minute emergency repairs may have to be made with scalpel and paste.

Nevertheless, digital make-up represents a huge advance in the technology available to the graphic designer. It is an immensely powerful tool, which brings with it a great deal of responsibility for the appearance of the finished product. Once the system is up and running, there will be no one to blame for a less than perfect layout except yourself, or perhaps a bug in the program. And there will be much to learn: about operating the system, making use of the flexibility it offers, and about computers in general.

So how does digital make-up work, and how does it differ from preparing mechanicals by hand? Not as much as you may think. As with the totally manual method, it will always pay to sit down with a pencil and paper to plan your layout. A layout pad has been designed for that purpose, with leaves thin enough for you to trace the best parts of a previously attempted design before it is consigned to the trash. Make a sketch layout of the page. It does not have to be completely accurate, but it should be good enough for you to see what a spread is going to look like at full

size. This should include the margins, columns, and the position of page numbers and running heads.

Next, select your typeface. This will depend on the type of job, and what's available – both on your system, and at the service bureau. Don't forget practical considerations, such as the number of words per line and the relative x-heights (see p. 36) of the different faces. Try running off some sample lines of type in the face and at the point size and measure that you have chosen, and place it on the layout. That way you will be able to judge whether you require more or less leading and tracking. Try out different sub-headings, and decide now whether the text is to be set justified or ranged left. Remember, type on the screen only approximates the output from the laser printer or imagesetter, so it is important to have a reasonable idea of what to expect.

Next, calculate how much space the type will occupy. If the text has been input using a word processor with a word counter, then that figure will be a good guide. Otherwise use one of the methods outlined in Chapter 2 (see p. 46). If it is going to be too long, or fall short, adjust the layout.

Now draw up a grid. Although the digital make-up system will have built-in rulers and construction lines, the page on the screen – even on a large format display – will look deceptively different from a piece of board on your desk. So double-check with a ruler and a same-size reference grid. Then you can key the specifications into the computer.

If the publication is mostly words, with few or no illustrations, then you

can start to place the text on to the page. If, however, there is a large number of illustrations, it is best to draw up a rough plan showing where you expect them to fall. It is much easier to manage the layout (and make sure that nothing is left out) if you know exactly which elements have to be included, and roughly where.

Finally, make a written record of your specification and keep it nearby. Although it is in the computer somewhere, it can be time-consuming and disruptive to have to stop what you are doing to find a reminder of what measure, margin, or horizontal division you have been using.

Page layout programs

It is possible to make up complete pages in some of the so-called drawing programs, such as FreeHand and Illustrator. Even off-the-shelf word processing programs can now handle several columns of text integrated with graphics. And there are some packages on the market developed for specific design tasks: producing display advertisements for newspapers and magazines, for example. These are not page-oriented like other programs, and contain built-in modules for text and image origination. If all you do is design ads, then you won't need to buy any other programs.

At the other extreme, there are programs such as FrameMaker, developed to handle very large but relatively unsophisticated publications, such as technical manuals.

Most designers come across all kinds of jobs, however, and need a

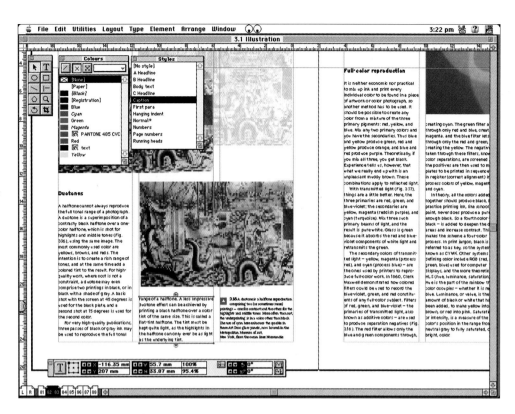

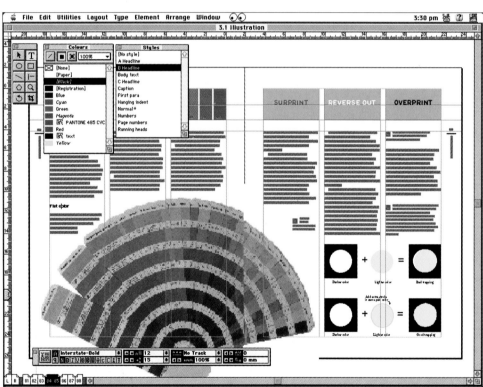

5.38 In a digital make-up system such as Adobe PageMaker the mechanical is replaced by an "electronic pasteboard." Text is imported from a word-processing system or in-built text editor and placed on to a grid. The windowshade allows you to pull down more text. Text can also be wrapped around illustrations.

more general-purpose program. The best-known and most versatile are Adobe PageMaker (Fig. **5.38**) and QuarkXPress (Fig. **5.39**). Aldus released the first version of Page-Maker for the Apple Macintosh in July 1985, and for the IBM PC in January 1987. QuarkXPress was not introduced until later in 1987. It was Aldus founder Paul Brainerd who coined the phrase "desktop publishing." PageMaker can thus rightly claim to be the original desktop publishing package. Aldus was taken over by Adobe in 1994.

Both boast a WYSIWYG (what you see is what you get) display, but the term is not strictly accurate. The

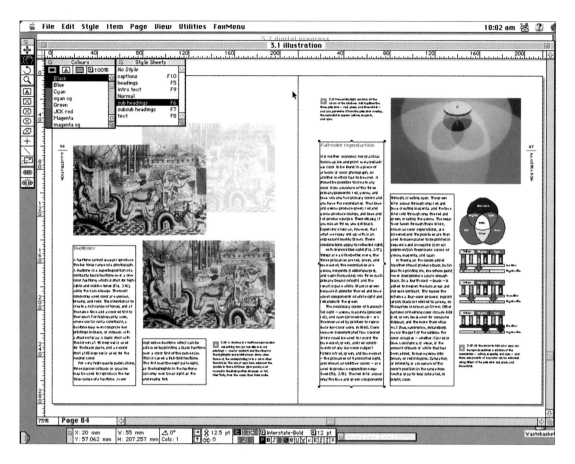

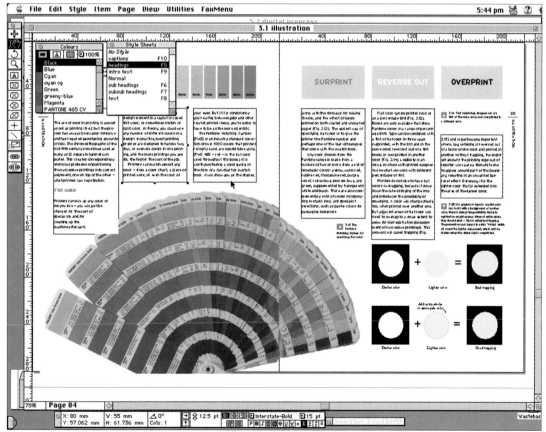

5.39
QuarkXPress is similar to PageMaker in many ways, but uses a different approach to placing text and graphics – XPress has linked text and graphic frames.

TEXT ARRIVING ON DISK
If someone is sending you copy on disk, ask them to save it as a text file or in ASCII text. That way, if you are opening up a file originated on a PC, say, in a Mac program, you will avoid having to edit out obscure formatting commands. Alternately, OCR (optical character recognition) programs are so accurate nowadays, it may be quicker to scan in the text from hard copy.

DIGITAL PREPRESS

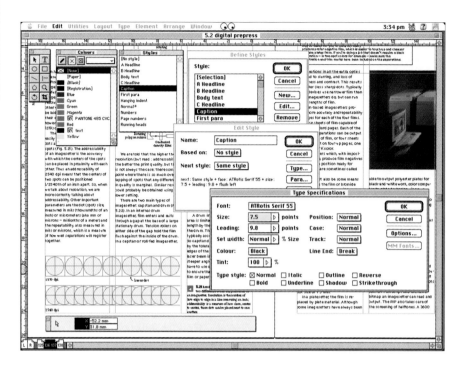

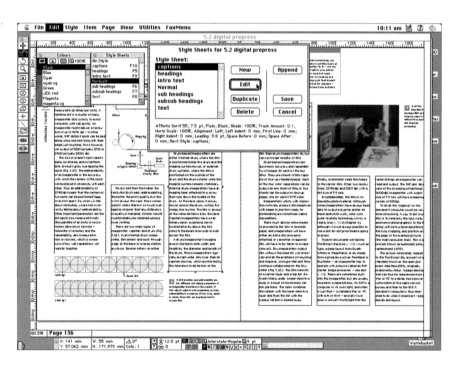

printed result is far superior to the page you see on the screen, even at full zoom (magnification), because screen fonts are fundamentally different from printer fonts (see p. 68). Nevertheless, what you see is far superior to what compositors have seen on screen at the type-setter's in the past. Both XPress and PageMaker make extensive use of the **WIMP** (windows, icons, mouse, and pull-down menus) facility, with "palettes" of tools (for drawing boxes, for example) and such things as style-sheet information that can be available on the screen all of the time (Fig. **5.40**).

Both systems enjoy equal popularity; however, they have different working methods. In general, XPress is favored by magazine designers, PageMaker by designers of publications with fewer pages. But there is no clear division, and designers will argue into the night about the relative merits of *their* program and its suitability to do a particular job.

In **PageMaker**, the user is presented with a picture on the screen of a "pasteboard" for electronically pasting on text or graphics. Any elements not being used can be placed outside the page area until they are needed. When you open a new **document** in PageMaker, you are asked to enter the page size and margins in a "dialog box." (In computer language, any job you are working on is called a document, whether it is a drawing, a piece of text, or a page layout.) You will also be asked how many pages the publication will have. It is then possible to specify the number of columns, their width, and the spacing between them. All of these parameters can

be changed later, if need be.

Text can be imported from a word processor document, and a symbol is placed in the position you wish the text to start. In "auto-flow" mode it will flow down the columns until all the text is in position. In regular mode, text will flow down the first column, and then stop. The text

5.40 Both PageMaker and XPress allow you to compile and edit a style sheet outlining highly specific instructions for components such as the font, leading, and tracking of body text, headlines, and captions. Thus you can maintain consistency between publications.

block takes the appearance of a window-shade (roller blind). A little ▼ in the "handle" indicates that there is more text in there. A blank handle indicates that all the text is accounted for. Once placed, the text can be moved around en masse, and edited in an integral story editor.

There are several aids to consistency. Anything placed on "master pages" (there are 256 of them) will appear on every page selected. This is useful for positioning construction lines, effectively creating a grid, and for inserting running heads and folios. (Pressing the command, option, and letter p keys together will invoke automatic page numbering throughout the document.) Style sheets allow you to specify body text, captions, headlines, and different grades of subheadings, as well as instructions about indents for paragraphs, kerning, and hyphenation. Entire "skeleton" documents can be saved as templates, which can be used over and over to produce documents that are going to look similar – future issues of a newsletter, for example.

PageMaker's story editor is virtually a word-processing package in itself, and can be used for fast text entry and last-minute editing while you are working on the layout of a publication. It includes a spelling checker, a search-and-replace command, and a word counter.

To achieve consistent predictable color from scanner to screen to proof, PageMaker has adopted Kodak's Precision Color Management System (CMS) – a library of scanner, monitor, and output device profiles. It also supports Kodak's PhotoCD, automatically color correcting and

sharpening images as they are imported to the layout.

PageMaker can handle process and flat (spot) color, which can be specified by Pantone number (the color library includes the expanded gamut of Pantone's Hexachrome six-color process, as well as metallic, pastel, and fluorescent inks), percentages of CMYK, and also in terms of RGB (red, green, and blue) values or HLS (hue, luminance, and saturation). Percentage tints can be applied to objects straight from the color palette. And as the functionality of programs like PageMaker and Photoshop begin to merge, PageMaker has the ability to color separate RGB TIFFs, without having to export them first to Photoshop.

Objects can be grouped, resized, rotated, or cropped – and text can still be edited while remaining in the group. Any part of the layout can be masked using objects created with the drawing tools: ovals, rectangles and polygons. Kerning can be to 0·0001 em and tracking can be edited in 0·1 pt increments.

Output will generally be to a laser printer or desktop color printer for proofing and low-grade output (for a newsletter, for example), or to an imagesetter for bromide or film. It has built-in automatic trapping, and non-printing objects, such as production notes, can be defined. A "print fit" preview shows where the document will fit on the output page, complete with register and trim marks. Limited imposition schemes can be set up, to produce booklets, for example. The program can also add OPI (open prepress interface) comments to linked EPSs.

With each new upgrade, Page-Maker and XPress continue to leap-frog each other – if a feature in one of them proves popular, then the rival will adopt its own interpretation. PageMaker has introduced frames and a control palette like in XPress; and XPress has changed over to the pasteboard metaphor. (It is a truism in computing that you only realize what something cannot do when they bring out a new version.) PageMaker has Plug-ins to add functionality to the basic program; XPress has its equivalent Xtensions. Both are also expanding from print into newer media such as CD-rom production and the Internet, with features that help convert page layouts into HTML (Hyper Text Mark-up Language – see Chapter 7, p. 209) and Adobe Acrobat's PDF (Portable Document Format).

In XPress, you start a layout by creating text and graphics boxes or frames for the design elements. It now has more sophisticated drawing tools – Bézier and freeform shapes no longer have to be imported from programs such as Illustrator and FreeHand. Complex shapes can be created by using Boolean operations (intersection, union, difference) to carve away or merge together simpler shapes – and a picture box can be created from the shape of a selection of text, to be filled, say, with an imported graphic. Text can be set on a path, can flow around all sides of an object, and clipping paths can be built around, say, the non-white areas of an imported TIFF image file. It can deal with text styles at the character level, rather than just at paragraph level: the styles palette shows the two current

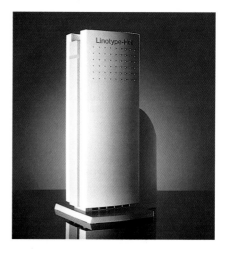

5.41 A RIP (raster image processor) is a computer dedicated to converting Postscript files like page layouts into bitmaps that an imagesetter can understand: this is Linotype-Hell's Delta RIP.

styles simultaneously. XPress also includes the agate measurement system, used in newspapers for classified ads.

Both XPress and PageMaker are based on the PostScript page description language. At the time of writing, neither PageMaker nor XPress were planning to support Apple's QuickDraw GX. The first page layout system to do so was SoftPress Systems' UniQorn. Like XPress, it is a frame-based system, but uses one type of frame for both text and graphics. It allows multiple custom-page-size setups, and both trapping and separations can be previewed live on-screen.

Layouts can be "repurposed" – if you change the paper or trim size of a page, the layout will automatically readjust itself, maintaining the correct bleed orientation and so forth. Frames can relate in proportion to other frames, rather than just to the page dimensions. It updates style sheets automatically as you go along, and it has a Fonts Extras palette for all those extra GX-specific typographical controls.

The essence of digital make-up is that you can be as rigid or as flexible as you choose. PageMaker is said to be more intuitive than XPress, but some designers are convinced that XPress has more functionality, with just about every typographic control you could wish for. The above can only give you a flavor of what both Adobe and Quark have to offer. Check with a dealer for the specification of the latest update. Both will continue to improve, however, and ultimately the choice is going to be a personal one.

Full-color digital prepress

All page-layout systems can handle color to some extent. XPress, for example, can separate files imported from Illustrator and FreeHand, or images from retouching programs such as Photoshop. But full color is extremely expensive on computer memory and can slow down the most powerful desktop computer to a snail's pace if it constantly has to manipulate and redraw pages with many full-color images.

It is recommended, therefore, that layouts are designed on a system using only low-resolution images, in the same way that photocopies of halftones on a mechanical are used "for position only." Send transparencies to the repro house to be electronically "stripped-in" later.

Printers and repro houses have been using digital scanners coupled with computers for many years. This is one of graphic design's best kept secrets. Organizations with digital prepress systems from suppliers such as Scitex, Du Pont, Linotype-Hell, and Dainippon have been able to scan in and retouch color transparencies since the early 1970s. Of course, these systems have been capable of much more, but were so expensive to buy and run that printers, afraid that designers might develop the "bad habit" of asking for alterations to their images, adopted an almost conspiratorial silence.

All this has changed, however. Designers are now able to effect similar changes to their images before the prepress stage, using desktop systems running programs such as Photoshop. The scanner manufacturers have also introduced less expensive "front-ends" to their systems, aimed specifically for designers to use.

With a so-called **CEPS (color electronic publishing system)**, you the designer use low-resolution images as for-position-only visuals to produce the "electronic mechanicals" on your desktop make-up system. High-resolution scans, straight from the original transparencies, are reunited with the layouts in the imagesetter at the repro house.

The low-resolution scans used in the computer until the proofing stage can be straight from your desktop scanner, or they can be "compressed" versions of scans from the repro house's system. As you lay out the images, the system remembers all the scaling, rotating, and cropping alterations made to the image, and conveys them to the operator at the repro house. This makes considerable savings on set-up time compared with conventional repro techniques, in which the operator has to check and measure position mark-ups on overlays.

Complex cut-outs and masks can be made and these are automatically translated into smooth high-resolution masks at the repro house, using a technique called mask-density substitution. In the same way, graduated tints (called degradés in Scitex talk) are recreated automatically in high-resolution versions.

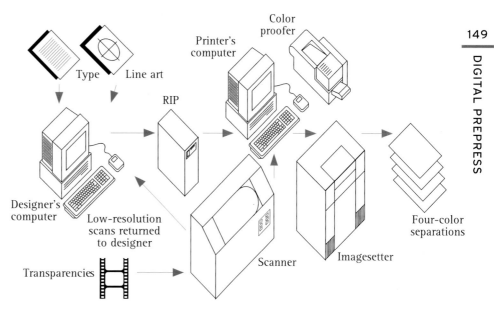

5.42 A regular desktop design system can be used as a front-end to the system at the repro house, mixing and matching the abilities of both to the best and most economical advantage. Transparencies are sent to the repro house where both high- and low-resolution scans are made. The low-res scans are used in your layouts and the high-res ones are substituted later, when the final pages are made up.

Most page layouts are output to an imagesetter via a RIP (see p. 137), which changes the PostScript outlines of the letters and drawings into a bitmap (an array of dots) that the imagesetter can print out (Fig. 5.41). Once all color and mono elements are in place, the page can be proofed on a digital proofing system, such as an Iris inkjet printer.

After corrections have been made (remember, one of the great advantages of CEPS is that no repro or film costs have been incurred at this stage), the PostScript file can be sent via removable hard disk or down line to the repro house. This assumes of course that the repro house already holds the original transparencies! At the repro house, all type, tints, and images are plotted directly on to final output film, with no need for intermediate typesetting, imagesetting, or stripping-in.

A CEPS is built around a top-quality drum scanner, a RIP and a high-resolution imagesetter (Fig. 5.42), and one difference between it and the kind of system you may find in a designer's studio is that at the repro house all operations are carried out in CMYK. Desktop systems use RGB for image capture and manipulation and only convert to CMYK right at the end of the process. Color management systems, such as Kodak's Precision Color Management (CMS) and constant calibration, are critical for the color you see on your screen to end up on the printed page.

Digital prepress is more than just a matter of processing the page layouts from a designer's desktop system. Systems such as Scitex's Brisque (Fig. 5.43) is built around a

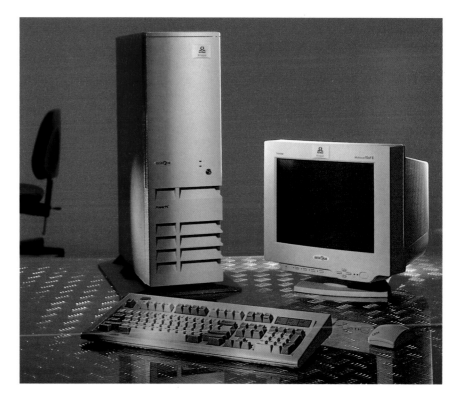

5.43 The Scitex Brisque is a digital front-end to the repro house's RIP and imagesetter that also manages the workflow through the prepress process.

MAKE A PRE-FLIGHT CHECK
Your printer isn't telepathic, so before handing off the completed job on a removable
hard disk along with laser proofs and/or thumbnails, take time to produce a list of all the
settings, files, fonts, colors, bleeds etc. – in a pre-flight check. Some programs, such as
Adobe PageMaker and QuarkXPress can produce lists automatically, but they can
become unwieldy and too full of detail. Account for every page in the publication, even
blank ones. Indicate the number of color separations expected for each page, and note
any details requiring special attention, such as instructions to position the saddle wires
to avoid spoiling an illustration on the center spread. Keep notes brief – and include
your name and telephone number just in case there are any unforeseen problems.

RIP, but also takes care of much of the production control in prepress. It uses electronic "job tickets" to plan the particular operations that need to be processed in the right order and to specific parameters. Prepress operators can set up "hot folders" to watch for certain file types, which then, say, can be automatically ripped from PostScript to editable continuous tone and linework, trapped, previewed (soft-proofed), imposed, held in a queue until approved, then exposed with on-the-fly screening on a designated imagesetter. CEPS should make last-minute corrections much easier, without the designer having to go back and change the original XPress or PageMaker files.

Late binding is the term used to mean last-minute changes within PostScript files while they are in the RIP, such as adding trapping and imposition information, particularly for digital presses.

CHOOSING A SYSTEM

Turnkey systems

A **turnkey system** is a complete package of hardware and software dedicated to a particular task. You turn the (imaginary) key, and off you drive. The system may be assembled from standard pieces of equipment, bought in from well-known manufacturers and "badge engineered" (i.e. the turnkey vendor's logo is stuck on the front). Or perhaps the vendor will have modified it somewhat. The software that does the job is usually only available from the turnkey vendor. (If it is subsequently sold separately from the turnkey system, it is said to be unbundled.)

The attraction to the user is that everything needed for a working system is purchased from one source, with a single maintenance contract and one technical support person to call if things go wrong. The disadvantages are that the system cannot usually be used for other tasks – to run the studio administration, for example. And you are "locked in" to one supplier for any future updates of the hardware and software. The trend today is toward "open systems" with standardized GUIs, and the ability for programs to be able to pass information between each other. This may not be possible with a turnkey. It may have a quirky interface, and once you have learnt to use it, that knowledge will apply to that system only.

Nevertheless, there are still several turnkey systems around, aimed at highly specialized applications. There are systems targeted at packaging designers, with their need to design in three dimensions and then produce flat-pattern developments of cartons, for example. Another group of turnkeys is aimed at screenprinters and signwriters, who need to cut letters and masks out of vinyl and Rubylith.

Turnkey systems are usually much more expensive than an equivalent system assembled from component parts selected by you. The vendors have been guilty of trading on people's fear of computers by stressing that their menus, for example, make use of the terms and language peculiar to that trade. But these days, much more flexible systems can be assembled quite painlessly from standard PCs or Macs, plus any make of plotter or cutter and inexpensive, off-the-shelf software.

Selecting, upgrading, and networking the system

Selecting and cost-justifying a system is a very personal business. Read the computer magazines, visit trade shows, and talk to other users doing similar work to that of your studio. Methodologies exist that use spreadsheet programs to enable you to quantify the benefits of introducing a computer system into your studio. These may be understandable to an accountant or bank manager and be instrumental in securing you a loan to make the purchase. But of course they cannot predict the future. Ultimately, the success of an installation is down to you. You will have to understand what the system is capable of doing, and how it can save you time and materials, while producing a quality product.

Once a successful installation has been established, however, expansion happens rapidly. This can take two forms: expansion of hardware – adding more systems, more memory, more output devices – and expansion into new application areas. On the Macintosh, particularly, programs have a common look and feel, which reduces the culture shock when you encounter new software. With the enormous number of "desk accessories" available, it is difficult to resist becoming addicted to every latest application that comes along.

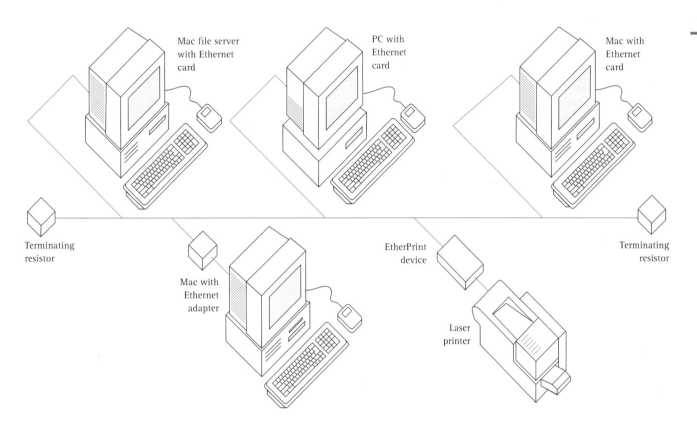

Mac file server with Ethernet card

PC with Ethernet card

Mac with Ethernet card

Terminating resistor

Mac with Ethernet adapter

EtherPrint device

Laser printer

Terminating resistor

5.44 Networking means that you can link computers together to send electronic mail or to share resources, such as a laser printer. You can also work with others on large projects.

As soon as you have more than one system, they can be networked together (Fig. **5.44**). There are three main reasons for **networking**: (1) to exchange files and messages with nearby members of your team using email (electronic mail); (2) to share expensive resources such as laser printers and disk drives; and (3) to co-operate jointly with others in your studio on a large-scale project – in a workgroup.

Networking has a language all of its own, and acronyms like ISO/OSI and TCP/IP abound. All you need to know is that the most famous LAN (local-area network) is called Ethernet. It operates via a single length of coaxial cable or twisted-pair telephone cable, and was developed by Xerox, DEC, and Intel and introduced in 1980. Other kinds of LAN include IBM's token ring system.

Workstations were designed from the outset to be networked, so there should be no problem there. On the Macintosh, networking is fairly straightforward. For email, one system is designated email server – the place where messages are stored and forwarded – and the others are called clients. Full networking is achieved when a "file server" is set up. Any computer in the network can act as a server. (In larger networks the file server is a dedicated computer with a large disk drive, but with no screen.) This provides shared storage for programs (though it is faster to keep your own local copy),

files, or fonts that everyone on the network can access. It is the responsibility of the applications software to say who has read-only access, and who has the authority to make changes to the master files.

Ethernet is faster, but is also more expensive to implement. It is possible to mix PCs and Macs on the same network. Sitka's TOPS (there is no official explanation of the acronym, except that it may have started life as "transparent operating

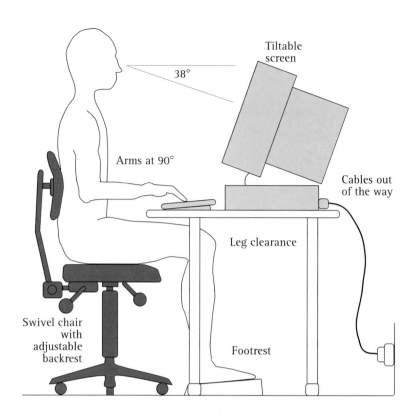

5.45 If you are to be working at the computer for long periods, it is vitally important to have the correct ergonomic conditions to reduce the possibility of computer-related health problems such as repetitive strain injury, backache, and eyestrain.

Tiltable screen

38°

Arms at 90°

Cables out of the way

Leg clearance

Swivel chair with adjustable backrest

Footrest

system") was developed by Sun, and is the oldest of the mixed environment networks.

A **modem** (the word is short for modulator/demodulator) is a device that allows you to send files down the telephone to the systems of your clients and typesetters. It is also possible to send and receive faxes direct from your hard disk (no paper is needed), and, of course, you can use a modem to connect to the Internet (see Chapter 7, p. 204).

Networking, though complicated, is not really difficult. It does, however, ultimately take you into a new league of computer management. While your studio may not want or be able to afford a systems manager, someone will have to take responsibility for the smooth operation of the system: developing filing systems, watching out for viruses, maintaining the shared resources, and so on.

Health and safety

As computers become commonplace, so must health and safety issues be taken seriously. It is rare indeed, for example, to find ergonomically adjustable desks and chairs in large organizations, so what chance does the smaller design studio have? But they cost little compared with the total investment in hardware and software, and can prevent lower-back damage to the most valuable component of the system – the designer. If that is not an incentive, then it should be noted that many of the recommendations are or will become legal requirements (Fig. **5.45**).

Desks should be as thin as possible and adjustable for height; chairs

should be grounded sturdily and give good lumbar (lower-back) support. When you sit on your chair, upper and lower legs should be at right angles and feet comfortably on the floor. A footrest may have to be provided, subject to sufficient leg clearance, if desk height is not adjustable. The display screen should, ideally, be tiltable to an optimum 38 degrees below the horizontal. The angle between your upper and lower arm, when typing, should be 90 degrees.

There is a body of knowledge existing on such hazards as WRULD (work-related upper-limb disorders) and RSI (repetitive strain injury) – a disorder of the hands and wrists causing numbness, swelling, tingling, and ultimately complete seizure. Keyboard operators have already suffered severe damage, and employers have already been sued for large sums, so do not wait until it is too late. Educate everyone to take frequent "thinking" breaks away from the system. To rest the eyes, a break of 15 minutes in every 75 minutes of continuous computer use is recommended.

Lighting should be diffuse and indirect. Fluorescent lights should have diffuser shades and should run parallel to the user's line of vision. Avoid glare and reflections, and excessively bright or dark color schemes. No user should have to face a window directly, and vertical blinds should be fitted, to be closed on sunny days. Regular eye tests are recommended. Because of the possibility of radiation, pregnant women should have the right to keep away from computers during pregnancy, without loss of pay or career prospects.

The health risk from static build-up and electromagnetic radiation from computers is an issue still hotly debated. Emissions from the front of a computer, i.e. through the screen, are in fact lower than from the sides or back. The computer screen should be at arm's length from your body – anyone sitting closer than 28 inches (711 mm) from the front is at some risk. Nobody should sit closer than 36 inches (914 mm) from the sides or back of a computer screen. Anti-glare screens do not help to cut down harmful radiation, unless they

specifically say that they do. Radiation from mono and grayscale screens is lower than from color ones, and larger screens do not seem to emit any more radiation than smaller ones.

Photocopiers and laser printers should be placed where the air is changed at least once an hour, at least $3\frac{1}{4}$ yards (3 m) away from the nearest person, and preferably in a separate, well-ventilated room to disperse the fumes produced by the toner. Noisy printers should also be fitted with hoods and be kept well away from the workers.

Finally, stress and anxiety can be reduced through appropriate and thorough training. This can be as simple as sitting down with the software manual for an hour or two each week to practice shortcuts, or spen-ding time looking over the shoulder of the "resident guru" at work. Or it can involve taking time off from your paying projects regularly, to attend more formal training courses.

SUMMARY

Computers are here to stay. You may not be able to purchase your own – yet. But you probably have access to a system at school or college, or in the design studio where you are working.

Of course, there will be designers and typographers who are reluctant to take the plunge, and there will always be a place for those who can conceptualize designs using just a pencil and paper. But they will miss out on the flexibility and control that a computer system can offer.

However, there is no such thing as a free lunch. There is a price to be paid for working on computers. The machinery will never be a panacea. It will never do the design work for you – in fact, it will probably make you work harder! You will have to do things that maybe before you left for the typesetter or printer to sort out. If you choose to go the computer route, the entire print production process will become your concern ... and your responsibility. The benefits are enormous, not only in cost savings, increased creativity, and improved quality, but also in job satisfaction and personal fulfillment.

Investing in computer technology is no longer a risky venture; there is a huge body of experience within the graphics design industry for you to draw upon.

P. SCOTT MAKELA

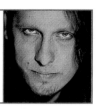

LIFE STORY Like many computer-literate designers, P. Scott Makela is a media hybrid: a graphic designer, typographer, product designer, video director, writer – and musician. His design work has appeared regularly in design and culture magazines, such as *Eye* (London), *Studio Voice* (Tokyo), *How*, *Semiotext(e)*, *Emigre* and *Ray Gun* (USA). He has written for journals such as *ID* (New York), *Industrieel Ontwerper* (Amsterdam), and the Walker Art Center's *Design Quarterly*.

Makela was born in 1961, a Minnesota farmboy, and as a teenager traveled the country playing with a "fervent Pentecostal rock band." After a mixture of art school and performing/recording post-punk music in Minneapolis, in 1984 Makela was inspired by April Greiman's new-wave typography to move to Los Angeles to practice graphic design. At the age of twenty-four, he was invited to teach at the California Institute of the Arts (CalArts) and Otis Art Institute, and in 1985 he opened a professional studio, Commbine. Makela claims to have been the first person in Minnesota to own a Mac.

In 1989, after four years at CalArts, Makela "went back to school" to the Cranbrook Academy of Art, where he combined "wirehead/hacker technologies and cyberpunk anti-hero philosophies" to establish the eclectic visual language of generated images, sound, and typography for which he is known. His 1990 poster, Cranbrook Design: The New Discourse, depicts a screaming orange human brain above a melting machinist's tool, combining the creative organic with the analytical inorganic – humanity meets technology.

After Cranbook, he moved back to Minneapolis where his wife Laurie Haycock was art director at the Walker Art Center, and set up a studio named, aptly and ironically, Words + Pictures for Business + Culture. He has contributed guest typography to Michael Jackson's Scream video for Sony, and designed two typefaces: Dead History, based on VAG Rounded and Centennial; and Carmela, named after his daughter – both in the Emigre catalog. In 1994, he was honored as one of the "ID Forty," in *ID* magazine's second annual selection of leading design innovators. In 1996 he returned to Cranbrook, along with Laurie Haycock, to run the design course.

Makela's studio is crammed with state-of-the-art technology plus software such as Photoshop, Illustrator, Fontographer, plus a whole suite of 3D programs. Video accounts for about a third of Makela's output, in effect funding the rest of his work. He's at ease working for both the screen and print: "cathode and wood," as he calls them. His trippy and liquid commercials with Los Angeles director Jeffery Plansker for the Canadian cable station UTV and Vans Shoes mix edgy surreal imagery and buzzing type with faux-naif camerawork and quickfire editing and have received many international awards.

> "My mantra is it must bleed on all four sides"

MANIFESTO **A Fragmented Message**
"Makela makes extravagantly ornamented paraphernalia for art schools, cable stations, and cultural institutions in a quasi-electro-futurist style that is increasingly making its way into mainstream media and design competitions, and passes for our avant-garde," said an article in *Eye* magazine.

Makela says of his work: "I'm trying to make it more like a dream or a hallucination. My mantra is it must bleed on all four sides." So type lies on top of type, pictures dissolve and radiate, mundane objects slide into and out of the frame. Metallic inks, drop shadows, and superbold type push the information to the surface. Says Michael Rock in *Eye*: "The typography floats above the images like bright leaves on an iridescent puddle of oil."

Clients seek him out whenever they require a zeitgeist of music, fashion, technology, and culture to be aimed at a global TV-savvy audience. Makela's 1991 prospectus design for the Minneapolis College of Art and Design delivered graphic muscularity and psychedelic images to prospective art students (after its release, enrolment went up by 26 percent) – but was also in demand from curious designers, film directors, and critics.

The Wild Next, cover of *How* magazine, 1994.

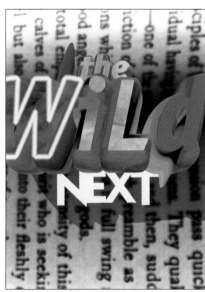

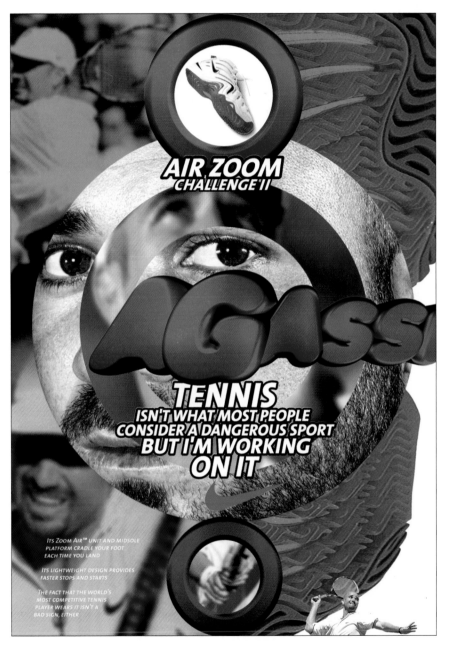

Poster advertising Nike tennis shoes, 1996–97, featuring Andre Agassi. Makela's distinctive design vision has here been softened in the service of corporate promotion, but the poster still captures the essence of his style. The superbold type, the use of overlapping shapes, bleeds, and acid colors are all pure Makela. In much of his earlier design work the language was more fractured and subjective and the individual elements represented – pieces of machinery, tools, blurry video scenes, fuzzy textures – were combined in a surreal way, to signify the idea of complexity itself. Here the dreamlike texture turns out, after all, to be the corrugated sole of a tennis shoe. (The project was co-designed with Laurie Makela.)

WORKSTATION
• Michael Rock, "P. Scott Makela is wired," in *Eye*, 12/94, pp. 26-35
• Web site <http://www.grfn.org/~makela/PSM_bio.html>

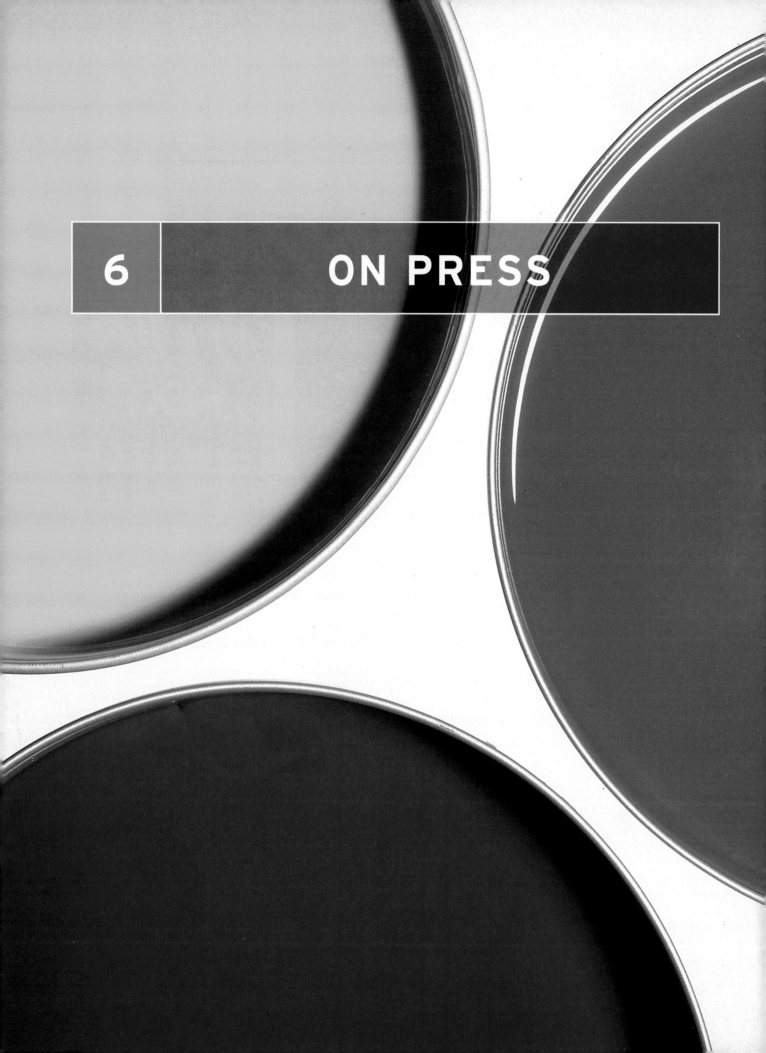

6 ON PRESS

The secret of a successful print job is a well-designed layout, some good scans for color repro, and the correct choice of paper and ink. Get all these right, and a good printing company can be relied upon to produce a pleasing result.

On press is the one part of the process that the graphic designer scarcely influences. It's now time to say goodbye to the layouts, leaving the printing work in the experienced hands of the printer.

Paper is one of the basic foundations of a good print job, but so often its choice is an afterthought. The first task in specifying paper is to think hard about what the finished item has to achieve. Then, after carefully considering the budget and availability of the stock, the designer can decide which particular characteristics of a paper are required.

Ink, too, plays a crucial role in the printing process, and the right formulation must be used for the right technology. Knowing about how inks perform will allow you to predict accurately how a job will come out. We discuss the effect of varnishing and laminating on an ink's performance, and explain the difference between die-stamping and thermography.

The printing process itself has a profound effect on print quality. The majority of designers will probably use offset litho for most applications, but in some circumstances, gravure can become a cost-effective possibility. And when should you use flexography, or even screen printing? What are the pros and cons? This chapter gives an insight into the process of choosing the right supplier, and suggests how to go about ensuring the best-quality job.

Finally, we come to finishing — all those operations of folding, gathering, stitching, and trimming that happen to a printed sheet after it leaves the press. What are the options? Is perfect binding better than saddle-stitching? This chapter explains.

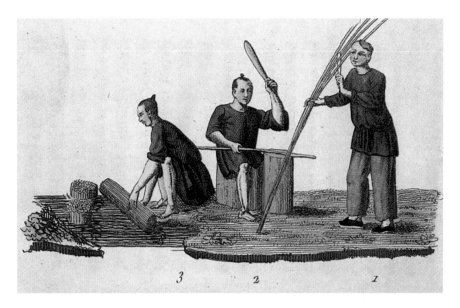

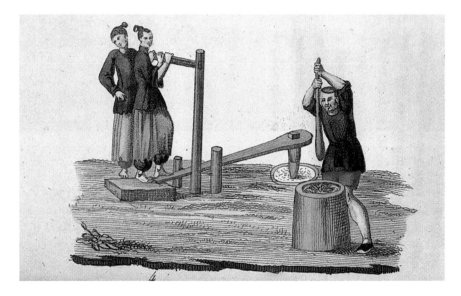

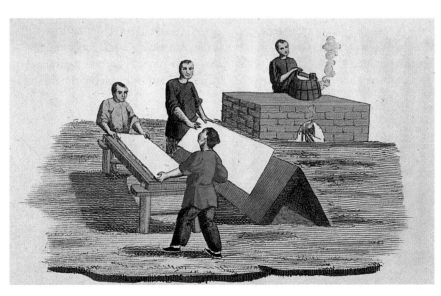

6.1 Papermaking in China, from a sequence of miniatures dating from 1811. Note that two people are required to make large sheets, a feat of coordination usually avoided by Western papermakers.

PAPER

Papermaking is older than any of the other printing crafts. Paper is largely a natural product – organic fibers held together by their own molecular forces. It is easy to make, but hard to make well. You can make it at home, with the help of a blender, some torn-up paper and other fibrous material (flowers, straw, cotton), and some kind of mesh to let the water drip through. Whether it will have the right degree of absorbency, strength, and surface finish required for fine printing is quite another matter.

The word "paper" comes from the Greek word "papyrus," the name of a plant that grows on the banks of the River Nile in Egypt. The writing material made from papyrus was not the kind of paper we are familiar with today. It was produced from strips peeled from the stem of the plant and pounded together into sheets.

The invention of paper made entirely from vegetable fibers – in this case tree bark, hemp, rags, and fishing nets – was announced to the Emperor of China in AD 105. However, a quasi-paper, made from pulped silk, was being made at least 200 years before that date.

Papermaking flourished in China (Fig. 6.1), but the techniques took a thousand years to reach Europe. The first documented paper mill was established in Spain, at Xativa, in around 1150. Mills were later set up in Italy, at Fabriano (a name still famous for the manufacture of beautiful paper) in around 1260, and in Hertfordshire, England, in around 1490. Papermaking was brought

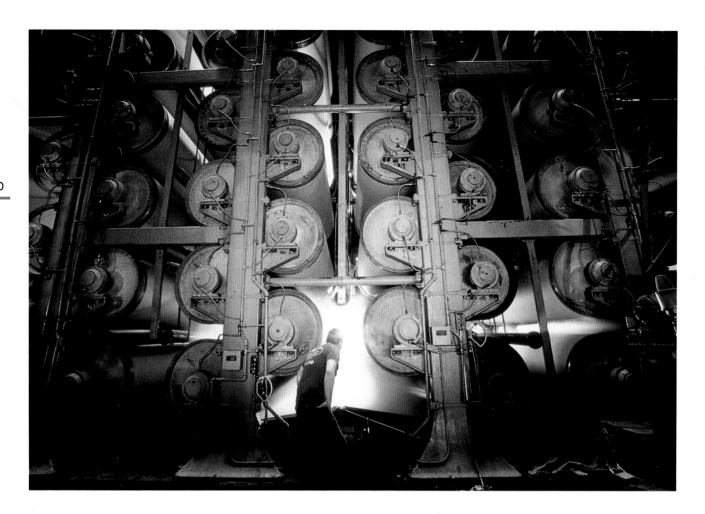

▲ **6.2** Papermaking is a continuous process, producing huge webs, or rolls, of paper. These are cut into sheets or made into smaller webs to feed the huge web litho, gravure, or flexo presses. Here, recycled paper is shown drying, in a mill in Minnesota.

to America by a German, William Rittenhouse. The first American papermill was established in Germantown, Pennsylvania, in 1690. Papermills couldn't be built just anywhere. The process depends on huge amounts of pure running water – 15,000 US gallons (120,000 UK gallons or about 500,000 liters) of water, for example, are required to manufacture just one ton (or metric tonne) of handmade paper.

Until the 19th century, all paper was made by hand. The first paper-making machine was invented by Nicholas-Louis Robert in 1798 and built in France. His patents were taken up by Henry and Sealy Fourdrinier, and further developed in England. The Fourdrinier process, as it is known, allowed paper to be made in a continuous operation, producing a web (Fig. **6.2**), or roll, at the end of what are still some of the largest machines in existence.

The raw materials

Paper is made from cellulose fibers, and these come from plants or trees. Cellulose is a chemical compound of the elements carbon, hydrogen, and oxygen, and constitutes the cell

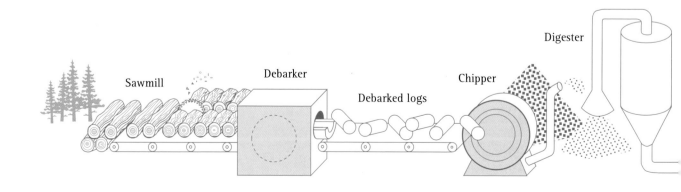

Sawmill   Debarker   Debarked logs   Chipper   Digester

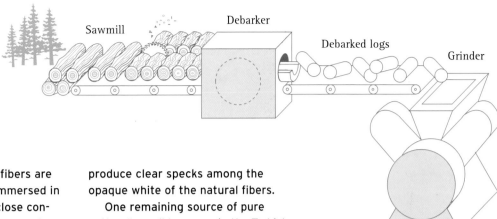

6.3 Mechanical woodpulp is made directly from logs. They are first debarked, then cut into smaller logs, and finally ground into fibers to be mixed with water and made into low-grade newsprint.

walls of plants. Cellulose fibers are tubular, and swell when immersed in water. Allowed to dry in close contact with one another, they create their own gelatin "adhesive." Along with the bonding from the fibrillation (splitting and fraying) of the fibers, this produces an extremely strong material. The resulting paper is naturally porous and will absorb the inks and dyes used in printing. And it can be made less porous by adding a substance called **size**. It is also inert enough not to be affected by inks or photographic chemicals. The fibers are colorless and transparent, yet produce paper that is white and opaque.

Early papermills made paper from rags. Textile production requires strong, long fibers for spinning and weaving. Papermaking is not so exacting, so papermills could recycle the shorter fibers from de-buttoned cast-off clothing and offcuts from shirt manufacturers, turning them into paper. Synthetic fibers such as nylon and rayon have put a stop to that. Artificial fibers (and animal fibers such as wool) are much more inert than cellulose. They do not bond as it does, and if they find their way into paper, they weaken it and

produce clear specks among the opaque white of the natural fibers.

One remaining source of pure cotton "rags," however, is the T-shirt industry, and its waste clippings are used to produce some of the finest papers. Another source of cotton for papermaking is from **linters**. These are the fibers left on the seed once the longer fibers for yarnmaking have been removed. The best linters come from the southern states of the USA, and from Egypt.

Clippings and linters are sorted, shredded, and placed in a large boiler. Under pressure and steam, any contaminants are removed. The fibers are washed and pulped. The dirty water is then drained off, clarified, and re-used. The pulp is bleached, and any chemicals left over are recycled into the next batch.

Chlorine bleaches, harmful to the environment, are gradually being replaced by **TCF (totally chlorine-free)** bleaches, such as hydrogen peroxide and **ECF (elemental chlorine-free)** bleaches, such as chlorine dioxide. Although ECF bleaches do not release hazardous dioxins into the waste stream, the resulting process water is often too corrosive to be recirculated. The pulp is then

felted into board-like sheets, for ease of transport to the papermill.

Most paper for general-purpose use is produced from wood. There are two kinds of **woodpulp**: mechanical and chemical. Mechanical, or groundwood, woodpulp is made by grinding logs under a stream of water, after first removing the bark (Fig. **6.3**). This results in the cheap but not very strong pulp used in **newsprint** and rougher grades of wrapping paper. It is the lignin left in mechanical pulp that makes the resulting paper turn brown and brittle in sunlight.

Chemical pulp relies on chemical agents such as calcium or sodium bisulfite to separate the wood fibers (Fig. **6.4**). This way they are damaged less than in mechanical

6.4 Chemical woodpulp is also debarked, but then the chips are cooked in chemicals to remove the lignin that makes newsprint brittle and turn brown. The pulp is reduced to fibers, washed, screened to remove knots and splinters, bleached, beaten, and mixed with various additives.

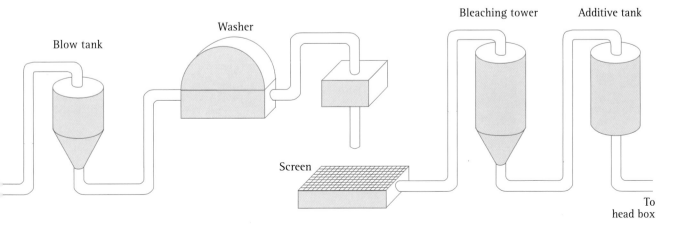

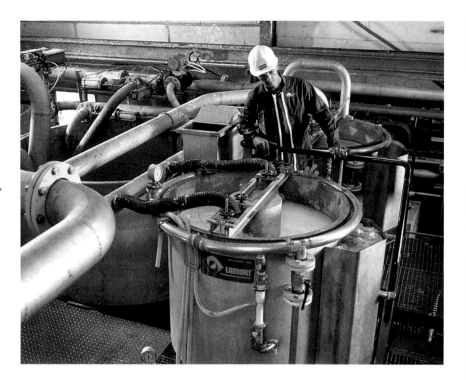

6.5 More and more paper is being produced from recycled material, but it is ironical that removing and disposing of the ink can produce an ecological cost of its own.

pulping, and thus paper from chemical pulp is of a higher quality. Oddly, chemical pulp is sometimes known as **woodfree**.

There are two sources of wood-pulp: from softwood (coniferous) and hardwood trees. When softwood is beaten, it loses opacity. Well-beaten softwood is thus used for hard trans-lucent papers, such as glassine (in the windows of envelopes, and also used to wrap after-dinner mints), greaseproof, and tracing papers. Hardwoods, such as eucalyptus, produce more opaque and bulky pulp than softwoods, and can be used to produce a wide range of different papers.

Cotton products and woodpulp are the most common raw materials for papermaking. Other plants are used for producing specialized papers. Esparto grass from North Africa and Spain is used in Europe for the body of the coated papers used in color work, and for good-quality writing papers. The fibers are small and flexible, and combine to form a paper with a closeness of texture and smoothness of surface. It also watermarks well. Straw is used for the rough board found in

book jackets, and in cigarette papers. Hemp has short fibers that bond well, and is used for papers that must be thin but strong – for Bibles and airmail paper.

Manilla fiber comes from the leaves of a plant that grows in the Philippines. It produces tough, almost untearable, paper mostly used for envelopes and wrapping papers. Other trees and plants that yield fibers for papermaking include corn (maize) stalks, bamboo, bagasse (from sugar cane), seaweed, citrus peel (a by-product of the food indus-try), and nettles.

Japanese papers are made from a wide range of plants, from the short-fibered *gampi*, which gives a thin, transparent paper with a fine smooth finish, to the longer-fibered and thus stronger *mitsumata*.

Recycled paper

All paper contains some recycled material, in the form of "broke," the waste from the papermaking process created within the papermill. This is returned to the refiner, beaten, and turned into more paper. So-called "post-consumer" waste has always

been used to manufacture board – the gray kind with specks of ink and sometimes whole letters visible.

Papermills specializing in recycled paper prefer good clean clippings from printers – all the trimmings, with no ink or other "pernicious contraries" present. That apart, the next best source is office or domes-tic paper. There is not very much demand for newsprint, which is low-grade stock to begin with. And what mills definitely do not want are fax paper, self-adhesive envelopes, and plastic-coated papers such as milk and fruit-juice cartons. Problems are also caused by foil-stamped papers, varnishes, and anything containing ultraviolet inks.

Material for recycling is first put through vibrating sieves and centrifuges, where metal objects such as staples and paperclips are removed. Next it is liquefied in a hydro-pulper, and washed to remove the fillers. The sludge then goes for de-inking (Fig. **6.5**). Steam and detergents are used to loosen the ink from the fibers. Air is blown through the sludge and the ink floc-culates (attaches to the bubbles) and floats to the surface, where it is scraped away.

The resulting pulp is mixed with a percentage of virgin stock and printers' waste and made into paper. Virgin pulp is added for strength, for the more times that fibers go through the process, the shorter they become. Recycled paper is never pure white. If the ink from previous usages has not been com-pletely removed but merely redis-tributed, then the paper will have a grayish tinge. This is something that

has to be allowed for in color printing. Good results can be achieved by reducing the black component in four-color work, but do not expect miracles. Recycled paper tends to have greater absorbency than conventional papers. This results in dot gain (see p. 191) and reduced sharpness, and it dries more quickly after printing. It is important that you discuss the use of recycled paper with your printer. Cylinder pressure may have to be adjusted, presses run slower, and different inks be used.

Off-whites and colored recycled paper can, however, have a subtlety of appearance and finish not found in conventional papers. One irony is that recycled papers are getting better all the time, and it is not always obvious to the purchaser that you are using them. Clients who want to demonstrate that they care about the environment by using recycled paper should print a statement to that effect somewhere on the publication.

Handmade paper

The tradition of handmade paper is still going strong (Fig. **6.6**). Handmade products are not only in demand from watercolor artists, but also from designers requiring exceptional strength and that slightly rough traditional finish, for limited edition books, prestigious corporate brochures, and stationery. Decorative papers incorporating plant fibers from linen, onion skins, and vine leaves are used for endpapers and book covers.

Handmade paper is always made from the finest ingredients. After all,

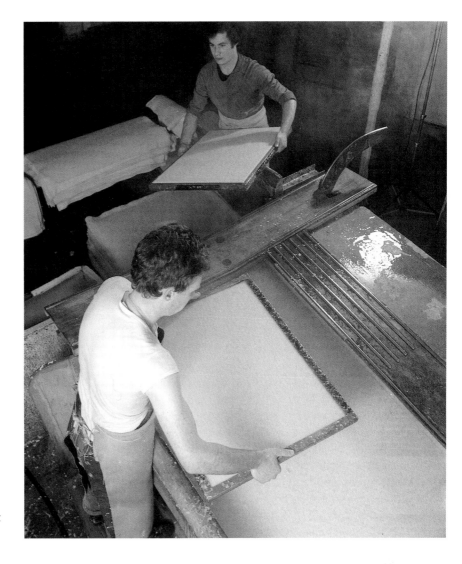

producing it is an expensive process, and so it makes no commercial sense to use inferior raw materials. Each sheet is slightly different, and therein lies its charm. Its extra strength comes from the process of manufacture, which requires a "vatman" to shake, or joggle, the mold to the left and to the right – an operation that the machine has been unable to imitate. This gives the paper strength in all directions, and no "grain."

One of the most obvious characteristics of handmade paper is its four **deckle** edges. The deckle, another word for the mold, is the name also given to the uneven tapering-off edge of the sheet seen sometimes on untrimmed books of poetry.

6.6 Paper is still being made by hand today. Handmade paper is particularly strong and durable. Here the "vatman" is scooping the pulp from the wooden vat to form a sheet of paper in the sieve-like mold at Hayle Mill in Maidstone, England. It takes a minute's rest to change from pulp to paper, it is said, but 30 years to get it right.

The size of a sheet is limited to the size a person can hold, the maximum being Antiquarian at 31 x 53 inches (787 x 1346 mm). Larger sheets would need two people.

Handmade paper is available in three finishes: HP (hot pressed), NOT (not hot pressed), and rough.

So-called **mold-made paper** uses a more automated procedure, producing the look and feel of handmade paper in a more consistent and reliable product.

Head box — Slice — Fourdrinier wire — Dandy roll — Press section — Pre-dryers — Size press — After-dryers — Calender stack — Jumbo reel or web

Machine-made paper

Most printing papers are produced on Fourdrinier machines (Figs **6.7** and **6.8**). This is a continuous process: pulp goes in at one end, and rolls of paper come out at the other. Fibers, whether from cotton linters or woodpulp, are bought by the papermill in the form of sheets. At this stage they have already undergone a kind of pre-papermaking felting process for ease of handling. These sheets are blended with lots of water for ten minutes or so to form a **slurry**. This is pumped into storage towers and then through conical refiners containing rotating bars. The amount of beating in these refiners determines the length of the fiber and the extent to which individual fibers are fibrillated. This in turn determines the kind of paper that will be manufactured: from highly beaten glassine and tracing paper to soft, bulky blotting paper that receives hardly any beating at all.

From the refiners, the pulp is moved to storage chests, and from there, via a large pump, through an internal sizing process. Next, it is put on to a moving conveyor belt made from a mesh, where the transformation takes place from creamy pulp to solid white paper.

A process called sizing controls the absorbency of the resulting paper, and is responsible for keeping the ink on the surface and preventing **feathering**. Internal sizing does this without blocking the pores or altering the porosity of the fibers. An acidic mixture of rosin (synthetic resin) and alum was traditionally used. More recently it has been replaced by synthetic sizes such as alkyl ketene dimer, which has a neutral pH (i.e. it is neither acidic nor alkaline). The paper may later be surface-sized with starch.

Other additives such as colored dyes are also introduced at this stage. Mineral **fillers**, or loading agents, such as china clay, increase the opacity of the paper and make its surface smooth. Printing papers commonly contain up to 30 percent of fillers.

As the pulp goes through the large pump, it comprises 99 percent water and 1 percent fibers. This is called the **furnish**. From a head box at the start proper of the paper-making machine, the furnish is released on to the wire mesh of

6.7 Fourdrinier machines convert pulp to paper. The first stage is the Fourdrinier wire — a conveyor belt of wire mesh that forms the paper and gives it texture. The rest of the machine is dedicated to drying and smoothing the paper.

the Fourdrinier. The rate of release and the speed the wire is traveling dictate the resulting weight of the paper. The slower the wire and greater the amount of furnish, the heavier the paper will be.

After forming on the wire, the paper is still around 70 percent water. Water drains through the mesh, and the screen is vibrated from side to side. The fibers thus tend to align in one direction, along the length of the roll, and this gives machine-made paper its characteristic **grain**. The pattern of the wire mesh give the paper its texture. **Laid** papers have a pattern of mainly horizontal or vertical stripes. **Wove** papers are created with a woven mesh.

6.8 Papermaking machines are among the biggest production machinery in existence — some are over a mile long. This No. 4 machine at James River Fine Papers at St Andrews in Scotland has since been modernized and largely enclosed to conserve heat.

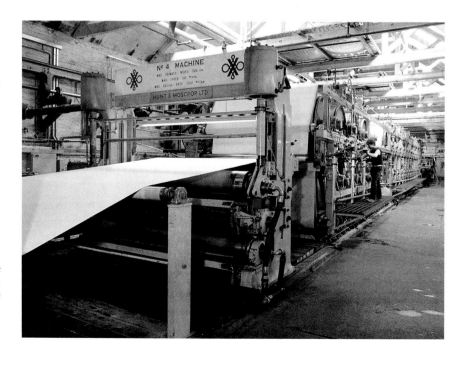

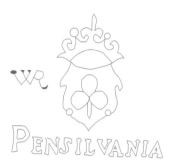

6.9 The watermark of William Rittenhouse, the first American paper-maker, and the fool's cap that gave foolscap writing paper its name. Some watermarks are quite complex; most are very simple.

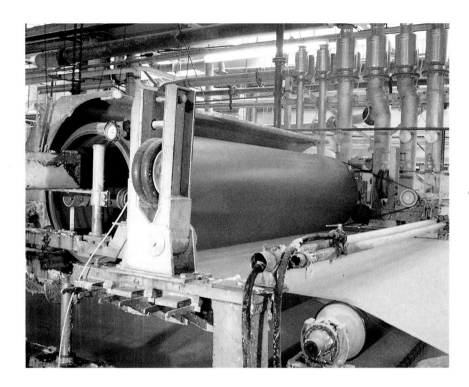

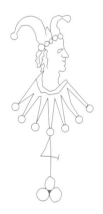

Paper is formed as it lies horizontally on top of the wire. To create texture on the top of the sheet, a hollow dandy roll is located above the wire. This device presses a pattern on to the top surface of the paper corresponding to the pattern on the wire.

A **watermark** is created by placing a raised symbol, fashioned in wire, on the dandy roll (Fig. **6.10**). In handmade paper production, it forms part of the mold. The watermark is thinner and thus more transparent than the rest of the sheet. For large print runs, it may be possible to have your own watermark incorporated into specially ordered paper stock. It can be an attractive design element in its own right (Fig. **6.9**), especially if it falls in the margins of a printed

publication. But it can interfere with the printing, for example, by weakening a solid area of ink.

From the Fourdrinier wire onward, most of the immense length of a papermaking machine is concerned with drying the damp paper. First, it passes through a series of presses that squeeze out most of the water. These presses can also be used to impart surface texture, and the amount of smoothing affects the final bulk (though not the weight) of the stock.

The paper can then be surface coated or sized with starch, and carried on a felt belt between staggered rows of huge steam-heated cylinders. It must not get too dry, however. After leaving this section, it will still contain 2 to 8 percent of water, necessary to ensure a paper stock with good printing and folding characteristics, and the ability to **cure** in balance with the relative humidity at the printers.

Once dry, the paper is pressed in a vertical row of polished steel calender rolls, or nips. This operation, called **calendering**, increases the smoothness and degree of gloss. The more calenders, the higher the gloss.

6.10 The dandy roll of a paper machine in the mill of James River Fine Papers at St Andrews.

The distance from headbox to calenders can be a mile or more. But the elapsed time of a fiber traveling that distance could be as little as two minutes. From the calender stack, the paper is wound into large rolls called webs. These are slit and rewound into more manageable smaller rolls for shipping. If the papermill has the capacity, they may be cut into sheets. Some papers may also require off-machine finishing such as **supercalendering** (polishing), **coating**, or embossing.

Cover paper, or board, is made in much the same way as book paper. The furnish contains more recycled material, and is beaten less, to ensure efficient drainage on the wire. Board can be single-ply, or multi-ply. Multi-ply board comprises a top liner, under liner, middle, and back liner. Generally, the liners are given conventional amounts of beating to develop strength. The middle stock, which is there as padding, is given very little. The plies may be combined on the machine or off it.

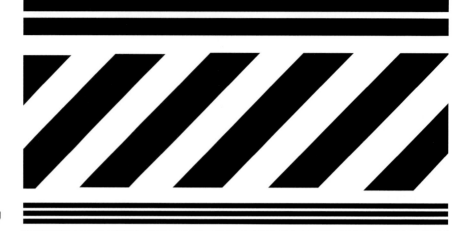

The characteristics of paper and board

By altering the furnish, and making adjustments to the papermaking machinery, mills are able to produce papers exhibiting very different characteristics. Which kind of paper you choose for a particular job will be determined mostly by the printing process. Offset litho presses require papers that are hard sized, whereas gravure presses need fast ink penetration, and hence "slack" sized paper. If you are dealing with high-quality halftones, you will need a smooth coated paper to do them justice. Economics, too, play a part. Newspapers are cheap and ephemeral, so mechanical woodpulp is a cost-effective choice. Legal documents have to last, so a good-quality rag paper is appropriate.

Paper is specified by its characteristics, and the main ones are weight, bulk, opacity, color, and finish. In the USA, the weight (also called basis weight, poundage, or substance) is measured in pounds per ream of paper cut to its basic size. A **ream** is 500 sheets. The basic size is 25 x 38 in for book papers, 24 x 36 in for newsprint, and 20 x 26 in for cover boards. To avoid misunderstandings, a 60 lb book paper is written 25 x 38 – 60 (500). In the rest of the world, the weight is measured in grams per square meter (g/m², gsm, or grammage). To convert lbs to g/m², multiply by 1·5 (the exact factor is 1·48), and to convert g/m² to lbs, multiply by two-thirds (or, more exactly, by 0·6757).

Another common measurement is the **M weight**, which is the weight of 1000 sheets. To convert poundage to M weight is simple: just double the poundage figure.

The **bulk**, or **caliper**, of the paper is its thickness. Rough papers tend to be thicker than smooth papers of the same weight. Thickness is measured by a bulking number – the number of sheets to the inch, under test conditions. The ppi (pages per inch) is twice the bulking number (because there are two pages to the sheet). Another way to describe bulk is to measure four sheets of paper with an instrument called a **micrometer**. This "four-sheet caliper" is expressed in thousandths of an inch, which are commonly referred to as **mils** or points. In both continental Europe and the UK, thickness is measured in micrometers and bulk in cm³/g.

Opacity is one characteristic not complicated by the metric system. It is the property of a paper affecting the **show-through** of printing from the other side of the sheet. Opacity is obviously influenced by both weight and bulk – the heavier and thicker a paper is, the more fibers there are blocking the passage of light. But it is also a function of the fillers added to the paper.

Visual opacity – the opacity of the unprinted sheet – is measured using an instrument called an **opacimeter**, and is expressed as a percentage. A sheet with 100 percent opacity is completely lightproof. A general idea of visual opacity can be gained by placing a printed opacity gauge under the sheet (Fig. **6.11**).

Printed opacity depends partly on how absorbent the paper is (the more absorbent, the more **strike-through** of ink), and on the paper's ink **holdout** (its capacity to keep ink on the surface). This is a difficult parameter to measure, and the subjective terms high, medium, or low strike-through are used.

The color of a paper is determined by dyes added during the papermaking process, or by coatings added afterward. Color can be affected by the raw materials used. Recycled papers are always grayer than those made from virgin pulp, but this and the speckled appearance can be used as design elements in their own right. Paper also comes in several grades of whiteness, produced by adding **optical brighteners** and other chemicals. The color of paper stock always affects the color

TOP DOTS ON UNCOATED STOCK

High-quality jobs can be successfully printed on uncoated paper stock – if you compensate for dot gain and choose the correct screen ruling. Ink dries partially by absorption, so the dots will spread. As they expand and merge, detail is lost in the shadow areas and the whole image flattens. Dot gain is especially critical in the case of textured papers and on darker or warmer-toned papers and dot-gain compensation might range from 2 to 3 percent in the highlights, to 7 to 10 percent in shadows to "open up" the dots on film. Waterless plates require less dot-gain compensation because the ink dot sits on the surface rather than being absorbed. The type of stock also dictates the screen ruling. Well-formed, ultrasmooth stock can take screens from 200 to 300 lpi; smooth vellum or wove 150-175 lpi; lightly textured stock, such as laid and antique, 120-135 lpi; while for heavily textured, open-fibered, and embossed stock, stick to 110-135 lpi.

of the ink printed on it, determining the lightest highlight in any halftone. You cannot have a highlight that is whiter than the paper, nor a shadow deeper than the color of the ink.

The finish of a paper is a description of its surface. Its texture first takes shape on the wire and under the dandy roll. As previously mentioned, wove and laid papers receive their characteristic texture here. Uncoated papers receive their smoothness in the calender stack. Coated papers are more likely to be calendered or super-calendered off the machine. Distinctive finishes such as ripple and stucco are created by embossing the paper.

For book papers, the roughest finish is called **antique**. This is an uncoated paper with high bulk. A smoother, pressed version is **eggshell**. **Machine finish (MF) paper** has been calendered and is smoother and less bulky than eggshell. **Machine glazed (MG) paper** has been dried against a highly polished

cylinder and has one glossy side with the other remaining relatively rough. It is an example of **duplex stock** – paper with a different finish or color on either side.

Coating covers the paper fibers with clay. Super-calendering coated paper gives it a highly glossy appearance. Coating produces a paper with excellent ink holdout, which is ideal for color reproduction. Thus coated papers are often called art papers.

The coating can be applied by rollers on the machine (film coating, or machine coating), or by rollers or blades off the machine (conversion coating). Conversion coated papers generally have a thicker coating and are of a higher quality. Blade coating produces a **matte** (dull) surface. Gloss is produced by calendering and super-calendering papers after they have been coated. The highest possible gloss is called **cast coated**: the wet coated web is dried in contact with a highly polished chromium drum. **Chromo paper** is polished on one side only.

Other important characteristics include strength and wet strength, dimensional stability (the ability to stay the same size), rigidity, and **picking** resistance (a binder is used in coatings to prevent fibers from lifting on the press).

And bear in mind that all machine-made papers have grain. Paper folds more easily with than **against the grain**, and ideally books should be designed so that the printed sheets have the grain parallel to the binding (Fig. **6.12**).

Stock can be ordered grain long, with the grain running lengthwise, or grain short, with the grain running

across the width of the sheet. Grain-long paper stretches less, so gives better color registration with web offset. Grain-short paper is better for fast print runs, because it bends easily around the press rollers and speeds up the printing process.

You can determine the direction of the grain by tearing a piece of paper – it will tear straighter along the grain than against it. Here are two other methods: run one edge of the sheet between the thumb and finger, through the fingernails. If it crinkles into a wavy pattern; that's the edge across the grain (Fig. **6.13**). Or mark a swatch and dampen it. It will curl in the direction of the grain. On paper specifications, machine direction is indicated by the symbol (m). Thus 25 x 38(m) is grain long, and 25(m) x 38 is grain short.

▼ **6.12** All machine-made paper has grain, caused by the orientation of the drying fibers. It is important to know the direction of grain, so that it can run parallel to any folds in your publication.

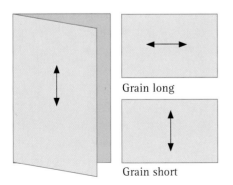

Grain long

Grain short

▼ **6.13** You can test for grain either by tearing a sheet of paper – it will tear more cleanly in the direction of the grain – or by running an edge between your finger and thumb – if it crinkles, then that's the edge across the grain.

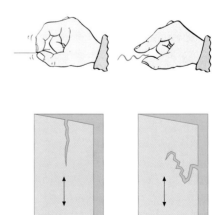

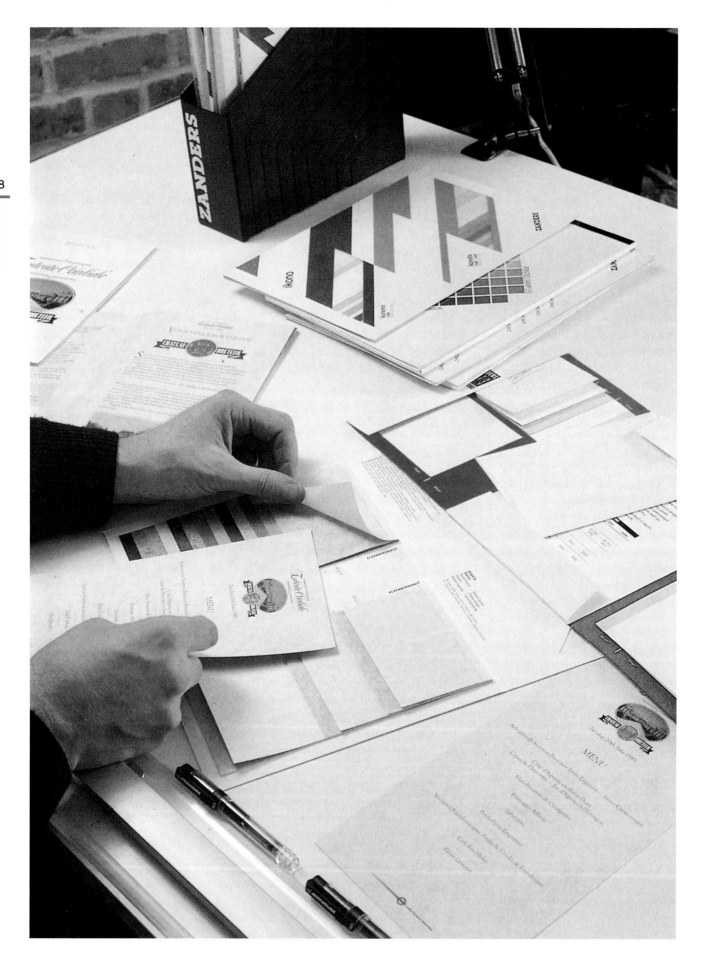

6.14 Every designer should aim to collect "designer packs" of paper samples at every opportunity. Try, too, to collect printed samples.

Choosing the right paper stock

There is ever a rich but bewildering range of papers available, and you should begin to collect samples, along with technical specifications on the characteristics described above. You can buy paper direct from the mill, or from a paper merchant. Paper merchants stock a wider variety of papers, obtained from many mills, both at home and abroad. Some merchants specialize in particular kinds of paper. Most mills and merchants will supply you with a designer's pack of samples (Fig. **6.14**). Collect printed samples of paper, too, and always choose a paper in consultation with the person who is going to have to print on it.

As mentioned earlier, for some jobs the printing process itself will narrow down your choice – you would never dream of putting blotting paper through a litho press, for example. Price, too, will be a limiting factor. Handmade paper must be reserved for the most prestigious jobs. And it is possible to over-specify paper. There is little point, for example, in specifying a high-gloss stock if it is to be laminated or varnished later.

Sheet-fed offset litho machines require papers with good surface strength and dimensional stability; web offset paper must also have a low moisture content. Surface finish is not such an issue, as modern offset presses can make a good impression on a wide range of surfaces. Offset ink is tacky, however,

and the paper should be well sized to prevent "picking" – the pulling out of surface fibers.

The prerequisites for letterpress printing are smoothness, absorbency, opacity, and compressibility. Paper has to be smooth enough to accept a uniform transfer of ink, and strong enough to take the pressure of the sharp edges of metal type without tearing.

The most important characteristic for gravure is smoothness. However, the paper must not contain any abrasive material on its surface – as matte coated stock does. It must also be absorbent enough to draw the ink out from the cells below the smooth surface of the cylinder.

And the silkscreen process demands that papers be not too absorbent.

The trick is to find the stock that matches the brief for the job – a paper just opaque enough to prevent strike-through, but not too heavy (remember the mailing bill), and with a finish appropriate to the design content. Antique may be fine for type and line illustrations, but for good halftone reproduction you will need a coated stock. Glossy is best for color reproduction, but its shine can interfere with readability in the type sections.

Glossy art paper can sometimes feel thinner than the same weight of matte-coated stock, so you may need to increase the weight when going for glossy. Increasing the weight of the stock on some jobs – on a small print run of small-scale booklets, for example – can be a

relatively inexpensive way of improving the overall quality of the print.

It is also important to think hard about what other rigors your paper will have to withstand. There may be a reply coupon on your booklet. If so, is it possible to write on the stock in ballpoint or felt-tip pen without it skipping or smudging? And will that exquisite set of corporate stationery accept additional text from a photocopier or laser printer? A print job may leave your studio looking good, but it also has to perform well in real-life conditions.

Odd-shaped booklets and posters can seem like a good idea at the time. But they can be wasteful on paper, so find out the sizes of stock that the printer can handle, and have a sheet in front of you when you are calculating the size and shape of your layout (see Appendix A, p. 221). Remember, however, that if the sheet is too large, this can affect the quality of color reproduction. And instead of requesting a paper by brand name, try asking printers what they have available – you may get a good deal. But beware – if you need reruns in the future, you may not be able to obtain that stock again.

Paper can represent a large proportion of the cost of any printed job, but, in the words of British typographer Ruari McLean, "can be a relatively inexpensive luxury, when luxuries – so often illegal, immoral, or fattening – are also harder and harder to obtain." Paper can give pleasure, and should always be chosen with a great deal of care.

INKS

Printing inks are completely different from the inks used for drawing and writing. They are generally thick and sticky – similar to the consistency of paint.

The various printing processes make very different demands of the characteristics of the ink: its formulation, viscosity (degree of runniness), tackiness, and rate of drying. Of course, a printer running an offset litho machine will buy ink specially formulated for offset litho (Fig. **6.15**). What a designer has to know, however, is that not all offset litho inks are the same, nor do they act in the same way. Even the standard process colors can vary subtly from manufacturer to manufacturer, and from different countries of origin. Until the discovery of phthalocyanine blue in the 1950s, process colors could be very variable indeed.

Formulation

So what are printers' inks made of? All inks are made from three basic constituents: pigments and dyes, a vehicle (or binding substance), and some additives. The **pigments and dyes** give an ink its color. Like the pigments in paint, they come from a wide range of natural and synthetic sources, some organic and some inorganic. Pigments are usually dry and powdery, and have to be ground finely. Dyes are liquid and have to be "coated" (attached to solid particles) before they can be mixed with the other ingredients. Black ink is made from carbon-black, manufactured by burning mineral oil in a restricted air supply.

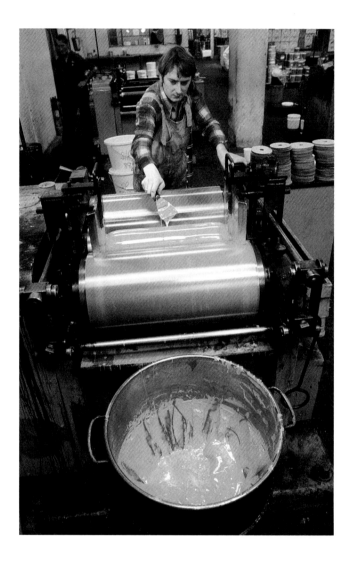

6.15 Inks for offset litho are generally manufactured on three-roll mills.

Colored pigments come from so many different sources and have such individual characteristics that there has to be a great deal of adjustment to the vehicle and additives in order to make them behave with any kind of consistency. Different colored inks behave differently on the press, and dry at different rates. And because of the scarcity of certain pigments, there are variations in price between different colors. Metallic inks, in

particular, are expensive. The choice of inks has been made simpler, however, by the adoption of the four process colors for full-color work, and by Pantone's standardization of 11 basic colors, from which over 1000 flat colors can be mixed to formula (see p. 84).

The **vehicle** is the carrier that binds the dry, powdery pigment together. It can be an oil, a natural resin, or an alkyd (a synthetic resin). The type of vehicle is determined by

6.16 The slip resistance of many forms of printed packaging is important.

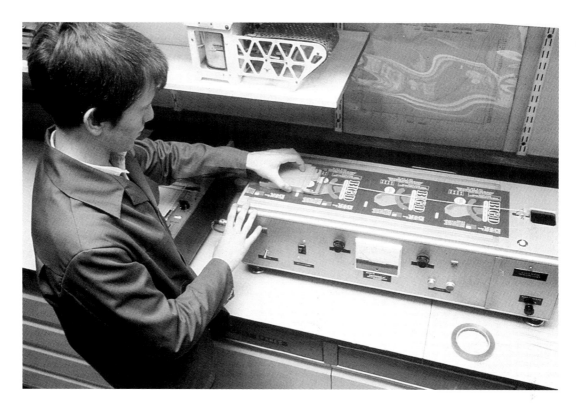

the process. Litho and letterpress inks are oil-based. Screenprint, gravure, and flexographic inks are resin-based and are thinned with a highly volatile solvent, such as alcohol. Non-tainting formulations have to be specified for food packaging.

Very few printing inks are water-based, though a water-based ink would be welcomed by those caring about the environment. Litho could never use a water-based ink, because the process is based on the fact that oil and water do not mix. But water-based inks have been used, for example, for printing candy wrappers by gravure and in newspaper printing by flexography.

As well as the pigment and vehicle, printing inks contain various additives – mainly driers, but also a selection of anti-oxidants (added to

stop the ink from drying in the machine), fillers, and other agents that give the ink particular properties such as slip-resistance (Fig. **6.16**). Printers sometimes mix in further additives to meet the requirements of a specific job.

Different driers are used depending on the process, the material the job is being printed on, and the intended end use. They are metallic salts or compounds of cobalt and manganese, and speed the rate of drying chemically. Paradoxically, too much drier can slow down the rate of drying. And too much drier on the litho press will mix with the watery fountain solution and cause pigment particles to be deposited on the non-image portions of the plate.

Most inks dry by a process called oxidation. The drying oil of the vehi-

cle absorbs oxygen from the air, causing cross-polymerization (linking) within its molecular structure. This makes the ink gel, and then harden. Quick-drying inks and varnishes are "cured" by exposure to ultraviolet light, producing a hard and scuff-resistant film.

The quality of the paper has a marked effect on the ink's drying time. The vehicle soaks quickly into newsprint, leaving the pigment on the surface. That is why ink from most newspapers leaves your fingers (and clothes) dirty. But vegetable oils are now being used to replace the mineral oils, for improved rub resistance, as well as better brightness and sharper dots.

For the higher-quality coated stock used for magazines printed by web offset, the ink is dried in high-

temperature ovens and then chilled. The sheets are folded straight away, so the ink has to be dried quickly. Naturally, it has to be able to cope with this rough treatment, and a special solvent-based formulation called **heat-set ink** is used.

Other additives include extenders, which increase the coverage of the pigment and improve ink transfer from press to paper; distillates, which improve the flow characteristics of the ink; and waxes, which improve the slip and scuff resistance of inks employed in packaging. Inks with added wax cannot subsequently be varnished.

Viscosity and tackiness

The most important characteristic of an ink is its **viscosity** – how runny it is. This property is measured using an instrument called an **inkometer**, or tackoscope.

Litho inks have to be relatively viscous, with high **tack** (stickiness). They must also have a high concentration of pigment. The nature of the process demands the thinnest possible ink film of the strongest possible color. The amount of ink arriving at the paper during the offset litho process is half that of the more direct processes of letterpress and gravure. Litho inks are relatively transparent: yellow printed over blue will produce a recognizable green. They also have to perform well while being almost constantly "contaminated" with the water that coats the litho plate.

Letterpress inks are similar to litho inks, but contain a smaller proportion of pigments. They generally have a higher viscosity, but

lower tack. Because there is no water used in the process, the chemistry of letterpress ink can be far less complex.

Inks for gravure and flexography are much more fluid that litho and letterpress inks. Gravure inks are thinned down with additional solvent before printing begins, and deposit a similar amount of pigment on to paper as letterpress. Flexographic ink is the thinnest of all, and has to be formulated not to attack the rubber rollers used in the process.

Silkscreen inks are semi-liquid with good flow characteristics. They have to get through the holes of the screen, but not be so fluid as to spread into the non-image areas. These inks, too, have to be thinned before printing to arrive at the correct viscosity.

Specifying inks

Some inks react unpredictably with other finishes. Colored inks for **wet-on-wet** printing on a multicolor press, for example, must be "tack graded" to arrive at an ink film of full density. Some colors will **mottle**, or change shade, when varnished. Purples and reflex blue are particularly susceptible. Colors print differently on different substrates: inks on art paper will appear stronger and brighter than on recycled paper (Fig. **6.17**), and different again on plastic.

Colors appear different under different lighting conditions. Printers view colors under standard lighting conditions, an area surrounded by neutral gray and illuminated by a light source with a color temperature

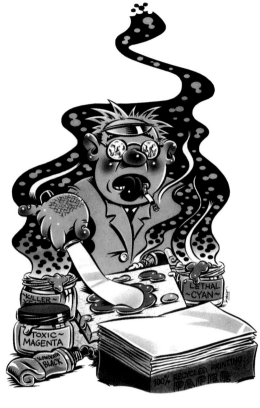

6.17 Recycled papers are more absorbent and less white than conventional stock, and printing on them can result in colors lacking in brilliance and saturation – hence the need for different ink formulations, which may themselves be helping to destroy the environment. Calculating the ecological cost of a print job is a complex process. (Cartoon by Phil Dobson.)

of 5000 Kelvin. If you are designing packaging destined for supermarkets, for example, standard conditions will give a false reading. Supermarkets use different colored lighting to seduce people into buying more things, and to make food look more succulent. The colors in the packaging must compensate for these effects – it is essential to view your designs under the lighting conditions for which they are being designed.

Lightfast inks should be specified if the job is to be exposed to sunlight. Magenta and yellow tend to fade faster than black and cyan (look at the covers of paperbacks in the windows of secondhand bookstores). Inks prone to fading are called **fugitive** inks. Silkscreen inks are more light-fast than the others.

Fluorescent and **metallic inks** often need to be underprinted to achieve a satisfactory result, just as black is often underprinted with a percentage of cyan to increase its density. Fluorescent dyes can be

CHOOSING A PRINTER
Are you printing a rough and ready circular, a company's stationery or a glossy lifestyle catalog? The type of job determines which of your regular printers to use. Jobbing printers have small-format machines able to print one or two colors in one pass. They will most likely use plastic plates and close registration can be a problem. They will happily print newsletters, letterheads and disposable pamphlets, but for more demanding jobs, they will have to send out for metal plates, and the price will rise. Better to use a mid-range printer with a press that can handle bigger plates and more colors — you might actually save money. Stick to standard paper and inks, the kind they always have in stock. For jobs where color matching and premium paper stock is really important, you will need to find a printer specializing in four-color or even hi-fi color work.

added to the process colors to improve the quality of reproduction of illustrations, particularly vibrant watercolors. "Metallic integrated process printing" is a term coined by Pantone to describe a method for adding percentages of gold and silver inks to the process colors. This results in an expensive six-color process, that is printed in the sequence silver, yellow, gold, followed by the remaining process colors. Since normal photography cannot record a metallic finish, the designer or repro house has to estimate the amounts to use, based on charts supplied by Pantone. (Gold and silver can also be applied by blocking and hot-foil stamping; see p. 193.)

Other specialty inks include the magnetic inks used on bank checks and business forms, microencapsulated or "scratch and sniff" inks that add a fragrance to printed work (but be aware of an allergic reaction by some innocent end user), invisible ink for children's books and fraud-resistant lottery tickets, and moisture-resistant inks for packaging applications. Varnishes are a kind of colorless ink used to add gloss to halftones, particularly in prestigious publications such as annual reports. They are also used to add ultraviolet protection to color work that will be exposed to sunlight. If you intend to **spot varnish** photographs or illustrations, you may need to provide artwork or keylines on the mechanical to indicate the areas to be covered. Be sure to discuss any special requirements in the design brief with your printer, and together you will be able to find the correct ink for the application.

SELECTING YOUR SUPPLIER

You may not be able to look over the shoulder of your printer as your design is being printed. But you can make sure that you have chosen the right supplier for the job, and that the printer is in no doubt as to your requirements. There are three main considerations: quality, cost, and the schedule. If you are running to tight deadlines, you may have to pay more. Similarly, quality means more care, and that too can cost money. This is not to say that you cannot produce beautiful printing on a small budget — there are plenty of examples of imaginative design that have used cost constraints to great advantage.

You can play your part by submitting clean, uncomplicated mechanicals and clear, unambiguous instructions, and by avoiding any superfluous processes that are going to add labor costs to your bill — unless you decide that a special shape or finish is absolutely necessary.

How do you select the supplier appropriate to the job in hand? First, clearly you should not think of asking a small jobbing printer to undertake a complicated color job for a prestigious client. Nor should you ask a fine-art printer to bid for a short-run black-and-white newsletter. There are horses for courses. Second, do not be afraid to ask around for personal recommendations from colleagues. Look for the name of the printer on the examples of printing jobs you have collected. If their credit line is not there, ask their client. Then obtain some competitive bids.

For small jobs, find printers somewhere nearby. If they consistently do good work, stick with them, and build up a friendly relationship. Ask them to bid for jobs, but don't make it too formal a process. They may be able to help you out of a jam one day.

For large-scale jobs, provide each prospective supplier with a clear specification of the job in writing, outlining the size, **print run**, and finish you want. Insist that their prices are to a format that you specify, so that you can compare like with like. Tell them that if they do not follow the rules, their bid will not even be considered. Listen to them, however, and give as much information as they need to make a sensible bid — you may end up working with them, after all. Listen to any suggestions they may have to reduce costs, and adapt your specification if you can. Ask what possible economies can be made, by adjusting the schedule, the imposition scheme, or the paper stock. Visit the print works if possible, to familiarize yourself with the company's equipment and its capabilities. Examine samples of work that have been done on stock similar to your job.

Indicate whether you or the prospective printer will supply color separations and film, and list the finishing operations you will require. Ask if the printer has these facilities in-house or will have to send out to sub-contractors. If the latter is the case, you may do better to negotiate finishing separately. Likewise, ascertain whose responsibility it will be to buy in the paper stock.

Show a detailed dummy to each company, and take no chances that they may misinterpret any aspect of the job. Decide also if you need a

simple bottom-line figure for the whole job, or whether you need a breakdown into ink, paper, plate-making, proofing, prepress, printing, mailing, and shipping.

When you have all the bids, make a decision, and inform everyone who has quoted. You may wish to negotiate a better price, but do not try to act the bigshot by playing one supplier off against another – you may wish to use several of them at a later date. But you may want to promise bigger jobs in future, conditional on this crucial one.

You must now draw up a contract. If the deal is done on the nod or handshake, the terms of a job in the USA will automatically revert to the Printing Trade Customs, originally drawn up in 1922 by the United Typothetae of America, and amended in 1994 by a consortium of US printing bodies (see p. 223). In the UK it will be governed by the Standard Conditions of Contract for Printers, published by the British Printing Industries Federation; there are other more specialist documents, for example the Customs of the Trade for the Manufacture of Books (see p. 224). Other countries have similar codes of conduct. It is as well to be familiar with them – ignorance is no defense.

The Printing Trade Customs formally set out the business relationship between the printer and the client. They state, for example, that quotations not accepted within 60 days are subject to review; that negatives, positives, flats, plates, and other items, when supplied by the printer, remain the printer's exclusive property unless otherwise agreed in writing; that a "reasonable variation" in color between color proofs and the completed job shall constitute acceptable delivery; and that "overruns and underruns not to exceed ten percent on quantities ordered, or the percentage agreed on, shall constitute acceptable delivery."

Any contract made between you and your printer will have legal standing, but if any of the terms contained in the Printing Trade Customs are to be adapted, they must be spelt out precisely, in writing. An underrun of ten percent, for example, on a print run of 10,000 is a perfectly legal shortfall of 1000 copies! You may want to prohibit a shortfall and instead risk a 20 percent **overrun**.

Make a realistic schedule that includes each stage in the process – design and mark-up of copy, typesetting, paste-up, prepress, **make-ready** (setting up the press), printing, and finishing – and let everyone concerned have a copy for comment. Anticipate any delays in ordering paper, vacations (use a calendar with weekends and holidays clearly marked), and shipping. Check proofs meticulously, bearing in mind that any error you miss will be multiplied hundreds or thousands of times. Things may go wrong, but careful planning and communication should eliminate too many surprises.

PRINTING PROCESSES

The various printing technologies have already been mentioned many times. Paper, ink, and printing process are all interdependent, and a choice of any one of them cannot be made in isolation. Once the decision to choose a particular printing process has been made, there is very little that a designer needs to or can do. If the mechanical is perfect, and the scans are good, then a good printer will produce a good result. There are things that can go wrong, however, and a little knowledge of how the printing processes work will go a long way in helping you to choose the right supplier and thus avoid any problems.

Printing processes can be categorized into one of four main types: relief, intaglio, planographic, and stencil (Fig. **6.18**). Letterpress is a form of **relief printing** invented by the ancient Chinese. Dating back to about AD 730, it is by far the oldest of the printing technologies. Flexography is another form of relief printing, which had to await recent advances in materials technology. In relief printing, the printed **impression** is made by a raised surface coated with ink and pressed against the paper, or other substrate.

Intaglio printing uses a plate with incised lines or grooves. Ink is applied, and then wiped from the surface. An impression is made when the substrate is pressed against the surface of the plate, drawing the ink out from the recesses. Gravure is a kind of intaglio process. The **planographic printing** process, of which lithography is the only example, is perhaps the most mysterious, as everything happens on the surface of the plate. It works simply because oil and water do not mix. **Stencil printing**, or screenprinting, is, like relief printing, an ancient technique; earlier Oriental stencils were held together by meshes of human hair.

Offset lithography is by far the most common form of printing nowadays. There will be some designers who in the course of their careers use nothing

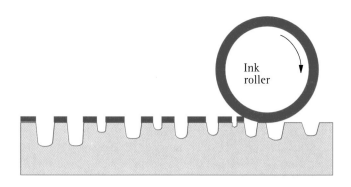

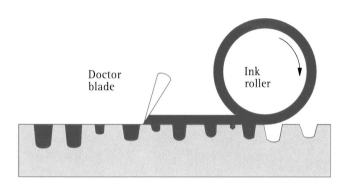

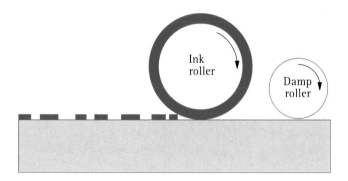

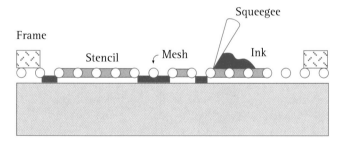

6.18 There are four main printing methods. Relief has ink sitting on the raised surface of the plate or type. Intaglio has ink in the grooves and recesses, while lithography is a planographic process with the ink on the surface, sticking only to the dry areas of the plate. And screenprinting forces the ink through a mask supported by a mesh.

else. It is rare these days for anyone to print by letterpress, but its historical significance is great. Unless you work in packaging design, it is unlikely that you will ever come across flexography or screenprinting. And unless you design mail-order catalogs or glossy magazines, you may never have to work with gravure. But you never can tell!

Offset lithography

In Prague (now in Czechoslovakia) in around 1798, Alois Senefelder was experimenting with Solnhofen limestone to find a cheaper alternative to engraving images on copper. His experiments with etching in relief were a failure, but he did notice that he could print just as well without

the relief. That discovery, along with the invention of photography in the mid-19th century, changed the course of printing history. It rendered letterpress virtually obsolete, and made **offset lithography** the predominant print technology of the 20th century.

The word **lithography** means "writing on stone." Senefelder discovered that if a design is drawn on a limestone surface using a greasy crayon, and then the surface is "etched" with a solution of gum arabic, water, and a few drops of nitric acid, the area that has been drawn on will become permanently receptive to grease. The undrawn area desensitized by the gum solution will be permanently resistant to grease. If the stone is later dampened and greasy ink is applied from a roller, the ink will stick to the design but not to the rest of the surface. Impressions can then be taken which are exact replicas of the original design.

Over the years, the same properties were discovered in more manageable zinc and aluminum plates. Then the **offset process** was developed to overcome the limitations of these metal plates. It involved taking an impression not directly from the plate but from an intermediate **blanket**. The offset process has several clear advantages. Metal plates are easily damaged, and offsetting the image on to rubber protects them from damage. The resilience of the rubber blanket enables impressions to be made on even quite rough papers, and other substrates such as tinplate. Furthermore, the design on the original stone had to be drawn as a

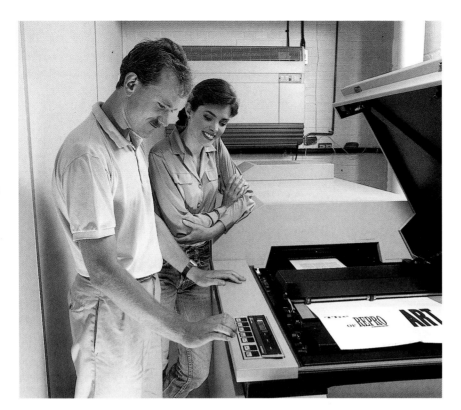

6.19 Plates for offset lithography are made in a printing down frame. The film or flat is put emulsion down, in direct contact with the plate, which is then developed either chemically or using a xerographic process.

mirror image of the finished design for it to print correctly. But because the image is first offset − printed to the blanket − and then on to the paper, the design for offset litho can be positive and "right reading."

Lithography would have become much more popular a lot sooner if it had not been for the fact that type-setting was a problem. It was poss-ible to transfer type set by letter-press on to the litho plate using paper with the ink still wet. But it wasn't until the invention of photo-graphy that type could be put on to a litho plate with any kind of quality control.

Platemaking is the process by which the design is transferred on to a printing **plate** from the artwork or mechanical, either photographically or electrostatically, by a process resembling photocopying (Fig. **6.19**). Offset litho plates have to be thin and flexible enough to wrap around a cylinder. Small plates are supplied pre-sensitized with a light-sensitive diazo compound or photopolymer, and are made from metal, plastic, or paper. Paper and plastic are used

for short runs, up to 1000 copies. Because they stretch and distort on the press, they are only suitable for single-color work. They are exposed under a process camera, "devel-oped" electrostatically, and then "fixed" by heat. Alternately, the plates are placed in direct contact with the artwork and the image is transferred using a photographic process similar to the production of PMTs (see p. 78).

Metal plates are made from aluminum with a granular surface, which gives the plate water-carrying properties, and provides anchorage to the image. Litho plates for larger machines and some smaller conven-tional metal plates can be exposed from either negative or positive film. As we have seen in Chapter 4, strip-ping and film make-up for black-and-white work is generally done using negative film. It follows that nega-tive-working plates will be used for single-color work. Negative-working plates are less expensive than posi-tive-working ones and are used in print runs of up to 100,000 copies. Most multicolor work, however,

makes use of flats assembled from positive film, because it is easier to keep the separations in register. In this case, positive-working plates are used.

The exposure or **burn** is made by ultraviolet light in a printing-down frame which holds the plate in direct vacuum contact with the flat. On exposure, the diazo or photopolymer resin coating of a **negative-working plate** radiated by the ultraviolet light undergoes a chemical reaction to become ink-attracting. This then forms the image on the plate that will print. The rest of the coating, unexposed to the ultraviolet light, is washed off during subsequent processing. Finally, a gum arabic solution is applied to the surface to make the non-image areas water-attracting and ink-rejecting.

When **positive-working plates** are exposed in the frame, it is the sensi-tized photopolymer coating radiated by the ultraviolet light that is made unstable on exposure, and it is this portion that is removed during pro-cessing. The unexposed areas are the ones that will print. Again, the plate is gummed to make the non-image areas unattractive to ink. Since the image can be further destabilized by light, positive-work-ing plates have a shorter life than negative-working ones. Some plates can be baked to "fix" and harden the image. Deletions can be made to a positive-working plate, by using a special eraser or brush-applied fluid. This can be useful for printing run-ons of a poster, for example, with dates or venues deleted.

All plates are subject to wear. After round 500,000 copies (or sometimes much lower numbers)

have been printed, both the image and the surface grain start to break up. Multi-metal plates with surfaces of hard-wearing chromium are specially designed for long print runs of between 800,000 and a million.

Positive-working plates produce less dot gain than plates made from negatives and are popular for web offset magazine printing. Bimetal plates are even better at controlling dot gain. Here in detail are the main types of plate:

■ **Electrophotographic plates** are produced like photocopies. The photoconductor is charged using a corona discharge, and on exposure to the artwork, the charge is dissipated in those areas struck by light. The charge remaining on the unexposed areas attracts a dry or liquid toner with an opposite charge. An organic photoconductor is coated on a substrate or paper, and the toned image either is fixed or transferred to another substrate. Plates used for laser imaging are coated on electrograined anodized aluminum. During processing, the coating is removed in the non-printing areas, and the plates are treated with etch and gum to make them water receptive. During the chemical removal process, the dots can become slightly ragged, so these plates are not recommended for fine screens and process color printing. It is also possible to make short-run polyester plates direct from a laser printer.

■ **Presensitized diazo plates** are coated with organic compounds and have a shelf life of about a year; wipe-on plates that are coated at the printers have a shelf life of one to two weeks. Most are made from negatives and, once exposed, are treated with an emulsion developer consisting of a lacquer and gum-etch in acid solution. As the unexposed diazo is dissolved by the solution, the gum deposits on the non-printing areas for water-receptivity, and lacquer deposits on the exposed images, making them ink-receptive. When developed, the plate is rinsed with water and coated with gum arabic solution. These are known as additive plates and can produce runs as long as 150,000. Some diazo plates are prelacquered and are capable of runs of up to 250,000. These plates are developed using a special solvent, and are known as subtractive plates.

■ **Photopolymer plates** are coated with inert and abrasion-resistant organic compounds and are capable of press runs up to 250,000. These too are available as negative- and positive-working plates. Some photopolymer plates can be baked after processing to produce runs of over a million. Dye-sensitized photopolymers that can be exposed by lasers are used in digital computer-to-plate systems.

■ **Silver halide plates** are coated with photosensitive compounds similar to slow photographic film. The emulsions are very light-sensitive to blue so must be handled in yellow-filtered light. The coatings can be exposed optically using negatives, or digitally by lasers. The processing solutions contain heavy metal pollutants (silver) which must be treated with silver-recovery chemicals before being discharged into municipal sewers.

■ **Bimetal plates** use presensitized polymer coatings consisting of a metal base with one or more metals plated on to it: either copper plated on to stainless steel or aluminum, or chromium plated on to copper, which may be plated on to a third metal base. These are almost indestructible, have good dot control and are capable of runs in the millions – they are also the most expensive. But should anything go wrong, a single acid treatment can restore the plate to its original condition.

■ **Waterless plates** consist of ink on aluminum for the image areas and a silicone rubber for the non-printing areas. Silicone rubber has very low surface tension and thus will repel ink. However, because of the pressure and heat of printing, regular litho ink will smear over the silicone and cause scumming or toning. Waterless printing must therefore use special inks and temperature control. The technique also demands good grades of paper in order to avoid debris accumulating on the blanket.

■ **Heat-sensitive plates** are made from polymers that respond to heat rather than light, so can be handled in daylight or artificial light. They are exposed using infrared laser diodes in special imagesetters and processed in an aqueous solution. With baking, they are capable of runs of over a million.

■ **Hybrid plates** use two separate photosensitive coatings on metal plates: a silver halide coating that can be exposed either optically to film or digitally by lasers over a

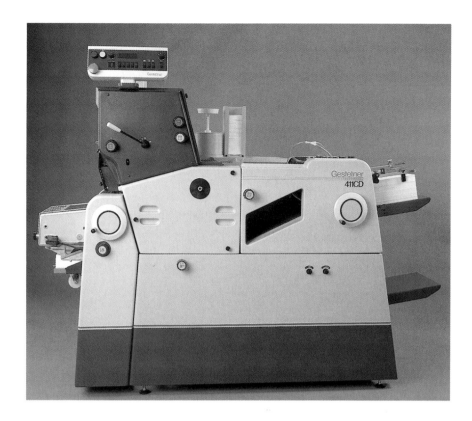

▶ **6.20** The Gestetner 411CD — a typical small offset litho machine.

bottom coating of conventional photopolymer. When the top coating is processed, the bottom coating is exposed to UV light. The top coating is then removed and the photopolymer (bottom) coating used for printing.

■ **Ablation plates** are made by a laser selectively burning tiny holes into thin coatings on a polyester or metal base. These can be produced digitally, require no chemical processing, and can be printed waterless. All the plates for a job can be imaged directly on the press, simultaneously and in register.

As you can see from the above, most plate coatings can be imaged digitally by laser. High-speed dye-sensitized photopolymers, silver halide, electrophotographic and ablation plates, coupled with PostScript-based digital systems have paved the way for **CTP (computer to plate)** systems. So say goodbye to the imagesetter and say hello to the platesetter. Your PostScript data comes in one end from the RIP, and out comes a plate ready for the press, with no need for film, stripping or further processing. The main debate at the time of writing is which technology will rule: visible light-sensitive plates such as Du Pont's Silverlith, versus infrared imaging with products such as Kodak's Direct Image Thermal Plate. Visible light is a tried and trusted technology; thermal plates offer better dots (as small as 3 microns), a faster turnround, and don't need a darkroom.

The litho press

Offset litho presses range from the small-scale **sheetfed** machines found in jobbing printers all over the world (Fig. **6.20**), to the huge presses used to print magazines and newspapers on to continuous webs, or rolls, of paper. The basic principles of the process are always the same (Fig. **6.21**). A litho machine comprises: a **plate cylinder** on to which the plate is securely clamped; a resilient rubber-coated cylinder, called the **blanket cylinder**; an **impression cylinder**; a system of inking rollers called the **ink pyramid**; and a **plate-damping unit**. The litho plate is dampened, and then inked. Next, the inked image is transferred (offset) to the blanket. The paper moves between the blanket and the impression cylinders, which are "packed" to ensure complete contact, and the

▶ **6.21** The layout of a small sheet-fed offset litho machine. The plate is first dampened by the fountain, then inked by the ink pyramid. The image is transferred to the rubber blanket cylinder and on to the paper, which is pressed between the blanket and the impression cylinder.

image in ink is transferred from the blanket on to the paper stock.

A single-color sheetfed machine prints single sheets in one color at a time. A mechanism called a feeder pushes each sheet in turn between the blanket and the impression cylinder. Sheets are lifted one by one by vacuum suckers, and are then sent through the machine by blasts of air and conveyor belts. High-speed presses use a **stream feeder**, which presents sheets to the rollers overlapping slightly. Detectors cut out the printing unit if a sheet is

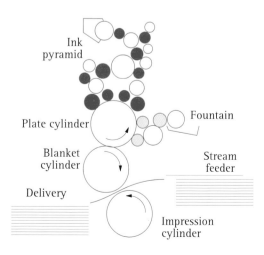

Ink pyramid

Plate cylinder

Fountain

Blanket cylinder

Stream feeder

Delivery

Impression cylinder

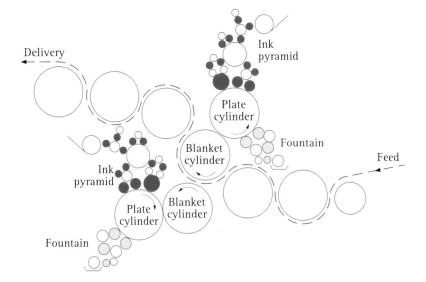

Delivery

Ink pyramid

Plate cylinder

Blanket cylinder

Fountain

Feed

Ink pyramid

Plate cylinder

Blanket cylinder

Fountain

6.22 A perfecting press can print both sides of the sheet in one pass. Here there is no impression cylinder — the two blanket cylinders press against one another.

defective or if two sheets are picked up together.

The front and side lays are adjustable stops which position the sheet before it enters the machine. The grippers – sets of metal fingers on the impression cylinder – grab the sheet and pull it through. A gripper allowance of ½ inch (15 mm) must be made when estimating the printed area of a sheet. After it has been printed, it is released, and the delivery mechanism stacks it with the others, **jogging** them constantly to neaten the pile. To stop the wet image from **offsetting** on to the next sheet in the pile, anti-**setoff** spray is applied as the sheet falls on to the pile, separating it from its neighbors by a layer of fine particles.

Meanwhile, inside the machine, the damping system deposits a fine layer of moisture on to the plate's surface before it passes under the inking rollers. One or two cloth-covered rollers, supplied by a **fountain** roller, are used to regulate the amount of dampening. Alcohol can be used for up to 20 percent of the solution, to lower the surface tension and lessen the moisture uptake of the paper. Damp paper stretches, and anything that reduces this effect will improve the quality of the printing, especially in close-register color work. Because of the cost of alcohol and environmental considerations,

new citrus-based fountain solutions have been developed.

Ink is introduced to the roller pyramid from a reservoir via an adjustable metal blade. Ink flow can be controlled by a computer taking densitometer readings from the printed sheets. This can also record ink settings that can be re-used if the job is to be reprinted. It is possible, though very messy and unpredictable, to print two colors from a single plate on a single-color offset press by using one color at one end of the fountain, another at the other end – the colors will blend in the middle. This is called **split fountain** printing.

A **perfecting press** (Fig. **6.22**) is a printing press that can print both sides of the sheet in one pass. One type of perfector is a **blanket-to-blanket press**, which has the two blanket cylinders printing at the same time, so that an impression cylinder is unnecessary.

Multicolor work can be printed in many different ways. An **in-line** machine has several single units arranged to print one color after another. Stock is conveyed to the next unit by grippers on transfer cylinders. A **converter** machine (Fig. **6.23**) has a drum mechanism that can reroute the paper so that it can print either two colors together on one side of a sheet or (when converted) one color on each side of the sheet. A four-unit converter can print four colors on one side, or two each on both sides.

6.23 Using a converter configuration, you can either print both sides of a sheet in one pass, or one side in two colors.

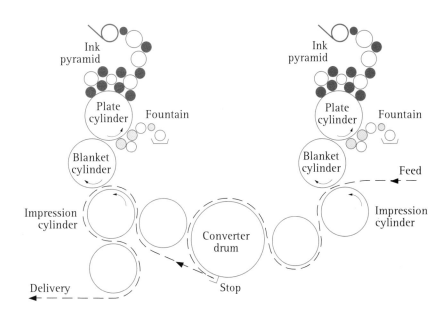

Ink pyramid

Plate cylinder

Fountain

Blanket cylinder

Impression cylinder

Converter drum

Delivery

Stop

Ink pyramid

Plate cylinder

Fountain

Blanket cylinder

Feed

Impression cylinder

Web path

Reel

Ink pyramid

Ink pyramid

Fountain

Plate cylinder

Plate cylinder

Fountain

Blanket cylinder

Blanket cylinder

To kite folder

6.24 In this web offset configuration, the web is printed on both sides in one pass. A typical web press consists of several units like this, one after the other.

Web-fed machines (Fig. **6.24**) print from a continuous roll of paper stock, which is printed and then folded and cut into sheets in a single pass. All web-fed machines print both sides of the sheet, and in web-offset, blanket-to-blanket designs are common. The length of the final sheet is determined by the circumference of the cutting cylinder. This cut-off length determines the press printing size you choose for a job. A single-width press with a width of 34 inches (850 mm) and a cut-off length of 24 inches (600 mm), produces eight $8\frac{1}{4}$ x $11\frac{11}{16}$ in (A4) pages to view, or 16 pages perfected (printed both sides) to a section.

A multiple-unit web-offset machine can have several web reels in operation. A five-unit web-offset machine with one reel in operation has the capacity to print four process colors plus one Pantone color, or one 16-page full-color section and one black-and-white 16-page section at the same time. A six-unit press, using only one or two printing units for each of two or three reels, can produce printings of flat color and black in many different permutations. On newspapers, for example, one cylinder might be reserved for printing late "stop press" items.

Web tension in the press is controlled by a dancer roller, which can apply a brake to the reel. When the reel runs out, the press is stopped and a new one is connected. On

larger presses, this can be done automatically by a "flying paster," which attaches the end of the old reel to the beginning of the new one, then accelerates the new reel up to press speed, all while the press is running.

After printing, the web is dried in a series of gas-fired ovens, then chilled (however, newspapers often use **cold-set ink**, which does not require this treatment). To avoid smudging, it is vital that the ink is dry before the web passes over a former, or kite, which makes the first fold in the direction of motion. This

is the part of the press always shown in old films, where it looks as though the web is disappearing into a slit (Fig. **6.25**). The paper is then cut into sections, and folded again down to the correct page size. Magazines are trimmed with a three-knife trimmer. Newspapers are usually left untrimmed. For books, the web is slit into ribbons, which are passed over polished turner bars on cushions of air, for better alignment during trimming.

Web machines are used for long print runs, typically over 20,000 copies, on jobs with tight deadlines. With web, all the colors can be printed, both sides, on one pass, with folding done in-line. However, registration is often not as accurate as on sheetfed presses. Trim sizes are restricted as well; non-standard sizes and finishes are better handled by sheetfed machines.

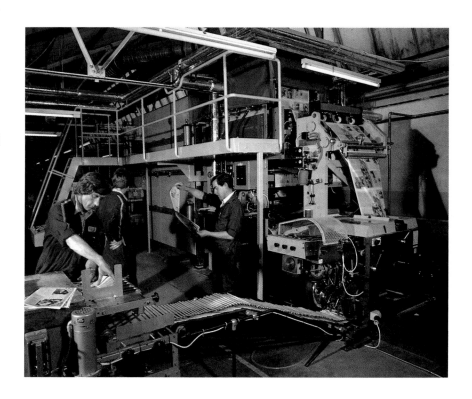

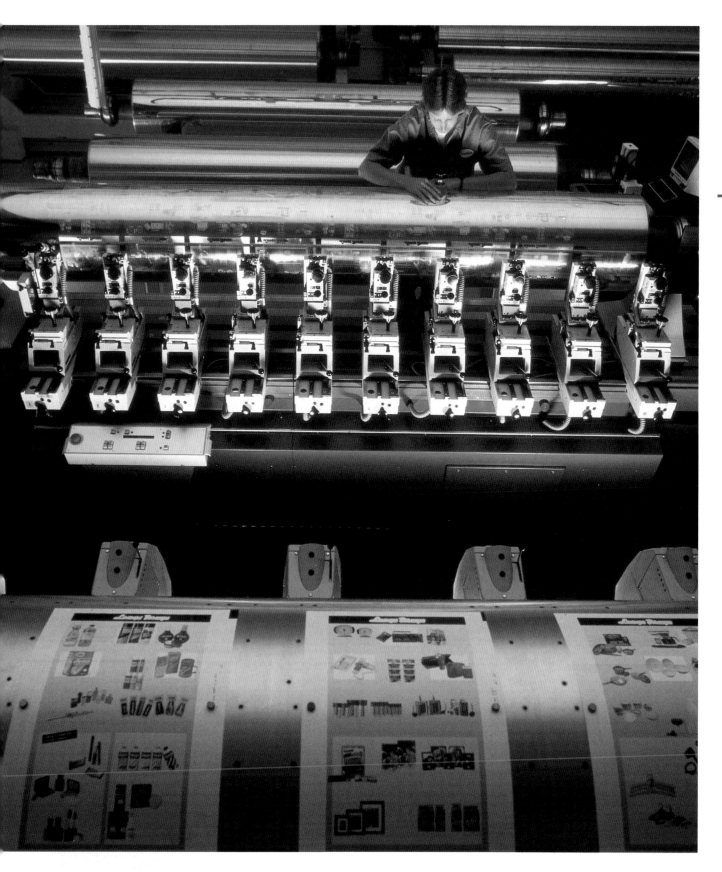

6.25 After printing and drying, the web is folded down the middle on a kite folder – as here at Headley Bros in Ashford, England.

6.26 Cylinders at the press of R. R. Donnelley in Chicago. Engraving gravure cylinders is very expensive, and thus the process is only economical for long runs.

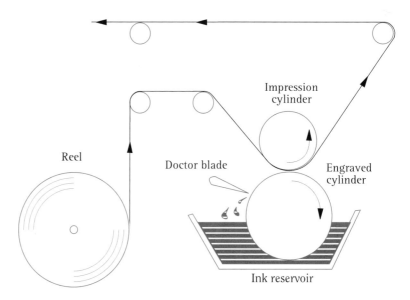

6.27 A gravure press is invariably web-fed. The engraved gravure cylinder is inked and then its surface is wiped clean by a doctor blade. The paper is printed as a result of pressure between the plate cylinder and the impression cylinder.

Gravure

The biggest rival to the huge web-offset presses is **gravure**. This is an intaglio process that is used to print everything from the highest quality postage stamps and banknotes, through glossy magazines and mail-order catalogs, down to rough-and-ready wallpapers and gift wrapping paper.

Although related to earlier inta-glio methods of printing, such as etching and copper engraving, gra-vure is a relatively recent process, invented in the middle of the 19th century by photographer Fox Talbot, as a means of reproducing **continu-ous tone** (see p. 19).

Present-day gravure machines are huge high-speed **rotary presses** that print from a web of paper. (Gravure is sometimes also called **roto-gravure**.) The engraved cylinder is partially immersed in a bath of thin, solvent-based ink (Fig. **6.27**). Its surface is flooded with ink, and as it revolves it is wiped clean with a flex-ible steel blade called a doctor blade, leaving ink only in the image areas. A web of paper is pressed against the surface of the engraved cylinder by a rubber-covered impression cylinder, and the ink is transferred to the paper. The web passes to a folder and then a drier, similar to those found on web-offset machines.

The important point about gra-vure is that it prints continuous tones by means of cells – containers of ink cut into the surface of the cylinder (Fig. **6.28**). Larger-diameter or deeper cells hold more ink, and thus deposit a thicker layer of ink, and hence make a darker printed image. This produces continuous-

tone images that are almost screen-less, as the ink from neighboring cells merges during printing. A draw-back is that type is also printed this way, so it is less sharp than that produced by offset litho.

In the original process, cells were of equal size but different depths. This arrangement has been super-seded either by cells of both varying depth and size, or by cells of con-stant depth but varying size. The latter method is used mainly for textiles and packaging design.

Preparing artwork for gravure is exactly the same as for offset litho (see Chapter 4), except that the typesetting is scanned as well as the tone. The complete artwork for the job is scanned in one pass. This is converted into signals that control a diamond engraving stylus which cuts into the surface of a blank copper cylinder, producing the pattern of cells (Fig. **6.26**, p. 181). After engrav-ing, the cylinder can be chromium-plated for extra durability. Cylinders coated with polymer resin can be cut directly by laser. These may prove to be cheaper in the long run, as the resin can be replaced and cut again.

Because of the considerable expensive involved in engraving the cylinders, gravure is reserved for jobs such as glossy magazines with very high print runs – typically 250,000 copies or more – or for

jobs demanding the highest quality of halftone reproduction.

Direct digital etching by laser uses an alloy that can be plated on steel like copper, but has much higher efficiency (copper reflects laser light). It is capable of etching 30,000 175 lpi cells per second.

Photopolymer plate systems for gravure consist of photopolymer coatings on stainless steel plates that can be mounted on magnetic

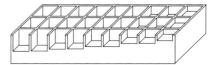

Constant area, variable depth

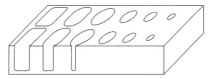

Variable area, constant depth

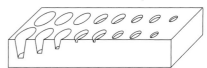

Variable area, variable depth

6.28 Conventional gravure cells have equal area but differing depth – the deeper the cell, the darker the impression (top). Other kinds of cell include those with variable area and equal depth, used mainly for packaging (center), and – for the highest quality work – those with variable area and variable depth (bottom).

cylinders. These plates make gravure a viable process for runs below 100,000 and can make gravure competitive with lithography and flexography for packaging runs.

Gravure was the first printing process to use digital imaging. Digital information from the prepress system is fed directly to the diamond styli in the engraving heads that produce the printing cells. This process is also called **filmless gravure**.

Letterpress

Until the 1960s, **letterpress** was the most popular form of printing. Now it is virtually obsolete, except for small limited-edition presses producing fine editions of books. The hot-metal typesetting side of the process survives, but mostly only to produce repro proofs that are then incorporated into mechanicals and printed by offset litho. Conversely, photoset mechanicals can be used to produce plates that print on letterpress machines. But increasingly, large letterpress machines are being converted to flexography (see below), in which the heritage of letterpress lingers on.

Letterpress is a relief process, invented by the Chinese. It was adapted to western use by Gutenberg, and perfected in the late 19th century, with the introduction of iron steam-powered presses. The beautifully crafted Stanhope, Columbian, and Albion presses from the golden age of letterpress, with their ornamental cast iron eagles and fanciful beasts, have long been relegated to science museums and the entrance halls of modern printers (Fig. **6.29**). But like steam locomotives, some

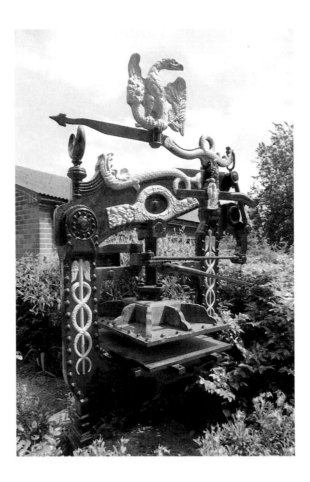

6.29 Most old iron letterpress machines, such as this Columbian, have been relegated to the foyers of large corporations, or gardens, as mere ornamental features. Thankfully, some are being restored and put back to work.

6.30 On a traditional letterpress machine, paper is laid face down on to the inked forme and the whole flatbed assembly is moved beneath a screw- or lever-powered press.

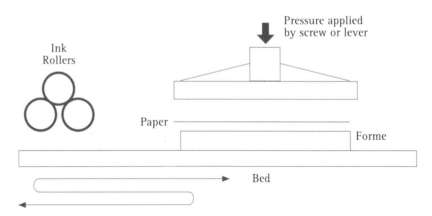

have been lovingly restored by enthusiasts and put to use. They create that three-dimensional tactile quality of impression that litho and gravure cannot achieve.

There are three types of letterpress machine: flatbed, platen, and rotary. The **flatbed** is the oldest, being derived from wine and textile presses (Fig. **6.30**). The forme containing the locked-up wrong-reading type and blocks is placed horizontally on the bed of the press. Paper

is placed over it, and a screw is turned or a lever pulled to apply pressure. The cylinder flatbed is a press that has the forme and paper on a bed that is inked and then moved under a heavy impression cylinder. The cylinder is lifted to allow the bed to return to its starting position.

The **platen** principle has the forme positioned vertically, with the platen – a heavy metal plate – swinging forward and upward with

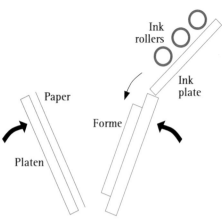

Ink rollers

Paper

Forme

Ink plate

Platen

6.31 The platen press operates like a pincer – the two halves are brought forcibly together into a vertical position by lever action.

the paper (Fig. **6.31**). It makes an impression as it snaps shut, like a clamshell, vertical and parallel with the forme. Platen presses can still be seen in operation, printing business cards.

A rotary press cannot print directly from the forme. A curved copy of the forme, called a stereotype, must first be cast. A *papier-mâché* mold, called a flong, is taken from the forme, and is used to make a one-piece metal, rubber, or plastic plate. It is then fixed around the cylinder. Rotary presses can be sheetfed or web-fed. During the changeover of newspapers from letterpress to offset litho, a process called photopolymer direct relief was used to make plastic or nylon plates for letterpress from photoset mechanicals. Flexography

(see the next section) uses a similar process.

Letterset is a process whereby the image is first offset on to a rubber blanket, as in offset litho. It is used for printing on metal and plastic cartons and cans.

Flexography

Flexography is a relief process, a form of letterpress, which prints using flexible rubber or photopolymer plates (Fig. **6.32**). The process was first demonstrated in 1890 by Bibby, Baron & Sons of Liverpool, UK, as a means of printing on non-absorbent packaging materials. It was further developed in the 1920s to make use of **aniline dyes**, derived from coal tar, and had various names. The term flexography was coined in 1952 as a result of a competition sponsored by the packaging industry. It was thought that

any name containing the words "coal tar" had connotations that would not be acceptable by the general public in the context of packaging for foodstuffs.

Flexography presses are rotary web-fed machines, similar in layout to gravure machines (Fig. **6.33**). Like gravure, flexo generally uses thin inks, usually solvent-based. Water-based inks containing fluorescent dyes can also be printed using flexography. It is an economical process only for very large print runs, typically measured in millions of copies.

Artwork is prepared exactly as for offset litho. The plates are produced in the same way as the stereotypes for letterpress, and are flexible

6.33 The configuration of a flexography machine is very similar to that of a gravure press. The Anilox roll even has a gravure-like cellular texture to carry the thin ink to the flexo plate.

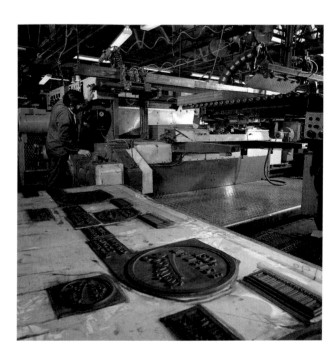

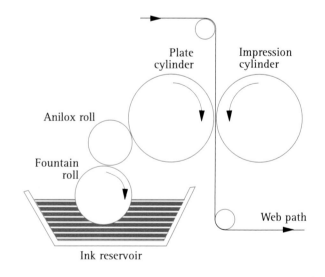

Plate cylinder

Impression cylinder

Anilox roll

Fountain roll

Web path

Ink reservoir

6.32 Many flexography machines are converted rotary letterpress machines.

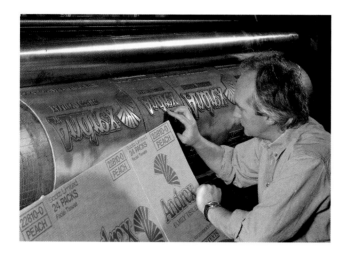

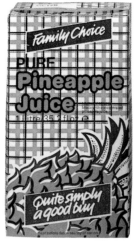

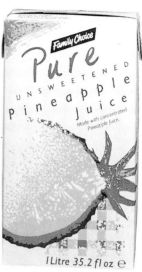

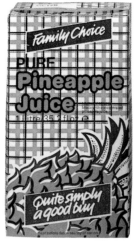

▲ **6.34** Flexography is used for unglamorous applications, such as cardboard boxes (above), and for difficult packaging materials such as waxed paper and plastic, as the examples (above right) designed by Stan Noble of designers Towers Noble show. Stan Noble often makes extensive use of a Quantel Paintbox in arriving at the concepts for his designs.

enough to be attached to the printing cylinder using adhesive. Corrections can be patched into existing plates. The plates do distort in use, and some image spread should be catered for in the design. Halftones and small type should be avoided, and so should any areas of reversed-out type, which could fill in.

Because of the plates' squashiness, flexo is used for food packaging applications that require flexibility – printing on plastic bags and other non-absorbent stock, such as cellophane and metal foil, and corrugated surfaces (Fig. **6.34**).

The process competes with gravure for printing magazines and paperback books on cheap newsprint. The plates do have a tendency to "plug up" with fibers from rougher stocks, however.

Screenprinting

At the other end of the spectrum, the **silkscreen** process, or **screenprinting**, is used for only relatively short print runs of up to 15,000 copies. The name derives from its craft origins when a screen of silk material was used to support the stencil bearing the image through which ink was squeezed (Fig. **6.35**, p. 186). Today, the screen is made from synthetic gauzes or metal meshes.

Despite its almost exclusive associations with poster design and the prints of Andy Warhol, screenprinting is an extremely versatile process. It is a simple and direct method of delivering ink, and can thus be used to print on any kind of substrate, even on curved and uneven surfaces. It can produce thick and opaque deposits of ink, in brilliant saturated colors, and with high chemical and abrasion resistance. Applications for screen printing range from printed circuit-boards in electronics, through bottles and cartons, to T-shirts, point-of-display advertising, compact discs, and logos on the sides of vehicles.

The screen has two functions: to support the stencil, and to regulate the ink. The screen itself is supported in a wooden or metal frame, evenly tensioned using air-powered or mechanical devices. Most screens are made from polyester. This is a precision woven mesh for close register work, with high stability and low sensitivity to variations in temperature and humidity. Other screen materials include polyamide, which has good wear resistance and elasticity. It is used for printing three-dimensional objects. Stainless steel screens have the highest dimensional stability, plus chemical and physical resistance. They are used for ceramic decoration and printed circuit-boards.

The mesh has two main characteristics: the count and the grade. The **mesh count** is the number of threads per inch. The lower the count, the less support there will be for detail, and the heavier the deposit of ink. The **mesh grade** relates to thread thickness, which influences the weight of the ink film. There are four grades: S, M, T and

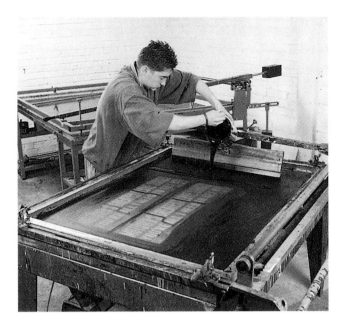

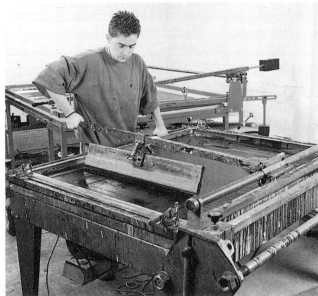

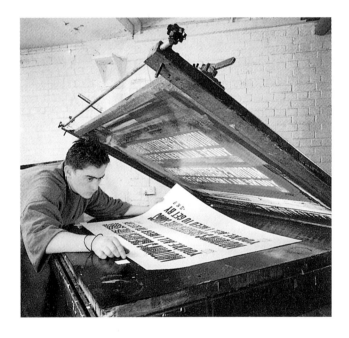

▲ ▶ **6.35**
Screen-
printing is mainly
associated with
poster and T-shirt
printing, but can also
be used where a non-
impact process is
required, for printing
directly on to the
surfaces of compact
discs and CD-roms,
for example.

A more direct method uses a screen coated on both sides (more thickly on the underside) with a light-sensitive polymer emulsion. After exposure to ultraviolet light in contact with positive film, the image areas are washed away with water. This leaves a stencil that completely encapsulates the screen mesh.

Presses for screenprinting range from simple bench-mounted configurations operated by hand (using a rubber squeegee to force ink through the mesh) to fully automatic rotary machines (Fig. **6.36**). On bench presses, a metal blade called a flo-coater, which is mounted behind the squeegee, returns the ink to its pre-printing position. The angle, pressure, and speed of both the squeegee and the flo-coater can be adjusted. Once set, the machine will produce consistent results throughout the print run. Fast cylinder-bed presses have the squeegee and flo-coater stationary. The stock, supported on a vacuum bed, moves in unison with the screen.

Screenprinting is a direct non-impact process producing thick, bright colors, but it is not recommended for close registration work, nor for smaller sizes of type. Half-tones pose problems because of possible moiré effects caused by the

HD. S is the thinnest, giving a 50 to 70 percent open area; HD is the heaviest, giving a 20 to 35 percent open area. One chooses a count and grade depending on the application, ink, and halftone screen being used.

Stencils can be cut by hand from water- or solvent-soluble laminate film, and are either ironed on to the screen using heat or mounted using a solvent. A pen plotter equipped with a cutting knife can be used by the designer to cut out "line" stencils direct from a computer system. The unwanted areas are "weeded out" and

discarded (don't forget enclosed areas like the bowls of letters such as b).

More complex stencils are made photomechanically. Artwork is prepared as for offset litho, and a film positive is made at the repro house. One method uses presensitized gelatin film exposed to ultraviolet light in contact with the positive. This is then hardened in hydrogen peroxide, and the sticky stencil is mounted to the underside of the frame. When it has dried, the polyester base is peeled off and discarded.

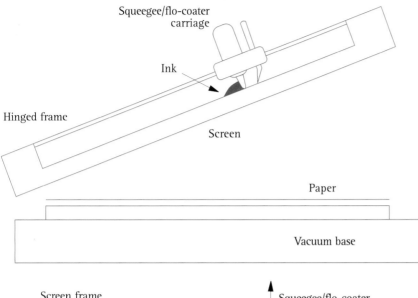

Squeegee/flo-coater carriage

Ink

Hinged frame

Screen

Paper

Vacuum base

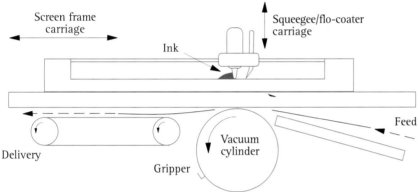

Screen frame carriage

Ink

Squeegee/flo-coater carriage

Delivery

Gripper

Vacuum cylinder

Feed

6.36 Most screenprinting is very labor-intensive, using a hand-operated bench configuration – literally pulling the squeegee across the surface of the screen. The process can be automated on a rotary machine – the squeegee and flo-coater remain in the same position while the screen moves. Paper is pulled by a gripper between the screen and a vacuum cylinder.

6.37 Collotype is the only process that can print a full tonal range without screening. it is relatively rare, and examples are impossible to show in a book that has been printed by offset litho (see also Fig. 1.9).

gauze of the mesh interfering with the screen. Moiré can be minimized, however, by using a stencil production system with good dot formation; by angling the mesh between four and nine degrees to the axis of the frame; or by using a "grained" or textured screen rather than a pattern of dots.

Collotype

Collotype, or photogelatin, was and is still the only process that can print continuous tone without screening (Fig. **6.37**) It is used for limited-edition art prints of exceptional quality. It is a slow process capable of only small print runs.

To produce a collotype, a right-reading unscreened negative is first made from the original. This is contact printed to an aluminum plate coated with light-sensitive gelatin. The gelatin hardens in proportion to

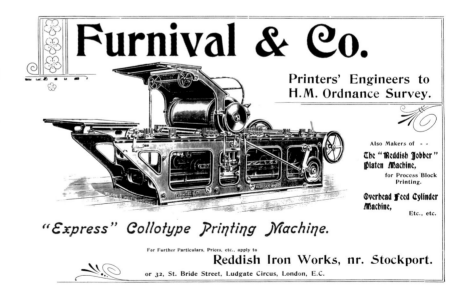

the amount of light falling on it: highlights remain soft, darker areas are harder. The plate is prepared for printing by flooding it with a solution of water containing glycerine – the soft areas absorb more than the

harder ones. Ink is then applied. It adheres to the hardened areas, and progressively less in the softer parts. An impression is made, producing a continuous tone image with a mottled grain.

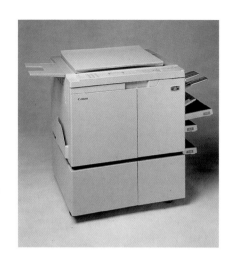

6.38 The ubiquitous photocopier – this is a Canon CLC 320 laser copier – is the print technology of the future. Already you can print direct from a mechanical or a disk, and the quality and cost per sheet will soon be on a par with offset litho.

6.39 *Margot* by Helen J. Holroyd, created by photocopying an ink drawing on to colored paper using different colored toners and collaging the resulting prints.

Xerography

Xerography, or photocopying, promises to replace small-scale offset litho in the near future. A photocopier can print direct from artwork or a mechanical, enlarging and reducing instantly. For small print runs, photocopying is cheaper than offset litho, with all its set-up costs. The results are dense and black, and photocopiers can now print on a wide range of paper stock. Systems such as the Xerox DocuTech are used for small-scale (less than 1000) "on-demand" runs of monochrome manuals and books.

Machines such as the Canon Color Laser Copier can produce full-color work direct from artwork, or from a disk from a computer system (Fig. **6.38**). They can scan halftones too. The cost per sheet is relatively expensive, but falling all the time.

Xerography was invented in 1938 by Chester Carlson, and developed by the Xerox Corporation. Artwork is placed face down on a glass plate, and is illuminated by a fluorescent light which travels the length of the image. The reflected image is directed through lenses on to an electrostatically charged drum. This charge leaks away where light from the image falls on the drum. A resin-based powder, called toner, is attracted to the image areas. This pattern of toner is transferred to a sheet of paper, where it is fixed by heat (Fig. **6.40**).

Laser copiers work like combined scanners and imagesetters by scanning the image digitally, and using a laser to write the image on to the electrostatic drum.

Creative photocopying
The photocopier can be more than just a means of duplicating precious proofs, or enlarging and reducing "for position only" prints. It is also a creative medium in its own right.

Helen J. Holroyd uses a standard mono photocopier to produce her colorful collages (Fig. **6.39**). She starts with a black-on-white ink

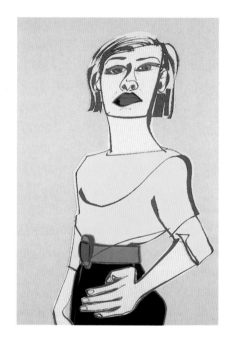

drawing and copies it several times using different colored toner, and on different colored papers. The copies are then cut up in different ways and combined with parts of the drawing in other colors to form the collage. It is possible to produce several prints from one set of photocopies.

Another technique is to copy the drawing on to acetate and color in the back of the photocopy – a

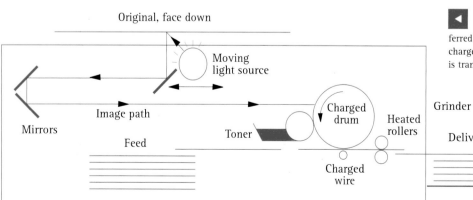

Original, face down

Moving light source

Mirrors

Image path

Feed

Toner

Charged drum

Heated rollers

Charged wire

Grinder

Delivery

6.40 Inside a photocopier, a light source scans the artwork and this image is transferred via mirrors on to an electrostatically charged drum. Toner adheres to the image, and is transferred to the paper and fixed by heat. In a laser copier, all this is done digitally, just like a combination laser scanner and laser printer.

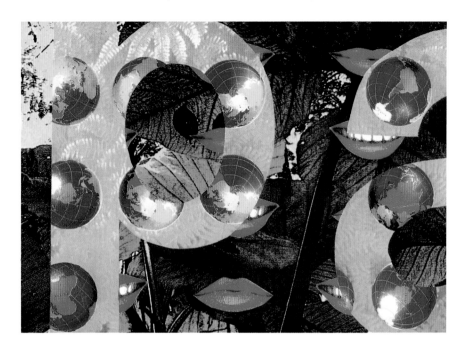

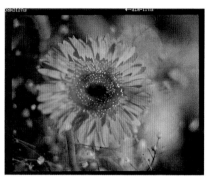

6.41 A Canon-created "still" from a storyboard for an animated film entitled Apathy Rex being made by Paul Nunneley in conjunction with brother Mark.

6.42 From the original transparency shown here, Paul Nunneley made these prints by adjusting the colors, contrast, and shape on a Canon CLC 500.

process akin to the coloring of cells in animation. The result can range from a subtle stained-glass effect to a vivid cartoon-style illustration, depending on the type and texture of paint employed.

Paul Nunneley uses the capabilities of the Canon Color Laser Copier to recolor, distort, and manipulate original transparencies (Fig. **6.41**). The Canon CLC is a combination scanner, copier, and printer. It can copy from either flat artwork or transparencies, and enlarge or reduce the whole image or a portion of it from 50 to 400 percent. For larger sizes, it will "tile," for example, a series of 16 A3 copies to make an A1 poster. It can also combine two originals into one copy, color black-and-white originals, and convert a color on the original to any other (Fig. **6.42**). The shape of the original can be changed too – stretched or condensed.

Nunneley uses a combination of all these techniques in making his illustrations. He will also interrupt the scanner, alter the focus, and change the image from positive to negative to achieve the effects shown here. It is even possible to create images with no originals, using colors and masks generated by the copier itself.

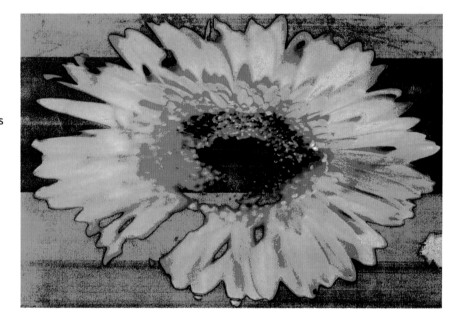

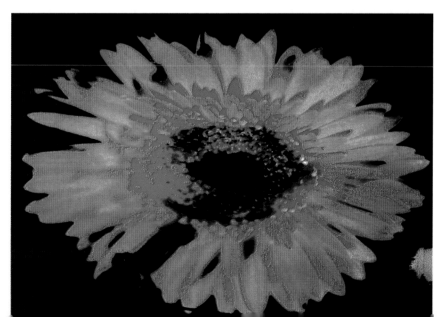

Printing processes:
the pros and cons

Offset litho
Advantages Extremely flexible and cost-effective for most jobs, wide range of presses from jobbing sheetfed machines to large web-fed presses, short set-up time, positive-working or negative-working, prints effectively on wide range of stock.
Disadvantages Needs more attention than gravure for consistency over long print runs, ink translucent and prone to more problems than in the other processes.

Gravure
Advantages High-quality high-speed continuous-tone reproduction and rich blacks, prints well on cheaper stock, very economical for long print runs, fast process after make-ready.
Disadvantages Type is screened, solvent-based inks, only viable for large print runs, expensive to set up, corrections require new cylinder, proofing expensive.

Flexography
Advantages Fast make-ready, prints well on non-absorbent stock, possibility of using water-based ink, prints well on cheap paper stock.
Disadvantages Image spread, poor halftones, usually have to use solvent-based ink, expensive to set up.

Screenprinting
Advantages Non-impact process, versatile, prints on any kind of substrate and on curved or uneven surfaces, can be used to produce thick and opaque deposits of ink, in brilliant saturated colors, and with high chemical and abrasion resistance.

Disadvantages Small print runs, not recommended for halftones because of the possibility of moiré effects, close registration and four-color work difficult, cannot print smaller sizes of type.

Letterpress
Advantages Quality of impression, wide range of original typeface designs (hand-set repro proofs can be taken for printing by offset litho).
Disadvantages Inflexible for design, expensive now that big presses have largely been taken out of service.

Collotype
Advantages High-quality screenless continuous-tone reproduction.
Disadvantages Slow, very expensive, short print runs only.

Xerography
Advantages Inexpensive for short print runs, no set-up costs, no film or plates, no ink, can print direct from computer disk.
Disadvantages Cannot print large sheets, color reproduction often poor and almost always variable, restricted paper stock.

Things that can go wrong

The printed publication can only be as good as your original artwork or mechanical. And that's why, if there's something wrong with the printed result, you should always check your artwork before you start blaming the printer. Of course, some jobs may *look* better, printed in color on beautiful paper, but they can never actually *be* better than the original. A printer may work miracles, but every time your copy goes through a pro-

cess it loses quality. That's why you should aim to get from artwork to plate with as few intermediate stages as possible.

If the typesetting you have produced is thin because the toner in the laser printer needs changing, then the printer can beef it up, but you will lose definition. The printer can't put back what was never there in the first place. Corrections to the mechanical can be a problem, too, introducing type of a different density, and cut lines where corrections have been pasted in. Okay, so your artwork is perfect. The type is crisp and black, all the hairline serifs are visible, and the halftones have a screen appropriate to the paper stock. What else can go wrong?

There are all kinds of problems associated with the paper, the ink, and the press, and how they interact with each other. Some of these have been mentioned earlier, but for the sake of completeness, they will be listed here in alphabetical order.

■ **Backing** is a lightening of color that occurs if ink removed from the fountain roller is not replaced by the flow of new ink.

■ **Catch-up** occurs in offset litho when insufficient water on the plate causes non-image areas to print (Fig. **6.43**).

■ **Chalking**, or powdering, happens mainly with matte coated stock and is caused when the vehicle from the ink is absorbed, leaving only pigment on the surface. It becomes apparent when dry ink starts to rub off the image or smudge, and unfortunately is only noticed after the job is finished. In emergencies, the original plate can be used to overprint a

layer of transparent size to try to bind the ink to the paper.

■ **Color variation** during a run is caused by altering ink-to-water balance, or by stopping the press.

■ **Crawling** is an imperfection in the surface of the ink, occurring when thick ink overprints wet ink.

■ **Crocking** is smudging or transfer of dry ink on to printed sheets.

■ **Crystallization** is a result of careless overprinting. If the ink of the first printing dries too hard before overprinting is done, it can repel the second color.

■ **Damper marks** are patterns over the print caused by worn damper covers or too much pressure.

■ **Dot gain** shows when halftone shadows fill in or if the print looks too dark, and is caused by bad film-to-plate contact, over-exposure of the plate, over-absorbent paper, or overinking. However, it will always occur to some degree, so an allowance should be made at the proofing stage.

■ **Doubling** – two dots where there should be only one – is caused when wet ink is picked up by the blanket on a subsequent printing. If it is slightly off register, it prints as a ghost dot nearby.

■ **Emulsification** is what happens when water gets into the litho ink. Most litho inks are designed to accept some emulsification, but too much results in a wishy-washy appearance.

■ **Flocculation** produces a surface like orange peel, and is an ink defect. It occurs when the pigment is not properly dispersed in the vehicle.

■ **Ghosting** is the word for faint areas, usually in solid blocks of color, caused by some parts of the image taking more than their fair share of ink, leaving other areas deficient. Some ghosting problems can be foreseen, and imposition schemes can be changed to prevent them. On small-format jobs, try to distribute solid areas evenly. Ghosting is also the term used to describe the dull image on the reverse side of a sheet caused by a printed image that has affected the drying and trapping of ink applied to the other side.

■ **Halation** appears in halftones as a halo-like light around a dark area, and is a prepress problem that should be picked up before plates are made.

■ **Hickies** are dark spots surrounded by uninked halos, or just plain white specks, that appear at random (Fig. **6.44**). They are caused by dust, paper fibers, or foreign bodies from the ink that have found their way on to the blanket. A solution is to run uninked paper through the press, and then wash the blanket.

■ **Linting** is a problem created by paper fibers that get on to the blanket, plate, or rollers of a press.

■ **Low spot** is a loss of image caused by an indentation on the blanket, often because plate and blanket are insufficiently packed.

■ **Moiré patterns** are unwanted "basket-weave" effects. They occur when the screen angles on multi-

▼ **6.43** Catch-up.

▼ **6.44** Hickies.

ON PRESS

▼ **6.45** Setoff.

▼ **6.46** Misregistration.

color work have not been set cor-rectly, or sometimes when there is regular patterning on an image, or when a halftone has been rescreened.

■ **Mottle** is an uneven, blotchy application of ink, caused by a mismatch between ink and paper stock, or too much dampening water on the blanket.

■ **Offset** see setoff.

■ **Paper curl** can be caused by too much dampening water, or can hap-pen because the stock has not accli-matized to the relative humidity of the press room. Wavy edges appear if the stack of paper has a lower moisture level than the surround-ings. Tight edges are caused by a higher moisture level in the stack.

See also tail-end hook.

■ **Picking** is a lifting of the paper's surface most noticeable in solid areas, caused by ink that is too tacky, a press running too fast, or a paper surface with too low a "picking resistance."

■ **Piling** is caused by a build-up of ink on the press rollers, or by particles from uncoated stock which adhere to the blanket and break up the image on the following sheets.

■ **Registration problems** are caused by poor stripping at the flat stage (check the proofs) or by paper stretching on the press (Fig. **6.46**).

■ **Scuffing** is a problem in packaging design, where print is likely to receive rough handling. Choose a scuff-proof ink or try a coat of varnish.

■ **Scumming** is when ink starts to appear on the non-image parts of the plate. It can be caused by a badly done deletion, or more likely it's time for the plate to be replaced.

■ **Setoff**, or offset, occurs when the

wet image on a sheet of paper prints on to the paper above or below it in the pile, or later rubs off in a bound book (Fig. **6.45**). Anti-setoff spray should separate each sheet by a fine layer of particles.

■ **Show-through** is when you can see right through a sheet of paper to the printing on the other side. Choose a more opaque stock next time.

■ **Skewing** is a problem that occurs during printing if the paper, blanket, and cylinder are not in proper contact.

■ **Slurring** is when halftones start to fill in, and is caused by too much ink, or slippage from smooth paper. There is a portion of the color bar on the proof specifically for indicating slurring.

■ **Snowflaking** in solid areas is a problem caused by water droplets in the litho ink. In gravure it can happen because inadequate pressure prevents the paper from taking the ink from one or more cells.

■ **Spreading** is an enlarging of the

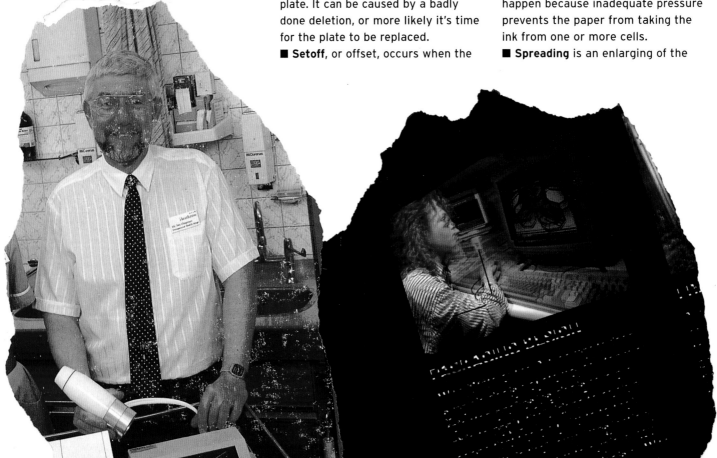

6.47 Die-stamping is used to add glamor to the kind of blockbuster paperback book you see on airport magazine booths. They can be stamped blind, giving a subtle three-dimensional effect, or inked, or foil blocked in gold, silver, or other metallic colors.

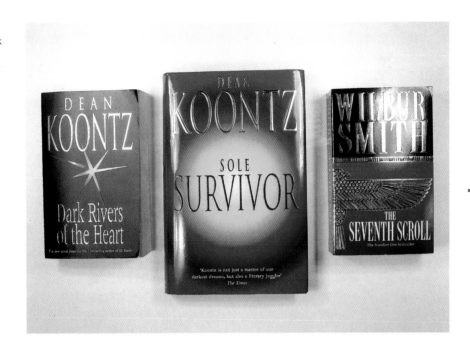

image caused by too much ink, or too much pressure between blanket and plate.

■ **Sticking**, or blocking, occurs when there is so much setoff that the sheets stick together.

■ **Strike-through** is like show-through, only worse – it is when the ink penetrates the whole thickness of the sheet. Change stock, or use a different ink formulation.

■ **Tail-end hook** – when solid areas near the back edge of a sheet make it curl down – is caused by paper adhering to the blanket too tightly as it is pulled off by the delivery grippers, and it happens if the ink is too tacky.

■ **Tinting** happens when pigment finds its way into the fountain, discoloring the background.

■ **Tracking**, or stripping, is when several colored images are printed in a row and inking becomes uneven as a result.

FINISHING

All the processes that convert the printed sheets into folded and bound publications are collectively known as **finishing** operations. These can also include print-related operations such as die-stamping, thermography, varnishing, and laminating.

Die-stamping is a process for producing a three-dimensional low relief effect on paper or cover board (Fig. **6.47**). It works as a kind of heavy-handed letterpress, with the additional assistance of a hollowed out recess on the other side. The hollowed out recess is in fact the die; the stamping part, the counter-die. The die is placed face upward beneath the paper. It is made in steel

from artwork, either etched photographically like a process block, or engraved by a computer-controlled machine tool.

Die-stamping can be used **blind**, to produce the subtle effect found on letterheads, or inked. Or the die can be used with metal foil, to make the bold impression that is so popular on the covers of blockbuster paperback books. **Die-cutting** uses sharp steel rules in a wooden die to cut shapes from paper.

Laser die-cutting is used to produce intricate patterns and designs on greetings cards and/or for see-through logos on business cards. Note that you must include small tabs of 0·3 to 0·5 mm to prevent the inner bowls of letters, for example, from falling out.

A cheaper way to obtain a low relief is by means of **thermography**. A freshly printed image is dusted with transparent thermography powder. This sticks to the ink and, when heated, swells into the third dimension. High-gloss and matte finishes are available. It is worth bearing in mind, however, that sheets printed using thermography can later be a problem when put through laser printers, as the thermographic printing can melt.

Embossing, similar to die-stamping, also gives the stock an area of texture. The lettering on the spine of a hardback book is formed by **blocking** in gold or silver leaf using a brass, or die. This time, the die is in relief and the effect is below the surface of the substrate.

Hot-foil stamping, or leaf stamping, transfers a foil coating from a carrier roll of polyester, by means of a heated die. The coating can be metallic, matte, pearl, or even a **hologram** (Fig. **6.48**).

Spot varnishing of halftones to add gloss and intensity has already been mentioned in the discussion of inks (see p. 173). Overall **varnishing**, as a finishing operation, is carried out by running printed sheets

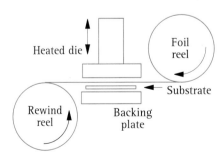

6.48 In hot-foil blocking, the foil passes from a roll and is stamped on to the substrate by the action of heat.

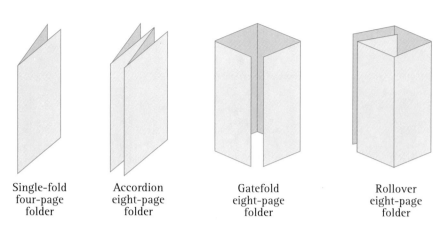

Single-fold
four-page
folder

Accordion
eight-page
folder

Gatefold
eight-page
folder

Rollover
eight-page
folder

6.49 There are many different ways to fold a folder. Here are some examples— but remember to make economical use of your printed sheet before you specify an exotic fold.

through rollers. Machine varnish (lacquer) can be applied using a conventional litho machine, but the sheen it produces is barely notice-able. High-gloss or liquid lamination is a nitrocellulose coating requiring a special machine. Ultraviolet varnish, which dries on exposure to ultravio-let light, also produces high gloss and scuff-resistance. Two layers of varnish, printed wet-on-wet, give a very smooth glossy finish.

Lamination adds strength as well as gloss. Film lamination is glued to the stock as it goes through a heated roller under high pressure. It is applied from a roll on to overlap-ping sheets, leaving the gripper edge and the sides free for any other processing. But laminated sheets must be left for two days for the adhesive to dry completely, before operations such as guillotining or embossing can be performed with confidence. Ultraviolet lamination cures more quickly.

Ink that is to be varnished or laminated should be quick drying, with little residual solvent, and absolutely no wax additives. Too much anti-setoff spray can have an adverse effect on either process. Metallic inks are a problem, and should be left alone. They have their own sheen, after all.

Folding and binding

After these print-related finishes have been applied, the stock can be folded (Fig. **6.49**). There are three types of folding machine. **Buckle folders** (Fig. **6.50**) are the most commonplace. The sheet enters a pre-set distance and is stopped and buckled back at the fold line by two inward-revolving rollers. These nip the flat sheet, then fold it and carry it forward to the next "plate," where the process is repeated. **Knife fold-ers** (Fig. **6.51**) are used in bookwork. Here a blunt knife is used to nip the sheet between two rollers. They are very precise, but slower than buckle folders. **Combination folders** give the best of both worlds.

Single-sheet jobs then go straight to the guillotine for trimming. Multi-page jobs first have to be united with the other pages, **gathered** on conveyor belts, bundled flat, and collated (put in order). For books, the sections are gathered one next to the other. Printed marks on the spines of sections, called backstep marks, indicate the correct sequence visually. Letters or numbers printed

on the signatures serve as a double check.

Loose **inserts** are single sheets of paper or even sometimes booklets, that are added, generally by hand, to a magazine. They fall out when the magazine is shaken.

Tipping-in is adding a single page to a publication, either by pasting down the inside edge, or by wrapping a short strip around the fold. This is a labor-intensive process, and thus very expensive. Illustrations that were printed intaglio, or on art paper, used to be tipped in to books. **Tipping-on** is pasting a smaller illus-tration, an errata slip, or a reply coupon on to a page.

Perforation can be done on the printing press, by means of a perforating strip attached to the impression cylinder (eventually ruin-ing the blanket), or on a special finishing machine.

Magazines and booklets are bound in one of two ways: by saddle-stitching or perfect binding. **Saddle-stitching** (Fig. **6.52**) is a fancy way of saying stapling, though the wire staples used in saddle-stitching are longer and rounder than office

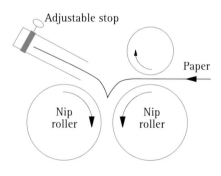

6.50 In a buckle folder, the sheet is brought to rest by an adjustable stop before being forced between a pair of nip rollers.

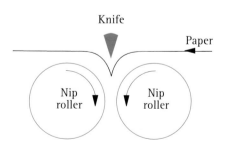

6.51 A knife folder is used for more exacting work — a knife-like device pushes the sheet between two nip rollers, producing a much sharper fold.

SCORE BEFORE FOLDING
Heavy paper or card should always be scored before folding – enough to produce a raised ridge. A fold should always be made with the ridge or hinge on the inside. Booklet covers must have a score wide enough to accommodate all the pages to be inserted inside.

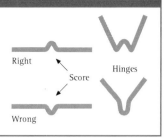

Right

Score

Wrong

Hinges

▼ **6.52** In saddle-stitching, the folded and collated signatures move along a conveyor on saddles the shape of inverted Vs. Wire staples are then inserted along the fold of the spine.

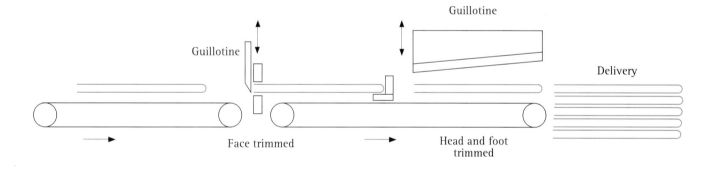

Signature feed

Signature feed

Wire stitchers

To trimmer ⟶

Guillotine

Guillotine

Delivery

Face trimmed ⟶ Head and foot trimmed

staples. Saddle-stitching gets its name from the inverted V saddle on to which the sections are placed. Sections are opened out and placed one inside another, inserting larger sections inside smaller ones, and with the cover on top. This is the least expensive form of **binding**, but can only be used with publications of up to around 128 pages, depending

on the paper stock. On thicker publications, take note of paper creep – pages near the center will be narrower after trimming than those near the covers (see p. 110). Specify stainless steel wires so that they don't rust.

Side-stabbing (Fig. **6.53**) inserts the wires from front to back, near the spine, disguised by the creased **hinges** of the covers.

Calendars, cookbooks, and technical manuals are usually **spiral-bound** (Fig. **6.54**) so as to lie flat. The sheets are punched with a line of round or slotted holes near the **spine**. Wire is then coiled through the holes and crimped. **Wire comb**, or Wire-O, bindings and **plastic comb** bindings give a more finished look.

▼ **6.54** Spiral binding is used for calendars, manuals, and cookery books – wherever the publication has to fold perfectly flat. Wire-O gives a neater finish.

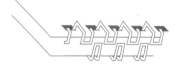

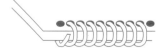

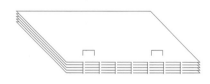

▲ **6.53** In side-stabbing, the wire staples are inserted through the front of the signature, along the back edge close to the spine.

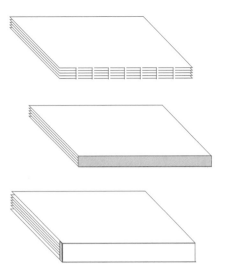

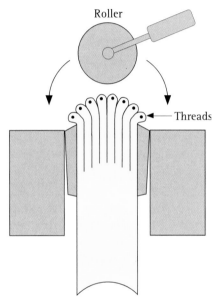

6.55 In perfect binding, the signatures are collated, then the spines are cut off, roughened, and spread with glue to attach the covers.

6.56 The thread used to sew the book block makes it thicker at the spine. Rounding keeps the book in good shape; backing produces a neat shoulder.

Roller

Threads

Perfect binding (Fig. **6.55**), unsewn binding, or cut-back binding, can be far from perfect unless a good glue is used. For this process, the sections are gathered and collated as before, and presented to the machine spine down. The edge is notched, or milled off and roughened, and adhesive is applied. The covers are folded, scored, and wrapped around the pages. The adhesive is then cured by heat, and the pages are trimmed. Perfect-bound magazines have a flat spine, on to which a title, date, and a résumé of the contents can be printed. But the process is slower and more expensive than saddle-stitching, and double-page spreads can be a problem with copy disappearing into the gutter. Fold the

magazine back and it falls apart! Mass-market paperback books are often printed two-up, head to head, and only cut apart after perfect binding.

Hardback books are sometimes perfect bound, but the sections can instead be sewn through the spine with thread – this is called **section sewing**. They are then gathered together into a book-block. **Thread-sealing** combines features of perfect

binding and section sewing (but no thread runs between sections).

Side-sewing is a method used for children's books, in which the thread goes front to back, as in side-stabbing. This produces a stronger binding than section sewing, with the disadvantage that the book will not lie flat when folded.

A case-bound, or hardback, book (Fig. **6.57**) has a hard case made apart from the pages. The book-block and cover are assembled,

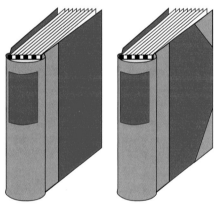

Quarter bound　　　　Half bound

6.57 Case-bound books consist of a book-block, a hard cover, and endpapers that are assembled at the final stage of binding.

6.58 A quarter-bound book and a half-bound book with its additional triangles at the corners.

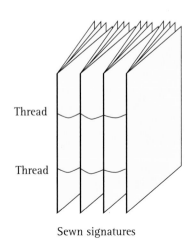

Thread

Thread

Sewn signatures

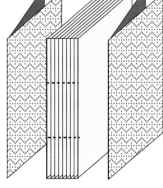

Endpapers　　　　Endpapers
Book block

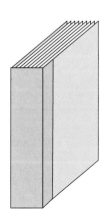

Strip of crash glued on

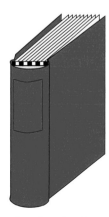

Headband and case added

along with tipped-on endpapers, at the final stage of binding. Endpapers are usually of heavier stock than the text pages, and are sometimes decorated. **Rounding and backing (R & B)** is a combined operation that puts a rounded shape into the spine of the book-block, and a joint below the shoulder (Fig. **6.56**). Some books are rounded; others are left with flat spines. Linings are glued to the spine; **headbands** and **tailbands** – and perhaps a bookmark – are added; and the endpapers are glued to the insides of the cases. Book jackets can be wrapped around the cased book by hand or by machine.

Cases are made from heavy board, with the grain parallel to the spine to prevent warping. The material used to make the case of a hardback book looks attractive is known as the covering. It can be of nonwoven material, such as embossed paper, fiberfelts, or plastic-coated fiber, or a form of starch-filled cloth or **buckram**. A **quarter bound** book (Fig. **6.58**) has the spine and an adjacent strip of the cover bound in an expensive material, maybe leather, with the rest of the sides in something cheaper. A **half binding** has, in addition, triangles at the corners in the expensive material. Leather, embellished with gold block-ing and tooled decorations, is reserved for expensive limited-edition books.

After binding and counting, the job is parceled up in waterproof packaging or shrink-wrapping, is boxed, correctly labeled, put on to pallets, and shipped to its destination – and your job is done.

SUMMARY

On press is that part of the production process over which the graphic designer has the least amount of hands-on control. What the designer does possess, however, is the power of *selection*. An appropriate choice of paper, ink, and printer should ensure a predictable outcome, given that the designer's input is as near perfect as can be, and bearing in mind the merits and limitations of the various printing processes.

Paper, ink, and printing process are all interlinked. The size of the print run and the budget for the job are also important considerations. Offset litho and letterpress demand thick and sticky inks; conversely, the inks for gravure and flexography need to be thin and runny. Consequently, gravure and flexo are able to print at high speed on to relatively poor stock – and flexo can print on to the most difficult surfaces, such as cellophane and waxy board. But there is a trade-off. Flexo and gravure cylinders are expensive to produce, and so the process is only viable for large print runs.

Most designers will spend most of their careers working with offset lithography, which is perhaps the most economical and versatile process of all. But there will perhaps come a time when you need to produce a design for a plastic carrier bag, for example, and have to evaluate the relative advantages and constraints of flexography and screenprinting, and modify the design appropriately. Or there may come a time when you wish to produce a high-quality invitation card on hand-made paper using letterpress. With the information outlined in this chapter, you will be confident of making the right choice.

So, too, with finishing. The expected end use of a printed product and the budget are key factors in the choice of perfect binding, say, over wire stitching, or varnishing over lamination. Only experience will teach you to make the correct choices every time, but, forearmed with the knowledge contained in this chapter, you will at least be aware of all the options open to you.

MALCOLM GARRETT

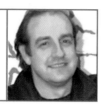

LIFE STORY Malcolm Garrett was born in Northwich, England, in 1956. He studied typography and psychology at Reading University from 1974 to 1975, and graphic design at Manchester Polytechnic from 1975 to 1978. His first professional work in 1977 made an immediate impact, with his album sleeves for Manchester punk rock band The Buzzcocks. In the late 1970s and early 1980s, Garrett was identified, along with colleagues Peter Saville, Jamie Reed, and Neville Brody, as one of the most influential designers working for youth culture clients. In 1983, with partner Kasper de Graaf, he set up Assorted Images (Ai).

In projects for Simple Minds, Duran Duran, and Culture Club, Garrett applied corporate identity to pop groups. Using logos, emblems, and other decorative typographical devices, he turned bands into brands. Other work in the entertainment industry followed, including television graphics. Over the years, Garrett has designed under every possible way of spelling his own name (one R, two Rs, one T, two Ts) and under various trade names including Aesthetic Images and Assorted Images. Ai could mean "love" in Japanese or stand as an acronym for artificial intelligence.

Ai was an early advocate of computer graphics – first with an Apple II-based CAD system (yes, Apple II not Mac II) called the Robocom Bitstik, used to distort and stretch logos, then more mainstream Macs. Garrett's past work also includes graphic identity for such clients as the London Symphony Orchestra, and the New Materials Workshop, Tokyo, as well as exhibition design, television graphics, and design for literature of all kinds. In the late 1980s, Garrett's focus shifted decisively in the direction of new technology and in 1994 he broke with Ai and joined up with multimedia director Alasdair Scott, with whom he has collaborated since 1989, in order to set up AMXdigital. The company's purpose is to design and develop web pages for clients such as Guinness (see spread). He is currently responsible primarily for interface and navigational design for interactive media at AMX. The company is based in London, with an office in Los Angeles, USA.

> "If you're going to succeed and move forward, you do have to be pigeonholed"

As well as Guinness, AMX has recently been commissioned to develop CD-based multimedia titles for clients such as EMI Records, Kodak Image Bank, D&AD, and internet sites for the BPI, Barclays Bank, Financial Times Television, UCI cinemas, Guinness Brewing (for Ogilvy & Mather), Malibu rum (for Lowe Howard Spink), *Dazed&Confused* magazine, and WEA records. He has taught multimedia design at the School of Visual Arts in New York, and Savannah College of Art & Design, Georgia, and is external examiner for MA Communication design at Central St Martins, London. He also maintains strong links with the Icelandic College of Arts and Crafts, Reykjavik; Space Invaders school of multimedia, Copenhagen; and CalArts school of design, California.

MANIFESTO A Pragmatic Anarchist
Garrett is a big believer in communication. His definition of good design is: does it do its job? Did message A get communicated to audience B? "If you don't speak to an audience in a language it can understand," says Garrett, "then communication is unlikely to take place. This either means that you educate an audience in the nuances of your own personal language, or you explore the languages that exist, which can be efficient yet conceptually restrictive." His work often seems to adopt a vernacular approach, but is not constrained by convention. He's a pragmatic anarchist.

Garrett has always loved technology. "If you're going to succeed and move forward, you do have to be pigeonholed. So despite calling myself Assorted images in an early idealistic vision of never being pigeonholed, I figured, well, if I'm to be pigeonholed anyway, it will be for computers, technology, something I'm good at, something I've got involved in early on, something I have a view about. I decided it was time perhaps to have people reappraise what they think I'm about. I would much rather be known as Malcom Garrett, the guy who plays with computers, than Malcolm Garrett, the guy who designs record sleeves.

"I'm genuinely excited by the things that are happening now and things that haven't happened yet. I figure it is my job to be this kind of blinkered believer. You know: I am the new futurist, I will live in the technological world. That appeals to me and I will ignore the current technical problems because somebody else will sort out the technology. That's the Japanese approach. You go to Japan and everybody is positive and optimistic and you look at what Japan's done in the last 50 years. If it can happen, it should. Is that irresponsible?"

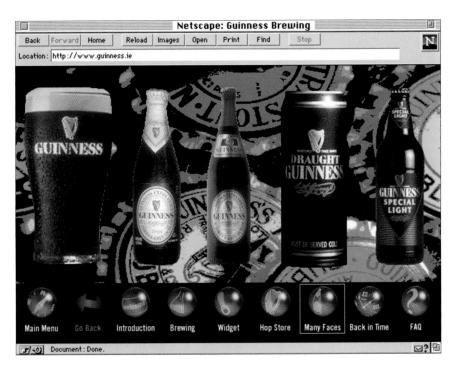

WORKSTATION

• Alan Pipes, interview in *Design*, July 1985, pp. 44-45.
• *Graphis*, Nov/Dec 1988, No. 258.
• *Emigre* 11, 1989 Ambition/Fear issue.
• *Emigre* 13, Redesigning stereotypes issue.
• "The book is dead," *Graphics World*, Feb 1991, No. 90.
• "Multimedia—who needs it?". *Baseline* No. 18 1994, pp. 30-33.
• Rick Poynor, interview in *Eye*, 12/94, pp. 11-16.
• Web site: <http://www.amxdigital.com/>

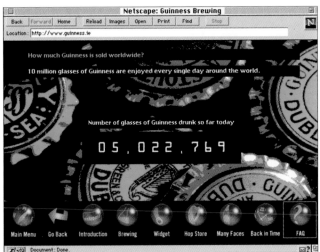

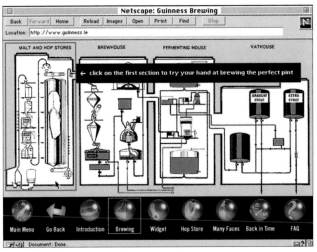

▲ The Irish company Guinness has developed a stout that sells all over the globe; throughout its long history, the company has been responsible for innovative advertising. The half of the Guinness site designed by AMXdigital is called The Brewery (the other half – The Local – was designed by Webfactory). The web site, like the drink, is very black and white – mainly white on black. At the home page you are greeted by an image map taking you to The Brewery (left) or to The Local (right). Recently, a signpost has been added in the middle, linking to other Irish sites.

In The Brewery, animated bubbles take you to see how beer-can technology can now re-create the distinctive texture of Guinness, and you can have a go at controlling the brewing process. A screensaver, based on a popular television commercial, can be downloaded. The HTML is minimal – all the animated graphics have been done using Macromedia's Director and the code embedded into the HTML using the <EMBED> tag. You will need a Shockwave plug-in to see everything work, but a non-shocked version is also available.

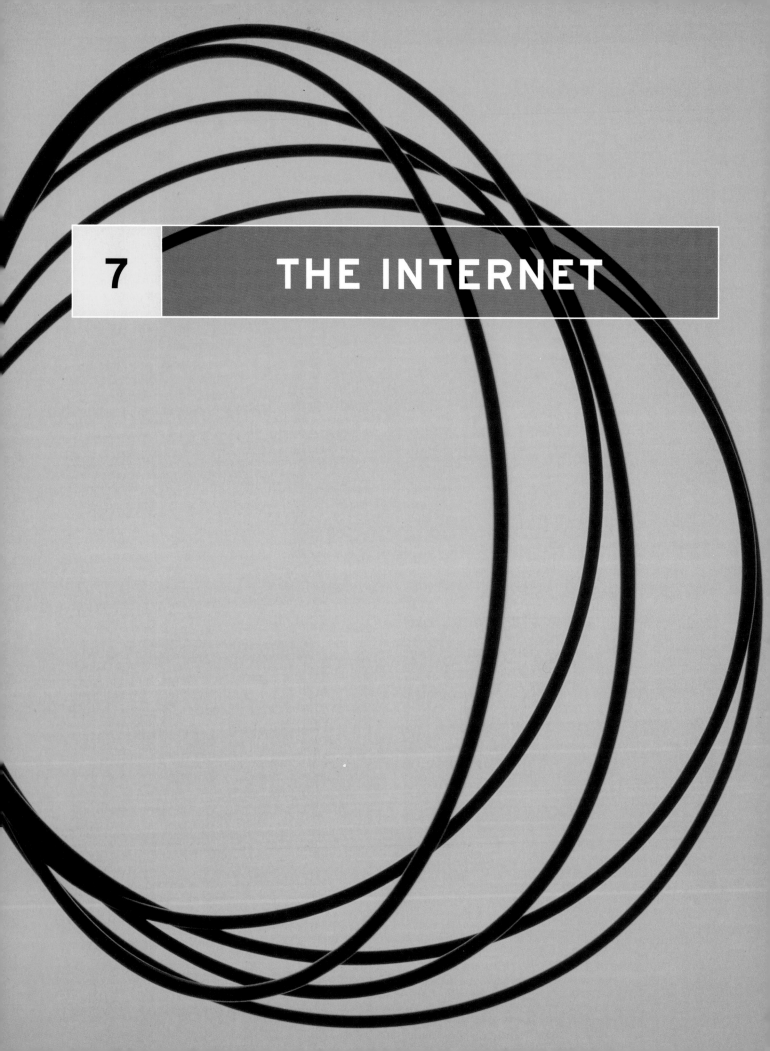

7 THE INTERNET

magine. you are reading this book and you come across a term you don't quite understand or the name of a person or place you'd like to know some more about. The words are highlighted by being in **bold type**, so that means you can flick to the back of the book and look them up in the glossary. But think how amazing it would be if you could just "click" on the word somehow and be transported to a place with all the answers in as much detail as you need! Well if you were online to the Internet, that's exactly what would happen.

What is the Internet? It is simply a global network of computers, and a means of connecting your computer (yes, you do need to have one!) to other computers via a telephone line. It is merely a medium. But on the Internet you'll find lots of useful tools: the main three being email (electronic mail), news-groups, and the World Wide Web.

With email, you can send messages to other people: you type a message on your computer, connect to the Internet using a piece of equipment called a modem, and send it off. It then waits in the recipient's "mailbox" until they check their mail. You can also send digital "attachments" – anything from computer-generated artwork to sound samples.

Newsgroups are online "bulletin boards" or discussion groups that enable you to keep in touch with other designers, exchange tips and experiences, or download "shareware" fonts and programs.

The World Wide Web (WWW) is a collection of "pages," probably running into several billions by now, containing text, images, sound, movies, and, most impor-tantly, "hot links" to other pages. You view these pages using a program called a "browser," such as Netscape Navigator. WWW pages can also have "forms" built in so that you can, say, order

books from an online bookshop or CDs from the Cyber Mall, or send fan mail (or a job offer) to the illustrator or photographer showing their virtual portfolio at an online gallery.

So what's in the Internet for the designer? First, it is a cheap and fast way to send artwork to the client and printer. Second, it's an inexpensive and effective way to advertise yourself and your work worldwide. Third, it is a potentially huge source of new clients.

WHAT IS THE INTERNET?

The Internet is a global network of computers or, more accurately, a network of computer networks — *the* network of networks — after all, there is only one Internet. It enables you to connect your computer (or, perhaps in the near future, a box attached to your television similar to a console games machine) to every other computer on the Internet, initially via a telephone line. It is basically a medium of communication, like the telephone network, but capable of much more. On the Internet you'll find many useful tools and resources, the main three being email (electronic mail), newsgroups, and the World Wide Web.

First, as always, some history. In 1962, Dr J. C. R. "Lick" Licklider was chosen to head research into improving the military's use of computer technology. The result was ARPAnet (ARPA stands for Advanced Research Projects Agency — the funding body), which was set up to connect together just four computers at sites around the United States in order to distribute the resources where they were needed. Computers were extremely expensive in those days (even though they probably only had around 12 k of memory each) and had to be shared around. The first ARPAnet mode was installed at the University of California at Los Angeles in September 1969. Additional notes were soon added at Stanford Research Institute, the University of California at Santa Barbara, and the University of Utah.

This was all made possible by packet switching. The reasoning went that in a nuclear war, the communi-cations infrastructure — the networks of wires, command centers, antennae — would become prime targets. By decentralizing the network, communications would keep flowing even if parts of the network were destroyed. The key idea is that messages are broken down into "packets" and sent off in the general direction of their destination, where they would then be reassembled. Paul Baran of the Rand Corporation published such a scheme in 1964. The National Physical Laboratory in the UK set up the first test network based on these principles in 1968.

ARPAnet was developed from the outset to be both resilient and de-centralized — designed, in other words, to survive a nuclear attack. By 1971 approximately twenty nodes had been installed. In 1972, the First International Conference on Computer Communications was held in Washington DC to discuss communication protocols in order that different kinds of networks around the world would be able to "talk" to each other. The International Network Working Group (INWG) was created and Vinton Cerf, who was involved with ARPAnet at UCLA, was chosen as the first chair. The first international connections to the ARPAnet were made in 1973: to University College, London, and the Royal Radar Establishment in Norway.

In September 1973, Bob Kahn and Vint Cerf presented their basic Internet ideas at a meeting of the INWG at the University of Sussex in Brighton, UK. The system of proto-cols they came up with became known as the TCP/IP, after the two

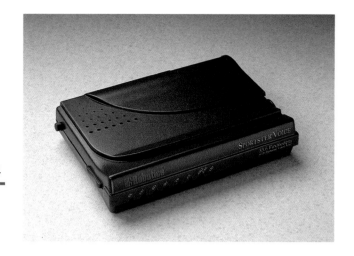

7.1 A modem converts the digital signal from your computer into an analog signal that can travel down the telephone line. This US Robotics Sportster can also be used to send faxes and voice mail.

initial protocols developed: Transmission Control Protocol (TCP) and Internet Protocol (IP). These were first published in September 1981, became the standard Internet protocols in January 1983, and are still used today.

The Internet was opened up to commercial networks such as CompuServe and America OnLine in 1991 and continues to grow and grow. The number of computers on the Internet reached a million in 1992 and by the end of 1993 this number had doubled. At the time of writing, the number of computers connected to the Internet was estimated at 41.9 million.

Who invented the Internet? Who coined that word? The definitive primary source for Internet history is the collection of email memos called RFCs (Requests for Comments). RFC791, for example, is the September 1981 specification for Internet Protocol (IP). The oldest reference to the word "Internet" that I could find was in the title of RFC675: V. Cerf, Y. Dalal, and C. Sunshine, "Specification of Internet Transmission Control Program," dated December 1st, 1974.

So who runs the Internet? No one actually owns the Internet and no one body runs it. That is both its strength and weakness. If a resilient network has been designed to find a route around physical damage, so it can always find a route around

censorship. Some people see the Internet as much more than a collection of co-operating computer networks. They see a new community called Cyberspace, with its own culture, language, and laws. But fascinating as that concept might be, it is really outside the scope of this book. Check out Further Reading, p. 00, if you'd like to know more.

In summary, the Internet is:
• A network of networks based on the TCP/IP protocols
• A community of people who use and develop those networks
• A collection of resources that can be reached from those networks.

HOW TO GET STARTED

You may already have access to the Internet at school or college. If not, you can rent time at a Cybercafé or invest in your own equipment. You will need a **modem** (Fig. **7.1**) and an account with an **ISP** (Internet Service Provider). The modem connects your (digital) computer to the (analog) telephone network and your ISP should be a local telephone call away. You will need **TCP/IP** (Transmission Control Protocol/Internet Protocol) software and either **SLIP** (Serial Line Internet Protocol) or **PPP** (Point to Point Protocol) soft-

ware. Don't worry, your ISP will usually supply you with all the software you need to get started, plus instructions on how to configure the software. Modems are rated by their data throughput – 33.6 kbits per second is the state of the art at the time of writing, with 56k on the way. Modems can also be used to send faxes directly from your computer or can be used to set up a direct connection (i.e. direct from your telephone to their telephone, not via the Internet) with your repro house. You can cut out the modem all together and gain a faster connection by leasing a dedicated digital **ISDN** (Integrated Services Digital Network) line. Use SLIP or PPP to get connected, and you're ready to explore the Internet.

EMAIL

With email (electronic mail) you can send messages and "attachments" to other people connected to the Internet: you type a message on your computer, connect to the Internet, and send it down the telephone line to your local ISP (Fig. **7.2**). It then finds its way to the destination computer and waits in the recipient's "mailbox" until they check their mail. If they wish to reply, they hit the "reply" button on their computer, type a message (perhaps highlighting parts of your original message) and – you have new mail.

Trivial, you may think. But it's much easier and faster than faxing, it's the cost of a quick local phone call, and you have a digital record of the correspondence. What's more, you can send "attachments," which could be scanned-in drawings or

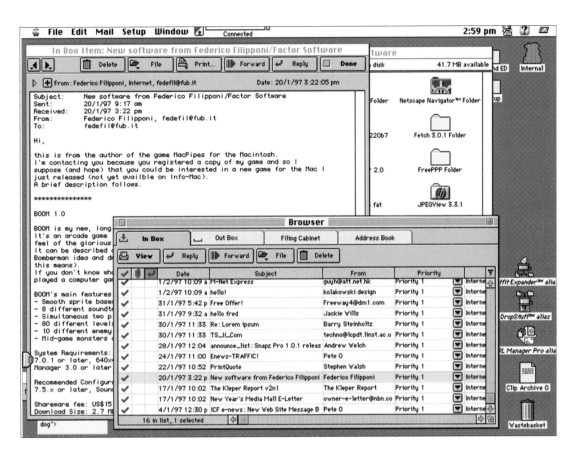

7.2 Email screenshot – the program being used is Claris Emailer.

photographs, digital artwork, programs, sound samples, anything that can be digitized. It's fast, cheap (the cost of a local phone call), energy-saving (green); another plus point is that precious artwork doesn't get delayed, lost, or bent in the mail.

In October 1963, computer-consulting company Bolt, Beranek, and Newman (BBN) published a paper demonstrating that users could communicate remotely with computers using ordinary tele-phones. BBN had already patented the modem earlier that year.

In 1971, Ray Tomlinson of BBN invented email. By the second year of ARPAnet's operation, the main traffic was news and personal messages. Researchers were using the network not only to collaborate on projects and trade notes on work, but to gossip. People had their own personal user accounts on the ARPAnet computers, and their own personal addresses for electronic mail. It wasn't long before the invention of the mailing list, with which a

message could be broadcast to anyone "subscribing" to a particular list. One of the first mailing lists was for science fiction fans.

Eudora (named after Eudora Welty, the author of "Why I live at the P.O.") is a popular email program for Macs; Pegasus Mail is an email program for Wintel PCs. Most email programs allow you to store "address lists" or "nicknames" of recipients and to add your "signature" to the end of each and every message.

Decoding Internet addresses

Everyone on the Internet has an email address of the form **user_name @site.dom**, in which **user_name** is your name or a nickname you have chosen, **site** locates your ISP or server computer, and **dom** is a "domain" type, possibly including subdomains. These are all separated by periods. (The exception is Compu-Serve, where your membership number is used instead of a user name

to make an address of the form: 101456.1525@compuserve.com.)

Domain types include:
.com commercial organizations
.edu educational institutions

Note that most of the sites in the .com and .edu domains are in the United States or Canada. Outside these functional domains, sites in the States have the .us domain, and there are subdomains for the fifty states, each generally with a name identical to the state's postal abbre-viation. Within the .uk domain, there is an .ac subdomain for academic sites and a .co domain for commer-cial ones. Note that .ca can be both California and Canada, depending on the context.

NEWSGROUPS

Usenet (Unix User Network) was established in 1979 between Duke University and the University of North Carolina to exchange news

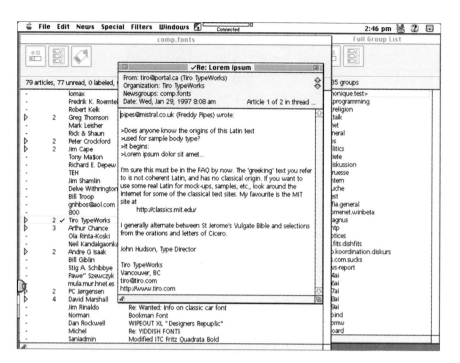

7.3 Newsgroup screenshot taken from a comp.fonts discussion thread. The program is Newswatcher.

and views. The original programs were written by graduate student Steve Bellovin. These were rewritten and extended by Steve Daniel and Tom Truscott.

Usenet is an example of a **client-server** architecture. A user (the client) connects to a machine (the server) where the Usenet postings for the past few days, weeks, or hours are stored. You can look at the headings of postings in the newsgroups of interest, and then request the full text of a particular posting (message or article) to be forwarded to your machine (Fig. **7.3**). You may then read or store the article, reply directly to the poster via email, or post a follow-up article (starting or joining a "thread"). You can also initiate a new subject heading with a new posting. The newsgroup program on your computer keeps track of which articles you have already read.

Newsgroups are supposed to be limited to a single topic, and the name of the group should give you some idea of the content to be expected. In 1986 to 1987, seven main hierarchies were created: **comp**, **misc**, **news**, **rec**, **sci**, **soc**, and **talk**. The alt hierarchy was proposed at a barbecue in Mountain View,

California, on May 7th, 1987, and implemented by subterfuge.

At the time of writing, there were over 13,000 different newsgroups, covering everything from keeping fish (rec.aquaria.freshwater.goldfish) to font design (comp.fonts). Not all ISPs carry all newsgroups, however. Some refuse to carry some sexually explicit groups, especially those used for posting "binaries" (image or sound files), which also take up a lot of "bandwidth" (here meaning throughput of traffic).

Newswatcher is a popular newsgroup program for Macs; Free Agent is a newsgroup program for Wintel PCs.

Chatting on the Net

There may be times when you'd like to communicate with other netizens live in almost real time. With **IRC** (Internet Relay Chat) you can. It is a text-based system, so you'll need to know lots of acronyms in order to keep up with the conversations. First you join a channel, #Brighton for example, and then you can either broadcast your comments to everyone else on that channel or choose a person to talk to in private. If you have prearranged a conference with someone, you can create your own

channel in which to speak privately. Homer is a popular IRC program for Macs; IRC2 is an IRC program for Wintel PCs.

You can even go one step further by entering a virtual world as an **avatar** (in Hindu mythology, an avatar is an earthly incarnation of a deity) to talk to other avatars in a virtual scene. You are presented with a 3D VRML (Virtual Reality Modeling Language) room or landscape or, in the case of Microsoft's Comic Chat, a two-dimensional black-and-white cartoon strip in which your representative interacts with other people appearing as robot Barbie dolls or teddy bears (Fig. **7.4**). The chat appears as text in speech bubbles. Avatar chat may be fun, but it can be very slow – you'll need a fast connection and powerful computer – and in highly populated channels you may find yourself talking to someone with the same "character" as yourself!

With a microphone attached to your computer, you can speak to other net users anywhere in the world for the price of a local call. Video conferencing is possible on the net, using a program such as CuSee-Me, so long as you also have a video camera attached to your computer.

Netiquette

Network etiquette, or **netiquette**, is something that a **newbie** (new user) will come across sooner or later. In the absence of any governing body, certain netizens take it upon themselves to police the newsgroups and will **flame** (post a harshly criticizing message in public on Usenet or send very long messages to you via email)

any transgressors. Newbies are encouraged to **lurk** for a while (a lurker is someone who reads but never posts) and consult the newsgroup's FAQ (Frequently Asked Questions) list before posting for the first time.

Postings that are "off topic" often elicit a flaming. **Crossposting** (posting the same message to several groups) is particularly frowned upon, but real venom is reserved for **spamming** (from the Monty Python song "Spam"), which is crossposting a carelessly inappropriate message or advertisement to many different groups or individuals. Messages set all in capitals (interpreted as "shouting") or with overlong signatures (especially ones containing so-called ASCII art) are discouraged, but it is considered very bad form to criticize a poster's poor grammar or spelling. The latest versions of newsreading programs, such as Newswatcher, have useful "kill files" which enable you to filter out unwanted messages from particular people or on particular topics.

Acronyms and smileys

Because of the need to conserve bandwidth, and for speed of typing, many acronyms are in common use. Here are a few you may encounter:

AFAIK   as far as I know
BTW   by the way
FYI   for your information
IMHO   in my humble opinion
ROFL   rolls on the floor
            laughing
RT*M   read the * manual
            (clean version!)
YMMV   your mileage may vary

And because gestures or inflections of speech are impossible on the net, symbols made from ASCII characters, called smileys or "emoticons" have evolved. These are particularly useful to avoid causing offense – your harmless joke may be taken literally, but a smiley makes every-

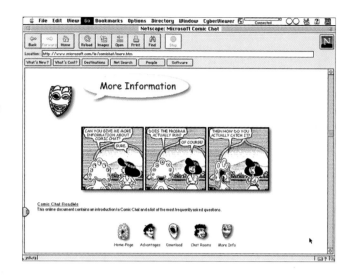

7.4 IRC screenshot, with atavars. This is Microsoft's Comic Chat, with characters designed by Jim Woodring.

thing OK! Here are a few (turn your head 90 degrees to the left):

:-) or :) basic smiley
;-) or ;) winking smiley (for irony)
:-(or :(sad smiley

You may also see these non-smileys:

<g>   grins
<s>   sighs

Ftp: uploading and downloading

Ftp (File Transfer Protocol) lets users transfer files between computers. There are many sites around the Internet where users can **download** programs, documents, and images (Fig. **7.5**). **Mirror sites** keep copies

of the files from the main sites, but may be geographically closer to you. If you have a **WWW** site (see next section), you will use ftp to **upload** your files to the server. Fetch is a popular ftp program for Macs; Ws_ftp is an ftp program for Wintel PCs.

Telnet lets you log on to another computer, anywhere on the Internet, as if you were using a terminal attached to that computer. You may use Telnet, for example, to check your email while round at a friend's house or run programs remotely. Gopher and Archie are other terms you may come across: they are ways of locating files via ftp. However, they are becoming much less important as the World Wide Web and all-in-one browsers such as Netscape Navigator take over their original role.

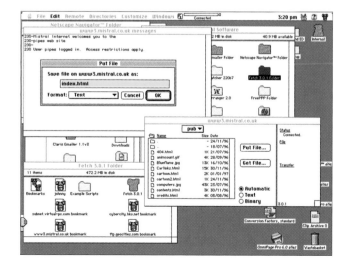

7.5 You can download software or upload your home page to your ISP's server using an ftp program such as Fetch .

MAKE YOURSELF KNOWN

Search engines such as Alta Vista and Lycos send out robots to rove the web, reading the first few words of web sites and then try to classify them so that someone initiating a search with a few key words will not be inundated with thousands of likely matches to plow through. Help them out by using the <META> tag in your HTML document so that search engines will know all about you. Placing something like this in your document will stand a good chance of coming top of the list in an Alta Vista search for Palo Alto poodle parlors:

```
<HEAD>
<TITLE>Acme Pet Parlor</TITLE>
<META NAME="description"
CONTENT="We specialize in grooming pink poodles.">
<META NAME="keywords"
CONTENT="pet grooming, Palo Alto, dog">
</HEAD>
```

WORLD WIDE WEB (WWW)

While consulting for CERN (the European Laboratory for Particle Physics) between June and December 1980, Tim Berners-Lee wrote a hypertext-based program called "Enquire-Within-Upon-Everything." In October 1990, the name **World Wide Web (WWW)** was decided, and in November, with Robert Cailliau as co-author, the first WWW program was developed. On April 30th, 1993, CERN placed the software for the WWW in the public domain.

In September 1993 a group of graduate students from the University of Illinois at Champaign-Urbana developed Mosaic, a software package that used the WWW protocol. Mosaic was a major factor in the explosion of business interest on the Internet, because it made the Internet accessible to inexperienced users. Many other browsers have evolved since Mosaic's development, including its direct descendant Netscape Navigator and the more recent Microsoft Explorer.

The World Wide Web is a huge collection of interconnected "pages," probably running into several billions by now. These pages are viewed by a program called a **browser**, such as Netscape Navigator (which, like most Internet software, can be downloaded for free) and can contain text, images, sound, movies, and hypertext "hot links" to other pages, which may reside on servers anywhere around the world (Fig. **7.6**). These pages can be about anything: football, recipes, bands, illustration. The biggest growth area is in commercial sites (see Malcolm

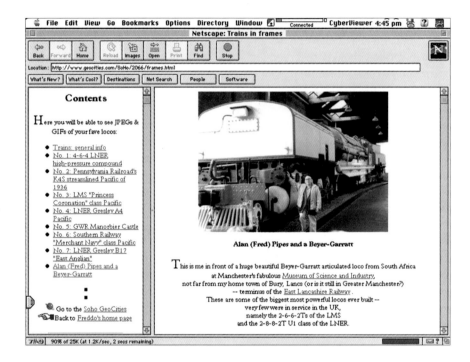

Garrett, p. 198), where corporations entice users to visit their online "advertisements" with the promise of free screensavers and other entertaining programs to download. Pages may also have built-in "forms," so that you can, say, order books from an online bookshop or CDs from the Cyber Mall pages, or send fan mail (or a job) to the artist showing at an online gallery. Many sites encourage you to register (giving them valuable marketing information) and you are issued with a password for subsequent visits.

Most people on the net have a **home page**. Your ISP or college may provide you with disk space on their server and there are many sites around the world that offer free space for home pages. These can also be used as test areas to develop your web design skills.

The WWW is based on a client-server model where the client (your

▲ **7.6** Netscape screenshot showing the use of frames to create a separate scrollable contents list to a site on steam locomotives.

browser) communicates with the servers (the sites storing the web pages you want to view) using **HTTP** (Hyper Text Transport Protocol). HTML (Hyper Text Markup Language) is used to create and communicate the page. The address of a page or its **URL** (Uniform Resource Locator) is thus of the form: http://www.your_ISP.com/user_name/index.html.

Designing for the World Wide Web

The World Wide Web is a wonderful opportunity for the graphic designer, but it does have some curious challenges. For a start, you don't have a lot of control over how your designs and layouts will be seen! You can't specify fonts, their sizes or the

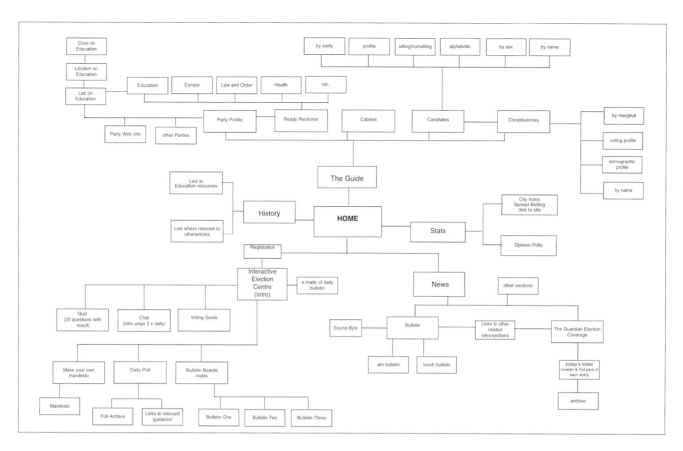

measure used. You have very little influence over the use of white space, and there are many trade-offs to be made to keep downloading time to a minimum (if your page doesn't download quickly then it won't be seen – the user will just carry on surfing!)

You have to accept that your design is going to appear differently on different browsers and on different machines. On some browsers, for example, the user can increase or decrease the default text size – great for the partially sighted, but it can play havoc with your carefully crafted layouts. But on the upside, some designers find these constraints liberating, plus you don't have to worry about the resolution of images (everything is 72 dpi), CMYK concerns, or anything at all to do with print production! The web is an ideal publishing medium: it is cheap (almost free), global, instantaneous, and, despite what was said earlier in this paragraph, extremely versatile.

So what is there left for the designer to do? Basically what all graphic designers do all the time in any case: communicate the client's message in the most effective way; make it easy for the user to "navigate" around the site; and make the pages distinctive, attractive, eye-catching, and entertaining. You may have to use ingenious work-arounds to achieve all the results you envisaged at concept stage, but the web is also a great leveler – college graduates in their back bedrooms have exactly the same tools available to them as the most prestigious design groups working for the largest multinational corporations.

Perhaps the biggest difference between designing for print and for the WWW – and this applies equally to CD-rom design – is that the layouts for a book or magazine are designed linearly: readers are expected to start at the beginning and work their way through to the end. In interactive media like the WWW, the reader is encouraged to leap from one hot link to another, so page organization is important. Designing a WWW site is more akin

7.7 Concept design of a web site for the 1997 British General Election, designed by New Media Labs for the *Guardian* newspaper.

to making a movie, but one with multiple narratives, to boot. Remember, the reader may be entering any page in your site from an outside link, so every page must be self-contained, with all the navigational aids necessary to help them carry on surfing. A concept plan with flowcharts and maybe a storyboard is essential (Fig. **7.7**). WWW designers need directorial skills too – with sound and animation available, you may well be asked to coordinate the efforts of a whole team of other professionals.

Do designers really have to learn HTML?

Well, yes and no. The Internet at present is rather like the early days of automobiles, when you had to carry a toolkit around with you and know enough about the engine to make running repairs. There are plug-ins to QuarkXPress and PageMaker that can convert existing page layouts into HTML and there

7.8 Programs such as Claris Home Page enable you to create web pages quickly.

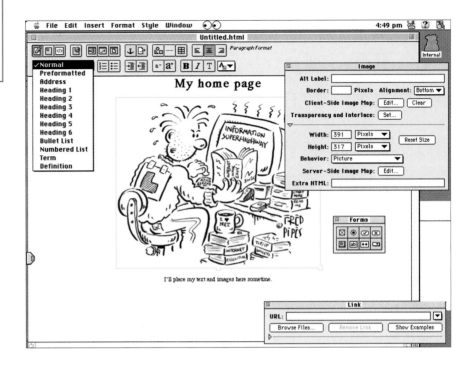

are stand-alone **WYSIWYG** web design programs, such as Adobe PageMill and Claris Home Page (Fig. **7.8**) that claim that you can design web pages without ever having to come into contact with HTML code – after all, you don't need to be able to program in PostScript to lay out pages in QuarkXPress, do you? In practice, however, these programs are of most use to get simple pages started; to fine-tune the layout of your pages, you do need a working knowledge of HTML.

A complete description of HTML is beyond the scope of this chapter, but there are many excellent books on the subject (see Further Reading, p.235) and the joy of the Internet is that there are many teaching resources available. To start with, your browser will have built-in links to "How to..." pages, and your ISP's home page is always a good place to start surfing for advice. If you do find a page that you like the look of, all you have to do is hit the "View document source" button on your browser for it to display the HTML code for the page you are viewing. It's then a relatively easy step to figure how that designer achieved that effect.

Writing your own home page
A good way to give a taste of the flavor of HTML is to design a simple **home page**. A first encounter with the Internet is often quite a culture shock. It's like going back twenty years in time to the days of ASCII-only typewriter terminals. Email and newsgroups are ASCII based – thus many characters are unavailable, and you have to remember to insert

carriage returns at the ends of lines. HTML is no exception; the simple reason is that the web is accessed by every possible kind of computer – the files that travel around the Internet must be of the lowest common denominator, and that means ASCII text. Likewise images have to be in a format understandable by all types of computer, and that means they are most commonly in **GIF** (Graphics Interchange Format) or **JPEG** (Joint Photographic Experts Group) format.

A simple web page will thus comprise a text document plus GIF and/or JPEG files all in the same directory (equivalent to a Mac folder). To create a home page, you will need either a simple text editor, such as Simpletext for a Mac or Notepad on a Wintel PC, a word processor that can output text files (but remember to turn "smart quotes" off), or a web page design program such as PageSpinner that will also provide menus of useful commands and options. You will also need a graphics program, such as Photoshop, that can export GIF and JPEG files. And finally, you will need ftp access to a server – you can create the pages on your computer,

but for anyone else to be able to see them they must first be "published" by uploading them to a server.

HTML works its magic by the use of **tags** that the browser interprets as the web page arrives from the server to the client. Tags nearly always have a start and an end, "containing" the item in question. The first part of the tag turns an attribute on and the second turns the attribute off. Tags themselves are surrounded by angled brackets (the < "less than" and > "greater than" symbols) and the closing tag is usually preceded by a slash symbol (/). For example, the tag for the title of your page is written in HTML like this:

```
<TITLE>My home page</TITLE>
```

All HTML documents contain the following code:

```
<HTML>
<HEAD>
<TITLE>My home page</TITLE>
</HEAD>
<BODY>
Text and images to be placed here?
</BODY>
</HTML>
```

GETTING YOURSELF ORGANIZED
Append notes to yourself in your HTML code by using the tag <!–a note to myself–> to make future debugging easier. It can be harder than you think to update complex HTML pages, even if you created them yourself. And use lots of white space between paragraphs – unless you use <P> or <BR> any formatting in the code will be ignored by the browser. And remember to turn off curly quotes if you're writing HTML on a word processor: browsers only understand feet (') and inches (").

DON'T BE A CLICHÉ
Avoid "Click here" links and try to make the hyperlink part of the description. For example, use: "Do you like **Elvis**?" instead of "Click **here** to go to the Elvis site." Don't just make lists of links, try to add content and narrative to your site. Some HTML tags are loathed by most users: never use the <BLINK> tag and steer well clear of Microsoft's <BGMUSIC> tag.

A program such as PageSpinner will present this sequence whenever you open a new document – it also colors the tags to distinguish them from the text (Fig. **7.9**). The <HTML> tag tells the browser that an HTML document is on the way. The name of the text document should end with the suffix ".html" (although PC users, restricted to file names of eight characters plus a three-letter suffix use just ".htm" for their extension). By default, the first page of a web site is always called index.html.

The text within the <TITLE> tags will appear at the head of your browser window and as the description of an URL in the bookmark file of your browser. Everything within the <BODY> tags will appear in the main window of the browser.

Note that HTML is not case sensitive: <title> will be interpreted exactly the same way as <TITLE> or even <TiTlE>, but for legibility, we will use

upper case. File names should always be in lowercase.

Now you can import or type in a heading and some text (Fig. **7.10**):

```
<HTML>
<!--This file was created on
1/1/98 by me-->
<HEAD>
<TITLE>My home
page</TITLE>
</HEAD>
<BODY>
<H1>Welcome to my
world!</H1>
This is my as yet still under
construction home page.<P>
It was last updated on
January 1st 1998.
</BODY>
</HTML>
```

Headings. Unlike in print, in web design you cannot specify the font and sizes of headings, all you can say about a heading in HTML is that it will (probably) be bigger and bolder than the regular text. There are six headings in HTML: H1 through H6. The default for an H1 heading is 24 pt Times. It is best always to start with an H1 heading and not to skip levels. If you miss off the </H1> end tag, the whole document will be one big heading! H6, strangely, will be smaller than the body text, at around 9 pt.

Anchors. The best thing about the web is that you can create hypertext "hot links" to other parts of your page, to other pages on your site, or to other unrelated pages on any other computer anywhere in the world. To do this, you insert anchors: either local relative ones pointing to another text file in the same directory, or absolute ones containing the

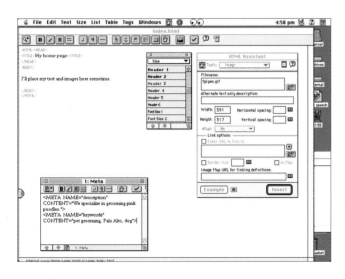

▲ **7.9** PageSpinner screenshot showing the HTML code of your home page document.

▶ **7.10** This is how the HTML code in the text will look when interpreted by the browser.

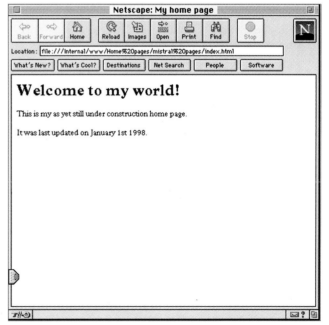

full URL of the page you want to link to. An anchor is of the form

```
<A HREF="URL">the hot text</A>
```

where the URL is either relative, i.e. music.html – another page on your site – or absolute, i.e. http://members.aol.com/elvisnet/index.html, the URL of the ElvisNet site. An example of anchors in use follows (Fig. **7.11**):

```
<HTML>
<!--This file was created on
1/1/98 by me-->
<HEAD>
<TITLE>My home
page</TITLE>
</HEAD>
<BODY>
<H1>Welcome to my
world!</H1>
This is my getting there
slowly home page.<P>
My favorite artiste of all time
is<A HREF="http://members.
aol.com/elvisnet/index.html">
Elvis</A><P>You can find more
musical links on my <A HREF=
"music.html"> Music</A>
page. <P>

This page was last updated on
January 1st, 1998. <BR>
Why not email me with your
comments on
<A HREF="MAILTO:pipes@
mistral.co.uk">pipes@mistral.
co.uk</A>
</BODY>
</HTML>
```

Note that other type of anchor at the end: the MAILTO: attribute automatically creates an email form within the browser.

Character formatting. You may not be able to influence the choice of font and formatting very much – those decisions are in the hands of the end user, but you can at least

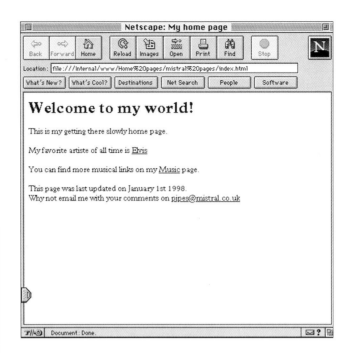

7.11 This is how the HTML code in the text will look when interpreted by your browser. Note that the hot links are underlined and in a different color to the regular text.

make words **bold** or *italic*. HTML, however, has two classes of styles: logical and physical. Logical styles, such as <STRONG> tag the text according to its meaning, while physical styles, such as <BOLD> indicate the specific typographical appearance of the text.

Logical tags are supposed to help enforce consistency in your documents. Remember, the WWW was developed by scientists used to the conventions of academic papers, not graphic designers with their own set of needs. Most browsers render the <STRONG> tag in **bold** text. However, it is possible that a browser might display the word in bright red instead. If you want something to be displayed in **bold** (for example) and do not want a browser's setting to display it differently, use physical styles. *Italic* is best avoided, however – the browser's version of *italic* is usually an oblique version of the roman font and nearly always illegible.

Try to be consistent about which type of style you use. If you tag with physical styles, do so within the whole document. If you use logical styles, stick with them throughout a document.

Here are some of the logical styles:

<EM>	for emphasis, typically displayed in *italics*
<CITE>	for titles of books, films, etc., typically displayed in *italics*
<STRONG>	for strong emphasis, typically displayed in **bold**.

And here are some examples of physical styles:

<B>	**bold** text
<I>	*italic* text
<TT>	typewriter text, i.e. fixed-width font, usually Courier.

Escape sequences. Three ASCII characters – the left angle bracket (<), the right angle bracket (>), and the ampersand (&) – have special meanings in HTML and therefore cannot be used "as is" in text. (The angle brackets are used to indicate the beginning and end of HTML tags, and the ampersand is used to indicate the beginning of an escape sequence.) Double quote marks may be used as is, but a character entity may also be used (").

To use any of these in an HTML document, you must enter their escape sequence instead:

< is the escape sequence for <
> is the escape sequence for >
& is the escape sequence for &

Color. By default, the background color in Netscape is gray and the text is black. Hot links are blue and these change to purple when that link has been visited (browsers have a cache, a portion of your hard disk, in which they store recently visited sites). These can be changed, how-ever, by adding attributes to the <BODY> tag. The bad news is that the RGB colors you specify must be converted to hexadecimal! (#FFFFFF is white and #000000 is black — there are shareware programs and calculators that allow you to do this quite painlessly.) For example,

<BODY TEXT="#000055"#
BGCOLOR="#EDEDFF"
LINK="#CC0000"
VLINK="#005522">

results in dark blue text, a light blue background, and red hypertext links which, when visited, change to green. You can use Netscape swatch colors, such as "RED," "GREEN," "BLUE," and so on, and you can color individual words or phrases by adding the COLOR attribute to the <FONT> tag.

Horizontal rules can be added to divide text, using the tag <HR>. In Netscape, a rule will always appear with a drop shadow (unless you tell it not to). Other attributes can be added to change the thickness and length of the rule. For example,

<HR SIZE=4 WIDTH=80%
ALIGN=CENTER NOSHADE>

creates a solid black centered rule, four pixels thick, across 80 percent of the screen.

Images. To add an image, use the tag <IMG SRC="picture.gif">, where picture.gif is the file name of the image, in this case a GIF file. IMG says place image here and SRC tells the browser that the source is an image in the same directory as the text file called picture.gif. By default, images are ranged left, but you can center them using the <CENTER> tag. It is also useful to specify the dimensions of the image, in pixels, using WIDTH and HEIGHT attributes. If you do this, the browser will leave a space for the image and display any text that follows without waiting for the image to load. Images always take longer to download than text and this gives the user something to read while waiting for the pictures. The ALT attribute describes the image in text and is a courtesy to users with a browser, such as Lynx, that doesn't support graphics. Other attributes define the space between the image and text and whether the image has a border or not. You can use an image as a link and the default is a blue rectangular border, which looks odd on an image with an irregular outline. For example,

<CENTER><IMG SRC="fido.gif"
ALT="my poodle Fido" WIDTH=200
HEIGHT=50 BORDER=0></CENTER>

displays a centered image without a border. If you were using a browser such as Lynx or had your images switched off, all you would see was the text "my poodle Fido."

Optional extras
You can also use GIFs to tile a back-ground, you can create tables of data, and forms for feedback using **CGI** (Common Gateway Interface) scripts. You can make a graphic into an "imagemap" — when users click on specified portions of the graphic they are linked to other pages. A feature called "frames" will divide the main window into lots of smaller scrollable ones (see Fig. **7.6**)— so that you can have a permanent table of contents in a sidebar, say, with the content in the main window (and a clock in the corner). With plug-ins, such as Shockwave from Macromedia, you can have anima-tions created in Director or zoomable vector drawings or maps from FreeHand. You can add audio, movies, and, with VRML (virtual real-ity modeling language) roam around 3D virtual-reality environments.

Sun's **Java** programming lan-guage (named after the amount of Mount Java coffee drunk during its development) allows you to incorporate "applets" (no relation to Apple computers) into your HTML code. These are tiny programs embedded into the HTML that when downloaded will run on any computer to produce animations, for example. Sun describes Java as a "simple, robust, object-oriented, platform-independent, multi-threaded, dynamic general-purpose programming environment." With

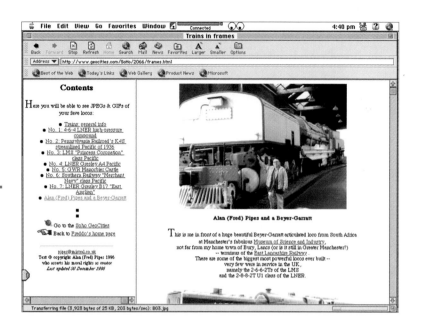

7.12 This is the same page as in Figure **7.6** but viewed in another browser — in this case Microsoft's Internet Explorer.

Java you don't need to download plug-ins – the ability to run Java is built into browsers such as Netscape's Navigator. There are also programs available with names like Café and Roaster that allow you to write applets without ever seeing Java's C++ type code.

Remember the automobile simile earlier? Web design is also like the early days of "desktop publishing" when anyone purchasing a copy of PageMaker or QuarkXPress and a handful of fonts was led to believe that they too could be a graphic designer. And the result? A lot of publications looking like Victorian handbills. Just because you can do something, you don't have to incorporate every feature into every document. Everything can be used appropriately somewhere, but in general: try to exercise some restraint!

There are sound reasons for this: the more features you add to your pages, the longer they will take to download and the more chance there is that the user will get bored and move on. It may be convenient for you to write the page in Director, say, but it can be a bore to have to download the latest version of a Shockwave plug-in first, and then to

have to wait ages for the Shocked "movie" to download before you can even decide whether to surf on to another page. Some of the better pages, in my opinion, have few frills, just plain white backgrounds, the minimum amount of graphics, a logical structure, and legible text.

Standard and non-standard HTML

HTML 2·0 sets out the specifications for "standard" HTML, as agreed by international committees. However, vendors such as Netscape, driven by the demands of graphic designers, have added so-called extensions or enhancements to their browsers plus the corresponding HTML code to make them work. As Netscape has a large market share of the browser-installed base, this is not seen as a problem, but it makes Internet purists mad! If a browser sees a tag it doesn't understand, it should ignore it – but unpredictable results can sometimes occur on non-Netscape browsers. To compound the problem, Microsoft has come out with its own browser, Internet Explorer, with its own "enhancements" (Fig. **7.12**).

Having said that, waiting for

committees to agree on standards takes time – if they can ever reach agreement. And many of the Netscape enhancements are of great interest to the graphic designer. As a result, a *de facto* standard is emerging, as other browser vendors adopt the more popular Netscape enhancements. Among these are the ability to specify font sizes with the <FONT SIZE=n></FONT> tag, where n = 1 to 7, with 3 being the default. You can also specify relative sizes; for example, a + 3 is very useful as an initial capital. The <BASEFONT SIZE=n> tag enlarges or reduces the body text. Note that headings will be affected, as they are set relative to the basefont.

Tables were originally introduced to display tabular matter. But they are also a useful workaround for laying out text. A table with a single row and a single column, for example, can be used to display a single column of text with some degree of control over the measure (set the border to zero: BORDER="0"). A table of two columns can be used to place a graphic, say, flush left with the text running alongside it.

Other ways of formatting the text include the <PRE> tag, which recognizes preformatted text containing carriage returns, tabs, and multiple spaces between characters, but only displays in a monospaced font such as Courier. The <BLOCKQUOTE> tag will generally indent text and is used as a workaround to achieve just that effect – but it might not work on all browsers.

So our nearly finished home page might now look like this (Fig. **7.13**):

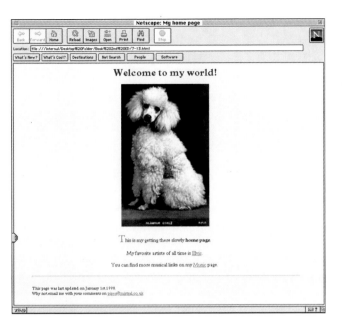

7.13 This is how the code below looks in Netscape.

most useful accessories will eventually become a part of the standard browser.

Graphics formats: GIFs and JPEGs

Another way to be in control of the look of your pages is to put all the typography into graphic images – and some web designers do. On a lot of web pages, you will find that headings are often GIFs, and so are other graphic devices such as bullets and buttons. The GIF (Graphics Interchange Format) was originally developed for CompuServe (it's still called CompuServe GIF on the Photoshop menu) and it is very good at compressing 8-bit (256 color) files that have areas containing flat color, such as logos and typographic headings. A later version, called GIF89a, also supports transparency (so that images with irregular outlines can appear to blend into the background), and interlacing, so that the image first appears as a highly pixelated picture that sharpens up as it downloads (Fig. **7.14**). GIF89a also allows animated GIFs to be

```
<HTML>
<!--This file was created on 1/1/98
by me-->
<HEAD>
<TITLE>My home page</TITLE>
</HEAD>
<BODY TEXT="#000055"
BGCOLOR ="#EDEDFF"
LINK="#CC0000"
VLINK="#005522">
<CENTER><H1> Welcome to my
world!</H1>

<IMG SRC="fido.gif" ALT="my
poodle Fido" WIDTH=200
HEIGHT= 150 BORDER=0><P>

<FONT SIZE="+3"
COLOR="RED">T </FONT>his is
my getting there slowly
<B>home page</B>. <P>
My favorite artiste of all time

is<AHREF="http://members.
aol.com /elvisnet/ index.html">
Elvis</A>. <P>
You can find more musical links
on my <A HREF= "music.html">
Music</A> page. </CENTER><P>

<HR SIZE=4 WIDTH=90%
ALIGN=CENTER>

<BLOCKQUOTE><FONT SIZE="-
1">This page was last updated on
January 1st, 1998. <BR>
Why not email me with your
comments on
<AHREF="MAILTO:pipes@mistral.
co.uk">
pipes@mistral.co.uk</A></FONT><
/BLOCKQUOTE>
</BODY>
</HTML>
```

The only way at present to have total control over the appearance of your layout is to use an Adobe Acrobat file in PDF (Portable Document Format), but once again this is yet another file to download and read later – you will need the proprietary software to create the files, and the user will need viewing software to read them.

One solution has been to run parallel sites: one for Netscape/ Shockwave users, another more basic one for the rest of the world. The proliferation of plug-ins and other helper programs, plus new technologies like Java and Acrobat only seem to exacerbate the situation. Time will tell, however, and the

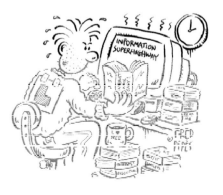

 7.14 An interlaced GIF looks rough at first, but sharpens up as the image downloads.

assembled from a series of still frames in programs such as Gifbuilder.

All browsers (except completely non-graphical ones like Lynx) support GIFs. Most now also support JPEG (Joint Photographic Experts Group) files. JPEGs (files with the suffix .JPEG, or .JPG for PC users) can display 24-bit color and are much better than GIFs for displaying photographic images. The file sizes are smaller too. JPEGs can also be made to download progressively and there are plug-ins to Photoshop, for example, that allow you to produce progressive JPEGs.

There are other formats in use, but these are the most common. Whichever you use (remember GIFs are good for graphics with areas of flat color; JPEGs are best for photographs) you must keep the file sizes to a minimum. and that means 30 k maximum for any one image. For designers dealing with print images of several megabytes, this may seem an impossible task, but remember you are only dealing with resolutions of 72 dpi and using as few colors as you can get away with. Programs such as DeBabelizer are useful tools for reducing the number of colors (and hence file size) without sacrificing too much quality.

GIFs have less obvious uses too. Graphic designer David Siegel (http://www.dsiegel.com/tips) has lots of tips for web designers, but his neatest trick is the single-pixel GIF. He has a clear (transparent) GIF for creating "white" space in a layout. Replacing x and y in the tag

```
<IMG HSPACE=x VSPACE=y
SRC="dot_clear.gif">
```

where x is the number of pixels horizontally and y is the number of pixels vertically, will create rectangles of space of any size, and because these tiny GIFs are cached in your hard disk, they can be used over and over with no drop in performance.

You can also use various colored ones to create solid blocks and bullets. The most ingenious single-pixel GIF trick is to use a black dot to construct an em rule, thus:

```
<IMG ALIGN=ABSMIDDLE WIDTH=11
HEIGHT=1 SRC="dot_black.gif">
```

What's more, you can download these GIFs from David Siegel's ftp site.

Testing your pages

Web pages are cheap and fast to produce and the temptation is to "publish" as soon as you possibly can. After all, if there are mistakes, then they can soon be rectified and the original files at the server overwritten. True, but it is still good practice to test, test, and then test again.

You can view your emerging pages on a browser such as Netscape without going online, and this should be the first step. Then try viewing your pages on another browser, such as Internet Explorer (they can all be downloaded free, or can be installed from CD-roms that come with computer magazines). Try uploading your pages to a home page site and go online to check that they still look OK.

If you designed the pages on a Mac, find a friend with a PC and see

how they look on that platform. PCs have different color tables, and your subtle background color could turn into a dithered mess, or even render the text illegible. A PC might have a 96 dpi monitor, so your 72 dpi graphic will appear smaller! The default font on most browsers is Times, and the Times New Roman on PCs is different from the version of Times on Macs!

Remember some users may have black-and-white screens, so increase the contrast in your graphics. And finally, pity those (few?) users out there whose only access to the Internet is via text-only browsers such as Lynx – at least give them something to read!

You may not need or want to start writing Java applets or CGI scripts, so make friends with your local HTML geek: the local newsgroups are a good place to start. And talk to the people at your ISP about what you can and can't do at the server end. You will at least now know what is possible.

Publicizing your pages

How do you tell the world that you have a web site? You can send out postcards, by snailmail. Add your URL to your letterheads and to the signature on your email and newsgroup postings. And you can make it easy for people searching for your site to find it!

Some people still seem to think that the Internet is one huge encyclopedia – you type in a word somehow and it comes up with an answer. Well, not yet. But there are search engines that can help. The best known is Yahoo, which is more a

7.15 Alta Vista is a popular search engine that presents you with possible sites based on keywords. Sometimes a good deal of lateral thinking is needed to find a particular site.

7.16 WebArranger is a personal organizer for the Internet, storing URLs, email addressses, and clippings of information.

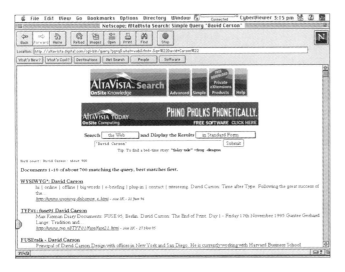

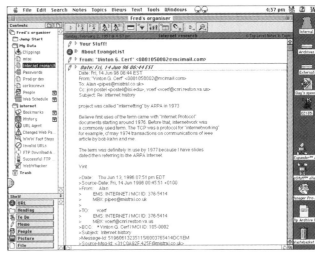

directory of web sites that have been nominated, reviewed, and indexed by its staff. You can speed up the process by sending them details of your site. Alta Vista, maintained by Digital Equipment, sends out "robots" to search out pages and then tries to classify them. Users can search for words and phrases using logical operators; for example, to find a bedtime story, type "fairy tale" + frog - dragon (Fig. **7.15**). Sometimes you have to use quite a lot of lateral thinking to find a site you know is there – and that's where the surfing comes in. It's like detective work: one page leads to another, nearer and nearer, until you find what you're looking for. Some search engines just look at the first few words of a page and you can have some influence by using the <META> tag at the head of your page:

<META NAME="description" CONTENT="We specialize in grooming pink poodles.">
<META NAME="keywords" CONTENT="pet grooming, Palo Alto, dog">

will result in a "hit" if you type in either poodle or dog.

Getting organized

Once you needed a whole folder of programs to get access to the different parts of the Internet: a TCP/IP program, SLIP (Serial Line Internet Protocol), or PPP (Point to Point Protocol) to access your Internet account, an email program, a newsgroup program, an ftp program, and a web browser for starters – plus a whole array of "helper" programs, such as Stuffit to expand the compressed files you've downloaded, JPEGView to view and save that photograph your friend has just sent you, and Soundmachine to play that sample from the latest CD of your favorite band. Browsers such as Netscape Navigator and Microsoft's Internet Explorer aim to become one-stop solutions, incorporating email and newswatching into their browsers. Plug-ins that add functionality to browsers are also gradually being incorporated into the fabric of the browsers themselves.

The problem is that browsers keep on getting bigger, new versions take up more memory on your hard disk and take longer to download. In the near future, technologies based on Java and Apple's OpenDoc may make things a little more manageable. OpenDoc is cross-platform

"component" architecture that uses mini-application "parts" called Live Objects for tasks such as text-editing – similar to Java applets. The idea is that third-party developers need only produce the component parts. Cyberdog is Apple's Internet container – one Live Object allows Cyberdog to work with Netscape bookmarks; another can import mailboxes and address books from Eudora. It's a pick and mix approach.

The conventional Internet model puts everything into a bloated browser. The Cyberdog model puts browsers and hot links into applications. It allows users to integrate live Internet data into their non-Internet desktop applications, by embedding Cyberdog components (such as a mini web browser) into any OpenDoc-compatible application, for example ClarisWorks. This adds a new dimension to traditional documents, adding live links and views of the Internet to any document, whether it's a monthly report, lesson plan, or executive information system.

In the meantime, web organizers such as WebArranger (Fig. **7.16**) can make some order out of your time on the web and work with your Internet applications rather than replacing them. It is not a lot different to other personal organizers, with "to do" lists and reminder alarms, it can import a

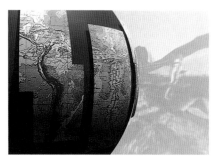
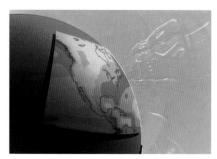

7.17 State-of-the-art computer graphics from London-based production house Digital Pictures. Alec Knox animated this 30-second title sequence, from a design by Andrew Sides of Baxter Hobbins Sides, for the current affairs program This Week. Seven colored globes – representing continents and days of the week – shatter and align to produce the final title frame.

Netscape bookmark list, which you can then sort and export back toNetscape. It has a "grabber" that captures text or images, from an email or web page for example, and puts it into a clippings file where they can be cut and pasted into an email addresses book, a list of URLs to visit or a user-defined whatever. URLs are highlighted in blue and a key combination can automatically launch your browser to find that particular page. It can keep trying busy ftp sites in the background. It can monitor sites for updates or changed addresses and a program called WebWhacker can download an entire web site complete with links (to a specified limit) so they can be viewed later, offline.

DESIGNING FOR THE SMALL SCREEN

Until recently, graphic design for print, and graphic design for screen-based applications, such as television and multimedia, were seen as two distinct disciplines, employing very different kinds of designer. Print designers have long been used to working with high-resolution but static visual information; screen designers have to think more like movie makers. The popularity of the Internet has been responsible for breaking down some of these divides and many designers are now expected to "repurpose" their layouts for use in many diverse and different kinds of media.

As we have seen earlier in this chapter, designing a web site is more than just feeding a QuarkXPress document into an HTML plug-in and

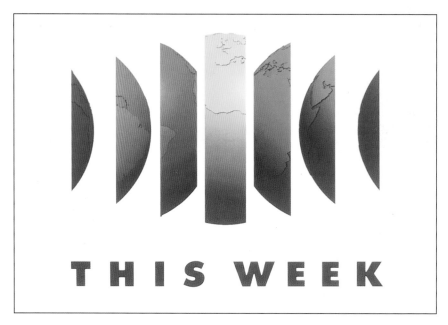

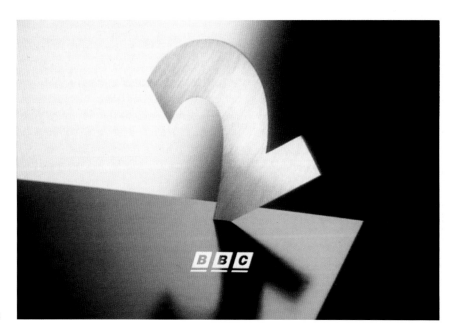

7.18 Martin Lambie-Nairn, best known for his computer graphics work, produced this award-winning station ident for British television's BBC2. What you can't see on the printed page is that the sequence is full of action.

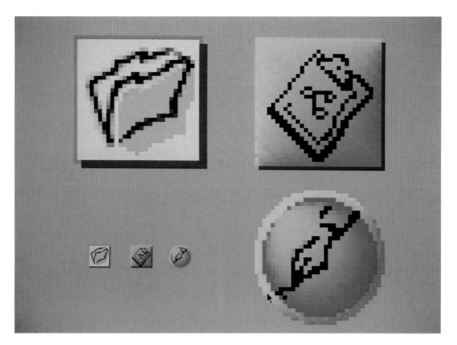

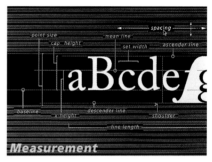

7.19 West-coast designers IDEO are at the forefront of interaction design, which aims to use graphic design to help users make sense of unfamiliar products. These screen icon designs are based on Claris's software packaging identity. To achieve the watercolor effect, Bruce Browne used a manual anti-aliasing technique – adding lighter tones to soften the jagged edges caused by the pixels on the screen.

7.21 Gary Stewart of the Royal College of Art, London, used Macromedia Director to create this interactive computer-based tutorial for users with no previous typographic training.

7.20 A "page" from an electronic encyclopedia for Cable & Wireless, designed by Rory Matthews of Brighton-based Cognitive Applications. The system uses a 19-inch touch-screen, and also makes use of sound, animation, and full motion video clips.

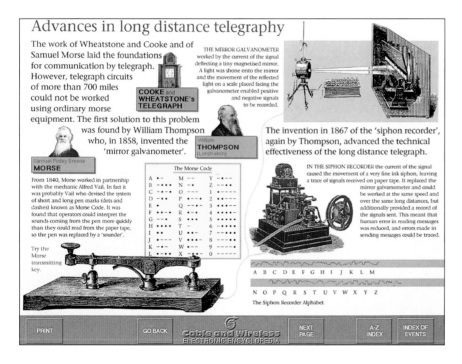

work, designers used to produce lettering on boards, which were then placed in front of the camera. Nowadays, everything is created on a computer system and output direct to video, or, in the case of sports and current affairs programs, broadcast live.

Design for television adds the time dimension to graphic design (Fig. 7.17) – the words and letters can move! Everyone is now familiar with the clichés of flying chrome-plated logos. But TV graphics still tend to overuse drop shadows and graduated tints, just because they are easy to do. You don't need to use sophisticated solid modeling with photorealistic rendering techniques such as ray tracing to achieve a memorable effect, as the award-winning idents for British TV's BBC2 by Martin Lambie-Nairn prove (Fig. **7.18**).

Other areas opening up to graphic designers include interaction design (Fig. **7.20**) – designing the icons and interfaces of software applications – and interactive database design (Figs **7.19** and **7.21**), for

uploading the result to an ISP. A job destined to be both published in print and on the Internet will have to be planned very carefully to take advantage of the strengths of both media while avoiding their relative weaknesses. And even if you can turn your hand to designing wonderful web pages, creating designs for television and multimedia means taking on an entirely new set of challenges. For television and film

TV DESIGN DANGERS
Computer monitors have non-interlaced screens; television sets are interlaced (see p. 128) – so avoid very thin horizontal lines (one pixel thick or a small odd number of pixels) and tight patterns (like herringbone) or they will flicker. The same applies to fonts with fine serifs, like Bodoni – use sturdy bold faces like Helvetica and Century Schoolbook instead. Avoid excessive kerning and type below 14pt. TV tubes aren't as sharp as computer monitors and have a narrower color gamut, and bright saturated colors, particularly yellows and reds, can cause problems of "blooming," so use the NTSC/PAL filter in Photoshop to make sure your colors are broadcast legal. And keep important elements away from the edge of the screen – they may be lost!

use in art galleries and museums, or for distribution on CD-rom. Collectively known as hypermedia, and created using computer programs such as HyperCard or Macromedia Director, these "stacks" mimic conventional books. The difference is that the "reader" can flip around at will, usually by pointing to a highlighted word in the text, or by choosing a new topic from a menu. The problem for the designer – apart from organizing the stack so as not to frustrate the reader by too many dead ends – is one of legibility. The amount of text on any one page must be kept to a minimum (although it is possible to scroll a large amount of text within a window) because low-resolution text on a screen is tiring to read. The graphics must also be carefully laid out to avoid unwanted effects such as "pixel beards" where a letter or graphic interacts unfavorably with a background tint.

SUMMARY

What's in the Internet for the designer? Many things. First, it is a cheap and fast way to transport artwork to the client. Magazine publishers have long been "macked up" and most have email: it's only a matter of time before design groups, advertising agencies, and publishers get online.

Second, it's a cheap and effective way to advertise yourself and your work worldwide, using online galleries of work. You don't have to wait for a source book or CD-rom to come out, and you can change round your portfolio daily, if need be. OK, putting lots of graphics on to WWW pages makes them slow at present, but technology is improving all the time.

Third, it is a source of new clients. The fastest growing area of graphic design is in making the WWW pages themselves. Everyone wants one – you only have to watch TV commercials to see how often http://www.something.com "addresses" come up these days. As with CD-rom design and production, huge opportunities exist for designers who understand and appreciate the possibilities (and limitations) of the medium.

You may not wish to learn all the ins and outs of HTML, but with the working knowledge you have gained here you will be able to assemble sample WWW pages quickly and clearly using a wysiwyg page designer and then be able to fine-tune the source code. You will at least be able to produce a working prototype of the look and feel for a site, which can then be completed by a team of other professionals. You may even be inspired to do it all yourself. In WWW design, the entire concept-to-production cycle is back in the designer's hands. Gutenberg must be smiling.

APPENDIX A Standard Sizes for Paper, Books, and Envelopes

US STANDARD PAPER SIZES

Grade classification	Basis size* in	mm	Weights, lb/ream	Design applications
Bond	17 x 22	432 x 559	13, 16, 20, 24, 28, 32, 36, 40	Letterheads, newsletters
Book	25 x 38	635 x 965	30, 40, 45, 50, 55, 60, 65, 70, 75, 80, 90, 100, 120	Books, catalogs, calendars, annual reports, brochures, magazines
Text	25 x 38	635 x 965	90, 100, 120, 140, 160, 180	Posters, self-mailers, announcements
Cover	20 x 26	508 x 660	25, 35, 40, 50, 55, 60, 65, 80, 90, 100	Business cards, annual report covers, greeting cards

*Basis size: the standard size in a particular grade that determines basis weight

US BOOK SIZES

Name	in	mm	Name	in	mm
Medium 32mo	3 x 4¾	76 x 121	Medium 12mo	5⅛ x 7⅔	130 x 195
Medium 24mo	3⅝ x 5½	92 x 140	Demy 8vo	5½ x 8	140 x 203
Medium 18mo	4 x 6⅔	102 x 169	Small 4to	7 x 8½	178 x 216
Cap 8vo	7 x 7¼	178 x 184	Broad 4to	7 x 8½	178 x 216
12mo	4½ x 7½	114 x 191	(up to 13 x 10) (330 x 254)		
Medium 16mo	4½ x 6¾	114 x 171	Medium 8vo	6 x 9½	152 x 241
Crown 8vo	5 x 7½	127 x 191	Royal 8vo	6½ x 10	165 x 254
Post 8vo	5½ x 7½	140 x 191	Super Royal 8vo	7 x 10½	178 x 267
			Imperial 8vo	8¼ x 11½	210 x 292

Note that American and European usage is to express the width dimension of the book first. In the UK and Far East, depth is shown first. Sizes quoted are not absolute and may vary slightly.

TRIMMED PAGE SIZES FROM STANDARD US SHEETS

Trimmed page size in (mm)	Number of pages	Number from sheet	Standard paper size in	mm
3½ x 6¼ (89 x 159)	4	24	28 x 44	711 x 1118
	8	12	28 x 44	711 x 1118
	12	8	28 x 44	711 x 1118
	16	6	28 x 44	711 x 1118
	24	4	28 x 44	711 x 1118
4 x 9 (102 x 229)	4	12	25 x 38	635 x 965
	8	12	38 x 50	965 x 1270
	12	4	25 x 38	635 x 965
	16	6	38 x 50	965 x 1270
	24	2	25 x 38	635 x 965
4½ x 6 (114 x 152)	4	16	25 x 38	635 x 965
	8	8	25 x 38	635 x 965
	16	4	25 x 38	635 x 965
	32	2	25 x 38	635 x 965
5¼ x 7⅝ (133 x 194)	4	16	32 x 44	813 x 1118
	8	8	32 x 44	813 x 1118
	16	4	32 x 44	813 x 1118
	32	2	32 x 44	813 x 1118
6 x 9 (152 x 229)	4	8	25 x 38	635 x 965
	8	4	25 x 38	635 x 965
	16	2	25 x 38	635 x 965
	32	2	38 x 50	965 x 1270
Oblong 7 x 5½ (178 x 140)	4	8	23 x 29	584 x 737
	8	4	23 x 29	584 x 737
	16	2	23 x 29	584 x 737
8½ x 11 (216 x 279)	4	4	23 x 35	584 x 889
	8	2	23 x 35	584 x 889
	16	2	35 x 45	889 x 1143
9 x 12 (229 x 305)	4	4	25 x 38	635 x 965
	8	2	25 x 38	635 x 965
	16	2	38 x 50	965 x 1270

US STANDARD ENVELOPE SIZES

Commercial/official Window Number	Size, in	Booklet Number	Size, in
6	3⅜ x 6	2½	4½ x 5⅞
6¼	3½ x 6	3	4¾ x 6½
6¾	3⅝ x 6½	4¼	5 x 7½
7	3¾ x 6¾	4½	5½ x 7½
7¾	3⅞ x 7½	5	5½ x 8½
Data Card	3½ x 7⅝	6	5¾ x 8⅞
8⅝	3⅝ x 8⅝	6½	6 x 9
9	3⅞ x 8⅞	6¾	6½ x 9½
10	4⅛ x 9½	7	6¼ x 9⅝
10½	4½ x 9½	7¼	7 x 10
11	4½ x 10⅜	7½	7½ x 10½
12	4¾ x 11	8	8 x 11⅛
14	5 x 11½	9	8¾ x 11½
		9½	9 x 12
		10	9½ x 12⅝
		13	10 x 13

Catalog Number	Size, in	Announcement Number	Size, in
1	6 x 9	A-2	4⅜ x 5⅝
1¾	6½ x 9½	A-6	4¾ x 6½
2	6½ x 10	A-7	5¼ x 7¼
3	7 x 10	A-8	5½ x 8⅛
6	7½ x 10½	A-10	6¼ x 9⅝
7	8 x 11	Slim	3⅞ x 8⅞
8	8¼ x 11¼		
9½	8½ x 10½		
9¾	8¾ x 11¼		
10½	9 x 12		
12½	9½ x 12½		
13½	10 x 13		
14¼	11¼ x 14¼		
14½	11½ x 14½		

INTERNATIONAL "A" SIZES OF PAPER

Size	mm	approx. in
4A0	1682 x 2378	66¼ x 93⅜
2A0	1189 x 1682	46¾ x 66¼
A0*	841 x 1189	33⅛ x 46¾
A1	594 x 841	23⅜ x 33⅛
A2	420 x 594	16½ x 23⅜
A3	297 x 420	11¾ x 16½
A4	210 x 297	8¼ x 11¾
A5	148 x 210	5⅞ x 8¼
A6	105 x 148	4⅛ x 5⅞
A7	74 x 105	2⅞ x 4⅛
A8	52 x 74	2 x 2⅞
A9	37 x 52	1½ x 2
A10	26 x 37	1 x 1½

*Nominal size: in the A series, this equals one square meter

All A series sizes mentioned here are trimmed. "A" sizes can be cut from two stock sizes – R, for trims, and SR, for extra trims or bleeds. A listing of R and SR metric sizes and inch equivalents is below.

Size	mm	approx. in
RA0	860 x 1220	33⅞ x 48⅛
RA1	610 x 860	24⅛ x 33⅞
RA2	430 x 610	17 x 24⅛
SRA0	900 x 1280	35½ x 50⅜
SRA1	640 x 900	25¼ x 35½
SRA2	450 x 640	17⅞ x 25¼

▼ Paper sizes.

ISO "B" AND "C" SIZES OF PAPER

Size	mm	approx. in
B0	1000 x 1414	39⅜ x 55⅝
B1	707 x 1000	27⅞ x 39⅜
B2	500 x 707	19⅝ x 27⅞
B3	353 x 500	12⅞ x 19⅝
B4	250 x 353	9⅞ x 12⅞
B5	176 x 250	7 x 9⅞
B6	125 x 176	5 x 7
B7	88 x 125	3½ x 5
B8	62 x 88	2½ x 3½
B9	44 x 62	1¾ x 2½
B10	31 x 44	1¼ x 1¾
C0	917 x 1297	36⅛ x 51
C1	648 x 917	25½ x 36⅛
C2	458 x 648	18 x 25½
C3	324 x 458	12¾ x 18
C4	229 x 324	9 x 12¾
C5	162 x 229	6⅜ x 9
C6	114 x 162	4½ x 6⅜
C7	81 x 114	3¼ x 4½
C8	57 x 81	2¼ x 3¼

ISO ENVELOPE STANDARDS

Sheets from the A series can be inserted in the C series envelope, flat or folded. For example, a C5 envelope will accommodate an A5 sheet flat, or an A4 folded once. ISO envelope sizes are all taken from B or C size sheets.

Envelope	mm	approx. in
C3	324 x 458	12¾ x 18
B4	250 x 353	9⅞ x 12⅞
C4	229 x 324	9 x 12¾
B5	176 x 250	7 x 9⅞
C5	162 x 229	6⅜ x 9
B6/C4	125 x 324	5 x 12¾
B6	125 x 176	5 x 7
C6	114 x 162	4½ x 6⅜
DL	110 x 220	4¼ x 8¾
C7/6	81 x 162	3¼ x 6⅜
C7	81 x 114	3¼ x 4½

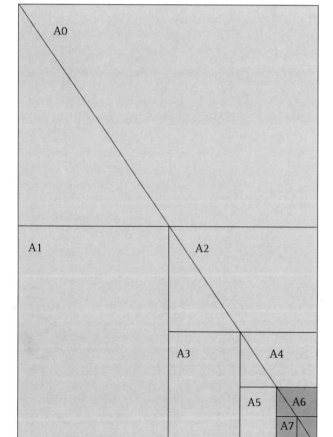

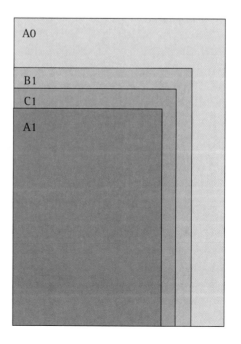

1. Quotation
A quotation not accepted within 30 days may be changed.

2. Orders
Acceptance of orders is subject to credit approval and contingencies such as fire, water, strikes, theft, vandalism, acts of God, and other causes beyond the provider's control. Canceled orders require compensation for incurred costs and related obligations.

3. Experimental work
Experimental or preliminary work performed at the customer's request will be charged to the customer at the provider's current rates. This work cannot be used without the provider's written consent.

4. Creative work
Sketches, copy, dummies, and all other creative work developed or furnished by the provider are the provider's exclusive property. The provider must give written approval for all use of this work and for any derivation of ideas from it.

5. Accuracy of specifications
Quotations are based on the accuracy of the specifications provided. The provider can requote a job at time of submission if copy, film, tapes, disks, or other input materials don't conform to the information on which the original quotation was based.

6. Preparatory materials
Art work, type, plates, negatives, positives, tapes, disks, and all other items supplied by the provider remain the provider's exclusive property.

7. Electronic manuscript or image
It is the customer's responsibility to maintain a copy of the original file. The provider is not responsible for accidental damage to media supplied by the customer or for the accuracy of furnished input or output. Until digital input can be evaluated by the provider, no claims or promises are made about the provider's ability to work with jobs submitted in digital format, and no liability is assumed for problems that may arise. Any additional translating, editing, or programming needed to utilize customer-supplied files will be charged at the prevailing rates.

8. Alterations/Corrections
Customer alterations include all work performed in addition to the original specifications. All such work will be charged at the provider's current rates.

9. Prepress proofs
The provider will submit prepress proofs along with original copy for the customer's review and approval. Corrections wil be returned to the provider on a "master set" marked "O.K.," "O.K. with corrections," or "Revised proof required" and signed by the customer. Until the master set is received, no additional work will be performed. The provider will not be responsible for undetected production errors if:
- proofs are not required by the customer;
- the work is printed per the customer's O.K.;
- requests for changes are communicated orally.

10. Press proofs
Press proofs will not be furnished unless they have been requested in writing in the provider's quotation. A press sheet can be submitted for the customer's approval as long as the customer is present at the press during make-ready. Any press time lost or alterations/corrections made because of the customer's delay or change of mind will be charged at the provider's current rates.

11. Color proofing
Because of differences in equipment, paper, inks, and other conditions between color proofing and production pressroom operations, a reasonable variation in color between color proofs and the completed job is to be expected. When variation of this type occurs, it will be considered acceptable performance.

12. Over-runs or under-runs
Over-runs or under-runs will not exceed 10 percent of the quantity ordered. The provider will bill for actual quantity delivered within this tolerance. If the customer requires a guaranteed quantity, the percentage of tolerance must be stated at the time of quotation.

13. Customer's property
The provider will only maintain fire and extended coverage on property belonging to the customer while the property is in the provider's possession. The provider's liability for this property will not exceed the amount recoverable from the insurance. Additional insurance coverage may be obtained if it is requested in writing, and if the premium is paid to the provider.

14. Delivery
Unless otherwise specified, the price quoted is for a single shipment, without storage, F.O.B. provider's platform. Proposals are based on continuous and uninterrupted delivery of the complete order. If the specifications state otherwise, the provider will charge accordingly at current rates. Charges for delivery of materials and supplies from the customer to the provider, or from the customer's supplier to the provider, are not included in quotations unless specified. Title for finished work passes to the customer upon delivery to the carrier at shipping point; or upon mailing of invoices for the finished work or its segments, whichever occurs first.

15. Production schedules
Production schedules will be established and followed by both the customer and the provider. In the event that production schedules are not adhered to by the customer, delivery dates will be subject to renegotiation. There will be no liability or penalty for delays due to state of war, riot, civil disorder, fire, strikes, accidents, action of government or civil authority, acts of God, or other causes beyond the control of the provider. In such cases, schedules will be extended by an amount of time equal to the delay incurred.

16. Customer-furnished materials
Materials furnished by customers or their suppliers are verified by delivery tickets. The provider bears no responsibility for discrepancies between delivery tickets and actual counts. Customer-supplied paper must be delivered according to specifications furnished by the provider. These specifications will include correct weight, thickness, pick resistance, and other technical requirements. Artwork, film, color separations, special dies, tapes, disks, or other materials furnished by the customer must be usable by the provider without alteration or repair. Items not meeting this requirement will be repaired by the customer, or by the provider at the provider's current rates.

17. Outside purchases
Unless otherwise agreed in writing, all outside purchases as requested or authorized by the customer are chargeable.

18. Terms/Claims/Liens
Payment is net cash 30 calendar days from date of invoice. Claims for defects, damages, or shortages must be made by the customer in writing no later than 10 calendar days after delivery. If no such claim is made, the provider and the customer will understand that the job has been accepted. By accepting the job, the customer acknowledges that the provider's performance has fully satisfied all terms, conditions, and specifications.

The provider's liability will be limited to the quoted selling price of defective goods, without additional liability for special or consequential damages. As security for payment of any sum due under the terms of an agreement, the provider has a right to hold and place a lien on all customer property in the provider's possession. This right applies even if credit has been extended, notes have been accepted, trade acceptances have been made, or payment has been guaranteed. If payment is not made, the customer is liable for all collection costs incurred.

19. Liability
1. Disclaimer of express warranties: The provider warrants that the work is as described in the purchase order. The customer understands that all sketches, copy, dummies, and preparatory work shown to the customer are intended only to illustrate the general type and quality of the work. They are not intended to represent the actual work performed.
2. Disclaimer of implied warranties: The provider warrants only that the work will conform to the description contained in the purchase order. The provider's maximum liability, whether by negligence, contract, or otherwise, will not exceed the return of the amount invoiced for the work in dispute. Under no circumstances will the provider be liable for specific, individual, or consequential damages.

20. Indemnification
The customer agrees to protect the provider from economic loss and any other harmful consequences

that could arise in connection with the work. This means that the customer will hold the provider harmless and save, indemnify, and otherwise defend him/her against claims, demands, actions, and proceedings on any and all grounds. This will apply regardless of responsibility of negligence.

1. Copyrights. The customer also warrants that the subject matter to be printed is not copyrighted by a third party. The customer also recognizes that because subject matter does not have to bear a copyright notice in order to be protected by copyright law, absence of such notice does not necessarily assure a right to reproduce. The customer further warrants that no copyright notice has been removed from any material used in preparing the subject matter for reproduction.

To support these warranties, the customer agrees to indemnify and hold the provider harmless for all liability, damages, and attorney fees that may be incurred in any legal action connected with copyright infringement involving the work produced or provided.

2. Personal or economic rights. The customer also warrants that the work does not contain anything that is libelous or scandalous, or anything that threatens anyone's right to privacy or other personal or economic rights. The customer will, at the customer's sole expense, promptly and thoroughly defend the provider in all legal actions on these grounds as long as the provider:

• promptly notifies the customer of the legal action;
• gives the customer reasonable time to undertake and conduct a defense.

The provider reserves the right to use his or her sole discretion in refusing to print anything he or she deems illegal, libelous, scandalous, improper, or infringing on copyright law.

21. Storage

The provider will retain intermediate materials until the related end product has been accepted by the customer. If requested by the customer, intermediate materials will be stored for an additional period at additional charge. The provider is not liable for

any loss or damage to stored material beyond what is recoverable by the provider's fire and extended insurance coverage.

22. Taxes

All amounts due for taxes and assessments will be added to the customer's invoice and are the responsibility of the customer. No tax exemption will be granted unless the customer's "Exemption Certificate" (or other official proof of exemption) accompanies the purchase order. If, after the customer has paid the invoice, it is determined that more tax is due, then the customer must promptly remit the required taxes to the taxing authority, or immediately reimburse the provider for any additional taxes paid.

23 Telecommunications

Unless otherwise agreed, the customer will pay for all transmission charges. The provider is not responsible for any errors, omissions, or extra costs resulting from faults in the transmission.

Reproduced courtesy of the Printing Industries of America, Inc.

APPENDIX C Customs of the Trade for the Manufacture of Books (UK)

Prepress, platemaking, printing and binding

(a) Litho plates made by the printer are the property of the printer and may be destroyed after completion of printing (unless otherwise agreed with the publisher).

(b) Both film and photoset material used for litho platemaking become the property of the publisher when payment has been made in full. Film is usually held without storage charge for two years after invoice. Before making a storage charge for film, the printer should offer the publisher an opportunity to make his own storage arrangement. A charge to recover removal costs may be made for any film transferred, but it will be the printer's responsibility to check that the film is complete before dispatch. All charges should be agreed with the publisher before implementation.

(c) Some film is produced by plate projection systems and cannot be processed without separate coded instructions, either on disk or in the form of magnetic cards. Where such instructions are individual to the work in question, rather than forming part of a more general database, these are also considered to be the publisher's property.

(d) Where offset printing is ordered separately from composition, the printer's responsibility is limited to reproducing the image supplied to him. However, any technical or other defect noticed by the printer in the material thus supplied should be brought to the publisher's attention as soon as possible.

(e) Estimates usually provide that material, when supplied by the customer, including artwork reproduction copy, tapes, films, plates, paper and binding materials shall be suitable for their purpose. Provided the publisher has been given adequate forewarning of cost, the printer or binder may charge for any additional work (such as retouching,

film spotting, excess blanket-washing, paper conditioning, handling pre-printed covers) incurred when materials are found during production to be inconsistent with the standards on which the estimates were based. Where it is not practical for such warning to be given, the publisher should be informed without delay and remedial costs passed on.

(f) Final intermediates used in the production of work for a publisher should not be destroyed or erased without the written agreement of the publisher, but the publisher should not expect the printer to store items indefinitely. The publisher is entitled to remove any such material on payment of appropriate handling charges.

(g) It is normally assumed that publisher's property (e.g. artwork, photographs, the property of third parties supplied by the publisher etc.) is held and worked on by the printer/binder at the publisher's risk. The printer/binder should, however, exercise great care in handling and storing such property and if it is damaged before the production process is completed, the question of restitution should be the subject of negotiation between the parties. Camera-ready copy, artwork, photographs etc. are normally returned to the publisher upon completion of manufacture unless otherwise agreed and should not be destroyed without the written agreement of the publisher.

(h) To avoid the possibility of subsequent disagreement, printing and binding orders should always be comprehensive, specifying precisely the materials the printer/binder is to use, and include the delivery date required and agreed price where appropriate.

(i) If a manufacturer folds more sheets than are covered by the publisher's initial instructions, he does so at his own risk. However, it is open to him to negotiate with the publisher to recover his fold-

ing costs if the sheets are then sold or bound.

(j) In the case of multi-volume sets, where individual volumes are not available separately, the manufacturer should charge for the production of complete sets only. Any surplus copies of individual volumes should be referred to the publisher for mutual agreement as to disposal.

(k) A storage charge may be proposed by the binder for any sheets, covers, bound stock and other material belonging to the publisher and kept on his behalf. A schedule of such items should be made to the publisher before any storage charge is made, and an opportunity given to the publisher to give disposal instructions.

(l) Incidental imperfections. It is the responsibility of the printer or binder to make good incidental imperfections or, should this be impractical or unduly costly, he may opt to offer the publisher financial compensation as an alternative, on the basis of a fully annotated title page. This is intended to reflect the full printing and binding cost of the book and is customarily set as 25 percent of the published price; it is, however, accepted that it is open to the manufacturer to negotiate alternative arrangements with publishers of mass-market paperbacks or specialized academic works with an extended stockholding life or where it is felt exceptional conditions apply.

(m) Edition imperfections. It is recognized that when substantial numbers of an edition are delivered in a faulty condition, and the fault lies with the supplier, the precise remedy must be a matter for individual negotiation between publisher and printer or binder.

(n) It is the responsibility of the supplier dispatching goods to ensure that accurate documentation is sent with them with a copy to the publisher.

(o) Covers. If the printer/binder has a specific manner in which he wants covers printed on a sheet, he should make it clear at the outset. Where covers are supplied to the binder it is the publisher's responsibility to ensure that imposition is correct. This might include the number of copies on a sheet, margins between covers for two-up binding etc.

Ownership, insurance and liability

(a) Ownership of the work will normally pass to the publisher at the moment of payment in full, but a different arrangement may be mutually agreed between publisher and manufacturer.

(b) The publisher and the typesetter/printer/binder is each normally responsible for the insurance of his own property, including property in transit. The publisher's responsibility for the insurance of work done is from the earlier of: (1) work delivered to the publisher, or to his nominated delivery address; (2) payment in full by the publisher. In this way the publisher insures the work from the moment when he has an insurable interest in it. The publisher is responsible for the insurance of material stored at his request in whatever form. The typesetter is responsible in the case of a failure or loss of work in progress and should insure against such a likelihood. The value for insurance purposes should cover the cost of replacement of tapes and disks to the same stage as when they were lost or damaged. The publisher should insure for any consequential loss as a result of loss or damage. The typesetter will not be responsible for any consequential loss.

(c) For insurance purposes the publisher's property on the supplier's premises includes all materials supplied by the publisher such as manuscripts, tapes and disks, artwork, photographs, transparencies, camera-ready copy, film, paper and, where a trade binder is used, printed sheets and printed covers that have been paid for by the publisher.

(d) The typesetter/printer/binder is entitled not to proceed with any work which, in his opinion, is or may be of an illegal or libellous nature, or an infringement of third-party rights.

Materials

(a) Storage. As part of his service the printer holds publisher's white paper free of charge for 60 days pending instructions to print. If he is required to hold it for a longer period he may implement a storage charge, unless it is agreed that special circumstances exist, such as stock papers which are delivered and used in regular quantities.

(b) Advice procedure. Paper supplied by the publisher should be advised to the printer before delivery and the advice note should specify the publisher and the title for which it is intended. On receipt of the paper, the printer should send the publisher an out-turn sheet quoting full details of the delivery and, if necessary, a report. Sheets and other goods provided by, or on behalf of, the publisher are not normally counted or checked when received, but the supplier should advise the publisher of any apparent shortages or damage as soon as discovered.

(c) Paper supplied on reel. Before ordering, the publisher should ask the printer to specify the type of reel centre required, maximum diameter of reel and type of splice and any other special requirements. The publisher should instruct the paper supplier to ensure that the end wrapping is flat, any joins are clearly marked, that a specification giving full details of each consignment, including the actual metre length per reel, is sent when the reels are delivered, and that delivery dates are arranged with the printer. The printer's spoilage is calculated on a length basis not on a weight basis. Reels are not checked when supplied, but the printer should advise the publisher of any shortage or damage as soon as possible.

(d) Spoilage allowances. Where the printer supplies the paper, the printer must specify in his estimate the quantity and sheet or reel size of paper required, including an allowance for printing and binding spoilage. It must be emphasized that this allowance should always be mutually agreed beforehand, particularly in the case of recycled or thin papers where higher than normal allowances may be required. Any use of material in excess of the specified quantity should be notified to the publisher and the cost borne by the printer, unless it is an agreed paper fault or change to the specification.

(e) Binding. If the binding is to be done in quantities smaller than the print run, it is the publisher's responsibility to allow for the extra binder's spoilage required, if necessary by increasing the print order. Each individual binding order will necessitate a spoilage allowance. For the first and last sections the publisher may need to allow the binder more spoilage than for the rest of the book.

General

A Outwork Certain elements of the work may have to be subcontracted because the supplier is not equipped to execute them. Where a supplier needs to subcontract work which he would normally do, he should consult his customer, where practical, before doing so. During the period of outwork the supplier retains sole responsibility for any costs incurred, the quality of the work, the production of the quantity of copies, and completion of the work by the date previously agreed; and for insurance in accordance with Section 3. A separate invoice must not be submitted, unless agreed in advance with the publisher.

B Schedules and delays (a) A production schedule, where timing is critical, should be submitted and agreed in writing, based on a realistic assessment of the circumstances at the time. Any delay on either side should be notified to the other parties concerned as soon as it is foreseen, and the remainder of the schedule negotiated. If the manufacturer has reserved machinery time for a particular order at the customer's request and the order is postponed, then the customer and the manufacturer should make every effort to find other suitable work to fill the reserved time. If neither party can find such suitable work, it is open to the manufacturer to seek to negotiate appropriate compensation. (b) A broken promise of delivery by an agreed date does not constitute a breach of contract if it is caused by force majeure (as generally recognized in the printing industry) nor, if caused in any other way, does it involve a penalty unless: (1) a penalty for any delay in completion has been agreed; and (2) the customer has not himself defaulted on any dates in the agreed schedule for the work.

C Cancellation Orders can only be cancelled on terms that compensate the supplier for any costs incurred for any materials purchased or services performed, unless the publisher can demonstrate that the supplier is responsible for the grounds of cancellation.

D Terms of payment Terms of payment, including any special arrangements such as stage payments and the charging of interest on overdue amounts etc., should be agreed between supplier and customer before the order is placed. In the absence of such prior agreement, payment will be in 30 days. The following are examples of current practice:

(a) Typesetting is customarily invoiced on completion of the contracted process. However, where a single supplier is responsible for composition and machining, the invoice may be rendered for the two processes if agreed in advance.

(b) Interim payments may, in certain circumstances, be negotiated for composition, machining or binding.

(c) It is normal practice to allow a plus or minus tolerance of 5 percent on the ordered quantity of books. If all books are bound in the first instance the invoice quantity printed should be the same as the invoice quantity bound when produced by the same supplier. If shortages occur, the publisher reserves the right to invoice the printer or binder for the excess use of materials (if supplied by the publisher) relative to that shortfall. It is a matter for negotiation between manufacturer and publisher as to how variations from these tolerances are dealt with.

(d) Except where covered by prior agreement, an invoice for composition may be rendered 60 days after completion of any proofing stage, where the proofs have not been returned to the supplier for further work to be done.

(e) Where materials are supplied by the printer, the charge for such materials shall be invoiced as part of the printing or binding as appropriate. Paper may only be invoiced in advance by the printer by prior agreement.

(f) The existence of an unresolved query on the invoices does not release the publisher from his obligation to pay the parts of the invoice not under query.

(g) VAT will be charged where appropriate whether or not it has been included in the estimate.

(Extracts reproduced courtesy of the British Printing Industry Federation and the Publishers Association)

ABLATION PLATES In offset litho printing, a laser is used to burn tiny holes into thin coatings on a polyester or metal base. These can be produced digitally, require no chemical processing, and can be printed waterless. All the plates for a job can be imaged directly on the press, simultaneously and in register

ACCORDION FOLD or **CONCERTINA FOLD** A folding method in which two or more parallel folds are made in opposite directions

ACETATE A clear film used as an overlay on a MECHANICAL, for the production of separations for flat color, for example, or KEYLINES

ACHROMATIC STABILIZATION See GRAY COMPONENT REPLACEMENT

ADDITIVE COLORS The primaries of transmitted light: red, green, and blue-violet

ADDRESSABILITY A measure of how close the centers of the dots that make up type or images can be placed next to each other on an output device such as a laser printer; see also RESOLUTION

AGAINST THE GRAIN Folding or feeding paper stock at right angles to the orientation of the fibers

AGFAPROOF A proprietary prepress color proofing system

ALIGNMENT Placing type or images so that they line up either horizontally or vertically

ALPHANUMERIC CHARACTER SET A complete set of letters, numbers, and associated punctuation marks; see also FONT

AM SCREENING (AMPLITUDE MODULATED) Conventional screening which uses an array of differently sized dots; see also FM SCREENING

ANCHOR In HTML code, a means of pointing your BROWSER to another web page. The TAG is of the form <A HREF="URL">the text to be linked</A> where the URL is either relative, such as music.html – another page on your site – or absolute, i.e. http://members.aol.com/elvisnet/index.html, a site elsewhere on the INTERNET

ANILINE DYE Synthetic dye used in flexographic ink

ANTI-ALIASING An optical trick to make hard jagged edges on low-resolution computer screens and color output look smoother

ANTIQUE PAPER A book paper with a rough finish

APPLICATION Computer software that does a particular task, such as page layout

APR (AUTOMATIC PICTURE REPLACEMENT) This uses a low-resolution halftone in a digital page layout, which will be relaced later at the repro house by a high-resolution scanned image

ASCENDER The part of a lower-case letter such as k or d that extends above the body of the type

ASCII (AMERICAN STANDARD CODE FOR INFORMATION INTERCHANGE) A text-only format of 256 codes used to represent alphanumeric characters with no additional information about size, font, or spacing

ASSEMBLER A low-level computer programming language that uses mnemonics, such as MPY for multiply

ASSEMBLY Collecting and arranging design elements on film to create the FLAT used for platemaking

AUTHOR'S CORRECTIONS Corrections that are made to a galley proof by the author or editor, which may contain new material or changes of mind that will have to be paid for

AUTO-REVERSING FILM Film that can be used to copy negative-working film to negative-working film without the need for an intermediate positive

AVATAR On the INTERNET, in IRC, your visual human-like representative, speaking your words in a virtual scene. In mythology, an avatar is an incarnation of a Hindu deity

BACK EDGE The margin closest to the spine

BACKING A problem of lightening of color in printing that occurs when ink removed from the fountain roller is not being replaced by the flow of fresh ink

BACKSTEP MARK Black mark printed on a SIGNATURE that shows where the final fold will be. After collation, the marks should fall in a stepped sequence

BACK UP Printing on the other side of the sheet; in computer terminology, to copy important work onto FLOPPY DISKS, REMOVABLE HARD DRIVES, or other storage media

BAD BREAK In justified setting, hyphenation of a word that looks wrong

BARYTA Smooth paper used for letterpress repro proofs

BASELINE The imaginary horizontal line on which letters sit

BASTARD SIZE Any non-standard size, especially of paper

BINDING Fixing together folded signatures into multipage publications, using glue, thread, or metal wires. Also the cover and backing of a book

BIT The primary unit in computing – a binary digit (a 1 or a 0)

BITMAP An image or letter made from a pattern of dots or PIXELS on a RASTER device such as a computer screen or laser printer

BLANKET The intermediate rubber roller on an offset litho press that transfers the image from the plate to the paper

BLANKET CYLINDER The cylinder on an offset litho press to which the blanket is attached

BLANKET-TO-BLANKET PRESS An offset litho press that can print both sides of a sheet in one pass – the sheet passes between two blanket cylinders and there is no need for an impression cylinder

BLEED Part of the image that extends beyond the trim marks of a page

BLIND A method of die stamping or embossing in three-dimensional low relief without foil or ink

BLOCKING Producing the lettering on the spine of a hardback book, usually in gold or silver leaf, by means of a die; see also STICKING

BLUE AND RED KEYS A method for ensuring the close registration of color separations using a key image in blue or red as a guide

BLUEPRINT or **BLUE** A dyeline proof for checking the position of design elements and stripped-in halftones before the plate is made, also called OZALID

BODY TYPE Type below 14 point, used for the main body of text, as opposed to DISPLAY type

BOND A durable grade of paper, used mostly for stationery

BRIGHTNESS The brilliance or light reflectivity of paper

BROMIDE Smooth high-contrast photographic paper used for PMTs and as output from imagesetters

BROWNLINE or **BROWNPRINT** A proof made from a lithographic negative similar to a BLUEPRINT but producing a brown image

BROWSER A computer program that allows you to view and interact with WWW pages on the INTERNET. An example is Netscape Navigator

BUBBLEJET PRINTER A form of inkjet printer in which a heating element causes bubbles to eject the ink

BUCKLE FOLDER A folding machine that uses an adjustable stop to buckle the sheet, which is then forced between two nip rollers

BUCKRAM A heavy coarse-thread binding cloth

BUG A mistake in a computer program which makes unexpected things happen

BULK See CALIPER

BURN Exposure of a litho plate

BURNISHING Rubbing down pressure-sensitive lettering such as Letraset

BYTE Eight bits, corresponding to one ASCII character

C++ A structured computer programming language, the basis of JAVA

CALENDERING Smoothing and compressing paper as it travels through the paper machine

CALIPER The thickness of paper, also called BULK

CAMERA-READY COPY or **MECHANICAL** A complete and finished layout of type and images ready to be scanned or photographed by a process camera

CAST COATED Paper with a high-gloss finish

CASTING OFF Calculating how much space the text in a manuscript will occupy when set into type

CATCH-UP Printing on non-image areas, caused by insufficient water

CD-ROM (COMPACT DISC – READ-ONLY MEMORY) A plastic disk, like an audio CD, on to which tiny holes are "written" by a laser beam to store digital data or programs

CEPS (COLOR ELECTRONIC PUBLISHING SYSTEM) Low-resolution images are used as for-position-only visuals. High-resolution scans, straight from the original transparencies, are reunited with the layouts in the imagesetter at the repro house.

CHALKING Pigments smudging or rubbing off, caused by improper curing of paper which results in too rapid an absorption of the binding vehicle in ink

CHASE In letterpress, the rectangular metal frame holding type and blocks; when locked up, it is called a FORME

CHROMO PAPER A type of paper polished on one side only

CLIENT-SERVER ARCHITECTURE A user or a user's program is the client and connects to a remote

machine (the server) where, for example, USENET postings or WWW pages are stored

CLIP ART Copyright-free illustrations

CLOCK SPEED The length of the processing cycle in a computer, measured in MHz

CMYK Cyan, magenta, yellow, and key (black). This is the system used to describe and separate colors for printing. Other color systems include RGB (red, green, blue) for transmitted color, such as for computer screens, and HLS (hue, luminance, saturation), a more theoretical description. The PANTONE MATCHING SYSTEM matches colors by mixing 11 basic colors

CMS (COLOR MANAGEMENT SYSTEM) A library of scanner, monitor, and output device profiles to ensure consistency of color reproduction by mapping color from the GAMUT of one device, such as a display, into a device-independent model, and then to the gamut of another device, such as a color printer

COATING Adding a layer of china clay to paper to increase its smoothness

COLD-METAL SETTING or **STRIKE-ON** Typesetting produced directly on to paper using a typewriter or rub-down lettering

COLD-SET INK Solid ink that is melted and used with a hot press, solidifying when it contacts the paper

COLLATING or **GATHERING** Bringing pages and signatures together for binding

COLLOTYPE Printing process using plate coated with gelatin, the only process to reproduce continuous-tone images without screening

COLOR BAR A printer's check appearing on color proofs to show up any faults in color registration, print density, dot gain, and slurring

COLOR CALIBRATE To adjust the output values of a computer screen to correspond more faithfully to printed colors

COLOR CAST An unfaithful color on a color image, often found on a subject photographed against a srongly colored background

COLOR DISPLAY SYSTEM The color computer display screen or monitor itself, and the graphics card that drives it

COLOR-KEY A 3M proprietary dry proofing system using plastic laminates

COLOR SEPARATIONS A set of films for the cyan, magenta, yellow, and black components of a full-color image

COLOR SPACE See GAMUT

COMBINATION FOLDER A folding machine that uses both the knife and buckle methods in combination

COMPOSING STICK A device used in hand setting for assembling a line of type

COMPOSITOR The person who sets type

CONCERTINA FOLD A type of fold in which two or more parallel folds are made in opposite directions, also called an ACCORDION FOLD

CONTINUOUS-TONE COPY Artwork or photography containing shades of gray, as opposed to LINE COPY, also called CONTONE

CONVERTER An offset litho press that can be converted to print either two colors on one side of a sheet or one color on both sides in one pass

COPY The raw material of the graphic designer: the text, type, artwork, and mechanicals

COPYFITTING Marking up type so that it fits a given space in a layout

COPY PREPARATION Adding the instructions to text that define how it is to be set; MARKING UP is the manual method of copy preparation

CPU (CENTRAL PROCESSING UNIT) The "brain" of a computer, a microprocessor chip, or chipset

CRAWLING An imperfection in the surface of the ink, occurring when thick ink overprints wet ink

CROCKING Smudging or transfer of dry ink on to printed sheets

CROMACHECK Proprietary off-press proofing system from Du Pont which uses plastic laminates

CROMALIN Proprietary off-press proofing system from Du Pont which uses dry toners and light-sensitive sheets

CROP MARKS Lines to indicate which portions of a photograph or illustration are surplus to requirements

CROPPING Choosing not to use portions of a photograph and marking an overlay on the original to indicate which portions of the image are to be printed

CROSS-HEADINGS Display type used to interest the reader and break up gray areas of body type

CROSSOVER When an image, text, or tint extends from one page of a publication to a facing page, which may or may not be from the same printed sheet

CROSSPOSTING Posting the same message to several newsgroups on the Internet – not a good idea, especially if it is off-topic

CRYSTALLIZATION When the ink of the first printing dries too hard before overprinting, it can repel the second ink and produce poor TRAPPING

CTP (COMPUTER-TO-PLATE) or **DIRECT TO PLATE** Making offset litho plates in a PLATESETTER direct from a PostScript file without the need for film

CURE Acclimatize paper to the temperature and humidity of the press room

CUT-OUT Remove irregular areas of a photograph to make a subject stand out

CYAN Process blue – really more a turquoise

DAMPER MARKS Patterns over the print caused by worn damper covers, or too much pressure.

DECKLE The natural wavy edge to paper; also the frame used to make handmade paper

DENSITOMETER An instrument used to measure the density of printed color

DESCENDER The part of a lower-case letter such as p or g that extends below the baseline

DIAZO Proof made by direct contact with film positives; see also BLUEPRINT and BROWNLINE

DIDOT POINT A unit of measurement used in continental Europe equivalent to 0.0148 inch (0.376mm), 7 percent larger than the American point

DIE-CUTTING Using sharp steel rules in a wooden die or laser to cut shapes from paper

DIE-STAMPING Producing a three-dimensional low relief effect on paper or cover board using a metal die and counter-die

DIFFUSION TRANSFER A semi-automatic process for making enlargements or reductions of line or halftone copy. A negative is produced in the process camera and transferred to a receiver sheet to create the BROMIDE positive; see also PMT and VELOX

DIGITAL CAMERA Instead of capturing an image on light-sensitive film that has to be sent away to be developed and printed, a digital camera uses an array of CCD (charge-coupled device) sensors to convert the image into a form that can be stored in the camera's RAM and then downloaded into your computer

DINGBAT A symbol or ornament such as ✣ or ☞ treated as characters in a font

DIRECT DIGITAL PRINTING PostScript files are sent directly to special offset plates (direct to press) on the press or to electrophotographic cylinders in xerography machines, without the need for artwork or film

DIRECT THERMAL PRINTER An output device that burns an image into special paper

DIRECT TO PLATE See COMPUTER-TO-PLATE (CTP)

DISPLAY TYPE Type above 14 point set for headlines or other display purposes; some fancy display faces are available in capitals only

DITHERING A crude computer method of screening. Thermal transfer and inkjet printers produce their colors by interspersing pixels of cyan, magenta, and yellow (and sometimes black) in regular patterns, grouped together in either two-by-two or four-by-four matrixes

DOCUMENT In computer language, any job you are working on is called a document, whether it is a drawing, a piece of text, or a page layout

DOT-FOR-DOT A method of screening an already screened halftone to prevent moiré patterns

DOT GAIN or **DOT SPREAD** As individual dots begin to join in darker areas of a halftone there can be an apparent jump in what should be a continuous tone

DOT-MATRIX PRINTER An output device that uses pins striking a ribbon to transfer ink on to the paper

DOUBLING Two dots where there should only be one. It is caused when wet ink is picked up by the blanket on a subsequent printing. If it is off register, it prints as a ghost dot nearby

DOWNLOAD Use FTP to transfer files from a remote server to your computer

DPI Dots per inch, a measure of the resolution or addressability of a raster device such as a laser printer

DPS Double-page spread, two facing pages treated as one design layout, also called a SPREAD or DOUBLE TRUCK

DRAWDOWN A smear of ink from a smooth blade used to check the quality of an ink on a particular paper stock

DRAW PROGRAM or **OBJECT-ORIENTED PROGRAM** A computer program that stores and manipulates images in terms of the lines and curves used to create them, usually in PostScript; see also PAINT PROGRAM

DROP CAP A large initial letter dropping into the lines below and signaling the beginning of the text

DROP-OUT Complete removal of the dots in highlight areas of a halftone

DRY PROOF A color proof made without ink, such as a Cromalin

DTP Desktop publishing – digital page make-up

DUMMY A "concept model" of a publication, usually a miniature folded version, showing the position of pages; also a book without printing made up to the correct number of pages in a particular paper stock for the purpose of weighing,

designing the dust jacket, and generally seeing how the finished product will look

DUOTONE A high-quality halftone with a full tonal range made from two printings, either black and one other color, or black twice

DUPLEX STOCK Paper that has different finishes or colors either side

DUSTING Accumulation of paper particles on the blanket of a litho press, also spraying powder on to sheets coming off the press to stop wet ink touching the other sheets above and below

DYELINE See DIAZO

DYE SUBLIMATION PRINTS Color proofs of near photographic quality produced by mixing vaporized dyes on the surface of the paper

EARMARKS Distinguishing features of a typeface used for identification, named after the ear of a lower-case g

ECF (ELEMENTAL CHLORINE FREE) In papermaking, chlorine-free bleaches, such as chlorine dioxide; see also TCF

EGGSHELL PAPER A smooth pressed type of book paper

EM The width of a letter M, or a square em-quad space, which will be different for each typeface unlike a PICA EM which is ⅙th of an inch

EMAIL (ELECTRONIC MAIL) A means of sending messages and "attachments" to other people, mainly connected to the INTERNET, but also within organizations on a local network, or INTRANET. You type a message on your computer, connect to the Internet using a MODEM, and send it down the telephone line to your local ISP

EMBOSSING A finishing process producing an image in low relief

EMULSIFICATION What happens when water gets into the litho ink. Most litho inks are designed to accept some emulsification, but too much results in a wishy-washy appearance

EMULSION SIDE The duller side of film, which can be scratched

EN The width of a letter N, half an EM

EPS Encapsulated PostScript, a format for transferring drawings created in Illustrator and Freehand, for example, into digital layout programs

ESCAPE SEQUENCES The left angle bracket (<), the right angle bracket (>), and the ampersand (&) have special meanings in HTML and cannot be used "as is," you must enter their escape sequence instead: &amp, for example, is the escape sequence for &

EZINE A magazine that exists only on the Internet or on CD-rom

FACE See TYPEFACE

FAMILY A set of fonts related to a basic roman typeface, which may include italic and bold plus a whole spectrum of different "weights"

FAQ (FREQUENTLY ASKED QUESTIONS) A list of questions and answers, usually relating to a particular newsgroup. Newbies are encouraged to consult the FAQ before posting, so as not to annoy the old hands

FEATHERING Ink spreading from the edges of type, caused by poor quality ink or paper

FILLERS Additives in papermaking that improve the properties of the stock, for example increasing bulk and preventing FEATHERING

FILLING IN When halftone dots or the bowls of letters such as a or b fill solid with ink

FILM High-contrast photographic film used to transfer the image to the plate, can be positive (when the image is the same as the mechanical) or negative (the white areas show black and vice versa)

FILMLESS GRAVURE In gravure printing, digital information from the prepress system is fed directly to the diamond styli in the engraving heads that produce the printing cells

FILM RECORDER Output device for making transparencies from an image created in the computer

FINAL Film containing all the pages and design elements assembled ready to make the plate

FINISHED ARTIST Person who makes a neat camera-ready mechanical from a designer's rough layout

FINISHING All the processes that convert printed sheets into folded and bound publications

FLAME (verb) To post a harshly criticizing message in public on Usenet or send very long abusive messages via email

FLAPPING An overlay of tissue or acetate protecting artwork and mechanicals

FLAT All the film assembled by the stripper to make a 16- or 32-page plate

FLAT COLOR, MATCH COLOR, OR SPOT COLOR A single printing of a Pantone color, printed solid or as tints, in register with the black

FLATPLAN A diagram showing the position of pages in a publication along with a brief description of their content, used mainly to identify full-color and flat-color sections

FLAT-TINT HALFTONE A black halftone printed over a tint of color, faking a DUOTONE

FLEXOGRAPHY (FLEXO) A form of relief printing, using fast-drying inks and rubber or plastic plates on a rotary letterpress

FLOCCULATION An ink defect that produces a surface like orange peel, caused by the pigment not being properly dispersed in the VEHICLE

FLOPPED Laterally inverted – normally applied to halftones that have been stripped into film wrongly

FLONG See MAT

FM SCREENING (FREQUENCY MODULATED) or **STOCHASTIC SCREENING** Using dots arranged randomly to reproduce continuous tone artwork; see also AM (amplitude modulated) or conventional screening, which uses an array of differently sized dots

FOLD LINES Marks usually in the trim areas showing where sheets are to be folded

FOLIO Page number, or a single sheet of a manuscript

FONT A complete set *in one size* of all the letters of the alphabet, complete with associated ligatures (joined letters), numerals, punctuation marks, and any other signs and symbols

FONT MASTERS A set of type designs in one or more sizes that are scaled (enlarged or reduced) to create all the intermediate sizes

FONT METRICS The information about horizontal spacing built into a typeface by its designer

FOOT The bottom margin of a page

FORE EDGE The margin of a page furthest from the spine

FORME A locked-up chase in letterpress; also another name for a FLAT

FOUNTAIN The ink reservoir in letterpress, or the container for the solution that dampens the rollers of an offset litho press

FOUR-COLOR PROCESS Full-color printing in which colors are approximated by various percentages of the process colors cyan, magenta, yellow, and black. A full-color image is separated by filters into four different films – one for each of the four process colors – and four plates are used for the printing

FRAME BUFFER Computer memory that holds the current image on the screen; see also VRAM

FRAME GRABBER An input device that uses a television camera to capture a picture or three-dimensional object, or a video frame; it converts it into digital form readable by a computer program

FTP (FILE TRANSFER PROTOCOL) A protocol to let users transfer files between computers

FUGITIVE Inks that fade when exposed to light

FURNISH The liquid pulp that is converted into paper

GALLEY A typesetting proof for checking the setting before the type is made up into pages; they are generally long and thin

GAMUT or **COLOR SPACE** The range of colors that can be reproduced on a color display, output device, or by a particular color printing method – some colors available on a computer screen may not be printable using the CMYK process

GANGING UP Grouping together several transparencies to be scanned together; also printing a group of different jobs on the same sheet of paper using a single plate

GATHERING See COLLATING

GHOSTING Printing fault of a repeated image appearing next to the correct image, caused by faulty imposition; also a dull image on the other side of the sheet – this happens when the printed image affects the drying and trapping of wet ink on the reverse

GIF (GRAPHICS INTERCHANGE FORMAT) A common format for graphics containing flat areas of color, see also JPEG

GOLDENROD Orange or yellow opaque masking paper used to make up a FINAL

GOLDEN SECTION An aesthetically pleasing proportion with many examples in nature; the ratio is 34:21 or 8.1:5

GRAIN The orientation of fibers in paper, which lie in the direction of flow in a papermaking machine. GRAIN LONG means the grain is in the direction of the sheet's length. GRAIN SHORT means the grain is in the direction of the sheet's width

GRAVURE or **PHOTOGRAVURE** An INTAGLIO printing process in which the image is etched below the surface of a cylinder. The deeper the ink, the darker the tone.

GRAY COMPONENT REPLACEMENT or **ACHROMATIC STABILIZATION** Removing percentages of cyan, magenta, and yellow that cancel each other out to produce neutral grays, and relacing them with a tint of black

GREEKING Gray lines that indicate the presence of type on a computer screen; also the nonsense setting (usually Latin!) used by designers to show the position of type on a rough layout or dummy

GRID The underlying structure for a page layout as prescribed by the designer; usually preprinted on to layout sheets or boards or programmed into MASTER PAGES in a digital page layout program

GRIPPER EDGE The edge of a sheet held by metal fingers in the press – a term used in imposition. The gripper margin is the allowance that avoids any damage by the grippers to the printed image

GUI (GRAPHICAL USER INTERFACE) What you see on the screen when you want to communicate with the program, the most famous of which is the WIMP (windows, icons, mouse, pull-down menus) interface of the Apple Macintosh, derived mostly from the Smalltalk project at Xerox's PARC. Other "standards" include Windows for the PC and X-Windows for workstations.

GUTTER The combined margin of a book or folder on each side of the spine; the margin on one side of the spine is called the BACK EDGE. The term gutter is also used for any vertical space, such as that between two columns

HAIRLINE RULE A rule thinner than 0.5 point

HALATION or HALO EFFECT When ink builds up around letters or dots, leaving the center lighter

HALF BINDING The spine, adjacent strips of the cover, and triangles at the corners are bound in one material, maybe leather, and the rest of the book in a less expensive material

HALFTONE A continuous-tone image converted to line by turning it into a pattern of dots, either digitally, by laser, or by photographing it through a screen

HARDCOPY Output from a computer system that you can hold in your hand – usually a paper proof

HARD DISK Permanent magnetic memory, usually within the computer

HARD DOT A clean, regular, and sharp halftone dot

HARDWARE The parts of a computer system that you can see and touch

HEAD The margin at the top of a page

HEADBAND A decorative feature added to a case-bound book at the top of the spine

HEAT-SET INK Web ink that is dried quickly by heat then chilled

HEXACHROME A proprietary six-color system from Pantone using brighter (fluorescent) versions of CMYK plus vivid orange and green; also referred to as HiFi color; see also FOUR-COLOR PROCESS.

HICKIES Imperfections in litho printing caused by any dry hard particles on the cylinder or blanket, also called fisheyes, bull's eyes, donuts, and Newton's rings

HIGH-FIDELITY PRINTING or HIFI PRINTING uses additional process inks to increase the GAMUT. Pantone's Hexachrome, for example, adds green and orange inks to the regular CMYK

HIGH-RESOLUTION See RESOLUTION

HINGE The crease in a book cover near the spine

HINTING In computer fonts, a method for changing the shapes of characters – especially those of small sizes – so that they look better on low-resolution printers

HLS (HUE, LUMINANCE, SATURATION) A method for specifying color; see CMYK and RGB

HOLDOUT The paper property that makes it resist the absorption of ink

HOLOGRAM A three-dimensional image created by laser photography, reproduced by hot-foil stamping or embossing on to reflective-backed mylar

HOME PAGE Your own WWW site, in which you can indulge your hobbies, try out your Internet skills or publish an EZINE

HOT-FOIL STAMPING Transferring a foil coating from a carrier roll of polyester to paper or cover board by means of a heated die

HOT-METAL SETTING Casting molten metal into molds to produce type for letterpress printing

HOUSE STYLE Standards of consistency concerning spelling and use of English (or any other language) as laid down by a particular publisher, or to be used within a particular publication

HTML (HYPER TEXT MARKUP LANGUAGE) Text-based language used to create and communicate WWW pages

HTTP (HYPER TEXT TRANSPORT PROTOCOL) The protocol of the World Wide Web

HUE The rainbow parameter of a color that distinguishes red, for example, from blue

HYPHENATION The division of words, usually between syllables, pairs of consonants or pairs of vowels

ICON A small picture on a computer screen representing an application, tool, or document

IMAGESETTER A high-resolution output device that produces film or bromide prints from a PostScript file, so called because it can output line art and halftone images as well as type; see also PLATESETTER

IMPOSETTER Imagesetter which, with imposition software, produces film negatives with pages in position ready for platemaking

IMPOSING TABLE In letterpress, the place where galleys are assembled

IMPOSITION The layout of pages such that after printing, folding, collating, and trimming, they will all end up in the correct order and the right way up

IMPRESSION The process of transferring ink from the plate to the paper during printing

IMPRESSION CYLINDER In an offset litho press, the cylinder that presses the paper against the BLANKET CYLINDER

INKJET PRINTER An output device that creates an image by spraying tiny drops of ink on to paper; see also BUBBLEJET PRINTER

INKOMETER or TACKOSCOPE An instrument for measuring the tackiness of ink

INK PYRAMID In an offset litho press, the system of rollers that conveys ink to the plate

IN-LINE An in-line press has several single units arranged to print one color after another; also a process, such as folding or gluing, that happens straight after the printing, in the same pass

INSERT Any printed material that is included during binding. Material wrapped around a signature is called a WRAP. A LOOSE INSERT is not attached to the "parent" publication and will fall out when it is shaken

INTAGLIO PRINTING A method in which the ink is contained in grooves below the surface of the plate and transferred to dampened paper by pressure

INTERNET A network of networks based on the TCP/IP protocols, a community of people who use and develop those networks, and a collection of resources that can be reached from those networks

INTRANET A local network, such as within a corporation, using the same tools as the Internet: EMAIL and WWW pages, for example

IRC (INTERNET RELAY CHAT) A means of communicating in text in real time with other Internet users using a program such as Homer

ISDN (INTEGRATED SERVICES DIGITAL NETWORK) A dedicated digital telephone line – you don't need a MODEM

ISP (INTERNET SERVICE PROVIDER) The company who you dial up to get on to the Internet

JAVA A C++ based programming language from Sun that is object-oriented and platform-independent – tiny programs called applets are downloaded and embedded in the HTML code

JOGGING Vibrating paper stock before trimming to bring all the edges into alignment

JPEG (JOINT PHOTOGRAPHIC EXPERTS GROUP) A common format for graphics containing continuous tones of color, such as photographs; see also GIF

JUSTIFIED Type set with edges that are aligned both left and right. Justified setting requires HYPHENATION, and variable spacing between words

KERNING Adjusting the spacing between pairs of letters, such as T and A, to improve the aesthetic appearance; see also TRACKING

KEY Black in four-color printing; see CMYK

KEYLINE The marks on a mechanical's overlay that indicate the position of tints, halftones, and bleeds. A keyline artist is a person who assembles the finished mechanical

KNIFE FOLDER A folding machine that uses a knife to force the sheet between two nip rollers

k-p DISTANCE The distance from the top of a letter k to the bottom of a letter p

LACQUER See VARNISHING

LAID A paper texture created on the Fourdrinier wire; it has a characteristic lined appearance

LAMINATION Coating paper or cover board with a clear film to add strength and gloss

LANDSCAPE The orientation of a page when the width is greater than the height

LASER PRINTER An output device in which toner is attracted to an image on a drum that has had electrostatic charge removed by the action of a laser; the image is transferred to paper and fixed by heat

LATE BINDING The term used to mean last-minute changes within PostScript files while they are in the RIP, such as adding trapping and imposition information, particularly for digital presses

LAYDOWN SEQUENCE The sequence colors are printed – usually yellow, magenta, cyan, and finally black

LAY EDGE The left side of the sheet as it passes through the press; the lay edge will change to the right side if the sheet is to be printed on the reverse

LEADING or INTERLINE SPACING The space between lines of type; in letterpress these were strips of lead

LEAVE EDGE The edge of a sheet opposite the GRIPPER EDGE

LETTERPRESS A RELIEF PRINTING process, in which ink is transferred from the raised surface of metal or wooden type directly on to paper

LETTERSET An indirect letterpress printing process, in which the image is first transferred to a blanket, and then on to the paper

LIGATURE Two or more letters, such as fi and ffl, joined together into one character

LINE Artwork in black (or any other single color) and white only, with no intermediate tones of gray, which will print without first being screened

LINEN TESTER See LOUPE

LINOTYPE A typesetting machine for letterpress in which a whole line of type (line o' type), or slug, is cast in one operation

LINTERS In papermaking, the fibers left on the cotton seed once the longer fibers have been removed for yarn making

LINTING A printing problem caused by paper fibers that get on to the blanket, plate, or rollers of a press

LITERALS In proofreading, the spelling mistakes and transposition of letters caused by typing errors

LITHOGRAPHY A PLANOGRAPHIC PRINTING process in which greasy ink is transferred from the surface of a dampened plate or stone directly on to paper. OFFSET LITHOGRAPHY, usually short-ened to offset litho, prints first on to a rubber or plastic blanket, and then on to the paper

LOUPE Designer's magnifying glass, also called a LINEN TESTER or eyeglass; used for checking color transparencies and halftone dots

LOW SPOT Loss of image caused by an indentation in the blanket of an offset press

LUMINANCE See VALUE

MACHINE CODE The lowest level of computer language – lists of hexadecimal numbers

MACHINE FINISH (MF) Paper that has been calen-dered and is smoother and less bulky than EGGSHELL PAPER

MACHINE GLAZED (MG) Paper that has been dried against a highly polished cylinder and has one glossy side while the other remains relatively rough

MAGENTA The process color red, really more a purple

MAILING LIST An email discussion group, in which a message sent to the list server is broadcast to anyone "subscribing" to the particular list

MAKE-READY Setting up the press ready to print

MAKE UP Assemble, position, and paste type and graphic elements to produce a mechanical or flat

MANUSCRIPT The original copy for typesetting, shortened to Ms

MARGINS The areas of white between the text and the edges of the page

MARK UP Write instructions on text to define how it is to be set in type

MASK Shape cut out of opaque material such as Rubylith or Goldenrod to shield film from expo-sure to light; also used in image manipulation programs such as Photoshop

MASTER PROOF A clean and neat proof on to which the corrections and comments of all interested parties are collated

MAT or **FLONG** In letterpress, a *papier-mâché* mold taken from the FORME and used to make a STEREOTYPE; an abbreviation for matrix

MATCH COLOR See FLAT COLOR

MATCHPRINT A proprietary prepress proofing system from 3M

MATRIX A metal mold used to cast metal type; also any array or pattern of pixels, as in DITHERING; see also MAT

MATTE Dull finish, the opposite of glossy

MEASURE The width of a line of type – usually the column width, specified in pica ems

MECHANICAL Camera-ready artwork on boards, or all the line artwork for a page layout with the halftones marked "for position only," also called CAMERA-READY COPY. Mechanical separations are sets of overlays in register containing the artwork for flat color

MECHANICAL TINTS Patterns of dots simulating shades of gray or flat color added by the process blockmaker (Ben Day tints) or printer according to the designer's instructions

MENU In computing, a list of options or commands from which you are invited to choose

MESH COUNT A measure of the fineness of the mesh in the screens used in screenprinting – the number of threads per inch

MESH GRADE Thread thickness in the screens used in screenprinting

METALLIC INKS Inks that contain metal dust, producing a sheen when printed

MICROMETER An instrument for measuring very small distances, such as the thickness of paper; also one millionth of a meter

MIL One thousandth of an inch

MIRROR SITE Stores copies of files from main sites, but may be geographically closer to you

MODEM (MODULATOR DEMODULATOR) A device to convert digital data from your computer into analog data that can travel down the telephone line

MOIRÉ PATTERNS Unwanted "basket-weave" effects caused by superimposed regular patterns, such as halftone dots. Screens must be set at angles that minimize the moiré effect

MOLD-MADE PAPER Paper made by a semi-auto-matic process to resemble handmade paper

MONO, MONOCHROME Black-and-white, or the vari-ous tones of one color

MONOTYPE A letterpress typesetting machine that casts individual metal letters in a two-stage process

MOTTLE An uneven IMPRESSION caused by too much dampening water or the wrong choice of paper and ink

MOUSE In computing, a small pointing device used to control a cursor on the screen

M WEIGHT The weight of paper as measured per thousand sheets

NEGATIVE-WORKING PLATE Offset litho plate prepared by exposure to negative film

NETIQUETTE A code of conduct or good manners for the Internet

NETWORKING Linking computers together so that they can communicate with each other and share output devices such as laser printers and file servers

NEWBIE A new user to the Internet, particularly to newsgroups

NEWSGROUP A "bulletin board" of articles on a specific topic, arranged in threads, see also USENET (UNIX USER NETWORK)

NEWSPRINT Inexpensive, rough, and absorbent paper used for printing newspapers and magazines

NTSC (NATIONAL TELEVISION SYSTEMS COMMITTEE) The US standard of the FCC (Federal Communications Commission) for broadcast television

OFFSET Abbreviation for offset lithography; also the same as setoff – when ink transfers from one printed sheet to the back of another

OFFSET LITHOGRAPHY or **OFFSET LITHO** A PLANO-GRAPHIC PRINTING process in which greasy ink is transferred from the surface of a dampened plate first on to a rubber or plastic blanket, and then on to the paper

OFFSET PROCESS See OFFSET LITHOGRAPHY

ONE-UP Printing a single job on one plate. Quality is better controlled, but it is usually more economi-cal to print two-up, i.e. two different jobs, or the same job in tandem, on one plate

OPACIMETER An instrument for measuring the opacity of paper

OPACITY The property of a paper affecting the show-through of printing from the other side of the sheet

OPERATING SYSTEM Behind-the-scenes computer software that takes care of the internal workings of the computer

OPI (OPEN PREPRESS INTERFACE) A protocol, origi-nally proposed by Aldus, which enables files from different digital prepress programs to be used together

OPTICAL BRIGHTENERS Additives to paper that increase its brightness by glowing under the influence of ultraviolet light

ORIENTED POLYPROPYLENE (OPP) LAMINATION The standard bookjacket lamination film

ORPHANS A single word or a few words, usually less than a third of the measure of the setting, form-ing a line of their own at the end of a paragraph; see also WIDOW

ORTHOCHROMATIC Film sensitive to the blue end of the spectrum used for line work – red records as black and marks in light-blue pencil are invisible; see also PANCHROMATIC

OUT OF REGISTER The blurred effect that occurs when film separations or plates are misaligned

OVERLAY A sheet of acetate or tissue over a photo-graph or in registration with a mechanical containing artwork for flat color, keylines, or instructions to the printer

OVERMATTER Setting or images that are excess to requirements, to be used in the next issue of a magazine, for example

OVERPRINT Color, usually black, printed over flat color

OVER RUNS or **RUN-ONS** Sheets printed beyond the quantity specified, to compensate for spoilage or for the client's own use

OZALID See BLUEPRINT and BROWNLINE

PAGEMAKER A page-layout program from Adobe, originally developed by Aldus

PAGE PROOF A proof showing type arranged on a page, along with folios, running headlines, captions, and sometimes the position of illustrations

PAGINATION The sequence of pages in a book or folder

PAINT PROGRAM or **PAINT SYSTEM** A computer program that stores the image on the screen as a bitmap; see also DRAW PROGRAM

PAL (PHASE ALTERNATION LINE) The standard in the UK and most of Europe for broadcast television

PANCHROMATIC Film that records all colors equally, as opposed to ORTHOCHROMATIC, which does not "see" the blue end of the spectrum

PANTONE MATCHING SYSTEM (PMS) A widely used proprietary system for specifying flat color in percentages of 11 standard colors; coordinating papers and markers corresponding to Pantone colors can also be purchased

PAPER CREEP ALLOWANCE Allowing for the thickness of paper at the spine of a thick saddle-stitched publication by shifting the margins on the mechanical so that the margins remain consistent after the sheets are trimmed

PAPER CURL Wavy edges caused by the stack of paper having a lower moisture level than the surroundings, or tight edges caused by the stack having a higher moisture level

PASTE UP To cut and assemble typesetting, line art, and halftones on to board using gum or wax, to produce a mechanical

PDF (PORTABLE DOCUMENT FORMAT) A document format which uses a reader such as Adobe Acrobat to recreate the appearance of fonts and spacing in your page layout

PEN PLOTTER A point-to-point output device used mainly for engineering drawings; if equipped with a knife in place of the pen it can be used to cut stencils for screenprinting or vinyl letters for signs

PERFECT BINDING Binding trimmed single sheets of paper with glue to produce a book or magazine with a flat spine

PERFECTING PRESS A press that prints both sides of the sheet at the same time

PERFORATION Producing the tear-along lines on coupons or stamps, for example, by piercing with sharp metal strips

PERSONAL COMPUTER A stand-alone desktop computer; a PC is an IBM Personal Computer or a software-compatible system from a vendor such as Compaq

PHOTOGRAVURE See GRAVURE

PHOTOTYPESETTING or **PHOTOSETTING** A process in which type is set on to bromide paper or film by exposure of light through a matrix containing tiny negatives of the letters, or directly by the action of a laser beam

PICA or **PICA EM** A unit for measuring type equal to 1/6th of an inch, or 12 points; on a typewriter, the normal pitch of ten characters per inch

PI CHARACTERS Greek and mathematical signs, used with but not typically part of a font

PICKING Removal of some of the surface of paper during printing

PIGMENTS AND DYES Components of printing inks that give it color

PILING Sticking or caking of ink pigment on the blanket or plate

PIN REGISTER Accurate positioning system for color separations – both films and plates – with punched holes and corresponding pins

PITCH On typewriters, the number of characters per inch

PIXEL Pixel is short for picture element and is the dot on a computer display. The resolution (sharpness) of a raster display is measured by the number of pixels horizontally by the number of scan lines vertically, e.g. 1280 x 1024

PLANOGRAPHIC PRINTING Any process using a plate on which both the printing and non-printing areas are on the same surface, e.g. lithography

PLASTIC COMB A type of ring binding found on reports and manuals

PLATE A metal or plastic sheet with a photo-sensitive face on to which an image is chemically etched, either changing the characteristics of the surface, as in LITHOGRAPHY, or cutting below the surface as in RELIEF or INTAGLIO PRINTING

PLATE CYLINDER In an offset litho press, the cylinder to which the plate is attached

PLATE-DAMPENING UNIT In offset litho, the system of rollers that dampens the plate before inking; see also FOUNTAIN

PLATEN A small letterpress that acts like a clamshell, bringing a flat plate and the paper together in an opening and closing motion, as opposed to a ROTARY PRESS

PLATESETTER A device that processes plates direct from a PostScript file; see also IMAGESETTER

PMT Photomechanical transfer, a DIFFUSION TRANSFER process for enlarging or reducing line art; also called a BROMIDE

POINT A unit for measuring type equal to approximately 1/72nd of an inch (exactly 1/72nd of an inch in computer systems), abbreviated pt; also a measure of paper bulk equivalent to one thousandth of an inch (a MIL)

PORTRAIT The orientation of a page when the height is greater than the width

POSITIVE-WORKING PLATE An offset litho plate prepared by exposure to positive film

POSTSCRIPT An outline description language for type developed by Adobe and licenced to suppliers such as Linotype, Monotype, Agfa, and AM Varityper. Type 1 PostScript fonts contain hinting and encryption; see also EPS and TRUETYPE

PPP (POINT TO POINT PROTOCOL) The gateway from your client software, i.e. Eudora for email, to the Internet; see also SLIP

PREPRESS PROOF A proof taken directly from the film separations, to check that the color will print correctly

PRESS PROOF A proof taken from the plates that will be used to print the finished job, and on the specified paper stock, usually on a special proofing press

PRINTING-DOWN FRAME In offset litho, a device for holding the film and plate in contact during exposure to ultraviolet light

PRINT RUN The number of copies to be produced in one printing, also called the press run

PROCESS CAMERA A camera designed to enlarge or reduce artwork and mechanicals, and produce film positives and negatives

PROCESS COLORS The four colors – cyan (process blue), magenta (process red), yellow, and key (black) – used to approximate full-color artwork

PROGRESSIVES A set of proofs showing the four color separations printed in various combinations; also called Hollywoods or progs

PROOF Hardcopy that allows you to check the accuracy of setting, the position of design elements on a page, or the fidelity of color after separation

PROOFING PRESS A small press used to produce proofs

PROPORTIONAL SCALE See REPRODUCTION CALCULATOR

QUAD A square space in typesetting used as a unit of measurement, such as an em quad or en quad

QUARTER BINDING The spine and adjacent strips of the cover are bound in one material, maybe leather, and the rest of the sides in a less expensive material

RAM (RANDOM ACCESS MEMORY) Quick-access temporary memory in a computer containing the job in hand, in the form of chips

RANGED LEFT/RIGHT Ranged left is a method of setting type in which the type is aligned on the left-hand side and ragged on the right. Ranged right is ragged on the left and aligned on the right

RASTER A horizontal scan line on a computer screen or output device

REAM 500 sheets of paper

RECTO The front of a sheet of paper, or the right-hand page of a publication; opposite of VERSO

REFLECTED LIGHT Colors from an object or flat artwork, as opposed to TRANSMITTED LIGHT from a light source or transparency

REFLECTION COPY Any original art viewed by light reflecting from its surface, as opposed to TRANSMISSION COPY, such as a 35mm slide

REGISTER or **REGISTRATION** Correct positioning of one color separation in relation to the others during printing. A register mark is a symbol used on copy and film to ensure accurate registration

RELIEF PRINTING A printing process, such as LETTERPRESS and FLEXOGRAPHY, in which ink lies on the raised surface of the plate but not in the grooves and is transferred to the paper by pressure

REPRODUCTION CALCULATOR or **PROPORTIONAL SCALE** A slide-rule-type instrument for estimating the size of an illustration after reduction or enlargement

REPRODUCTION PROOF or **REPRO PROOF** A crisp proof on art paper of letterpress setting to be used on a mechanical

REPURPOSING Adapting an existing page layout to become a different format or medium, such as a WWW page

RESIST A substance used on plates for preventing the non-printing areas from etching

RESOLUTION A measure of the fineness and quality of an output device, usually measured in dots per inch (dpi) – the number of dots that can be placed end to end in a line an inch long; see also ADDRESSABILITY

RETOUCHING Modifying or correcting photographic images either manually with dye and airbrush, or electronically to a scanned image using a program such as Photoshop or Quantel Paintbox

REVERSED OUT When type is set in white against a black or flat color background

RGB (RED, GREEN, BLUE) A system for specifying color on a computer screen; see also CMYK

RICH BLACK A black object or area that prints even darker through the use of undercolors

RIGHT-READING EMULSION DOWN (RRED) Film used for offset litho platemaking in which the image appears the correct way round when the film is viewed from the shiny (non-emulsion) side; also called wrong-reading emulsion up (WREU)

RIGHT-READING EMULSION UP (RREU) Film used for direct forms of platemaking, such as LETTER-PRESS and FLEXOGRAPHY, in which the image appears the correct way round when the film is viewed from the dull emulsion side, also called wrong reading emulsion down (WRED)

RIP Raster image processor – a device that converts a PostScript file into a bitmap that can be output from an IMAGESETTER or PLATESETTER

RIVERS Unwanted space running vertically and diagonally in chunks of (mainly justified) type – to be avoided

ROLLING BALL A pointing device that controls the position of a cursor on the computer screen

ROM (READ ONLY MEMORY) Permanent unalterable computer memory in the form of chips; also abbreviation for ROMAN

ROMAN Normal type, as opposed to italic or bold; also a kind of type with serifs such as Times New Roman

ROTARY PRESS A press that uses a cylinder as its printing surface, as opposed to a FLATBED or PLATEN press

ROTOGRAVURE See GRAVURE

ROUNDING AND BACKING (R&B) Putting a rounded shape into the spine of a bookblock, and a joint below the shoulder

RUBYLITH A red transparent masking material

RUNAROUND Type set around a photograph or other design element, deviating from the normal measure

RUNNING HEADS Headlines that appear in the same (or a symmetrical) position on every page of a publication except where chapter titles occur or if illustrations outside the grid area displace them

SADDLE STITCHING A binding method using wire staples along the fold of the publication

SANS SERIF A typeface without SERIFS

SATURATION or **INTENSITY** A measure of the color's position in the range from neutral gray to fully saturated, or bright, color

SCALING Enlarging or reducing – usually applied to an image – and calculating the percentage of enlargement or reduction so as to anticipate the space it will occupy in a layout

SCANNER An electronic device used to convert artwork or transparencies into halftone separations

SCATTER PROOFS Proofs with several illustrations printed randomly together on one sheet, not in their correct positions on the page

SCORE To crease a sheet of paper or board so that it will fold easily

SCREEN A piece of glass or plastic used to convert continuous tone copy into a halftone; also the frequency of dots, expressed in lines per inch or lpi

SCREENPRINTING A printing process using a stencil supported on a mesh or screen; ink is forced through the open mesh but is prevented from reaching the non-image areas of the paper by the stencil

SCUFFING A problem in packaging design, where print is more likely to receive rough handling; scuffproof ink, lamination, or a coat of varnish is the solution

SCUMMING A printing problem caused when the plate accepts ink where it shouldn't

SECTION SEWING A binding method in which signatures are sewn through the spine with thread before being casebound

SELF COVER A cover printed on the same paper stock as the rest of the publication, using the same plate as pages from the inside

SEPARATION Film in register relating to one of the four process colors; also artwork or film in register relating to flat color

SERIES A complete range of sizes in the same typeface

SERIF The mark that terminates the ends of the letters in some typefaces

SERVICE BUREAU A place where you can rent expensive equipment by the hour, or have laser prints, bromides, and film output from an imagesetter from your disk at a price per sheet

SET The width of a letter

SETOFF or **OFFSET** This occurs when the wet image on a sheet of paper prints on to the paper above or below it in the pile. Anti-setoff spray should separate each sheet by a fine layer of particles

SET SOLID Type set without leading, for example 10/10pt

SET-UP TIME The time it takes to make-ready and set up the press to run your job

SHEETFED A press taking single sheets of paper

SHEETWISE A form of imposition using one plate to print the front of a sheet, and another to print the back

SHINGLING See PAPER CREEP ALLOWANCE

SHOW-THROUGH or **STRIKE-THROUGH** Being able to see through a sheet of paper to the printed impression on the other side

SIDE BEARINGS The space allocated on either side of a letter by its designer to stop adjacent letters from touching and to achieve an aesthetically pleasing appearance when words are set

SIDE SEWING A form of binding used mainly for children's books in which the thread is sewn near the spine, front to back, as in SIDE STABBING

SIDE STABBING A form of binding in which wire staples are inserted near the spine from front to back

SIGNATURE Several pages for a book, printed from the same plate and arranged so that they can be folded and trimmed to make a section, usually of 16 pages. A BACKSTEP MARK on the spine shows how several signatures are to be arranged so they bind in the correct sequence

SILKSCREEN See SCREENPRINTING

SIZE In papermaking, substances added to the furnish to make the paper less absorbent, which can also be coated or sprayed on to the web at a later stage of the process at the size press; sizing can also be used to mean SCALING

SKEWING A printing problem that occurs when paper, blanket, and cylinder are not in proper contact

SLIP (SERIAL LINE INTERNET PROTOCOL) The gateway from your client software, i.e. Eudora for email, to the Internet; see also PPP

SLUG A line of letterpress type from a LINOTYPE machine, or a piece of metal used for word spacing

SLURRING Distortion of the image, with dots appearing elongated or smeared, caused by too much ink or slippage of stock

SLURRY In papermaking, fibers with lots of water

SMILEY Symbol made from ASCII characters meant to convey emotions, e.g. :-)

SNOWFLAKING In offset litho, a problem of water droplets in the litho ink that spoil solid areas; in gravure the effect is caused by inadequate pressure which prevents the paper from taking the ink from one or more cells

SOFT DOT Halftone dot slightly out of focus

SOFTWARE The list of instructions that turns a general-purpose computer into a machine for a particular purpose, such as digital page layout or image manipulation

SORTS In letterpress, individual pieces of metal type

SPAMMING (from the Monty Python song "Spam") CROSSPOSTING a carelessly inappropriate message or advertisement to many different groups or individuals

SPINE The bound edge of a book or magazine, where the fold is

SPIRAL-BOUND A method of binding used for calendars, cookery books, and manuals, using a wire spiral inserted through holes in the pages

SPLIT FOUNTAIN Printing two colors on an offset press by using one color at one end of the fountain and another at the other end – the colors blend in the middle

SPOILAGE Wasted printed sheets that are discarded

SPOT COLOR See FLAT COLOR

SPOT VARNISH Applying patches of varnish, often to make halftones glossy

SPREADING An enlarging of the image caused by too much ink, or too much pressure between blanket and plate

STANDARD LIGHTING CONDITIONS A light source with a color temperature of 5000 Kelvin

STANDARD VIEWING CONDITIONS An area to view color proofs, surrounded by neutral gray and illuminated by STANDARD LIGHTING CONDITIONS

STARVATION GHOSTING An unwelcome effect that results in uneven printing and is due to some extent to the placement of dense black elements in certain positions on the plate

STENCIL PRINTING A printing process, such as SCREENPRINTING, using a stencil supported on a mesh or screen; ink is forced through the open mesh but is prevented from reaching the non-image areas of the paper by the stencil

STEP-AND-REPEAT A method for copying film, so that two or more of the same job can be printed from one plate

STEREOTYPE or **STEREO** A letterpress plate made by casting lead in a *papier-mâché* mold (a MAT or flong) taken from the FORME. It can be flat for flatbed presses or curved for rotary machines

STET A proofreading mark meaning reinstate, or "let it stand," i.e. print what was there originally

STICKING or **BLOCKING** So much SETOFF that the sheets stick together

STOCHASTIC SCREENING or **FM SCREENING** Using dots arranged randomly to reproduce continuous tone artwork; see also AM (amplitude modulated) or conventional screening, which uses a regular array of differently sized dots

STREAM FEEDER A mechanism on highspeed sheetfed presses that presents sheets to the rollers overlapping slightly

STRIKE-ON SETTING See COLD-METAL SETTING

STRIKE-THROUGH See SHOW-THROUGH

STRIPPING IN Inserting halftones on film into the film made from a mechanical. A stripper is a person who assembles film into the final

STYLE SHEET A paper document or feature of a page layout program that sets out the specifications for a publication or series of publications, listing such things as the typeface, size, leading of body text, headlines, and captions

SUBSTRATE Any sheet material to be printed — paper, board, plastic, or another substance. Also the carrier material in film, for example, on to which a layer of emulsion is deposited

SUPER-CALENDERING Smoothing paper by pressing it between highly polished cylinders, done off the machine

SURPRINT Superimposing type on to a tint of the same color — they share the same film and are printed together

SWATCH BOOK A book of tear-off color samples; the most commonly used come from Pantone

SYSTEM A catch-all term meaning all the computer equipment you need to make things work (as in "the system's down"); also the operating system (as in System 7); or a set of software tools (as in a digital prepress system)

TACK The adhesive property of an ink

TAG HTML code that the BROWSER interprets "on the fly" as the web page arrives from the server to the client. Tags usually have a start and an end, "containing" the item in question. The first part of a tag turns an attribute on and the second turns the attribute off. Tags are surrounded by angled brackets (the "less than" and "greater than" symbols) and the closing tag is usually preceded by a slash symbol (/)

TAILBAND A decorative feature added to a case-bound book at the bottom of the spine

TAIL-END HOOK When solid areas near the back edge of a sheet make it curl down, caused by paper that adheres to the blanket too tightly as it is pulled off by the delivery grippers because the ink is too tacky

TCF (TOTALLY CHLORINE FREE) In papermaking, chlorine-free bleaches, such as hydrogen peroxide

TCP/IP (TRANSMISSION CONTROL PROTOCOL/INTERNET PROTOCOL) The standards that enable computers to pass information between each other on the Internet

TELNET A program that lets you log on to another computer, anywhere on the Internet, as if you were using a terminal attached to that computer

THERMAL-TRANSFER PLOTTER An output device that prints by "ironing" colored wax on to paper by the action of heat

THERMAL-TRANSFER PRINTS Color proofs produced by melting colored waxes on to paper

THERMOGRAPHY Creating a raised impression by using a heat-treated resinous powder

THERMOJET PLOTTER A form of inkjet printer which sprays melted plastic on to the paper; also known as a phase-change inkjet

THREAD-SEALING A combination of some of the features of perfect binding and section sewing, but no thread runs between sections

TIFF Tagged Image File Format, a protocol for dealing with scanned photographs in digital prepress programs

TINT Shades of a flat color created by patterns of dots similar to halftones, specified as a percentage of the solid color

TINTING A printing problem of pigment finding its way into the fountain, discoloring the background

TIP IN A page-size insert glued to the edge of a SIGNATURE

TIP ON A small insert glued to the surface of a page, such as a coupon

TOOL A facility in a computer program that makes something happen — a circle tool, for example, allows you to draw circles in different ways; tools are usually represented by ICONS

TRACKING Adjusting the spacing between all letters, as opposed to KERNING, which only adjusts the space between pairs of letters; also, when several colored images are printed in a row and inking becomes uneven as a result

TRANSMISSION COPY Copy, such as transparencies and film positives, viewed by TRANSMITTED LIGHT

TRANSMITTED LIGHT Colors from a light source or a transparency, as opposed to REFLECTED LIGHT from a print or flat artwork

TRANSPARENCY A color slide, usually either 35mm, 5in by 4in, or 10in by 8in, so-called TRANSMISSION COPY

TRAP A small nick in the design of letters to allow for ink spread, especially around junctions

TRAPPING Creating an overlap between areas of flat color to compensate for any misregistration — usually the lighter color overlaps the darker; also any area of color overlapping another. A SPREAD traps a light foreground object to a dark background; a CHOKE traps a light background to a dark foreground object. RICH BLACKS require KEEPAWAY: the undercolor is made smaller than the black, so that if the inks misregister the undercolor is covered by the black

TRIM AND CENTER MARKS Indications of where paper sheets are to be trimmed and folded; they mark out the finished page area

TRUETYPE An outline description format from Apple and Microsoft which rivals POSTSCRIPT

TURNKEY SYSTEM A packaged and integrated assembly of hardware, software, and support. Turnkey suppliers buy in equipment from third parties and repackage or "badge engineer" the components, perhaps adding some proprietary go-faster boards as well as their own software, before passing on the "value-added" system to the end user

TWO-UP See ONE-UP

TYPEFACE The design of a font

TYPE SPECIFICATION A list of all the typefaces, sizes, and leading to be used for body type, headlines, captions, and so on, in a publication or series of publications; see also STYLE SHEET

UNDERCOLOR ADDITION (UCA) Adding a tint of process color to add density to a black; see also RICH BLACK

UNDERCOLOR REMOVAL (UCR) Reducing the amount of color in areas of shadows, to save ink and improve trapping

UNITS Letters of different widths in a typeface are allocated different numbers of units in accordance with a scheme that is devised by the typographer and the type foundry and dependent on the output process being used

UPLOAD Using FTP to send a file from your computer, such as your WWW home page, to a remote server

URL (UNIFORM RESOURCE LOCATOR) The unique address of a WWW page, of the form: http://www.your_ISP.com/user_name/index.html

USENET (UNIX USER NETWORK) A collection of NEWSGROUPS, each containing articles on a specific topic, arranged in threads

VALUE or **LUMINANCE** The parameter of color describing the lightness or darkness, changed by adding black or white to a particular hue

VARNISHING Coating areas of a page with a colorless varnish or lacquer to improve gloss on halftones, for example

VEHICLE The component of a printing ink that carries and binds the pigment

VELOX A halftone on BROMIDE paper that can be pasted on to a mechanical and used for undemanding printing

VERSO The back of a sheet of paper, or the left-hand page of a publication, opposite of RECTO

VGA (VIDEO GRAPHICS ARRAY) Developed by IBM for the PS/2 computer. Its standard resolution is 640 x 480 pixels, extendible to 1024 x 768, and it can display 256 colors from a palette of 256k

VIGNETTE A halftone that fades to nothing around the edges

VIRUS A pernicious and self-replicating piece of mischief that can cause havoc in a computer, introduced on floppy disks of dubious origin

VISCOSITY The amount of flow and tack in an ink

VRAM Video random-access memory; see FRAME BUFFER

VRML (VIRTUAL REALITY MODELING LANGUAGE) A platform-independent language for describing 3D virtual reality scenes

WATERLESS PLATES In offset litho printing, waterless plates consist of ink on aluminum for the image areas and a silicone rubber for the non-printing areas. Silicone rubber has very low surface tension and thus will repel ink.

WATERMARK A symbol or mark manufactured into paper which can be seen when the sheet is held to the light

WEB A continuous roll of paper used on web-fed presses, cut into sheets after printing

WET-ON-WET One color is still wet as another is printed

WIDOW A single word or part of a word from the end of a paragraph left at the top of a new column or page; see also ORPHANS

WIMP Windows, icons, mouse, and pull-down menus (or windows, icons, menus, and pointing device), the original Mac GUI with which the user tells the computer what to do by pointing and clicking at icons (little pictures) and menu items (lists of available options) on the screen using a mouse or other pointing device

WINDOW A transparent hole in a negative awaiting a halftone to be stripped in; also an active and independent area of a computer screen

WINDOWS A Mac-like operating system for PCs developed by Microsoft

WINTEL A name for PCs that use WINDOWS and Intel microprocessor chips

WIRE COMB A form of spiral binding used for reports, cookery books, and manuals

WOODFREE Chemical woodpulp for papermaking

WOODPULP Wood that has been debarked and separated into fibers for papermaking, either by grinding (mechanical woodpulp) or by cooking in chemicals (chemical or woodfree woodpulp)

WORK-AND-TUMBLE An imposition scheme in which both sides of a job can be printed, in two passes, by a single plate: one side is printed, then the sheet is turned head-over-heels so that the gripper edge changes ends

WORK-AND-TURN An imposition scheme in which both sides of a job can be printed, in two passes, by a single plate: one side is printed, then the sheet is turned sideways so that the lay edge changes sides but the gripper edge remains the same

WORKSTATION A type of networkable computer, more powerful than a personal computer, made by vendors such as Sun and Silicon Graphics

WOVE A paper texture introduced on the Fourdrinier wire; it has a characteristic woven appearance (or sometimes no detectable texture); see also LAID

WRONG-READING EMULSION DOWN (WRED) See RIGHT-READING EMULSION UP (RREU)

WRONG-READING EMULSION UP (WREU) See RIGHT-READING EMULSION DOWN (RRED)

WWW (WORLD WIDE WEB) Interconnected Internet "pages" viewed by a BROWSER, such as Netscape Navigator, containing text, images, sound, movies, and hypertext "hot links" to other pages

WYSIWYG (WHAT YOU SEE IS WHAT YOU GET) In computer software, a screen-based representation of a printed or WWW page that approximates what you will see in the finished product, as opposed to a list of computer code

XEROGRAPHY A copying process using black toner attracted to an image on an electrostatically charged drum; the toner is transferred to paper and fixed by heat

X-HEIGHT The height of a letter x in a particular typeface – a typographic measurement which ignores the height of the ascenders and descenders

XPRESS A digital page-layout program from Quark

ABBREVIATIONS AND ACRONYMS

AFAIK	as far as I know
AM	amplitude modulated
APR	automatic picture replacement
ASCII	American Standard Code for Information Interchange
A/UX	a workstation operating system, a version of Unix
A/W	artwork
BTW	by the way
C++	a high-level computer language
CCD	charge-coupled device
CEPS	Color Electronic Publishing System
CMS	Color Management System
cm³/g	cubic centimeters per gram
CMYK	cyan, magenta, yellow, key (black)
cpu	central processing unit
CRC	camera-ready copy
CRT	cathode ray tube
CTP	computer-to-plate
DMA	direct memory access
dpi	dots per inch
DPS	double-page spread
dtp	desktop publishing
ECF	elemental chlorine free
EPS	Encapsulated PostScript
FAQ	Frequently Asked Questions
FM	frequency modulated
FTP	File Transfer Protocol
FYI	for your information
Gbyte	gigabyte
GIF	Graphics Interchange Format
g/m²	grams per square meter
gsm	grams per square meter
GUI	graphical user interface
HD	grade of mesh for screenprinting with 20–35% open area
HLS	hue, luminance, saturation
HP	hot-pressed, a handmade paper finish
HP-GL	Hewlett-Packard graphics language
HTML	Hyper Text Markup Language
HTTP	Hyper Text Transport Protocol
Hz	Hertz, or cycles per second
IBC	inside back cover

IBM PC	a make of personal computer
IFC	inside front cover
IMHO	in my humble opinion
IRC	Internet Relay Chat
ISDN	Integrated Services Digital Network
ISP	Internet Service Provider
JPEG	Joint Photographic Experts Group
k	kilobyte, 1024 bytes (kbyte is more accurate usage)
kbyte	kilobyte, 1024 bytes
LAN	local-area network
l.c.	lower case
lpi	lines per inch
M	grade of mesh for screenprinting
(m)	machine direction in paper
Mbyte	megabyte
MF	machine finish paper
MG	machine glazed paper
MHz	megahertz, or millions of cycles per second
MIPS	millions of instructions per second
Ms	manuscript
MS-DOS	Microsoft – Disk Operating System (PC's operating system)
NOT	not hot-pressed, a handmade paper finish
NTSC	National Television Systems Committee
OBC	outside back cover
OFC	outside front cover
OPI	open prepress interface
OPP	oriented polypropylene lamination
PAL	Phase Alternation Line – broadcast television standard in the UK
PC	personal computer
pcb	printed circuit-board
PDF	Portable Document Format
PMS	Pantone Matching System
PMT	photomechanical transfer
ppi	pages per inch
PPP	Point To Point Protocol
pt	point, a measurement of type size
RAM	random access memory – short-term computer memory

R&B	rounding and backing
RC	resin-coated
RGB	red, green, blue
RIP	raster image processor
RISC	reduced instruction set computer
ROFL	rolls on the floor laughing
ROM	read-only memory – permanent computer memory
RRED	right-reading emulsion down
RREU	right-reading emulsion up
RSI	repetitive strain injury
RT*M	read the * manual (clean version!)
S	grade of mesh for screenprinting with 50–70% open area
SIMM	single in-line memory module
SLIP	Serial Line Internet Protocol
SPARC	scalable processor architecture
S/S	same size
stet	reinstate deleted material
T	grade of mesh for screenprinting
TCF	totally chlorine free
TCP/IP	Transmission Control Protocol/Internet Protocol
TIFF	tagged image file format
TPD	two-page display
u.c.	upper case
UCA	undercolor addition
UCR	undercolor removal
URL	Uniform Resource Locator
UV	ultraviolet
VGA	video graphics array
VRML	Virtual Reality Modeling Language
VRAM	Video random-access memory
WIMP	windows, icons, mouse, and pull-down menus
WOB	white on black
WORM	write once read many – computer optical drives
WRED	wrong-reading emulsion down
WREU	wrong-reading emulsion up
WRULD	work-related upper-limb disorders
WWW	World Wide Web
WYSIWYG	what you see is what you get
YMMV	your mileage may vary

FURTHER READING

Nancy Aldrich-Ruenzel and John Fennell (eds) *Designer's Guide to Typography.* Phaidon, Oxford, 1991. A collection compiled from articles first published in *Step-by-step Graphics* magazine, including contributions from Neville Brody and April Greiman.

Nancy Aldrich-Ruenzel (ed.) *Designer's Guide to Print Production.* Watson-Guptill, New York, 1990. Another collection compiled from articles first published in *Step-by-step Graphics* magazine.

Fernand Baudin *How Typography Works (and Why It Is important).* Lund Humphries, London, 1989. An idiosyncratic handwritten text based on a series of blackboard lectures by the Belgian graphic designer.

Mark Beach *Graphically Speaking.* Elk Ridge, Manzanita, OR, 1992. A practical guide to avoiding common mistakes, cutting costs, and communicating effectively.

D. E. Bisset *et al. The Printing Ink Manual.* Northwood, London, 1961 (and subsequent editions). Everything you need to know about ink.

Lewis Blackwell *Twentieth-century Type.* Laurence King, London, 1992. Beginning just before the invention of mechanical typesetting, this is a study of typography and its spectacular development in the last hundred years.

Lewis Blackwell *The End of Print.* Laurence King, London, 1995. A book about and designed by innovative graphic designer David Carson.

Lewis Blackwell and Neville Brody *G1.* Laurence King, London, 1996. A collection of work by contemporary graphic designers, including Zuzana Licko and P. Scott Makela, along with the found images that have inspired them.

Michael H. Bruno (ed.) *Pocket Pal: A Graphic Arts Production Handbook* (16th edn). International Paper, Memphis, TN, 1995. A handy concise pocket-sized guide to graphic arts production.

Allistair Campbell *New Design Handbook.* Little, Brown and Co, London, 1993. Standard reference manual for all designers – complete with desktop computer graphics and four-color tint chart.

Rob Carter *American Typography Today.* Van Nostrand Reinhold, New York, 1989. A guide to the work of 24 contemporary American typographers, from Frank Armstrong to Dietmar Winkler, with a chronology of other important typographers.

Sebastian Carter *Twentieth-century Type Designers* (2nd edn). Lund Humphries, London, 1995. A standard reference work on the lives of 24 designers worldwide, from Frederic W. Goudy to Carol Twombly.

Mario Henri Chakhour *Painting with Computers* (inc. CD-rom). Rockport Publishers, Rockport, MA,

1996. Exploration of nine digital art techniques, including PixelPaintPro and Fractal Design Painter. A gallery of finished work follows each chapter.

Lee Chartier and Scott Mason *Creating Designs on a Limited Budget.* North Light Books, Cincinnati, OH, 1995. A drawing-board/work-station manual showing how to achieve impressive results in cost-effective ways.

Luanne Seymour Cohen and Tanya Wendling *Design Essentials* (2nd edn). Adobe Press, Mountain View, CA, 1995. Illustrated step-by-step procedures for creating graphic and photographic effects using Adobe Photoshop.

David Collier *Collier's Rules for Desktop Design and Typography.* Addison-Wesley, Wokingham, England, 1991. A lively and graphic look at digital design by a former partner of DeCode Design.

Bob Cotton (ed.) *The New Guide to Graphic Design.* Phaidon, Oxford, 1990. Part One covers basic design principles and procedures; Part Two consists of a series of case studies of designers at work on packaging, magazines, books, and videos.

James Craig *Production for the Graphic Designer* (revised edn 1990). Watson-Guptill, New York, 1976. An updated version of Craig's definitive work.

James Craig and William Bevington *Working with Graphic Designers.* Watson-Guptill, New York, 1989. Graphic design explained to lay people.

Terence Dalley (ed.) *The Complete Guide to Illustration and Design.* Phaidon, London, 1980. Well-illustrated guide to the practice of illustration and graphic design.

John Dreyfuss *Into Print.* The British Library, London, 1994. Selected writings on printing history, typography, and book production.

Adam C. Engst *Internet Starter Kit* (2nd edn). Hayden Books, Indianapolis, IN, 1994. This definitive guide to the Internet comes with a CD-rom of software to get you started.

April Greiman *Hybrid Imagery.* ADT Press, London, 1990. Lots of computerized trickery from the doyenne of the West Coast avant-garde.

Steven Heller and Anne Fink *Low-budget High-quality Design.* Watson Guptill, New York, 1990. Lots of tips on how to produce effective graphics on a low budget.

Jost Hochuli and Robin Kinross *Designing Books: Practice and Theory.* Hyphen Press, London, 1996. The basic principles of "macrotypography" by the Swiss designer, with a detailed commentary of 27 of his designs by a design historian.

Richard Hollis *Graphic Design: A Concise History.* Thames & Hudson, London, 1996. A documentary history that begins with the poster, then charts

the development of word and image in magazines, advertising, and corporate identity.

Dard Hunter *Papermaking: The History and Technique of an Ancient Craft.* Dover, New York, 1943. An authoritative history of papermaking.

Terry Jeavons and Michael Beaumont *An Introduction to Typography.* Quintet/The Apple Press, London, 1990. A colorful illustrated book on all kinds of type.

Ruari McLean *The Thames and Hudson Manual of Typography.* Thames & Hudson, London, 1980. An authoritative history of typography from an eminent typographer and designer.

Ruari McLean (ed.) *Typographers on Type.* Lund Humphries, London, 1995. An illustrated anthology of essays from type designers as diverse as William Morris and Matthew Carter.

Ellen Lupton *Mixing Messages: Contemporary Graphic Design in America.* Princeton Architectural Press, New York/Thames & Hudson, London, 1996. Catalog of an exhibition held at the Cooper Hewitt National Design Museum, Smithsonian Institution, New York.

Philip B. Meggs *History of Graphic Design.* Van Nostrand Reinhold, New York, 1983. A definitive and well-illustrated history of graphic design through the ages.

Jennifer Niederst *Designing for the Web.* O'Reilly & Associates, Sebastopol, CA, 1996. Clear introduction to writing HTML, aimed at graphic designers.

John Miles *Design for Desktop Publishing.* Gordon Fraser, London, 1987. Straightforward guide from a partner of Banks and Miles, explaining the fundamentals of layout to non-designers.

William Owen *Modern Magazine Design.* Wm C. Brown, Dubuque, IA, 1992. Magazine design from the turn of the century to the late 1980s.

John Peacock *et al. The Print and Production Manual* (5th edn). Blueprint, London, 1990. Dry but exhaustive manual for printers.

Rick Poyner (ed.) *Typography Now (2).* Booth-Clibborn Editions, London 1996. An updated survey of the most innovative designers in print, advertising, and the moving image.

David Siegel *Creating Killer Web Sites.* Hayden Books, Indianapolis, IN, 1996. Web design theory plus the nuts and bolts of successful page production.

Erik Spiekermann *Rhyme & Reason: A Typographic Novel.* H. Berthold AG, Berlin, 1987. A beautifully made treatise on typography in the style of *Tristram Shandy.*

Erik Spiekermann and E. M. Ginger *Stop Stealing Sheep & Find out How Type Works.* Adobe Press, Mountain View, CA, 1993. The title refers to a quotation by Frederic Goudy: "Anyone who would letterspace lower case would steal sheep."

USA

Communication Arts
410 Sherman Avenue
Palo Alto
CA 94306
ca@commarts.com

Computer Artist
Pen Well Publishing Co.
Ten Tara Blvd
5th Floor
Nashua, NH 03062-2801
Tomm@penwell.com

Emigre
4475 D Street
Sacramento
CA 95819
editor@emigre.com

Graphic Arts Monthly
245 West 17th Street
New York,
NY 10011
cross.gam@cahners.com

Graphic Design USA
Kaye Publications
120 E 56th Street,
New York
NY10022
gdusa@earthlink.net

Graphis
141 Lexington Avenue
New York
NY 10016

HOW
1507 Dana Avenue
Cincinnati, OH 45207
HOWEDIT@aol.com

ID
440 Park Avenue South
Floor 14
New York
NY 10016
IDMag@aol.com

Joint Venture
Emigre Inc.
4475 D Street
Sacramento, CA 95819
editor@emigre.com

MacWorld
IDG Publications
501 Second Avenue
San Francisco, CA 94107
andrea_dudro@macworld.com

Print
3200 Tower Oaks Blvd
Rockville
Maryland 20852
printmag@aol.com

Publish!
501 Second Avenue
San Francisco
CA 94107
candice_kronar@publish.com

Serif
Dept. W-1
976 W Foothill Blvd, Ste 529
Claremont
CA 91711
serif@quixote.com.

Step-by-step Graphics
6000 North Forest Park Drive,
Peoria IL 61614-3592
e-mail: 74431.1475@compuserve.com

3D Artist
Columbine Inc.
PO Box 4787
Santa Fe, NM 87502
http://www.3dartist.com/

u & lc
ITC
866 Second Avenue
New York
NY 10017
designedit@aol.com

X-Height
Font Haus
1375 Kings Highway East,
Fairfield
CT 06430
e-mail: fonthaus@aol.com

UK

Baseline
Bradbourne Publishing Ltd
East Malling
Kent ME19 6DZ
bradbourne@hdr-hans.demon.co.uk

CGI
Computer Generated Imaging
    Magazine
3rd Floor
30-31 Islington Green
London N1 8DU
nic@cgimag.demon.co.uk

Creative Review
Centaur Communications Ltd
50 Poland Street
London W1V 4AX
creativereview@centaur.co.uk

Creative Technology
10 Barley Mow Passage
London W4 4PH
create@atlas.co.uk

Design
The Design Council
1 Oxendon Street
London SW1Y 4EE
e-mail: mjohnson@atlas.co.uk

Design Week
St Giles House
Poland Street
London W1
lyndark@centaur.co.uk

Electronic Imaging
Market Link Publishing Ltd
The Mill
Bearwalden Business Park
Wendens Ambo
Saffron Walden
Essex CB11 4JX
market.link@dial.pipex.com

Eye
151 Rosebery Avenue
London EC1R 4QX
rpoyner@dircon.co.uk
US subscriptions: PO Box 1584
Birmingham
AL 5201-1584

Graphics World
Datastream Publishing Ltd
Fairmeadow
Maidstone
Kent ME14 1NG

Internet
Greater London House
Hampstead Road
London NW1 7QZ
info@ internet.emap.com

MacUser
19 Bolsover Street
London W1P 7HJ
edit@macuser.co.uk

MacWorld (UK edition)
IDG Publications
99 Gray's Inn Road
London WC1X 8UT
editor@uk.macworld.com

.net
Future Publishing
30 Monmouth Street
Bath BA1 2BW
netmag@futurenet.co.uk

PICTURE CREDITS

The author and publishers would like to thank all individuals, agencies, museums, and companies that supplied pictures for use in the book. Special thanks go to those designers – David Carson, Malcolm Garrett, Zuzana Licko, P. Scott Makela, Erik Spiekermann, and Lucille Tenazas – who provided material for the Design Trailblazer spreads.

Chapter 1: Figure 1.1 Mansell Collection, London; 1.3–5 Ann Ronan Picture Library, Taunton, Somerset; 1.6 Mansell Collection, London; 1.7 Nick Day, Brighton; 1.8–9 Ann Ronan Picture Library, Taunton, Somerset; 1.11 Mary Evans Picture Library, London; Photoshop manipulation by Dave Kemp; 1.12 David Foenander, Milton Keynes; 1.13 Linotype-Hell AG, Germany.

Chapter 2: Figure 2.2–3 Mansell Collection, London; 2.4 British Library, London; 2.5 Ann Ronan Picture Library, Taunton, Somerset; 2.7 Alan Pipes; 2.8 Mary Evans Picture Library, London; 2.14 Alan Pipes; 2.18 Alan Pipes; 2.23 Alan Pipes; 2.30 Alan Pipes; 2.35 Mary Evans Picture Library, London; 2.39 Carol Kemp; 2.40 Fontworks UK, London; 2.41 Zefa Picture Library, London; 2.42 Zefa Picture Library, London (J. Pfaff); 2.43 Art Directors Photo Library, London; 2.44 Zefa Picture Library, London; 2.45 Zefa Picture Library, London (J. Pfaff); 2.49–51 Alan Pipes.

Chapter 3: Figure 3.1 Mansell Collection, London; 3.3 Art Directors Photo Library, London; 3.4–5 US Embassy; 3.8 Roger-Viollet, Paris; 3.9–10 LD Publicity; 3.11 Hulton Getty Picture Collection Ltd, London; 3.16 Metropolitan Museum of Art, New York; 3.17 Paul Brierley, Harlow, Essex; 3.18–19 Alan Pipes; 3.20 Lefevre Gallery, London; 3.22 David Foenander, Milton Keynes; 3.23 Zefa Picture Library, London (J. Pfaff); 3.24 Kodak; 3.26 David Wood, Brighton; 3.27 Quantel; 3.28 Tapestry/BMPDDBNeedham; 3.29 Bob Harrington (left); Henry Lyndsey (right); 3.31 DC Comics Inc., New York.

Chapter 4: Figure 4.1–4 Alan Pipes; 4.9–10 Alan Pipes; 4.12–15 Alan Pipes; 4.17 Alan Pipes; 4.19 Alan Pipes; 4.20 Art Directors Photo Library, London; 4.21–2 Alan Pipes; 4.23 Du Pont UK Ltd; 4.24 Alan Pipes; 4.25 Scitex.

Chapter 5: Figure 5.1 Firefly Communications; 5.2 Apple UK; 5.3 Sun Microsystems, Inc.; 5.4 Silicon Graphics; 5.6 Performance Direct, Egham, Surrey; 5.7 Alan Pipes; 5.9 Radius; 5.10 Alan Pipes; 5.11 Radius; 5.12 Wacom; 5.13–14 Logitech; 5.15 Kodak; 5.16 Epson; 5.17 Linotype-Hell AG, Germany; 5.18 ICG; 5.19 Kodak; 5.20 Epson; 5.21 Scitex; 5.22 Alan Pipes; 5.23 Alan Pipes; 5.24 Linotype Hell AG, Germany; 5.25 Alan Pipes; 5.27 Tektronix; 5.28 Apple UK; 5.29 Alan Pipes; 5.30 Tektronix; 5.31–2 Alan Pipes; 5.34 Alan Pipes; 5.35 Fargo Electronics Inc./Bannerbridge PLC, Basildon, Essex; 5.36 Alan Pipes; 5.41 Linotype-Hell AG, Germany; 5.42 Alan Pipes; 5.43 Scitex; 5.44–5 Alan Pipes.

Chapter 6: Figure 6.1 Sonia Halliday, Weston Turville, Bucks; 6.2 Science Photo Library, London; 6.3–4 Alan Pipes; 6.5 Art Directors Photo Library, London; 6.6 Art Directors Photo Library (John Frye); 6.7 Alan Pipes; 6.8 James River Fine Papers, St Andrews, Scotland; 6.9 Alan Pipes; 6.10 James River Fine Papers, St Andrews, Scotland; 6.11–13 Alan Pipes; 6.14 Zefa Picture Library, London; 6.17 Phil Dobson, Brighton; 6.18 Alan Pipes; 6.19 Art Directors Photo Library, London; 6.21–4 Alan Pipes; 6.25 Art Directors Photo Library, London; 6.27–8 Alan Pipes; 6.29 Art Directors Photo Library, London (Archie Miles); 6.30–1 Alan Pipes; 6.32 Zefa Picture Library, London; 6.33 Alan Pipes; 6.36 Alan Pipes; 6.38 Canon; 6.39 Helen J. Holroyd, Brighton; 6.40 Alan Pipes; 6.41 Paul Nunneley, London; 6.42 Paul Nunneley, London; 6.47 (left to right) Hodder Headline, Hodder Headline, Pan Books; 6.48–58 Alan Pipes.

Chapter 7: Figure 7.1 US Robotics Ltd, Wokingham, Berks; 7.7 Simon Waldman, New Media Labs, *Guardian* newspapers, London; 7.18 Lambie-Nairn & Co., London /BBC, London; 7.19 IDEO, San Francisco; 7.20 Cognitive Applications, Brighton; 7.21 Royal College of Art, London.

240

INDEX